Inflation, Debt, and Indexation

Inflation, Debt, and Indexation

edited by
Rudiger Dornbusch
and
Mario Henrique Simonsen

The MIT Press
Cambridge, Massachusetts
London, England

First paperback edition, 1986
© 1983 by The Massachusetts Institute of Technology

This book was set in Times New Roman by Asco Trade Typesetting Ltd., Hong Kong and printed and bound by Halliday Litho Printing Company in the United States of America.

Library of Congress Cataloging in Publication Data
Main entry under title:

Inflation, debt, and indexation.

   Bibliography: p.
   Includes index.
   1. Indexation (Economics)—Addresses, essays, lectures.   I. Dornbusch, Rudiger.
II. Simonsen, Mario Henrique.   III. Fundaçao Getuilio Vargas.
HG229.5.I53   1983   339.5′2   83-43016
ISBN 0-262-04072-7 (hard)
      0-262-54044-4 (paper)

Contents

IV   Panel Discussion

Introduction

The chapters and discussions in this book were presented at a conference sponsored by the Getulio Vargas Foundation in Rio de Janeiro in December 1981. They cover problems in the area of inflation, debt, and indexation, with the latter as the focal point. The work reported here is in part theoretical, but it also includes analysis of the experience with widespread indexation and with inflation stabilization.

Price index links have long been recognized as a useful contractual arrangement in the face of price level uncertainties. Contingent clauses must be simple enough to be enforceable, and this explains the popularity of price level index contracts in high inflation economies. At least before the first oil shock in 1973–74, widespread indexation was often praised as a second best to price stability. It appeared to minimize the welfare losses caused by inflation. Among other virtues, widespread escalator clauses would make contracts independent of inflationary expectations, thus leading to a vertical Phillips curve even in the very short run. This would eliminate any temporary inflation-output trade-off, and all the uncomfortable side effects of anti-inflationary policies. In fact this was Milton Friedman's central argument in his enthusiastic defense of indexation.

The trouble with widespread indexation is that it represents an obstacle to relative price changes, specifically changes in real factor rewards. One cannot constrain a general equilibrium price vector by an arbitrary restriction and still obtain the Pareto efficiency properties of unconstrained equilibria. Only in one single case are indexed contracts fully efficient, namely, when all the states of nature just differ in terms of the general price level. This case of purely nominal shocks was often presented during the sixties as an adequate picture of inflationary economies. After the first oil shock it became clear that, far from being an approximate rule, it was a very uncommon exception.

The fact that indexed contracts can be inefficient in the face of relative price changes explains why escalator clauses are not pervasively and automatically introduced at the early stages of inflation. If the states of nature cannot be described by a single price index, there is no reason why contractual payments should be made contingent on such an index. Efficient contracts of the Arrow-Debreu type may be too complicated to be enforced, but economic agents can always minimize risks by reducing the length of their contracts. Price uncertainties usually destroy the market for long-term bonds but do not necessarily create a market for indexed bonds. The same applies to rent, labor, and other types of contracts.

One might argue for indexation by assuming that all states of nature can be described by a pair (P, X) where P is a particular price index and X a random vector independent of P. The problem is that P would be a very special price index that is not affected by real shocks and does not coincide with any of the regularly published price indicators. The fact that, at least until recently, no attempt was made to estimate such a price index explains at least three points: first, why indexation does not emerge very much in low inflation countries; second, why escalator clauses become universal when inflation rates reach a point where almost every price index appears as a good proxy for the ideal P; third, why highly indexed economies have faced serious problems of inflation, balance of payments, and unemployment since 1974.

Let us illustrate these problems with wage indexation. An indexed labor contract has two basic elements, the base wage and the nominal wage-adjustment rule. The latter must specify when money wages are changed and according to which price index. Now, a number of different arrangements can be found in terms of these two elements.

A first type of contract sets a very rigid wage base and a fixed time interval after which nominal wages are adjusted according to the accumulated increase in the consumer price index. This is imperfect wage indexation, since money wages are adjusted for past and not for current price changes. Real wages can be reduced, between adjustments, by an increase in the inflation rate, and the system opens the gate to monetary accommodation.

Contracts of this type have been discussed and applied in Brazil as well as in Italy. The rigidity of the wage base can be a problem, since there is no reason to believe that some Walrasian auctioneer could always make it consistent with full employment. Since monetary accommodation is possible, this sort of indexation may well become an inflation-perpetuating mechanism. It does not lead to a vertical Phillips curve in the short run because of the wage-adjustment lag, and it may produce highly unfavorable inflation-output trade-offs, which discourage anti-inflationary policies. An adverse supply shock, such as a bad crop, a real exchange rate devaluation, an increase in the real price of imported goods, or the introduction of an indirect tax can only be accommodated by an increase in the rate of inflation.

A second type of contract sets a rigid wage base and a threshold or trigger point: nominal wages are adjusted as soon as the consumer price index increases by x percent or more rather than at fixed intervals. For small inflation thresholds this practically means that real wages are kept unchanged all the time. This sort of arrangement finds its theoretical analysis in the Gray-Fischer model. Indexation leads to a vertical Phillips curve in the short run, leaving neither an inflation-output trade-off nor any possibility of monetary accommodation. This dissolves all the uncomfortable side effects of anti-inflationary policies but provides no support to Friedman's enthusiasm on escalator clauses. In a closed economy an adverse supply shock can produce persistent unemployment. In an open system real wage rigidity creates unfavorable trade-offs between full employment and external balance.

A third system, of more theoretical than practical interest, combines some indexation scheme with a flexible wages base. An attempt to implement such a system was made in Chile a few years ago, but wages proved to be less flexible than imagined by policy-makers. Of course, if the base wage was flexible enough, there would be no difference between wage indexation and money wage flexibility in the neoclassical line. This is the indexation concept of the non-Keynesian models of Barro and Liviatan.

A solution for the malfunctioning of indexation in periods of adverse supply shocks would be the automatic adjustment of wage and other incomes by price indexes corrected for real exchange devaluations, for indirect tax increases, for changes in the terms of trade, producing the ideal P of our earlier discussion. This would take care of the future but would not correct the existing disequilibria of the wage base. The latter should be realigned to the full-employment level, perhaps by skipping a number of automatic wage adjustments. Both suggestions were included in the recommendation of the Commission of the European Communities on the principles of indexation and have already been adopted by some countries.

Tax indexation must be analyzed from a different point of view, since it is not a market but an economic policy decision. It has also a different theoretical content, since the relevant variable is no longer the unanticipated part of the inflation rate but the inflation rate itself. Indexation can now be defended on welfare grounds. Bracket creep, the taxation of purely nominal capital gains, the underdepreciation of fixed assets, and subsidies from lenders to borrowers are hardly consistent with a welfare-maximizing fiscal policy. A practical problem has to be faced: tax indexation deprives the government of some revenue sources and should not be introduced without a previous fiscal reform. Even when such a reform is implemented to maintain public sector revenue, tax indexation weakens the fiscal drags on inflation. It also may reduce the political will to fight inflation, since life with permanent price increases is made less uncomfortable. The final decision depends very much on the inflation rate. High-inflation countries are forced to accept some degree of tax indexation in order to prevent low-income workers being shifted to the higher-income tax brackets.

Several of the chapters in this book address the question of indexed debt. Should the government issue such debt, will the existence of government indexed bonds promote stability and facilitate inflation control, or is it primarily desirable on equity grounds, if at all? An additional question is raised: Is there any reason at all to be concerned with public financial policy? The traditional arguments in favor of government indexed bonds would include two points: As a matter of equity the government should create a stable purchasing power asset for low-income savers. But in creating such *real* liabilities, the government would loose the incentive to use inflation taxes as a part of public finance and therefore indexed debt would promote price stability. The analysis weakens very much the case for indexed bonds once two issues are raised: first, why does the private sector not provide such assets if in fact it is correct that savers would value them, and, second, who pays the taxes to service the *real* liabilities that the government creates? This line of thinking takes one in the Miller-Modigliani direction to argue that government indexed debt cannot improve social welfare except for specified externalities in the packaging of debt or the certification of the state of nature, or else by systematic redistributive policies between income groups or between generations.

One of the themes that emerges from several of the chapters is that the beneficial effects of indexation are overrated. In many cases the private market does not need indexation, say, of wages, because as savers and investors, workers may be able to acquire even cheaper insurance than indexation could provide. In this perspective it becomes particularly clear that compulsory indexation of labor contracts cannot possibly be efficient in an economy facing real disturbances. Why, after all, should one factor face a perfectly riskless income while another group bears all the risk? Indexation, at best, makes its entry through the door of moral hazard problems, imperfect information, or transactions costs.

But once it is argued that the market can provide indexation, at least to some extent, the question arises why we observe so little indexed private debt. Is it the case that high uncertainty about relative prices leads the market for indexed bonds to "dry up"? A mutual fund could certainly diversify that risk, but it cannot provide a safe real return, independent of the state of the aggregate economy. Thus we return to the earlier point: indexation can perfectly cope with an economy that only has nominal disturbances. Via diversification it can also cope with real disturbances that arise from intersectoral shifts. But it cannot cope with aggregate real disturbances. If there is no real asset or portfolio of real assets that generates a safe real return, then the economy in the aggregate cannot pay a safe real return.

The chapters in this book are organized in four parts corresponding to their distinct focus. The first part deals primarily with the issue of wage contracting, inflation, and inflation stabilization. The chapters by Blanchard and Gray present extensions of the contract literature. Blanchard focuses on a realistic production structure where intermediate goods are introduced in a framework of staggered contracts to explain the stickiness of the general price level and the relative variability of prices and profits at different stages of the production process. Gray extends the labor market indexation literature by introducing explicitly intersectoral shifts in an imperfect information setting. Indexation now becomes hazardous once real variability is present and is large relative to monetary shocks. The chapter by Phelps brings in a link between contractual arrangements in the labor market and moral hazard issues: the interests of workers and firms are opposed, and an agency is needed to certify the state of nature and facilitate adjustment in the economy to a change in the state of nature. Rather than adjusting all wages and prices, Phelps argues, the social contract involves accommodating changes in the supply of money by the central bank acting in the impartial common interest.

The first part concludes with a chapter by Sargent who analyzes inflation stabilization in Great Britain today and in France in the 1920s. What, he asks, made stabilization so successful, and apparently rapid and untraumatic in France, and why is it so unsuccessful and controversial in Great Britain today? Sargent concludes that fiscal reforms, rather than monetarist gradualism, are the key to success.

Part II of the book presents an analysis of actual indexation experience and policy. The chapter by Simonsen opens with an analysis of Brazilian indexation, combining both the theory and the actual experience. Brazil is the laboratory of indexation experience and presents rich information in this area from the last fifteen years. Simonsen shows that indexation performed well, while real disturbances were minor. Once the oil shock brought a significant deterioration in the terms of trade, however, indexation problems emerged. Until 1979 import substitution still contained the problems, but by 1981 inflation had gone from 20 to 40 percent all the way to 100 percent. Therefore, to delay a foreign exchange crisis, the economy was forced into the deepest recession since the 1930s. The chapter by Macedo also deals with the Brazilian case and develops in detail the importance of changing the periodicity of wage settlements. It is shown that doubling the frequency of wage and adjustments doubles the rate of inflation. Emerson's view from Europe and excerpts from the recommendation issued by the Commission of the European Communities complete this part of the book.

Part III brings the chapters dealing with indexation and asset markets. Stiglitz introduces the Modigliani-Miller theorem to argue that public financial policy is irrelevant because the public must pay the taxes that service the debt. But then it is immediately recognized that intergenerational effects limit the scope of this theorem as does risk aversion. Two chapters by Fischer address the question of private and public debt. The case for government issue of indexed bonds finds only one and a half cheers out of a possible three. The cases where government financial intermediation through the issue of indexed bonds is beneficial turn out to be quite limited. In the accompanying chapter (from an earlier conference, reproduced here by permission) Fischer investigates whether it would have been profitable for various private firms in the United States to issue indexed debt. Interestingly, he concludes that, ex post, most of the firms analyzed would have had lower profits had they issued indexed debt.

The chapter by Liviatan recognizes the implications of assets markets for worker-savers ability to insure against fluctuations in wages. This raises the question to what extent indexation of wages and of assets are substitutes. Liviatan concludes that with perfect access to capital markets indexed bonds make wage indexation redundant. On the other side, however, even sophisticated forms of wage indexation cannot replace the role played by indexed bonds. Part III concludes with Levhari's chapter on the implications of indexed debt for the consumer. Levhari draws attention to the fact that indexed debt, through the debt service burden, imposes costs on the consumer that may more than outweigh the benefits of indexed debt. He also argues that indexed debt does not necessarily promote stability of inflation.

The volume concludes with a panel discussion covering the issues raised in the conference. An opening statement by Robert Barro reviews critically, from a free-market perspective, the arguments for government initiatives in the area of indexation. The following individual statements by Cavallo and Hahn take issue with the policy experience or highlight analytical problems that are recommended for further study.

I WAGES, PRICES, AND INFLATION STABILIZATION

1 Price Asynchronization and Price Level Inertia

Olivier J. Blanchard

1.1 Introduction

It is often informally argued that because of the complexity of the price system, and the inherent problems of coordination, the apparent inertia of the price level should come as no surprise.[1] A rather appealing argument along these lines is the following: when a nominal disturbance requires a change in the price level, what is required is not a change of a single price but of a complex structure of final good, intermediate good, and input prices. Price decisions for each of these goods are not taken continuously, and, price decisions across goods are not likely to be perfectly synchronized. The process of adjustment of all prices to a new nominal level will therefore imply movements of relative prices along the way. If price setters do not want large changes in relative prices, the path of adjustment of all prices may be slow, in other words, the price level may adjust slowly.

The purpose of this chapter is to formalize this argument and to see whether and how it survives formalization. We focus on three sets of questions. First, can asynchronization of individual price decisions generate "substantial" price inertia? It is obvious that, with so many price decisions, the price level will not adjust overnight to changes in aggregate demand; the question is whether, if each price is set for a relatively short period of time, say, a month or two at most, asynchronization can generate the degree of price inertia we appear to have in the United States. The answer is that this is indeed possible.

The second set of questions addresses whether the price level inertia so generated coincides with the usual notion of inertia or "stickiness." Does price level inertia, for example, imply that decreases in money or declerations in money growth necessarily lead to recessions? The answer is mixed. In general, movements in money will lead to movements in real money balances and economic activity. There are, however, paths of monetary deceleration that lead to disinflation with no output loss. These paths are reasonable and, apart from issues of credibility, easy to implement.

The third set of questions considers the implications of asynchronization for the relation between disturbances, the price level and the structure of relative prices. This is of interest both in itself and because it provides

4 Oliver J. Blanchard

a way of differentiating this theory of price inertia from other theories and potentially testing it.[2] Asynchronization implies snake effects, movements in factor prices slowly transmitted to intermediate and final good prices. It also implies more variability of profits and prices for primary inputs than for intermediate goods, for intermediate goods than for final goods; these implications seem to be in accordance with facts.

This chapter therefore suggests that asynchronization of price decisions is capable of generating price level inertia. If price level inertia is indeed partly due to asynchronization, the prospects for reducing it are not good. Given the time structure of price decisions, each price setter chooses its price optimally and frequently. Reducing inertia requires better overall synchronization of price decisions; this may be difficult to achieve, by agents or by policy.

1.2 The Model

In order to focus later on the effects of asynchronization, I start with an economy in which all price decisions are perfectly synchronized.

Equilibrium with Synchronized Prices

The economy is characterized by its technology and a specification of input supply and output demand.

Final output is produced in n stages, each carried under constant returns to scale by competitive firms. *Technology* is given by n relations:

$$y_i = y_{i-1} + \theta_i, \quad i = 1, \ldots, n, \tag{1.1}$$

where y_i denote good i so that y_0 denotes the primary input, and y_n the final output. All variables in this chapter are in logarithms. The θ_i are constants. They are unimportant for our purposes and will be deleted in what follows. Production is instantaneous, and to avoid issues of inventories, all goods are perishable.[3]

Competitive zero profit equilibrium implies that, if p_i is (the log of) the price of good i, the following relations hold (forgetting the θ_i):

$$p_i = p_{i-1}, \quad i = 1, \ldots, n \Rightarrow p_n = p_0 \tag{1.2}$$

Increasing the number of production stages, n, keeping the sum of θ_i's constant, allows us to increase the number of price decisions, while leaving the technology unchanged.[4,5] In this economy with synchronized prices, the number of price decisions is clearly irrelevant: y_n is always equal to y_0 and p_n to p_0.

The model is closed by a specification of *input supply* and *output demand*:

$$y_0 = \beta(p_0 - p_n) + \xi, \quad \beta \geq 0, \tag{1.3}$$

$$y_n = m - p_n. \tag{1.4}$$

Input supply is an increasing function of its real price and of a disturbance ξ.[6] Output demand depends positively on real money balances.[7]

Equilibrium is characterized by the price relations given by (1.2) and equilibrium in the primary input market; the derived demand for the primary input must equal the supply:

$$\beta(p_0 - p_n) + \xi = m - p_n. \tag{1.5}$$

Combining (1.2) and (1.5) gives

$$y_n = y_0 = \xi, \quad p_n = \cdots = p_i = \cdots = p_0 = m - \xi.$$

Money is neutral and affects only the level of all prices. Supply disturbances increase output, decrease all nominal prices and leave relative prices unchanged.

Price Asynchronization

I now relax the assumption that price decisions are taken every period and are perfectly synchronized. All price decisions are now taken every two periods. The basic period is presumably short and can be thought of as a month at most.[8] Price decisions are not all taken at the same time. Half of them are taken every period, in the following way: firms at the same stage of production take decisions at the same time for two periods. At even stages (i even) firms take decisions at $t, t + 2$, and so on; at odd stages (i odd) firms take decisions at $t - 1, t + 1$, and so on. For convenience, n is assumed to be even, so that firms producing y_n take decisions at $t, t + 2, \ldots$, firms producing y_{n-1} take decisions at $t - 1, t + 1, \ldots$, suppliers of the primary input take decisions at $t, t + 2, \ldots$.

Firms choosing p_i at time t for periods t and $t + 1$ face two possibly different input prices for t and $t + 1$. The competitive zero profit condition (1.2) is now replaced by an expected zero profit condition over the two periods. This is formalized by[9]

$$p_{it} = \tfrac{1}{2}[p_{i-1\,t-1} + E(p_{i-1\,t+1}|t)], \quad i = 2, 4, \ldots, n. \tag{1.6}$$

$E(\cdot|t)$ denotes the expectation conditional on information available at time t. $p_{i-1\,t-1}$ is the current input price in period t which was set in period $t-1$ and $E(p_{i-1\,t+1}|t)$ the expected input price for period $t+1$. A corresponding formula holds for i odd, at time $t-1$ or $t+1$.

Since nominal prices are fixed at each stage for two periods, they may not clear the market in both periods, and an assumption must be made about quantity determination. I assume the outcome to be demand determined: when a firm fixes its price for two periods, it stands ready to supply on demand. This is feasible as production is instantaneous and all input suppliers also supply on demand. Demand for the final good determines the demand for intermediate inputs and for the primary input.[10]

Prices in the primary input market are set in period t at the average expected market-clearing levels over periods t and $t+1$. For convenience, we assume m and ξ to move only every two periods, so that $m_t = m_{t+1}$ and $\xi_t = \xi_{t+1}$. As $p_{nt} = p_{nt+1}$, the derived demand and the supply of the primary input are the same in periods t and $t+1$. The primary input price for t and $t+1$ is therefore given by[11]

$$\beta(p_{0t} - p_{nt}) + \xi_t = m_t - p_{nt}. \tag{1.7}$$

To summarize, all firms choose their relative price every two periods. Their price decision depends on current and expected input prices for the next two periods. Half of the prices change every period.

The only deviation from the flexible price world is the presence of asynchronization: other sources of price inertia are excluded in order to isolate the effects of asynchronization. This excludes in particular such elements as labor contracts with nominal wages predetermined for long periods of time.[12] As a result it is not clear whether the primary input should be thought of as labor or as a raw material. If thought of as labor, its price has probably more inertia than formalized in equation (1.7).

Equilibrium with Asynchronized Prices

Equilibrium is now characterized by equations (1.6) and (1.7). Input market equilibrium, equation (1.7), gives us a first relation between p_{0t} and p_{nt}, given m_t and ξ_t. The other relation between p_{nt} and p_{0t} follows from the set of pricing relations given by (1.6). We now derive it by recursive substitution.

Starting from $i = n$, equation (1.6) gives

$$p_{nt} = \tfrac{1}{2}[p_{n-1\,t-1} + E(p_{n-1\,t+1}|t)].\tag{1.8}$$

For $i = n - 1$, it gives for $t - 1$ and $t + 1$

$$p_{n-1\,t-1} = \tfrac{1}{2}[p_{n-2\,t-2} + E(p_{n-2t}|t - 1)],$$

$$p_{n-1\,t+1} = \tfrac{1}{2}[p_{n-2t} + E(p_{n-2\,t+2}|t + 1)].$$

Assuming rational expectations, taking expectations of $p_{n-1\,t+1}$ at time t, using iterated expectations, and replacing in equation (1.8) gives

$$p_{nt} = (\tfrac{1}{2})^2[p_{n-2\,t-2} + E(p_{n-2t}|t - 1) + p_{n-2t} + E(p_{n-2\,t+2}|t)].\tag{1.9}$$

By induction, we can express p_n as a function of p_0:

$$p_{nt} = 2^{-n}\left[\sum_{i=1}^{n/2}\sum_{j=0}^{(n/2)-i} b_{nj}E\left(p_{0t-2i}\middle| t - \frac{n}{2} - i + j\right)\right.$$

$$+ \sum_{j=0}^{n/2} b_{nj}E\left(p_{0t}\middle| t - \frac{n}{2} + j\right)$$

$$\left. + \sum_{i=1}^{n/2}\sum_{j=0}^{(n/2)-i} b_{nj}E\left(p_{0t+2i}\middle| t - \frac{n}{2} + i + j\right)\right],\tag{1.10}$$

with

$$b_{nj} \equiv \binom{n}{j} - \binom{n}{j-1}, \quad b_{n0} \equiv 1.$$

This formula is quite formidable but has a simple structure. Consider first the case of perfect foresight, so that expectations are equal to actual values. This gives

$$p_{nt} = 2^{-n}\left[\sum_{i=1}^{n/2}\binom{n}{(n/2)-i}p_{0t-2i} + \binom{n}{n/2}p_{0t} + \sum_{i=1}^{n/2}\binom{n}{(n/2)-i}p_{0t+2i}\right].\tag{1.11}$$

This shows the first effect of asynchronization: the price level depends on input prices up to n periods in the past and n periods in the future. The weights are simply the coefficients of a binomial expansion, normalized by their sum, 2^n.

When we relax the assumption of perfect foresight and allow for uncertainty, actual values of input prices in (1.11) are replaced by expectations.

8   Oliver J. Blanchard

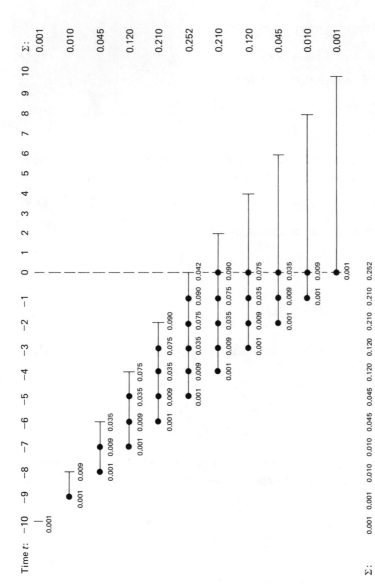

Figure 1.1
Weights on the primary input price for $n = 10$

The price level depends then on three sets of terms. The first double sum involves past input prices, both actual and expected; the term in p_{0t-2i}, for example, includes both the actual value of p_{0t-2i} and the values of p_{0t-2i} expected prior to $t-2i$, from $t-(n/2)-i$ to $t-2i-1$. The second sum involves both the actual value and past expectations of the current input price. The third involves both past and current expectations of future input prices. Note, and we shall return to this later, that many terms in this last double sum are past expectations of future prices and thus are predetermined at time t. Thus the symmetry between the effects of the future and the past which obtains under perfect foresight (equation 1.11) does not obtain under uncertainty and rational expectations.

A visually more explicit representation of (1.10) is given in figure 1.1 for $n = 10$. Each line represents a set of terms in equation (1.10). The right end of a line indicates for what period the expectation of p_0 is held. The dots on each line indicate when these expectations were formed. The numbers under the dots are the relative weights, $2^{-n}b_{nj}$. All elements strictly to the left of the vertical line $t = 0$ are predetermined at time t.

1.3 Price Level Inertia and the Number of Price Decisions

A Simple Measure of Inertia

Producers of the final good freely choose their own nominal price, the price level, every two periods and would not characterize it as sluggish. Their price decision, however, depends directly and indirectly on past input prices, and in a well-defined sense the price level is sluggish. Looking at equation (1.10), we can usefully think of the price level as the sum of 2^n components, some determined in the past and thus predetermined at time t, some free to move at time t.

This suggests a simple measure of price level inertia, namely, the ratio of the number of predetermined components to the number of non-predetermined components in (1.10). From equation (1.10), this ratio, R, is[13]

$$R = 1 - 2^{-n}\binom{n}{n/2},$$

which gives 0.5 for $n = 2$, 0.75 for $n = 10$, and 0.92 for $n = 100$. Thus this ratio is higher than the proportion of prices, which are not free to

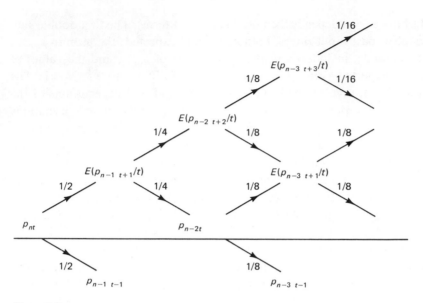

Figure 1.2
The degree of predetermination of the price level p_n

adjust at any given time—one-half—and is increasing with the number of price decisions. If n is large, most of the elements that compose the price level are predetermined.

As n increases, asynchronization implies a dependence of the price level on input prices further in the past and expected further in the future that is quite intuitive. That as n increases, the degree of predetermination increases is less intuitive. Figure 1.2 helps us understand why by showing how the price level depends on input prices as we go down the chain of production. Any element below the line is predetermined and thus can only depend in turn on predetermined elements. Any element above the line is not predetermined and may in turn depend both on predetermined and nonpredetermined elements. p_{nt} depends on predetermined $p_{n-1\,t-1}$ and nonpredetermined $E(p_{n-1\,t+1}|t)$. $E(p_{n-1\,t+1}|t)$, however, depends on partly predetermined elements such as $p_{n-3\,t-1}$. As we extend the graph to the right, more and more elements go below the line: the ratio, R, of predetermined to nonpredetermined elements increases and tends to 1 as n gets large.

This measure of price level inertia is a bit crude: it tells us how much of the price level is predetermined and cannot change in response to disturbances in the current period but tells us nothing about the path of price level adjustment thereafter. We now look at the complete path; this requires solving the model.

The Effects of an Increase in Money

As characterized by (1.10), the effect of the input price, actual or expected, on the price level is unambiguously positive. The effect of the price level on the input price is however ambiguous, as shown in (1.7). An increase in the price level decreases real balances, aggregate demand, the derived input demand and thus the equilibrium real input price; the net effect of a higher price level and a lower real price is ambiguous. If $\beta = 1$, the net effect is zero, and the input price does not depend on the price level. The system is then recursive, the price level depending on the input price and the input price on money and the supply disturbance. We start with this case; the general case will be analyzed in the next section. If $\beta = 1$, replacing p_{0t} from (1.7) in (1.10) gives

$$p_{nt} = 2^{-n}\left[\sum_{i=1}^{n/2}\sum_{j=0}^{(n/2)-i} b_{nj}E\left(\psi_{t-2i}\Big|t-\frac{n}{2}-i+j\right)\right.$$
$$\left.+ \sum_{j=0}^{n/2} E\left(\psi_t\Big|t-\frac{n}{2}+j\right) + \sum_{i=1}^{n/2}\sum_{j=0}^{(n/2)-i} b_{nj}E\left(\psi_{t+2i}\Big|t-\frac{n}{2}+i+j\right)\right],$$

$$(1.12)$$

with

$$\psi_t \equiv m_t - \xi_t.$$

Consider a permanent unanticipated increase in money at time t_0. Because of the long-run neutrality of money in this model, the long-run elasticity of the price level with respect to money is unity. We can derive from (1.12) incremental and cumulative price level elasticities over time. Denoting the proportional increase in money by dm we get

$$p_{nt_0+2i} - p_{nt_0+2i-2} = 0 \qquad \text{if } i < 0,$$
$$= \binom{n}{n/2} dm, \qquad \text{if } i = 0,$$
$$= 2\binom{n}{(n/2)-i} dm, \quad \text{if } i = 1, \ldots, n/2,$$
$$= 0 \qquad \text{if } i > n/2.$$

Oliver J. Blanchard

Table 1.1
Effects of an unanticipated increase in money at time t_0: incremental effects on p_n

n		t_0	t_0+2	t_0+4	t_0+6	⋯	t_0+10	⋯	t_0+20	⋯	t_0+50
2	p_2	0.5	0.5	0							
4	p_4	0.375	0.5	0.125	0						
6	p_6	0.312	0.468	0.187	0.031	⋯	0				
10	p_{10}	0.247	0.410	0.234	0.086	⋯	0				
20	p_{20}	0.176	0.322	0.240	0.148	⋯	0.028	⋯	0		
50	p_{50}	0.113	0.214	0.192	0.158	⋯	0.084	⋯	0.004	⋯	0
100	p_{100}	0.079	0.156	0.148	0.132	⋯	0.098	⋯	0.022	⋯	0
500	p_{500}	0.035	0.072	0.070	0.068	⋯	0.064	⋯	0.048	⋯	0.006

Table 1.2
Effects of an unanticipated increase in money at time t_0: cumulative effects on p_n

n		t_0	t_0+2	t_0+4	t_0+6	⋯	t_0+10	⋯	t_0+20	⋯	t_0+50
2	p_2	0.5	1.0	1.0							
4	p_4	0.375	0.875	1.0	1.0						
6	p_6	0.312	0.770	0.957	0.988	⋯	1.0				
10	p_{10}	0.247	0.547	0.891	0.977	⋯	1.0				
20	p_{20}	0.176	0.498	0.738	0.886	⋯	0.988	⋯	0.997		
50	p_{50}	0.113	0.327	0.519	0.677	⋯	0.881	⋯	0.966	⋯	1.0
100	p_{100}	0.079	0.235	0.383	0.515	⋯	0.730	⋯		⋯	0.999
500	p_{500}	0.035	0.107	0.177	0.245	⋯	0.378	⋯	0.654	⋯	0.998

Tables 1.1 and 1.2 give incremental and cumulative elasticities of p_n over time for different values of n. They show a monotonic adjustment with the rate of adjustment increasing initially before decreasing later.

The adjustment of the price of its higher level takes exactly n periods. The adjustment is, however, substantially complete before that: assuming the period to be a month, the adjustment after a year is 99 percent complete if $n = 20$, 90 percent complete if $n = 50$, and 75 percent complete if $n = 100$. Values of n of 100 may therefore generate the amount of price inertia we observe in the United States. Given the highly idealized nature of the model, it is difficult to decide whether such values for n are or are not reasonable.

There is an interesting distinction between demand disturbances, m, and supply disturbances, ξ. Note from equation (1.12) that they have an identical dynamic effect on the price level. Demand disturbances, however, affect demand and production along the chain of production and thus are immediately perceived by all producers. The assumption made above about the change in money being immediately known by all is therefore reasonable. Supply disturbances, on the other hand, have no direct effect on demand (this results from the assumption of demand determination). Thus producers of y_i, $i - 2, \ldots, n$, will perceive no change in their demand or input price at time t_0. If their information included only the demand they face and the input price they pay, they would not revise expectations. In this case the increase in the primary input price would slowly be transmitted to the structure of prices. p_n would not be given by equation (1.12) but by $p_{nt} = p_{0t-n}$, which implies substantially more inertia.

The Effects of Money Deceleration

Characterizing the effects of a change in the level of money is a useful first step but the experiment lacks empirical relevance. Of more direct relevance are the effects of money deceleration. Suppose that money and prices are both growing at rate g per period and that this rate of inflation is considered too high by policy-makers. What are the effects on real output of a sudden deceleration, say, sudden zero growth of money?[14] The effects differ, depending on whether this change is anticipated or not. Let's first assume that the policy is announced at time t_0 to take place at time $t_0 + n$: the rate of money growth remains equal to g until $t_0 + n$ and is equal to zero thereafter. From (1.12), real money balances from t_0 on are given by

$$(m - p)_{t_0 + 2i} = (2^{n-1}g) \sum_{j=0}^{i-1} (i - j) \binom{n}{j}, \qquad \text{for } i = 1, \ldots, \frac{n}{2},$$

$$= (2^{n-1}g) \sum_{j=0}^{i-1} \left(\frac{n}{2} - j\right)\binom{n}{j}, \quad \text{for } i = \frac{n}{2}, \ldots, n.$$

The paths of money and prices are plotted in figure 1.3. Real money balances, and therefore output, increase slowly after the announcement. They reach their maximum value at $t_0 + n$ when money growth stops. If, for example, $n = 50$ and $g = 1$ percent, which corresponds, if the basic period is a month, to 12 percent annually, real money balances are higher by 1.3 percent at time $t_0 + 50$. They decrease thereafter and return to their normal level at $t_0 + 2n$. Thus deflation is achieved not with a recession but with a mild expansion!

What is this due to? The announcement of a lower money growth leads price setters to slow down their rate of increase of prices before money deceleration takes place. When zero money growth actually takes place, real money balances are higher but progressively return to their normal level as prices keep increasing until $t_0 + 2n$. This is a very general feature of the "new" models of price inertia and holds for example also in the Taylor-Phelps (Taylor 1980, Phelps 1979) model of overlapping labor contracts.[15] What is required, however, is a decrease in inflation before the decrease in money growth: for this to happen, the announcement of the future change in policy must be credible. In practice, the lack of credibility is probably what makes this result unlikely to occur. If, for example, agents do not believe zero money growth before it is actually implemented, this deceleration leads to a temporary loss in output. The path of prices in this case is also plotted in figure 1.3.

1.4 Price Level Inertia and the Elasticity of Input Supply

In traditional empirical macroeconometric models prices are approximately markups over wages. Wages in turn depend on labor market conditions; of central importance for price inertia and the effects of money on real activity is the elasticity of nominal wages to the unemployment rate, the slope of the short-run Phillips curve. These models have, however, been criticized for their formalization of expectations. The critque is that expectations of inflation should be included in the Phillips

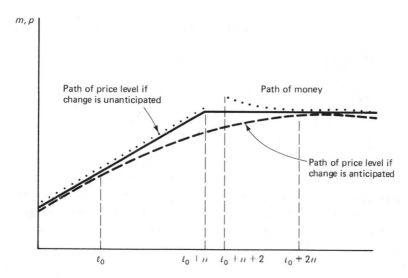

Figure 1.3
The effects of money deceleration

curve and that, with rational expectations, anticipated movements in money will have no effect on output, independently of the slope of the short-run Phillips curve.

This section shows that, if prices are asynchronized, the slope of the short-run Phillips curve is, even with rational expectation, an important determinant of the degree of price inertia. More precisely, it shows that the flatter the input supply, the slower the price level will adjust and the larger the effect of money on real output will be.

The case $n = 2$ can be solved analytically. Since β is not necessarily equal to unity, the model is no longer recursive and is a little more difficult to solve. To focus on the effects of demand disturbances, ξ is put equal to zero. Replacing (1.7) in (1.9) gives us an equation in p_{nt}:

$$p_{nt} = \frac{1 - \beta^{-1}}{4}[p_{nt-2} + E(p_{nt}|t - 2) + p_{nt} + E(p_{nt+2}|t)]$$

$$+ \frac{\beta^{-1}}{4}[m_{t-2} + E(m_t|t - 2) + m_t + E(m_{t+2}|t)]. \tag{1.13}$$

Taking expectations at time $t - 2$, denoting $E(\cdot|t - 2)$ by a hat and defining $\hat{\phi}_t \equiv \beta^{-1}(\hat{m}_{t-2} + 2\hat{m}_t + \hat{m}_{t+2})$:

$$(1 - \beta^{-1})\hat{p}_{nt+2} - 2(1 + \beta^{-1})\hat{p}_{nt} + (1 - \beta^{-1})\hat{p}_{nt-2} = -\hat{\phi}_t. \quad (1.14)$$

Equation (1.14) can be solved by factorization to give

$$\hat{p}_{nt} = \lambda\hat{p}_{nt-2} + \lambda(1 - \beta^{-1})^{-1} \sum_{i=0}^{\infty} \lambda^i \hat{\phi}_{t+2i}, \quad (1.15)$$

with $\lambda \equiv (1 - \beta^{-1/2})^2(1 - \beta^{-1})^{-1}$.

λ gives the direct dependence of $\hat{p}_{nt}$ on $\hat{p}_{nt-2}$; it is an increasing function of β. For $\beta = 1$ (the value assumed in the previous section), taking limits appropriately, $\lambda = 0$ and equation (1.15) reduces to the equation of the previous section. If input supply is relatively inelastic, that is, for β between 0 and 1, λ is negative and tends to -1 as β tends to zero. If input supply is relatively elastic, that is, for β greater than 1, λ is positive and tends to 1 as β tends to infinity. Thus the flatter input supply, the larger the direct dependence of the price level on the past.

What we want, however, is not $\hat{p}_{nt}$ but the actual value of p_{nt}. Consider as in the previous section an unanticipated permanent increase in money at time t_0, and assume for notational convenience that the increase is from zero to unity. Since there are no unanticipated movements in money or prices after t_0, equation (1.15) together with the assumed path of money, implies in this case

$$p_{nt+2} = \lambda p_{nt} + (1 - \lambda), \quad t \geq t_0. \quad (1.16)$$

Thus, given p_{nt_0}, we can solve for the sequence of prices after t_0. Equation (1.13) and the assumptions about the path of money give us another relation between p_{nt_0+2} and p_{nt_0} and thus the initial condition we need:

$$p_{nt_0} = \frac{1 - \beta^{-1}}{4}(p_{nt_0} + p_{nt_0+2}) + \frac{\beta^{-1}}{2}. \quad (1.17)$$

Equations (1.16) and (1.17) allow us to solve for the path of prices at and after t_0.

Table 1.3 gives the path of prices for different values of β. It shows in particular that, if real input prices are insensitive to market conditions, that is, if β is large, the price level reacts less and adjusts more slowly to changes in money: money has larger and more lasting effects on output. If we think of the input as labor, this shows the importance of the short-run Phillips curve slope, even in an economy with rational expectations.

Extending the analysis to values of n larger than 2 presents no particular

Table 1.3
Cumulative effects of a permanent unanticipated increase in money at time t

	$\beta = 10.0$	$\beta = 2.0$	$\beta = 1.25$	$\beta = 1.0$	$\beta = 0.80$	$\beta = 0.66$	$\beta = 0.50$	$\beta = 0.10$
$n = 2$								
p_t	0.24	0.41	0.47	0.50	0.52	0.55	0.58	0.76
p_{t+2}	0.73	0.90	0.97	1.00	1.02	1.05	1.07	1.12
p_{t+4}	0.86	0.98	0.99	1.00	0.99	0.99	0.99	0.93
p_{t+6}	0.92	1.00	1.00	1.00	1.00	1.00	1.00	1.03
$n = 10$								
p_t		0.19	0.23	0.25	0.26	0.27	0.30	
p_{t+2}		0.55	0.62	0.66	0.68	0.72	0.77	
p_{t+4}		0.77	0.85	0.89	0.92	0.95	0.99	
p_{t+6}		0.90	0.96	0.98	0.99	1.01	1.03	
p_{t+8}		0.95	0.99	1.00	1.00	1.01	0.99	
p_{t+10}		0.98	1.00	1.00	1.00	1.00	1.00	

difficulty, and the method is sketched in the appendix. Results for $n = 10$ and different values of β are presented in table 1.3. The conclusions are the same. Since the analysis is substantially simpler when $\beta = 1$, the last section makes this assumption; this section has shown how the results would be modified if the assumption were relaxed.

1.5 Variability of Relative Prices and Profits

Asynchronization of price decisions has implications not only for the dynamics of the price level but for the dynamics of the structure of relative prices. The equation giving the behavior of any nominal price p_k is, if k is even, the same equation as for p_n, that is, equation (1.10) with n replaced by k. The formula for k odd is slightly different but, as there are no particular insights to be obtained from it, we shall limit our attention to prices for which k is even.

Snake Effects

To see the effects of a permanent increase in money on the structure of prices, we can return to tables 1.1 and 1.2: they can also be interpreted as giving the cross-section time series of prices. The first column gives the values of p_{kt} for values of k ranging from 2 to 500, the second column the values of p_{kt+2} for the same values of k, and so on.

Table 1.2 shows how the increase in money twists the structure of prices. Prices early in the chain of production move more and adjust faster; prices farther in the chain move less and adjust more slowly. If we measure profit rates by $(p_k - p_{k-2})$ for sector k, it also appears that profit rates move more for low values of k.[16] These results would be unchanged if we were looking at a supply disturbance, ξ, instead of a demand disturbance, m.

Variance of Prices and Profits

Instead of looking at effects of once-and-for-all changes in m or ξ, we may look at the stochastic behavior of prices for a given process for m or ξ. Assume for example that ξ and m are white—assuming for convenience that for t even realizations of ξ and m are the same for t and $t + 1$. If, as before, we define ψ_t as $m_t - \xi_t$, the behavior of p_{kt} is, from (1.10),

$$p_{kt} = 2^{-k}\left[\sum_{i=0}^{k/2} b_{k,(k/2)-i}\psi_{t-2i}\right].$$

(1.18)

Table 1.4
Standard deviations of prices and profits

Sector	Nominal prices	Real prices	Profits
$n = k = 10$	0.126	0	0.025
$k = 8$	0.146	0.025	0.044
$k = 6$	0.178	0.067	0.070
$k = 4$	0.253	0.135	0.153
$k = 2$	0.353	0.276	0.790
$k = 0$	1.00	0.966	—

Note: $\sigma_\psi^2 = \sigma_\xi^2 + \sigma_m^2$ is normalized to unity.

Thus the standard deviations of nominal prices, real prices, and profit rates are given by

$$\sigma(p_k) = 2^{-k} \left[\sum_{i=0}^{k/2} (b_{k,\,(k/2)-i})^2 \right]^{1/2} \sigma_\psi,$$

$$\sigma(p_k - p_n) = \left[\sum_{i=0}^{n/2} (2^{-k} b_{k,\,(k/2)-i} - 2^{-n} b_{n,\,(n/2)-i})^2 \right]^{1/2} \sigma_\psi, \quad b_{kj} = 0, \text{if } j < 0,$$

$$\sigma(p_k - p_{k-2}) = 2^{-k} \left[\sum_{i=0}^{k/2} (b_{k,\,(k/2)-i} - 4 h_{k-2,\,(k/2)-i})^2 \right]^{1/2} \sigma_\psi, \quad h_{kj} = 0 \text{ if } j < 0.$$

Using identities associated with the hypergeometric distribution (Feller 1950, p. 62), the first expression can be rewritten as

$$\sigma(p_k) = 2^{-k} \left(\binom{2k}{k} - \binom{2k}{k-1} \right)^{1/2} \sigma_\psi.$$

The values of these standard deviations, for $n = 10$ and $k = 0, \ldots, 10$, are reported in table 1.4. The standard deviations of nominal prices, real prices, and profit rates are all decreasing in k. This ordering is again independent of whether the economy is affected by supply or demand disturbances.

This result is fairly robust, being due to asynchronization rather than to the other assumptions of the model. There are two ways to potentially reverse it. The first is to relax the assumptions of constant returns and no inventory. In this case, faced for example with a temporary increase in demand, a firm may decrease its price, decumulate inventory, and not change its derived demand; it would therefore not transmit the disturbance farther down the chain of production. Its price may then vary more than prices farther down the chain. The second is to allow for disturbances to the technology itself, for example, to allow the θ_i in equation (1.1) to be stochastic. In this case sectors affected by large technological disturbances may experience more price variability than the others.

If we think of the primary input as raw materials—there are clearly other factors at work in the labor market—the result is in accordance with facts. In the United States the variance in raw material prices is larger than the variance in intermediate product prices, which is itself larger than the variance in the WPI, both for periods dominated by demand disturbances and periods dominated by supply disturbances.[17]

1.6 Conclusions and Extensions

This chapter has shown that asynchronization of individual price decisions generates both inertia of the price level and movements in relative prices which appear in accordance with the facts.

It is time to return to the assumptions and face the questions addressed to other models of price inertia. Are there obvious opportunities for profit left unused? Is every agent acting optimally? There are two crucial assumptions in the model.

The first is that price setters choose the same nominal price for two periods rather than different nominal prices for both periods, or allow the second-period price to be contingent. We have purposefully chosen a basic period short enough for such schemes to have costs that outweigh their benefits. Indexation of the second-period price on the price level is clearly unfeasible if the basic period is short: there may well be no reliable price level index.

The second is the structure of timing decisions. Given the timing decisions of others, does an agent have an incentive to maintain his own timing decision? In our model the answer is that he has an incentive to change it: each producer has an incentive to synchronize his price decisions with those of his supplier. This feature is, however, a characteristic of the simple structure of the model and is easily removed: if, for example, each producer uses two inputs, the prices of which change at different times, he cannot achieve synchronization with both. It is easy to construct such structures of timing decisions that no price setter has an incentive to change his own timing, given the timing of others. With such structures, asynchronization and the implied inertia of the price level will remain: no agent has an incentive to change his timing or behavior.

This model can be seen as an alternative to the model of overlapping labor contracts developed by Akerlof (1969), Phelps (1979), and Taylor (1980). Both explanations of price inertia are, however, probably empirically relevant. The comparative advantage of this model is twofold. The first is that it is more explicitly grounded in maximizing behavior; this allows for an easier treatment of normative aspects of policies. The second, and more important, is that it derives the complete structure of prices together with the price level. Thus it is well adapted to analyze questions involving both nominal and relative prices. It can, for example, easily be used to look at the desirability of exchange rate indexation under various sources of disturbances, a question analyzed by Dornbusch (1982) using the Taylor model.

Appendix: Price Solution for Arbitrary n and β

Replacing equation (1.7), with $\xi_t \equiv 0$, in equation (1.10) gives

$$p_{nt} = 2^{-n}\left\{\sum_{i=1}^{n/2}\sum_{j=0}^{(n/2)-i} b_{nj}E\left[(1-\beta^{-1})p_{nt-2i} - \beta^{-1}m_{t-2i}\middle| t - \frac{n}{2} - i + j\right]\right.$$

$$+ \sum_{j=0}^{(n/2)-t} b_{nj}E\left[(1-\beta^{-1})p_{nt} - \beta^{-1}m_t\middle| t - \frac{n}{2} + j\right]$$

$$\left. + \sum_{i=1}^{n/2}\sum_{j=0}^{(n/2)-i} b_{nj}E\left[(1-\beta)^{-1}p_{nt+2i} - \beta^{-1}m_{t+2i}\middle| t - \frac{n}{2} + i + j\right]\right\}.$$

$$(1.A1)$$

We proceed in two steps. The first is to derive the behavior of $E(p_{nt}|t-n)$. Taking expectations in (1.A1) at time $t-n$ and denoting them with a hat:

$$\hat{p}_{nt} = 2^{-n}(1-\beta^{-1})A(L)\hat{p}_{nt} + 2^{-n}\beta^{-1}A(L)\hat{m}_t, \qquad (1.A2)$$

with

$$L: Lx_t = x_{t-2}$$

and

$$A(L) \equiv \sum_{i=-n/2}^{n/2}\binom{n}{(n/2)+i}L^i.$$

Consider the polynomial $1 - 2^{-n}(1 - \beta^{-1})A(L)$ associated with the homogenous part of this difference equation. It is symmetric so that, if λ is a root, λ^{-1} is also a root. Thus it can be factorized as

$$1 - 2^{-n}(1 - \beta^{-1})A(L) = \sigma B(L)B(L^{-1}),$$

where σ is a scalar and $B(L) = 1 + b_1 L + \cdots + b_{n/2}L^{n/2}$ has all roots inside the unit circle.

This implies that $E(p_{nt}|t - n)$ follows:

$$B(L)\hat{p}_{nt} = 2^{-n}\beta^{-1}\sigma^{-1}[B(L^{-1})]^{-1}A(L)\hat{m}_t. \tag{1.A3}$$

The second step is to solve for the actual value of p_{nt}. This is easily done for any specific path of—or process for—money. In the case of a permanent unanticipated increase in money at time t_0 from zero to unity, it is derived as follows:

Since there are no unanticipated movements of money or prices after t_0, equation (1.A3) implies for $t \geq t_0 + n$

$$B(L)p_{nt} = 2^{-n}\beta^{-1}\sigma^{-1}[B(L^{-1})]^{-1}A(L)m_t$$

The path of money considered here is such that all values of m_t on the right hand side are equal to unity. Thus:

$$B(L)p_{nt} = 2^{-n}\beta^{-1}\sigma^{-1}[B(1)]^{-1}A(1)$$

$$\Rightarrow B(L)p_{nt} = [\beta\sigma B(1)]^{-1} \quad \text{as } 2^{-n}A(1) = 1 \tag{1.A4}$$

For $t = t_0 + n, \ldots, t_0 + 2n - 2$ this gives a system of $n/2$ equations in n unknowns, $p_{0t_0+2n-2}, \ldots, p_{0t_0}$. In turn equation (1.A1) gives, for $t = t_0, \ldots, t_0 + n - 2$ and, given the path of money, $n/2$ equations in the same unknowns. This gives a system of n equations in n unknowns. Once this system is solved, values of p_{0t} for $t \geq t_0 + 2n$ can be derived using (1.A4). This is the method used to construct the second part of table 1.3.

Notes

I thank Stanley Fischer, Danny Quah, and Jose Scheinkman for comments and suggestions. Financial assistance from the National Science Foundation and the Sloan Foundation is gratefully acknowledged.

1. Many arguments along this line are presented in Gordon (1981).

2. The implications of various theories for the relation between disturbances, the price level and relative prices are presented in Fischer (1981).

3. It is sometimes argued that a source of price inertia is the length of the production process (for example, Coutts et al. 1978). The argument is that, if price is based on historical cost, a longer production process will lead to longer lags in price adjustment. Although this argument seems to have some empirical success, it appears difficult to reconcile with rational behavior on the part of firms.

4. An alternative formalization, which would extend work by Akerlof (1969), would postulate a large number of imperfectly substitutable final outputs produced under monopolistic competition. An increase in the number of price decisions would be obtained by increasing the number of products. The problem for our purposes is that the "technology" would not remain invariant as the number of price decisions increased. Otherwise, results are very similar.

5. An alternative is to formalize production as iterations of an input-output matrix. This turns out to be difficult to analyze.

6. The supply disturbance ξ does not affect the technology. It would be easy to allow for technological disturbances as well, by letting the θ_i be stochastic in equation (1.1).

7. It is well known that this relation can either be seen as a velocity equation or as a reduced form ISLM. Allowing for an interest rate would complicate the analysis but bring few insights. The unitary elasticity of output with respect to money balances assumption can be easily relaxed.

8. Although we do not derive the decision about period length from an optimization problem, this can be done by equalizing the marginal cost of more frequent changes to the marginal benefit of more accurate relative prices. This analysis has been pursued by Sheshinski and Weiss (for example, 1981).

9. This voluntarily abstracts from issues of monopoly power which may arise with asynchronized price setting. Condition (1.6) differs in two minor ways from the correct expected zero-profit condition: it neglects the fact that the second-period expected profit should be discounted by the interest rate; equivalently it assumes the real interest rate to be equal to zero. It assumes that the firm sells the same quantities in both periods, so that the weights on profit rates in period t ($p_{it} - p_{i-1\,t-1}$) and period $t + 1$ ($p_{it} - E(p_{i-1\,t+1}|t)$) are equal. Both shortcuts simplify the analysis considerably and are not the source of its main results.

10. In a more realistic model, firms would have the choice of supplying demand out of production or inventories. The initial effect of an increase in aggregate demand on the derived demand for the primary input would in general be smaller.

11. Using the fixed-price equilibrium terminology, our model allows for overemployment or underemployment of the primary input but not for unemployment since the input market is always in equilibrium. If we allowed for changes in m and ξ every period, the price would not necessarily clear the market in both periods, and there could be unemployment.

12. The nominal rigidity of labor contracts is of a different nature from the rigidities considered in this chapter. It is usually of much longer duration, and the assumption of demand determination is certainly more questionable.

13. All the expressions in this chapter are computed using binomial distribution tables (Aiken 1955). These give $F(n,r,p) = \text{Prob}\,(x > r)$ if x follows an n-binomial distribution with probability p. Then

$$2^{-n}\binom{n}{r} = F\left(n,r,\frac{1}{2}\right) - F\left(n,r+1,\frac{1}{2}\right).$$

14. The usual caveat about policy invariance of the structure applies. Such a drastic change may lead price setters to change price decisions more often or to try to achieve better synchronization.

15. In his paper (1979) Phelps considers a slightly different question. The question is whether, starting from steady inflation, there is a path of money such that inflation disappears over time and there is no change, positive or negative, in output. Phelps shows that there is such a path in his model but that the path is unappealing, involving oscillations in the rate of inflation along the way. Our model also has such a path, with the same unappealing features for $n > 2$.

16. This is more precisely the profit rate of the consolidated sector $(k, k - 1)$. We use this definition to avoid having to introduce p_k for odd k. The change in definition does not affect any of the conclusions.

17. This statement is based on comparisons of standard deviations of residuals from regressions on a quadratic trend, for subsamples of 47–1 to 80–1, for the following three series, "finished goods" producer price index (WPISOP3000NS in the DRI U.S. price bank), "intermediate materials, supplies and components" index (WPISOP2000NS), and "crude materials for further processing" index (WPISOP1000NS).

References

Aiken, H. *Tables of the Cumulative Binomial Probability Distribution*. Harvard University Press, Cambridge, 1955.

Akerlof, G. "Relative Wages and the Rate of Inflation." *Quarterly Journal of Economics* (August 1969): 353–374.

Coutts, K., W. Godley, and W. Nordhaus. *Industrial Pricing in the United Kingdom*. Cambridge University Press, Cambridge, 1978.

Dornbusch, R. "PPP Exchange Rate Rules and Macroeconomic Stability." *Journal of Political Economy* (1982), in press.

Feller, W. *An Introduction to Probability Theory and Its Applications*. Vol. 1. 2d ed., Wiley, New York, 1957.

Fischer, S. "Relative Shocks, Relative Price Variability and Inflation." *Brookings Papers on Economic Activity* 2 (1981): 381–442.

Gordon, R. "Output Fluctuations and Gradual Price Adjustment," *Journal of Economic Literature* (June 1981): 493–530.

Phelps, E. "Disinflation without Recession: Adaptive Guideposts and Monetary Policy." *Studies in Macroeconomic Theory*. Academic Press, New York, 1979.

Sheshinski, E., and Y. Weiss. Optimum Pricing Policy under Stochastic Inflation. Mimeographed, October 1981.

Taylor, J.: "Aggregate Dynamics and Staggered Contracts." *Journal of Political Economy* (February 1980): 1–23.

2 Wage Indexation, Incomplete Information, and the Aggregate Supply Curve

Jo Anna Gray

2.1 Introduction

This chapter examines the role of wage indexation in a framework that synthesizes two popular classes of models of output determination: models with a contractually fixed nominal wage rate as the central feature, and models with information confusion as the central feature. The effectiveness of wage indexation in damping macroeconomic fluctuations has been explored independently in each of these two classes. The role of indexing in the composite framework presented here differs significantly from its role in these earlier models.

The macroeconomic effects of wage indexation in models in which nominal wage rates are contractually fixed are well-known.[1] Because production decisions are made on the basis of complete information while wage decisions are not, indexation of the negotiated wage rate to the price level allows some response of the wage rate to contemporaneous aggregate disturbances. Under full indexation, this response produces a fixed real wage rate. Accordingly, it is found in these models that full indexation insulates the real sector of the economy from the effects of aggregate disturbances that leave the equilibrium real wage unchanged. Examples of such disturbances include unanticipated changes in the demand or supply of money—monetary disturbances. By contrast, full indexation may exacerbate the real effects of aggregate disturbances that change the equilibrium real wage. Examples of such disturbances include supply shocks such as an oil embargo or a change in labor productivity. In the presence of both types of aggregate disturbances, the optimal degree of wage indexation is generally less than one.

Studies of wage indexation in the context of simple models of incomplete information are relatively rare. The work that has been done suggests that wage indexation should have no effect at all on the response of the real sector to disturbances of any kind.[2] This is because labor demanders (firms) and labor suppliers (workers) are typically assumed to base their decisions on the same (incomplete) information set. Indexing arrangements have no effect on this information set: indexing in no way alters the information available to firms and workers at the time production decisions are made. In models of this kind then, the response of output and employment to disturbances is independent of the degree of wage indexation.

The framework developed here contains elements of both classes of models described above. It combines the contractual arrangements of the first class with an information structure similar to that of the second class. Specifically, one-period contracts stipulate a base nominal wage rate and an indexing parameter for each of the markets (industries) composing the aggregate economy. At the time contracts are signed, firms and workers know only the structure of the economy and the (unconditional) distributions of the two disturbance terms that impinge on their industry. These disturbance terms represent two types of shocks to the industry's demand curve—an aggregate demand (or monetary) shock that affects all industries identically and a relative demand shock that is industry-specific. Once contracts are signed, each firm observes the position of its own industry's demand curve. This observation provides the firm with partial information on the values of the two disturbances terms underlying the position of that curve. On the basis of this (incomplete) information firms make their production and employment decisions. After production has taken place, the actual values of all disturbance terms are revealed, and prices adjust to clear markets for goods. An essential feature of the model is the fact that firms do not make their production decisions on the basis of realized wage rates and output prices. Rather production decision are based on the expected values of these variables.

This framework produces results that differ significantly in some respects from those found in earlier work. Since the only aggregate disturbance in the model is a monetary one, the appropriate degree of wage indexation is not an issue. As long as indexing is costless, full indexing is optimal in the sense that it minimizes deviations of aggregate output from its full employment level. Full indexation will not, however, entirely eliminate such deviations. Indexing does not, in this model, completely insulate the real sector from monetary shocks. This is because indexing can neutralize only that portion of a monetary disturbance that is correctly perceived to be a monetary disturbance. If relative demand shocks are part of the the stochastic structure of the economy, and if information is incomplete, then some part of every monetary disturbance will be mistakenly perceived as a relative demand disturbance. This misperception leads to an output response even if wages are fully indexed.

The effectiveness of indexing in neutralizing the real effects of a given monetary disturbance increases with increased monetary variability. This is because the fraction of any change in industry demand that is perceived to be monetary is an increasing function of the variance of monetary shocks relative to the variance of industry-specific shocks. This result reinforces the existing arguments for a positive correlation between the variance of monetary disturbances and the incentives to index.

2.2 The Model

The one-period framework described in this section incorporates short-term wage rigidities and incomplete information. The model is "rational" in the usual sense: economic agents are assumed to know the structure of the model and the distributions of the disturbance terms that enter the model and then to form expectations that fully reflect that knowledge. The aggregate economy is composed of n industries, each containing h firms. Output and employment are explicitly determined by aggregating the profit-maximizing decisions of the $n \cdot h$ firms in the economy. Uncertainty enters in the form of two types of shocks to industry demand curves, aggregate demand disturbances that affect all industries identically and relative demand disturbances that are industry-specific. The chronology of events occurring for each firm over one period are as follows. First, a nominal base wage and an indexing parameter are contractually fixed for the period. Firms then observe the position of their industry demand curve, which reflects the sum of the realized disturbances to aggregate demand and relative demands. They do not observe the underlying demand disturbances themselves. Next, production decisions are made and carried out. These decisions are consistent with expected profit maximization. Finally, firms go to market with their output. At this point the actual values of the disturbance terms are revealed, and prices adjust to equate the supply and demand for each industry's output. There are no inventories of goods.

For simplicity, firms are assumed to have identical production functions of the form

$$X_{ij}^S = AL_{ij}^a, \quad 0 > a > 1, \tag{2.1}$$

where

$$i = 1, 2, \ldots, n,$$

$$j = 1, 2, \ldots, h.$$

The notation X_{ij}^S denotes the output of the jth firm of the ith industry. Similarly, L_{ij} denotes labor employed by firm j of industry i. Each industry faces a downward sloping demand curve of the form

$$X_i^D = \left(\frac{1}{n}\right)\left(\frac{P}{P_i}\right)e^{\alpha_i}Z, \tag{2.2}$$

where

$$Z = \sum_{i=1}^{n} \frac{P_i X_i}{P}.$$

Equation (2.2) may be interpreted as follows: industry demand is a share of total (aggregate) real expenditure, Z, where the size of the share depends on the number of industries in the economy, n, the industry's relative price, P_i/P, and a disturbance term, α_i. The disturbance term, α_i, is normally distributed with zero mean and variance σ_α^2 for all i. In addition it is assumed that the α_i's sum to zero across industries. The price level, P, is a geometrically weighted average of the individual industry prices, P_i:[3,4]

$$P = P_1^{(1/n)} P_2^{(1/n)} \cdots P_n^{(1/n)}. \tag{2.3}$$

And, finally, the level of real aggregate expenditure, Z, must be consistent with macroeconomic equilibrium. The macroeconomic specification of the model is discussed at the end of this section. As indicated earlier, that specification produces a stochastic aggregate demand function.

From equations (2.1) and (2.2) it is evident that all industries and all firms are identical, ex ante. Accordingly, the (homogeneous) labor force is assumed to distribute itself evenly across firms and to negotiate a common base nominal wage rate, W^*, and indexing parameter, λ, at the beginning of each period. The base wage is assumed to be set at the level that would correspond to equilibrium in the labor market if the realized values of all disturbance terms were zero. This level is designated by an asterisk and is referred to as the certainty equivalent of the nominal wage rate. The indexing parameter specifies the degree to which the base wage is adjusted for unexpected changes in the price level. Specifically,

$$\lambda = \frac{(W - W^*)/W^*}{(P - P^*)/P^*}, \tag{2.4}$$

where $0 \leq \lambda \leq 1$. Here P^* is the certainty equivalent value of the price level. Note that the indexing parameter has been restricted to values lying between zero and one, inclusive.

Calculation of the base wage, W^*, requires knowledge of the supply and demand functions for labor. Mobility costs are assumed to prevent workers from obtaining employment with any firm other than the one they contract with at the beginning of the period. Accordingly, W^* is assumed to be negotiated on the basis of an upward sloping labor supply schedule of the form

$$L_{ij}^s = \left(\frac{W}{P}\right)^e, \tag{2.5}$$

where e is the elasticity of labor supply with respect to the real wage. A labor demand schedule is developed later from the solution to the firm's maximization problem.

Once contracts have been signed, the level of employment becomes completely demand determined for the rest period. That is, workers are assumed to supply whatever amount of labor is demanded by firms at the negotiated wage rate. Equation (2.5) is in effect dropped from the system at this point. Each firm then observes the deviation of its own industry's demand curve from its expected position and forms conditional estimates of the (unobserved) relative and aggregate disturbances underlying the deviation. Using those estimates, the firm chooses production and employment levels in such a way as to maximize expected profits. Specifically, the problem faced by the jth firm of the ith industry is given by

$$\max_{X_{ij}L_{ij}} E(P_i X_{ij} - W L_{ij}),$$

subject to $X_{ij} = A L_{ij}^a$. This formulation of the firm's problem is appropriate only if the firm assumes that the price of its output and the wage rate it pays are independent of its actions—only if the firm acts as a perfect competitor. For simplicity, it is assumed that the number of firms, n, composing each industry is large enough to make this assumption acceptable.

The solution of the firm's optimization problem yields the following condition for a maximum:

$$[(aAL_{ij}^{(a-1)})]E(P_i) = E(W).$$

With the exception of the expectations operators, this is just the usual requirement that the value marginal product of labor be set equal to the wage rate. Rearranging this equation gives the labor demand function for firm j of industry i:

$$L_{ij}^D = \left(\frac{1}{Aa}\right)\left[\frac{E(W)}{E(P_i)}\right]^{-\phi},\tag{2.6}$$

where $\phi = \dfrac{1}{1-a}$.

Finally, note that industrywide equilibrium requires that the total supply of each good be demanded, or

$$X_i^D = X_i^S = \sum_{j=1}^{h} X_{ij}^S \quad \text{for all } i.\tag{2.7}$$

This completes the discussion of the microeconomic components of the model. We turn next to the requirements of macroeconomic equilibrium.

The aggregate economy consists of a money market and a goods market. From Walras' law, we know that equilibrium in one of these two markets insures equilibrium in the other. Accordingly, only the goods market is explicitly modeled here.

Aggregate demand for output (real expenditure) is assumed to be an increasing function of the level of real money balances, the velocity of money, and a disturbance term:

$$Z = \left(\frac{M}{P}\right)Ve^{\beta}.\tag{2.8}$$

Here M denotes the component of the nominal money supply controlled by the monetary authority. For simplicity, the velocity of money, V, is assumed to be a constant. The disturbance term, β, is normally distributed with zero mean and variance σ_{β}^2. It is intended to represent a variety of possible disturbances to aggregate demand—such as velocity shifts, changes in savings behavior, or fluctuations in export demand.

Goods market equilibrium requires that aggregate demand, Z, be equal to aggregate supply, X_T^S, as described in equation (2.9):

$$X_T^D = X_T^S = \sum_{i=1}^{n} X_i^S.\tag{2.9}$$

2.3 The Full-Information Solution

The main results of this chapter are derived in the next section under the assumption of incomplete current information. Before turning to that analysis, however, it will be useful to describe the full-information solution of the model, since it will serve as a benchmark for the discussion of the effects of incomplete information. This section then explores the response of prices and outputs to both aggregate and relative demand shocks, under the assumption of complete current information. The results are well-known: it is found that positive (negative) disturbances to aggregate demand leads to increases (decreases) in both the price level and aggregate output as long as wages are not fully indexed. In the special case of full indexation, aggregate demand shocks affect only the price level; they have no effect on output. Relative demand shocks, by contrast, have no impact on aggregate output or the price level. They do, however, generate changes in industry outputs and prices of the usual sort. In particular, a rise (fall) in demand for an industry's output leads to a rise (fall) in that industry's price and output. The degree of wage indexation has no affect on the response of the system to relative demand shocks. On the basis of these results an aggregate supply curve relating the price level and aggregate output is constructed. The slope of this curve is shown to depend on the degree of wage indexation, becoming vertical under full indexation.

In the analysis that follows it is convenient to use as a reference point the situation that would have occurred in the absence of shocks. For example, the impact of an aggregate demand shock on aggregate output is measured by the percentage deviation of actual output from the level of output that would have been produced if the shock had been zero. For small changes, these deviations can be approximated by log differences. Accordingly, the framework set out in the preceding section is rewritten below in terms of log differences. Lowercase letters, when they identify a variable, denote log value. Thus dx_T is the difference between the log value of actual aggregate output and the log value of the level of aggregate output that would have been produced if the realized value of all shocks had been zero. All coefficients are positive:

$$dx_i^S = dx_{ij}^S = adl_{ij}, \tag{2.10}$$

$$dx_i^D = dZ + (dp - dp_i) + \alpha_i, \tag{2.11}$$

$$dp = \frac{1}{n}\sum dp_i, \tag{2.12}$$

$$dw = \lambda dp, \tag{2.13}$$

$$dl_{ij} = -\phi(dw - dp_i) \quad \text{where } \phi = \frac{1}{1-a}, \tag{2.14}$$

$$dx_i^D = dx_i^S, \tag{2.15}$$

$$dZ = dm - dp + \beta. \tag{2.16}$$

Several comments on this reformulation of the model are in order. First, because all firms composing an industry are identical, the proportional change in production following a shock is the same for all firms in an industry, and is equal to the proportional change in the industry's output. Thus equation (2.10) determines changes in output for the firm and the industry to which it belongs. Second, the assumption of complete information is explicitly employed in deriving equation (2.14) from equation (2.6). To arrive at (2.14) the expected values of variables that appear in (2.6) are replaced by actual values. Log linearization of the resulting relationship gives (2.14). Third, no labor supply function corresponding to equation (2.5) is included in this formulation of the problem because the labor supply function is used only in determining the *level* of the base wage, W^*. It is not required in solving for dw, the proportional deviation of the realized wage from W^*. Finally, a condition corresponding to equation (2.9), which equates aggregate supply to aggregate demand, does not appear here. It is redundant as long as equation (2.15) is satisfied for every industry.

The solution of the complete information version of the model set out in (2.10) through (2.16) is a matter of straightforward algebraic manipulation. The results are summarized in equations (2.17) through (2.20):

$$dp = (dm + \beta)\left[\frac{1}{1 + a\phi(1-\lambda)}\right], \tag{2.17}$$

$$dx_T = (dm + \beta)\left[\frac{a\phi(1-\lambda)}{1 + a\phi(1-\lambda)}\right], \tag{2.18}$$

$$dp_i = (dm + \beta)\left[\frac{1}{1 + a\phi(1-\lambda)}\right] + \alpha_i\left[\frac{1}{1 + a\phi}\right], \tag{2.19}$$

$$dx_i = (dm + \beta)\left[\frac{a\phi(1 - \lambda)}{1 + a\phi(1 - \lambda)}\right] + \alpha_i\left[\frac{a\phi}{1 + a\phi}\right]. \qquad (2.20)$$

As indicated earlier, the response of aggregate output and the price level to aggregate demand shocks depends critically on the indexing parameter, λ. The larger λ, the greater the response of the price level, and the smaller the response of aggregate output, to a change in aggregate demand. In the special case of full indexation ($\lambda = 1$), output is unaffected by aggregate demand shocks. Note also that unanticipated changes in the component of the money supply controlled by the monetary authority cause changes in prices and outputs identical to those produced by the stochastic term, β. In this model then, monetary policy can be used to stabilize output if the monetary authority is able to react to current information—to produce changes in the money supply that offset β. These are familiar results. The response of industry outputs and prices to aggregate demand shocks is of course precisely the same as the response of aggregate output and the price level.

Relative demand shocks have no effect on the price level or aggregate output but do cause movements in relative prices and outputs. Since the price level is unaffected by these shocks, the degree of wage indexation is irrelevant to the price and output responses they generate. Accordingly, the indexing parameter, λ, does not appear in the coefficient on α_i in either equation (2.19) or (2.20).

From equations (2.17) and (2.18) we can construct an aggregate supply relationship—a Phillips curve—for the case of complete current information. Positive deviations of the price level from its certainty equivalent value are associated with positive deviations of output from its certainty equivalent value. Thus the relationship between the price level and output (in logs) can be represented by a positively sloped curve in (p, x_T) space. This relationship, depicted in figure 2.1, will be referred to as the aggregate supply curve throughout the rest of the paper. The slope of the schedule depends on the indexing parameter, λ. The larger λ, the steeper the curve, and the smaller the rise in output associated with an increase in the price level. In the special case of full indexation the aggregate supply curve is vertical.

The economic rationale underlying this curve is straightforward. An increase (decrease) in aggregate demand leads to a uniform, and perfectly predicted, increase (decrease) in all prices. If nominal wage rates are not

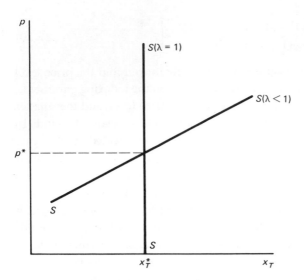

Figure 2.1
The aggregate supply curve for the case of complete information

fully indexed, the real wage falls (rises), producing a rise (fall) in the profit maximizing level of output for all firms. The greater the degree of wage indexation, the smaller the change in the real wage rate and therefore output. In the special case of full indexation the real wage is unaffected by price level movements, and output is fixed at its certainty equivalent value.

   This kind of aggregate supply curve has been incorporated in many of the models used to analyze the effects of wage indexation. Those models, like the one analyzed in this section, typically imply that full indexation completely insulates the real sector from monetary disturbances.

2.4 The Case of Incomplete Information

The response of prices and outputs to both aggregate and relative demand shocks is now explored under the assumption of incomplete current information. Specifically, it is assumed that firms make their production and employment decisions knowing only the position of their own industry's demand curve. They do not know the realized values of either of the disturbance terms that jointly determine the position of the curve.

The results of the section may be summarized as follows. As in the case of complete information, the response of prices and outputs to an aggregate demand shock implies an aggregate supply curve. Under incomplete information, however, the slope of this curve depends not only on the extent to which wages are indexed but also on the stochastic structure of the economy. Further, although the curve is positively sloped and becomes steeper as the degree of wage indexation rises, it does not become vertical under full indexation. This reflects the fact that full indexing does not completely insulate the real sector from monetary shocks when relative shocks are also part of the stochastic structure of the economy and information is incomplete.

In deriving these results, it is again convenient to deal with a model expressed in log differences. The model appropriate for the case of incomplete information differs from that of the preceding section in one important way: firms must make their employment and production decisions on the basis of uncertain output prices and labor costs. Equation (2.14) of the last section, which specifies the dependence of labor demand on the realized deviation of wages and prices from their certainty equivalent values, is not applicable here. It is replaced by equation (2.21), which relates labor demand to the *expected* deviation of wages and prices from their certainty equivalent values:[5]

$$dl_{ij} = -\phi(Edw - Edp_i). \tag{2.21}$$

With the exception of equation (2.14), the model set out in the preceding section is correct for the case of incomplete information as well as for the case of complete information. Equations (2.10) through (2.13) and equations (2.15) and (2.16) describe behavioral relations and equilibrium conditions that must hold ex post. They determine the actual levels of wages and prices once production decisions are made and firms "go to market" with their output. Further, because the disturbance terms entering the log derivative form of the model are additive, each of the equations of the model must also hold ex ante in expected values. For example, if equation (2.10) holds, it must also be true that

$$E(dx_i) = E(dx_{ij}) = aE(dl_{ij}). \tag{2.22}$$

The solution of the incomplete information version of the model just described is summarized by equations (2.23) through (2.28) (see appendix for details):

$$dp = \beta\left[1 - \pi\left(\frac{a\phi(1-\lambda)}{1+a\phi(1-\lambda)}\right) - (1-\pi)\left(\frac{a\phi}{1+a\phi}\right)\right], \tag{2.23}$$

$$dx_T = \beta\left[\pi\left(\frac{a\phi(1-\lambda)}{1+a\phi(1-\lambda)}\right) + (1-\pi)\left(\frac{a\phi}{1+a\phi}\right)\right], \tag{2.24}$$

$$dp_i = (\beta + \alpha_i)\left[1 - \pi\left(\frac{a\phi(1-\lambda)}{1+a\phi(1-\lambda)}\right) - (1-\pi)\left(\frac{a\phi}{1+a\phi}\right)\right], \tag{2.25}$$

$$dx_i = (\beta + \alpha_i)\left[\pi\left(\frac{a\phi(1-\lambda)}{1+a\phi(1-\lambda)}\right) + (1-\pi)\left(\frac{a\phi}{1+a\phi}\right)\right], \tag{2.26}$$

where

$$\pi = \frac{\sigma_\beta^2}{\sigma_\beta^2 + \sigma_\alpha^2}.$$

Note that the model has been solved under the assumption that monetary policy is completely predictable, that is, with dm equal to zero. The implications of an "active" monetary rule—where dm is manipulated to neutralize the effects of β—are discussed in section 2.6.

The interpretation of equations (2.23) through (2.26) is facilitated if they are compared to the results of the preceding section. Consider the solution for the individual industry's (and firm's) output given by equation (2.26). The first term in (2.26) represents the shift in the industry's demand curve relative to its "no-shock" position. This shift is correctly perceived by all firms in the industry. It reflects the combined affects of an aggregate demand shock (given by β) and a relative demand shock (given by α_i). knowledge of this shift provides firms with some current information. The second expression (in square brackets) gives the individual firm's (and the industry's) response to the shift. That response is a weighted average of the industry's full-information responses to aggregate and relative demand shocks, which are given in equation (2.21) of the preceding section. The weight associated with the full-information response to an aggregate shock is π, and the weight associated with the full-information response to a relative demand shock is $(1 - \pi)$. The weights involve the relative size of the variance of the two shocks in the system. Thus the greater the variance of aggregate shocks compared to relative shocks, the greater π, and the more firms respond to a shift in demand as though it were due to an aggregate demand shock. Conversely, the greater the variance of relative shocks compared to aggregate shocks, the smaller is π, and the more firms respond to a shift in demand as though it were specific to their own industry.

The economic intuition underlying these results is similar to the intuition underlying many of the results of the rational expectations literature of the past decade (see Lecas 1973). The fundamental problem facing firms is one of information confusion. They must estimate the size of two shocks (an aggregate shock and a relative shock) given one piece of information (the position of their industry's demand curve). Their estimate depends on the expected relative size (measured by relative variances) of the two shocks. The larger the variance of aggregate shocks, the more likely it is that a given change in demand is due to a change in aggregate demand, and the less likely it is that it is due to a change in relative demand. The converse is true for an increase in the variance of relative demand shocks. Accordingly, the weight π, which is the proportion of the shift in their industry's demand curve that firms estimate to be due a change in aggregate demand, is an increasing function of the variance of monetary shocks and a decreasing function of the variance of relative shocks.

The foregoing discussion also serves to motivate equation (2.24), which gives the solution for aggregate output. The response of aggregate output to either type of shock is simply the average of the individual industry responses. For aggregate shocks then, the proportional response of aggregate output is identical to the proportional response of any of the n (identical) industries. Relative shocks, however, have no affect on aggregate output because, by construction, relative demand shocks sum to zero across industries. It follows from the linearity of the model that the individual industry responses also sum to zero across industries. Thus the only disturbance term entering equation (2.21) is the aggregate demand shock, β.

The response of the price level to an aggregate demand shock may be regarded as the mathematical complement of the response of aggregate output. An increase in demand must be fully met by an increase in output or an increase in prices or both. Equation (2.23) simply states that the fraction of a demand shift which is reflected in a price level change is one minus the fraction that is reflected in an aggregate output change. The interpretation of equation (2.25) for the individual industry's price response is analogous.

From equations (2.23) and (2.24) we can construct an aggregate supply

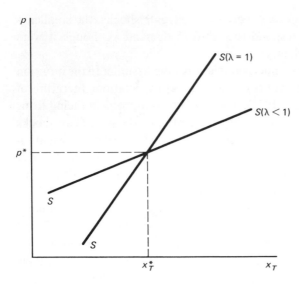

Figure 2.2
The aggregate supply curve for the case of incomplete information

relationship for the case of incomplete information. As in the case of complete information, the relationship can be represented by a positively sloped curve in (p, x_T) space (see figure 2.2). The slope of the schedule, however, depends on the stochastic structure of the economy, as summarized by the parameter π, as well as the indexing parameter, λ:

$$\frac{dp}{dx_t} = \frac{1 - \Delta(\pi, \lambda)}{\Delta(\pi, \lambda)}, \tag{2.27}$$

where

$$\Delta(\pi, \lambda) = \pi \left[\frac{a\phi(1 - \lambda)}{1 + a\phi(1 - \lambda)} \right] + (1 - \pi) \left[\frac{a\phi}{1 + a\phi} \right],$$

$$\pi = \frac{\sigma_\beta^2}{\sigma_\beta^2 + \sigma_\alpha^2}.$$

One of the important differences between this aggregate supply curve and the one of the preceding section is that full indexation does not, in general, make it vertical. From (2.27) it is evident that an infinite slope is possible only if $\Delta(\pi, \lambda)$ is equal to zero. For $\Delta(\pi, \lambda)$ to equal zero requires not only full indexation ($\lambda = 1$) but also a stochastic structure where aggregate disturbances completely dominate relative shocks ($\pi = 1$).[6] Accordingly, full indexing cannot completely insulate the real sector from monetary shocks if relative shocks are also part of the stochastic structure of the economy.

The intuition behind this result rests again on the assumption of incomplete information. In an economy where relative demand shocks are of measurable importance (π is less than one), changes in demand due to aggregate demand disturbances will be partially misperceived. Only a fraction π of any aggregate disturbance will actually be treated as an aggregate disturbance. A fraction $(1 - \pi)$ will be treated as a relative demand disturbance. If wages are fully indexed, the firm's profit maximizing level of output is unaffected by the component of the shock that is perceived to be aggregate because it expects its wage costs to rise in the same proportion as the price it receives for its output following an aggregate demand shock. The firm's profit maximizing level of output is, however, affected by the component of the aggregate demand shock that is perceived to be relative, regardless of the degree of wage indexation. This is because the firm expects the price of its output, but not its wage costs, to change following a relative demand shock. Wages are not expected to change because they change only in response to price level changes, and relative demand disturbances are not expected to affect the price level. In any stochastic environment that includes relative demand shocks then, some part of every aggregate demand shock will be misperceived as a relative demand shock. This misperception leads to an output response even if wages are fully indexed.

2.5 The Incentives to Index Wage Rates

The analysis of this section is concerned with measuring the benefits of wage indexation and the effect of increased monetary (or aggregate demand) variability on those benefits. Two reasons to expect a positive association between the degree of monetary variability and the incentives to index are identified. The first is already well documented in the existing literature: to the extent that indexing reduces the real effects of aggregate demand shocks, increased monetary variability generates a larger stabilizing role for indexing. The second reason is one of the contributions of this chapter: greater monetary variability increases the effectiveness of indexing in neutralizing the real effects of particular monetary disturbances.

In much of the recent literature on wage indexing the benefits of indexing have been assessed by its impact on welfare, as measured by the variance of aggregate output around an optimal, or full-equilibrium, value. This measure is motivated by the observation that deviations of output and employment from their full-equilibrium levels typically involve resource misallocation, regardless of whether the deviations are positive or negative. The dead weight welfare loss associated with this misallocation typically has the same qualitative properties as the measured variance of output around its full-equilibrium value: Positive and negative deviations in output are treated symmetrically, and the loss associated with a deviation increases more than proportionately with the size of the deviation. Here, an analogous measure can be constructed for either the individual firm or the economy as a whole. For the individual firm, for example, the full-equilibrium level of its output is that level that it would produce, given complete current information and flexible wages. The variance of the firm's output around this optimal level is given by[7]

$$\sigma_x^2 = \sigma_\beta^2 \left[\pi \left(\frac{a\phi(1-\lambda)}{1+a\phi(1-\lambda)} \right) + (1-\pi) \left(\frac{a\phi}{1+a\phi} \right) \right]^2$$
$$+ \sigma_\alpha^2 \left[\pi \left(\frac{a\phi(1-\lambda)}{1+a\phi(1-\lambda)} \right) + (1-\pi) \left(\frac{a\phi}{1+\phi} \right) - \frac{a\phi}{[(e+\phi)/e] + a\phi} \right]^2,$$
$$(2.28)$$

where

$$\pi = \frac{\sigma_\beta^2}{\sigma_\beta^2 + \sigma_\alpha^2}.$$

The gains associated with full-wage indexation are found by subtracting the variance of output for the case of full indexation ($\lambda = 1$) from the variance of output for the case of no indexation ($\lambda = 0$):

$$\rho = \sigma_x^2 \big|_{\lambda=0} - \sigma_x^2 \big|_{\lambda=1}$$
$$= (\sigma_\beta^2) \pi \left(\frac{a\phi}{1+a\phi} \right)^2 + 2(\sigma_\alpha^2) \pi \left(\frac{a\phi}{1+a\phi} \right) \left[\frac{a\phi}{1+a\phi} - \frac{a\phi}{[(e+\phi)/e] + a\phi} \right]^2,$$
$$(2.29)$$

where ρ represents the benefits associated with full-wage indexation. Note that these gains are calculated under the assumption that all firms share the same indexing parameter. It may be regarded as a measure of the increase in social welfare associated with moving from a nonindexed economy to a fully indexed economy, provided of course that indexing is costless.

Examination of the terms entering equation (2.29) reveals that an increase in monetary variability results in an increase in this measure of the benefits of indexation. The total effect of an increase in σ_β^2 on ρ may be usefully viewed as the result of two distinct partial affects. The first of these is the effect of σ_β^2 on ρ, holding π constant. This corresponds, for instance, to the exercise of doubling the variances of both shocks in the system, which leaves the relative size of the variances of the two shocks (and therefore π) unchanged. It is evident from (2.29) that this partial effect is positive. The second partial effect is the impact off σ_β^2 on ρ through its impact on π. An increase in σ_β^2 causes an increase in π which in turn causes an increase in ρ. This partial effect is then also positive.

The relationship of this work to much of the existing literature on wage indexation can be framed in terms of the two partial effects outlined here. The first of the two is already well-known from earlier papers. If indexing neutralizes the real effects of some fixed proportion of any aggregate demand shock, then an increase in the average size of the demand shocks impinging on the system generates a larger stabilizing role for indexing. In most models of wage indexation indexing neutralizes all of any aggregate demand shock that occurs.[8] In these models then, as well as in the present one, increased monetary variability generates a greater incentive to index wage rates by increasing the size of the problem—output and employment fluctuations—that indexing is used to correct.

The present model differs from previous ones in that it suggests a second link between the variability of aggregate demand and the incentive to index wage rates. An increase in aggregate demand variability causes an increase in π—in the proportion of any demand shift that is attributed to a change in aggregate demand. It is only this fraction of any demand shift that indexing is capable of neutralizing. Indexing has no affect at all on the economy's response to the fraction $(1 - \pi)$ of such shifts that are attributed to changes in relative demands. The parameter π then measure the effectiveness of wage indexation in neutralizing the real effects of a given shift in aggregate demand. In contrast to other models, this parameter is endogenously determined and is, in general, less than one.

2.6 Conclusions and Further Research

In this chapter, the role of wage indexation in neutralizing monetary disturbances was explored in a model characterized by incomplete information. It was found that indexing cannot fully insulate the real sector of an economy from monetary shocks if relative demand shocks are part of the stochastic structure of the economy. Further the *effectiveness* of indexing is neutralizing monetary (or more generally aggregate demand) disturbances increases as the size of monetary disturbances increases relative to the size of industry-specific demand disturbances. The latter result reinforces the existing theoretical arguments for a postive association between monetary uncertainty and the prevalance of indexing arrangements.

Research on two extensions of this basic framework is currently underway. One involves the role of monetary policy in the model, and the other the cyclical movement of real wages. Work on the first of these suggests that the role of monetary policy in this model differs importantly from its role in most well-known rational expectations models. If the monetary authority has better current information than the private sector, an active monetary policy can succeed in stabilizing the level of aggregate demand, thereby improving the quality of the information on which the private sector acts. This is the conventional result.[9] However, it does not follow that such a reduction in information confusion improves private welfare. It is possible under some circumstances for the monetary authority to improve private welfare by running monetary policy in a way that increases the amount of information confusion in the system. The assumption of contractually fixed nominal wage rates is crucial for this result. Because of the nominal wage rigidities, the full-information solution to this model is a second best solution. The model's full-information solution differs from its full-equilibrium, or optimal, solution. Consequently, a deterioration in the quality of information on which privates agents act does not necessarily decrease private welfare, as measured by the variance of output around its optimal level.

The behavior of real wages in the model is countercyclical unless wages are fully indexed. In the extreme case of full indexation the real wage rate shows no cyclical pattern. This result is the usual one for models in which nominal wages are contractually fixed and employment is determined along the firm's labor demand schedule. In the present model, however, it is possible to generate procyclical real wage movements by including in labor contracts a provision for paying higher nominal wage rates, the larger the quantity of labor supplied, as a kind of nominal overtime schedule. The combined effect of the overtime schedule, indexing, and information confusion is a cyclical real wage pattern that could, in principle, take any form. However, the steeper the overtime schedule and the greater the degree of wage indexation, the more likely is a procyclical pattern of real wage movements.

Appendix: Solution of Incomplete Information

The incomplete information model consists of equations (2.10) through (2.13), (2.15), (2.16), and (2.21). The variables to be solved for are dp, dx_T, dp_i, and dx_i.

As noted earlier, each of the equations of the model holds in expected value terms. By manipulating the expected value version of the model, it is possible to derive expressions for Edw and Edp_i, both of which enter (2.21):

$$Edw = \lambda Edp = E\beta \left[\frac{1}{1 + a\phi(1 - \lambda)} \right], \tag{2.A1}$$

$$Edp_i = E\beta \left[\frac{1}{1 + a\phi(1 - \lambda)} \right] + E\alpha_i \left(\frac{a\phi}{1 + a\phi} \right). \tag{2.A2}$$

Note that expectations are formed after firms see the position of their industry demand curves, which provides them with partial information on the two disturbances, α_i and β. Specifically, each firm is assumed to observe the sum $\alpha_i + \beta$ for its own industry and on the basis of that information to form an estimate of the two individual disturbances. If the two shocks are normally distributed with zero means, their conditional expectations are given by

$$E(\alpha_i | \alpha_i + \beta) = \left(\frac{\sigma_\alpha^2}{\sigma_\beta^2 + \sigma_\alpha^2} \right)(\alpha_i + \beta) = (1 - \pi)(\alpha_i + \beta) \tag{2.A3}$$

and

$$E(\beta|\alpha_i + \beta) = \left(\frac{\sigma_\beta^2}{\sigma_\beta^2 + \sigma_\alpha^2}\right)(\alpha_i + \beta) = \pi(\alpha_i + \beta). \tag{2.A4}$$

Substituting (2.A1) through (2.A4) into (2.21) produces (2.A5):

$$dl_{ij} = (\alpha_i + \beta)\left[\pi\left(\frac{\phi(1 - \lambda)}{1 + a\phi(1 - \lambda)}\right) + (1 - \pi)\left(\frac{\phi}{1 + a\phi}\right)\right] \tag{2.A5}$$

The solution of equations (2.10) through (2.13), (2.15), (2.16), and (2.A5) to obtain equations (2.23) through (2.26) is a matter of straighforward algebraic manipulation.

Notes

The author is a member of the staff of the Board of Governors of the Federal Reserve System. I am grateful to Fernando de Holanda Barbosa, Matthew Canzoneri, Robert Flood, Dale Henderson, and Ken Rogoff for helpful conversations in the course of writing this paper. The views expressed in this chapter are mine alone. They do not represent the official views of the Federal Reserve System, its Board of Governors, or its staff.

1. See, for example, Fischer (1977), Gray (1976 and 1978), and Cukierman (1980).

2. Barro (1976) analyzes wage indexation in a model of incomplete information adopted from Lucas (1973). However, his paper differs from this one in other important ways. In particular, in his framework the wage rate is fully flexible, and the distribution of prices is exogenous.

3. Since supply and demand conditions are identical for all industries, the expected (or certainty equivalent) levels of price and production are the same for all industries. Accordingly, equal weights are assigned to all prices in the price index.

4. The demand function given by equation (2.2) and the price index defined by equation (2.3) can be derived from the optimization problem of a household that has a Cobb-Douglas utility function with equal shares:
$U = C_1^{(1/n)} C_2^{(1/n)} \cdots C_n^{(1/n)}$,
where C_i denotes the household's consumption of good i.

5. To obtain equation (2.21), first take the log derivative of equation (2.6), which gives
$d\ln L_{ij} = -\phi[d\ln E(W) - d\ln E(P_i)]$.
Next, the log derivative of the expected value of W is approximated by the expectation of the log derivative of W itself:
$d\ln E(W) = Ed\ln W = Edw$.
Similarly,
$d\ln E(P_i) = Ed\ln P_i = Edp_i$.
Substituting these expressions into the equation above gives equation (2.21). The approximation used becomes more exact as the mean value of the variable in question becomes large relative to its variance.

6. If values of λ greater than unity are permitted, a vertical aggregate supply curve can also be achieved by setting λ equal to Λ, where Λ is given by

$$\Lambda = \frac{(a\phi)^2 + a\phi}{(a\phi)^2 + a\phi\pi}.$$

However, the value of λ that minimizes the variance of the individual firm's output around its full-equilibrium level is generally less than Λ. Accordingly, even under "optimal" indexing, which is designed to minimize deviations of the firm's output from its full-equilibrium level, the aggregate supply curve will not be vertical.

7. The full-equilibrium level of output for industry i is calculated by equating labor supply and demand for firm j of the industry (equations 2.5 and 2.6), solving for the firm's equilibrium level of employment, substituting that solution into the production function (equation 2.1), and multiplying the result by h, the number of firms in the industry. In terms of log differences, full-equilibrium, or optimal output is given by

$$dx_i^0 = \alpha_i \left\{ \frac{a\phi}{[(e + \phi)/e] + a\phi} \right\}.$$

Equation (2.28) is calculated by subtracting dx_i^0 from dx_i, (given by equation (2.26)), squaring the result, and taking its expected value:

$$\sigma_x^2 - E[(dx_i - dx_i^0)^2]$$

8. Again, see Fischer (1977), Gray (1976 and 1978), or Cukierman (1980).

9. It is not necessary that the monetary authority possess superior information in order to conduct effective policy. For an extensive discussion of these issues, see McCallum (1981).

References

Barro, Robert J. "Indexation in a Rational Expectations Model." *Journal of Economic Theory* 13 (October 1976): 229–244.

Cukierman, Alex. "The Effects of Wage Indexation on Macroeconomic Equilibrium: A Generalization." *Journal of Monetary Economics* 6, no. 2 (April 1980): 147–170.

Fischer, Stanley. "Wage indexation and Macroeconomic Stability." *Journal of Monetary Economics* 5, supplement (1977): 107–147.

Gray, Jo A. "On Indexation and Contract Length." *Journal of Political Economy* 86, no. 1 (February 1978): 1–18.

Gray, Jo A. "Wage Indexation: A Macroeconomic Approach." *Journal of Monetary Economics* 2, no. 2 (April 1976); 221–235.

Lucas, Robert E., Jr. "Some International Evidence on Output-Inflation Tradeoffs." *American Economic Review* 63 (June 1973), 326–334.

McCallum, Bennett T. "Rational Expectations and Macroeconomic Stabilization Policy." *Journal of Money, Credit, and Banking* 12, no. 4 (November 1980, part 2): 716–746.

3 Implicit Contracts and the Social Contract: Toward a Welfare Economics without Costless Mobility

Edmund S. Phelps

My first essay in contract theory, much of it in collaboration with Guillermo Calvo and with helpful feedback from John Taylor, introduced a modern setting in which to analyze wage and employment determination (Phelps 1977, Calvo and Phelps 1977).

Once the fledgling workers have made the long journey required for a career at one of the enterprises, it would be too costly, maybe too late, for them to make another one. So a worker choosing among the many competing firms will want to be assured in advance of what the terms of the employment will be under each of the envisionable contingencies else the worker would anticipate being a sitting duck for wage "economies" by the firm, so firms, to compete for labor, are driven to indicate (or tacitly acknowledge) beforehand their policy in this regard and to "contract" (at least implicitly) to carry out the indicated policy. Further, and here is the modernistic element, the worker will require that the contingencies on which the worker's remuneration (and any other rewards) are to depend *must be observable to the worker*, else the (effectively) immobilized worker would be exposed to a moral hazard—the enterprise might claim that some contingency unobservable to the worker had occurred that sanctioned (according to the firm's stated policy) a wage cut with no visible *quid pro quo*.[1] It is posited, in that spirit, that the optimal contract will specify the wage for full-time work as a function of the number of employees called up for work, a contingency the workers can readily measure, while leaving the management free to make the layoff decisions using its guesses of business prospects. In a monetary economy the present money wage will also be a function of the latest reported consumer price index (unless the method of retroactive correction of the previous wage is used) and, possibly, other easily observed data.

If consequently I am seen as the father of modernist (post-classical) contract theory, and Calvo the mother, it may also be said that the offspring bear less than the expected resemblance to their forebears.[2] Hall and Lilien (1979) deduced from their assumptions that the number of employees idle, who are laid off, will always be Pareto optimal (more accurately, Edgeworth optimal) in the ideal first-best sense—the firm will equate the marginal revenue product of labor to the extra wage payment that must be paid an employee when he is called to work, and that variable wage component will equal the disutility of working (in terms of money); this is contrary to the latent implications of Calvo and Phelps. A recent draft by Arnott, Hosios, and Stiglitz (1980) restored the theme of possible underemployment, by introducing some new considerations (which will not be taken up here), although the result encounters qualifications in Newbery and Stiglitz (1982). A paper by Grossman and Hart (1981) adduces underemployment outcomes (in bad times) by invoking risk aversion on the part of the firm—which directs the firm to overpay in good times if it can then underpay in bad times; see also Azariadis (1980). However, Green and Kahn (1981) argue that the underemployment result also depends on the further invocation of the no-income-effect-on-leisure utility function on the part of employees, so that equating the marginal utility of income across states also equates their total utility. Finally, analysts now speak of "risk sharing" as if risk aversion were the central feature of the problem rather than immobility as Calvo and I conceived the crux of the problem to be.

What follows is a "thought-piece" that attempts to return our perspective to the one I adopted to begin with:

1. Workers and firms alike are risk-neutral.

2. Firms control layoffs presumably because their managers are specialists on the stochastic cost and demand conditions they face, hence the expected profitability of greater or lesser work.

3. Workers control their own bodies, dodging work if they choose, because they are the specialists on what they feel like, hence the "expected utility" of reporting for work.

4. The contract is to make the full-time wage for full-time work a function of observable variables, such as the number of employees called up to work and possibly certain (lagged) macro data.

The focus in this sequel, however, is on the role of government in this modernistic contract-theoretic setting.

3.1 Underemployment and the Question of a Remedy

Let $f(n, s)$ denote the real value, in units of bread, of the production obtainable by the firm when it "works" n employees and state s occurs. Both f and f_n are increasing in s, and $f(\cdot)$ is a concave increasing function of n. We think of n as a continuous variable, $0 \leq n \leq m$, where m is the stock of employees attracted by the firm's contract and general prospects. Let the real wage bill associated with working (laying on) n employees be written $v_e(n) \cdot n + v_u(n) \cdot (m - n) \equiv V(n)$, where $v_e(n)$ is the wage to a working employee when n are working and $v_u(n)$ is the wage to an idle employee. Then the optimal layoff (on) rule, $n^*(s)$, maximizes $f(n, s) - V(n)$, subject to $0 \leq n \leq m$. The selection of the workers to layoff is random. Lastly it will be supposed that the nonpecuniary reward from *not* being called to report to work, though in a position to report, equals the nonpecuniary reward from being called to work.

In Calvo and Phelps the condition $v_u(n) = 0$ for all n is imposed without defense.[3] Then the optimal contract sets forth the schedules $v_e(n)$ solves the problem:

$$\max E_s\{f[n^*(s), s] - v_e(n^*(s))n^*(s)\} \quad \text{subject to}$$

$$E_s[v_e(n^*(s)) - R]\frac{n^*(s)}{m} = c$$

where R is the employees' reservation wage and c is the competitive level of expected rent, which the firm is constrained to meet (in the expected value sense). I shall interpret R as the pecuniary cost of working—the car fare to get to the job. Of course, in the aggregate the other firms must be promising positive expected rents, lest they fail to attract anyone from his garden! Hence $c > 0$. So our firm, if it makes v_u zero, must ensure the $Ev_e > R$. On the whole the firm will overcompensate the employee at work. (It will never undercompensate for fear of inviting absenteeism—"My phone has not been working, I think"—or sabotage, as an object lesson). It is shown that either $v_e(n)$ is a *constant*, greater than R, or else (somewhere at least) an increasing function of n.

Grossman and Hart call the imposition of $v_u = 0$ an "artificial assumption." Certainly it leans heavily on the "risk neutrality" of the worker. But is it indefensible? Calvo and I must have felt it natural to impose the condition because we both had 'come from" theories in which the firm is impelled to offer *incentive wages* to deter quitting or shirking, hence to offer v_e in excess of R. True, in the present model where workers cannot relocate, the proposed alternative policy $v_u > 0$ and $v_e - v_u = R$ might appear to be optimal; it need not tempt a worker to resign nor perhaps to risk dismissal. Nevertheless, the policy $v_e - v_u = R$ would fail to induce workers to report reliably when called up to work, and since profit is strictly concave in n in the neighborhood of $n^*(s)$, the resulting variability of worker response would reduce expected profit.[4] Hence it may be *optimal* for the firm to set $v_e(n) - v_u(n) > R$ for all or most n. Then the firm can set v_u at or near zero while still meeting the expected rent requirement. This contract assures the workers that they will enjoy a certain v_u if laid off and that they will have a nondiscriminatory chance at v_e. The logic of this contract is that the higher bonus, $v_e(n) - v_u(n)$, induces the employee to reduce the risk he is willing to run of being caught unprepared to report.

With $v_e - v_u > R$ for all or more n—and the further possibility that the $v_e(n)$ schedule will be an increasing function, as in Calvo-Phelps—the underemployment outcome comes back into existence, on an improved footing. At interior outcomes, where $n < m$, the firm chooses n to equate $f_n(n, s)$ to $V'(n)$ rather than to $R < V'(n) \le v_e - v_u$. So n is generally too small in the "ideal" first-best sense.

What can the government do to achieve a Pareto improvement of at least the expected-value type? The government could subsidize the call-up of employees to the working (laid on) status, perhaps by means of a subsidy to output. The subsidy could be financed through a tax on interest, saving, or wealth, earned by workers. (Taxing wages in excess of layoff benefits would undo the intended incentive effect of the subsidy.)

3.2 Intervening on the Side of Equalizing Life Prospects

It is clear that, whatever the identical policy practiced by the firms, which we may take to be identical ex ante, it will be Pareto efficient ex ante for the population of fledgling workers to distribute themselves evenly over the identical firms thus to equalize the labor-land or labor-capital ratio at every "firm" or production outpost. It will be *just* as well, for the identical employees will then have identical life prospects—the same expected value of wage income net of the reservation wage, the same c. Of course the competition among firms for the workers, and the competition among workers for "contracts," is capable (under auction conditions, or the like) of achieving precisely this ex ante social optimum.

However, suppose that once the workers reached their places, ready for the call to work at their chosen enterprises, something happened: some enterprises estimated or predicted higher nonlabor costs—a water shortage, a rise of fuel costs, etc., in their region—or maybe they sensed a worsened outlook for consumer demand for their brand of goods. As a result the workers located at these stricken enterprises now face worse prospects than they originally expected: in the case of the two-part wage policy, these unlucky workers now face precisely the same v_u and v_e that their enterprise contracted to pay to idle and working employees, respectively, but they now face a smaller (conditional) probability, P, of working and thus earning v_e ($> R$) than they anticipated facing—smaller than the unconditional ex ante probability. Hence the unlucky workers who find themselves joined to the afflicted enterprises now face a smaller chance of earning the working wage, v_e ($> R$), than do the more fortunate workers aligned to the other enterprises.

What is the just social policy toward the workers randomly cast on a course with inferior life prospects? What, we may ask in the spirit of social contract theory, would the fledgling workers agree to if they recognized the possibility of such an ensuing inequality in life prospects, as measured by the two disparate probabilities of working? To facilitate discussion, let us call these conditional probabilities P_1 and P_2, where $P_1 < P_2$ and let P_1^0 and P_2^0 denote these probabilities if no government action is taken.

I suggest that ex ante the workers would prefer to see remedial government action to reduce the inequality in the two probabilities, but not beyond the point where even

$$\min_{i=1,2} \left[(1 - P_i)v_u^i + P_i(v_e^i - R^i) \right],$$

the lesser of the two life prospects, would begin to suffer from a further move toward equalization of the probabilities. Since any public policy to "protect" the distressed group of enterprises may cost resources, such as a governmental relocation program (expenditure or subsidy voucher), or may distort resources, such as a subsidy to the purchase of the output of the distressed firms or a tax on competing goods, it should be expected that public measures to reduce the aforementioned inequality will reduce the aftertax worth of the wages (to the laid-off and the working) in both the lucky and unlucky enterprises. Hence there may come a point at which further closing of the disparity between P_2 and P_1 would be damaging on the whole for the intended beneficiaries as well as the more fortunate workers. This suggested answer of mine to the question posed is a rendering of Rawls's conception of economic justice, known as "maximin."

Most economists instinctively reject such a suggestion: if minimizing, or merely moderating, the no-intervention inequality in life prospects would reduce the average prospect, they say, then the practice of such a social policy can be seen to decrease the ex ante life prospect of each of the (identical) workers before he allocates himself among the firms, and that decrease of the ex ante prospect, they say, would be rejected ex ante by every worker since he is by hypothesis indifferent to risk. Only if he were risk-phobic, some economists say, would he agree to Rawls's "maximin" criterion for judging the optimum government intervention.

I think this analysis poses the question clearly. I believe, further, that I am right to focus upon the conditional expectations of the workers, once they have cast their lot with this or that region or trade, rather than their ex ante expectations. Why ignore the latest available information about supply shocks and demand shifts ex post? Why should that information be morally immaterial? One does not need to be risk-averse to be equality-loving or pro-underdog.

Yet there is a conundrum. Still later, some workers may find they are *experiencing* the ultimate bad luck of being laid off, declared redundant. Ex post facto ultimo, therefore, *they* are the worst off. Does "maximin" require that they have their prospect maximized by the government? And if so, doesn't that expose the absurdity of "maximin"? First, I am not certain it is absurd to maximize v_u. "They also serve who only early retire." Why shouldn't those least regarded ex post be paid as well as possible? However, in the present setting, the contractual market will—at least to a good approximation—be maximizing v_u, subject to the constraint the firms do not suffer a loss, thus earn the competitive world real rate of return on their capital; the bonus, $v_e - v_u$, though it will tend to exceed R for the reasons given, may so boost efficiency that it raises v_u as well as v_e. Taxing the bonus to raise funds for subsidizing layoffs may be counterproductive.

3.3 Underemployment Resulting from Monetary Disturbances

In a monetary economy the contracts could set a real wage by retroactively adjusting this period's money wage in proportion to this period's price level once the latter is known. Then a purely monetary downside disturbance "this period" would still reduce sales and possibly cause layoffs within the period if prices were preannounced for some period of time or if firms' pricing reflected their beliefs that all or most of other firms were not lowering their prices for some interval (and hence they were unwilling to reduce their own prices by enough to maintain sales). But *next period*, despite expected permanency of the shock, a restoration of the undisturbed level of sales and employment would be theoretically possible; its realization would depend upon the presence of equilibrating expectations (for example, rational expectations).

Thus it may be argued that for such idealized contracts, just as is commonly claimed, the indexing of money wage rates to the price level in optimal contracts makes monetary policy unnecessary for stabilizing employment against demand disturbances and insufficient for stabilizing employment against supply shocks. Obviously, the former contention exaggerates if the indexation makes next period's nominal wage, not (retroactively) this period's, depend on this period's price level. But let us focus on idealized contracts.

Here I will argue that these contentions misconstrue the optimal contract. It makes money-wage rates, w_u and $w_e(n)$, some function of the consumer price index, the economywide nominal-wage index, and the "money supply" (somehow measured). The elasticity of the money-wage rates, the $w_e(n)$, with respect to the general price level is usually less than one. Hence, when the price level drops, the firm knows that real wage rates will increase at least transiently. The rationale for the inelasticity is that such a disturbance is often a (good!) supply disturbance, which justifies a real wage rise; similarly, when the price level rises the real wage is at first reduced because the disturbance often reflects a (bad) supply shock, which justifies a real wage cut. (At most money-wage rates are linear homogeneous in all three variables: the general price level, the general wage level and money supply; the sum of the elasticities may even be less than one.)

But if the drop of the price level, by rising real wage rates, lowers production—because in fact the disturbance is purely monetary—there is a rationale for an "activist" increase of the money supply to raise the price level and raise output—to hasten the process of recovery to the normal output level.

Obviously, this proposition assumes that the central bank knows as much as the firms know. There is *no* asymmetry of information *there*. Why doesn't each firm simply disclose to the workers its belief that the disturbance is purely monetary, thus to persuade them to abandon the formula calling for a real wage rise? Because the workers know the firm has a reason to lie! The workers would want an agent to certify the state of the world for them. To a degree the central bank can function as such an agent. True, the bank could "call out the disturbance terms," but the simplicity of merely adjusting the money supply has much merit.

This chapter has examined possible types of underemployment in a contract-theoretic setting, and studied the rationale for some kind of governmental intervention that each of these types suggests. How extraordinary that this is very nearly the first attempt at a welfare analysis of proposed policy corrections! It is certain, however, that it will not be the last.

Notes

1. In contrast, what I call the classical type of contract theory posits that the parties to the contract can costlessly obtain perfect information about the state of the world and hence will observe all facets of every contingency. This is the contract theory originated by Azariadis, Baily, and D. F. Gordon.

2. Of course the contract problem is conceptually akin to some earlier incentive-compatibility problems, such as the insurance problem, the income tax problem, and the principal-agent problem.

3. The idle workers can survive somehow, by growing foodstuffs in their home gardens, perhaps. Hence, if there is a positive disutility of working—in terms of money, a positive reservation wage—it could be interpreted as an opportunity cost, such as the loss of opportunity to earn at home ("net" of the fun of doing something in the firm).

4. In addition production may be organized into modules or teams of complementary Smithian workers. Shooting may have to stop if, once on location, a member of the cast or crew has stayed up too late or reports ill.

References

Arnott, R., H. Hosios, and J. E. Stiglitz. 1980. Implicit Contracts, Labor Mobility, and Unemployment, Mimeographed. Princeton University.

Calvo, G. A., and E. S. Phelps. 1977. "Employment Contingent Wage Contracts." *Journal of Monetary Economics*, Supplement, pp. 160–168.

Green, J., and C. M. Kahn. 1981. Wage-Employment Contracts: Global Results. Working Paper 675. National Bureau of Economic Research.

Grossman, S. J., and O. D. Hart. 1981. "Implicit Contracts, Moral Hazard and Unemployment." *Papers and Proceedings of the American Economic Association*, pp. (May): 301–307.

Hall. R. E., and D. M. Lillien. 1979. "Efficient Wage Bargains Under Uncertain Supply and Demand." *American Economic Review* 69: 868–879.

Newbery, D., and J. E. Stiglitz. 1981. "Wage Rigidity, Implicit Contracts and Economic Efficiency: Are Market Wages Too Flexible." Working Paper. Princeton University.

Phelps. E. S. 1977. "Indexation Issues." *Journal of Monetary Economics*, Supplement, pp. 149–159.

4 Stopping Moderate Inflations: The Methods of Poincaré and Thatcher

Thomas J. Sargent

4.1 Introduction

In June 1979 Margaret Thatcher's administration began governing Great Britain. One of her primary goals was markedly to reduce the rate of inflation, an understandable goal in view of the experience of the past decade when Great Britain's rate of inflation had on average exceeded the rate of inflation in other industrial countries. Advocates of the two main groups of contemporary theories about inflation dynamics could have told Mrs. Thatcher that achieving that goal would be difficult, although each group would have characterized the nature of the difficulties quite differently. The first group consists of the "momentum" or "core inflation" theories.[1] The second group comprises the rational expectations-equilibrium theories.[2]

The first group of theories posits that there is some inherent momentum in the process of inflation itself, and that this momentum or persistence is neither superficial nor merely a reflection of slowly moving deeper forces that themselves cause inflation to behave as it does. Two distinct possible sources of sluggishness in inflation have been proposed. One is the notion of adaptive or autoregressive expectations. According to this doctrine workers and firms form expectations about future rates of inflation by computing a moving average of current and lagged rates of inflation. The moving average makes expected inflation a simple function of current and past rates of inflation. Further the weights in the moving average are assumed to be fixed numbers that are independent of the economic environment, including government monetary and fiscal policy, and are taken to characterize the psychology of expectations. Since firms and workers set current and future nominal wages and prices partly as functions of their expected rates of inflation, this model of inflationary expectations determines the actual rate of inflation partly as a long weighted average of past inflation rates. The other main determinant of inflation is the unemployment rate with which, by means of a Phillips curve mechanism, inflation varies inversely. According to this theory the only way to eliminate inflation through conventional monetary and fiscal restraint is by moving along the short-run Phillips curve and suffering a period of high unemployment that is long enough to break the slowly moving inflationary expectations. In this model the momentum in the inflation process and the high cost in unemployment of ending inflation is caused by the irrational nature of agents' expectations. Reductions in inflation are costly because it takes agents a long time to understand that they are in a less inflationary environment. If they learned faster, reducing inflation would be less costly.

A second, more sophisticated mechanism that can lead to a notion of intrinsic momentum in inflation is the staggered wage contract model of John Taylor [42] and Phelps and Taylor [33]. Taylor posits rational expectations, so that agents in his model form expectations of inflation as functions of all of the variables relevant for forecasting future inflation. As a result of positing rationality, the particular function that agents optimally use to forecast inflation responds systematically and predictably to the economic environment, including the monetary policy and fiscal policy regimes, contrary to the fixed-function forecasts assumed under adaptive expectations. The source of momentum or persistence in Taylor's model comes from the overlapping structure of multiperiod wage contracts, and a particular nonstate contingent form that he imposes on contracts. In this class of models, in terms of unemployment it is costly to end inflation because firms and workers are now locked into long-term wage contracts that were negotiated on the basis of wage and price expectations that prevailed in the past. In Taylor's model, as in all rational expectations models, the observed momentum or serial correlation in the inflation process partly reflects the serial correlation in the "first causes" of inflation, such as monetary and fiscal variables. In addition, however, the wage-contracting mechanism contributes some momentum of its own to the process, so that the resulting sluggishness in inflation cannot be completely eliminated or overcome by appropriate changes in monetary and fiscal policies. The wage-contracting process gives rise to a nontrivial trade-off between the variance of inflation and the variance of unemployment.

Although they both embody a measure of momentum in wage and price dynamics, the adaptive expectations and Taylor wage-contract models have substantially different implications about the unemployment costs of deflationary policies. The adaptive expectations or "core inflation" theory implies that inflation can be reduced only through a more or less extended period of higher unemployment. On the other hand, the wage-contracting models of Taylor and others imply the existence of a variety of alternative policy strategies, each of which could successfully deflate the economy with *no* costs in items of higher unemployment. The classes of strategies that eliminate inflation without imposing unemployment costs are all characterized by a policy of gradual tightening of monetary and fiscal policy. How gradual to make this process depends precisely on the dynamics of the wage contracts. To avoid increases in unemployment, the deflationary actions must respect the persistence in nominal wages built in by the old wage contracts. Thus an inflation can be eliminated costlessly, but only if it is done gradually. For such a policy to work, it is necessary that the strategy of gradual tightening of aggregate demand be pre-committed by the demand management authorities in a way that is sufficiently forceful and binding that it assures private agents' belief in the plan. Later in this chapter, I shall argue that there is a tension inherent in this kind of gradual policy, since promises to take strong contractionary actions in the more distant future in the face of very mild or contractionary actions in the present and near future are open to skepticism. (Recall the campaign promises of Presidents Carter and Reagan to balance the federal budget in the last year of their respective administrations.) At this point it is sufficient to emphasize that adaptive expectations and Taylor-like contracting models with rational expectations have different practical implications about the feasibility of relatively painless disinflations. The reason for these important differences in implications resides in the difference between the assumptions of adaptive and rational expectations. The latter hypothesis has private agents' decision rules responding in a particular stabilizing way with respect to changes in the government's strategy for demand management, while the former does not.

We now turn to the second group of theories of inflation, which are the rational expectations, and equilibrium theories. These theories maintain that essentially all of the characteristics of the serial correlation of inflation are inherited from the random properties of the deeper causes of inflation, such as monetary and fiscal policy variables. These theories differ from Taylor's kind of theory in viewing wage and price contracts, whether implicit or explicit, as more state contingent, and contracting procedures as more responsive to the economic environment.[3] In order to explain observed Phillips curve trade-offs, these theories resort to the Phelps-Lucas device of information limitations and the temporary confusions that they cause. When measures of aggregate demand and/or variables that partially reflect them such as prices and interest rates are realized to differ from what they had previously been rationally expected to be, it sets in motion movements in real economic variables. On this view the first cause of business cycle fluctuations is uncertainty about the position of future and maybe even current relative prices and productivity disturbances.

Although differing among themselves in many important substantive details, members of the second group of theories are united by their assertion that under the proper hypothetical conditions a government could eliminate inflation very rapidly and with virtually no Phillips-curve costs in terms of foregone real output or increased unemployment. The "measure" that would accomplish this would be a once-and-for-all, widely understood and widely agreed upon, change in the monetary or fiscal policy regime. Here a regime is taken to be a function or rule for repeatedly selecting the economic policy variable or variables in question as a function of the state of the economy. Particular models within this class differ widely with respect to the particular policy variables (e.g., high-powered money, a wider monetary aggregate, or total government debt) which are focused upon. However, all the theories require that the change in the rule for the pertinent variable be widely understood and uncontroversial, and therefore unlikely to be reversed. These characteristics are essential in eliminating the costs in terms of foregone output that information limitations and confusions cause with the Phelps-Lucas version of the Phillips curve.

According to each of these two theories, Mrs. Thatcher has faced a formidable task. The momentum view obviously implies that she could use monetary and fiscal variables to depress inflation only at the cost of also depressing real economic activity. The rational expectations, equilibrium view suggests that it is not in the power of a Prime Minister or even a united political party to create the circumstances required to bring about a quick and costless end to inflation. Whether or not the stage is set for successfully implementing a significant new policy regime is the result of intellectual and historical forces that individual political figures influence only marginally. Mrs. Thatcher comes to power against the background of over twenty years of stop-go or reversible government policy actions.[4] Her economic policy actions are vigorously opposed both by members of the Labor Party and by a strong new party, the Social Democrats. Thus the economic spokesman for the Labor Party, Mr. Peter Shore, advocates an immediate 40 percent devaluation and a larger government deficit. Mrs. Thatcher's party now runs third in the political opinion polls. In addition, throughout her administration, speculation has waxed and waned about whether Mrs. Thatcher herself would be driven to implement a U-turn in macroeconomic policy actions, and whether her stringent monetary policy actions would be reversed by the Conservative Party itself, by choosing a new party leader. Furthermore there is widespread dissent from Thatcher's actions among British macroeconomic scholars, so that she cannot be regarded as implementing a widely agreed upon theory. For all of these reasons, it is difficult to interpret Thatcher's policy actions in terms of the kind of once-and-for-all, widely believed, uncontroversial, and irreversible regime change that rational expectations equilibrium theories assert can cure inflation at little or no cost in terms of real output.[5] This is not to render a negative judgment on Thatcher's goal or her methods, but only to indicate that the preconditions for the applicability of rational expectations "neutrality" or "policy irrelevance" theorems don't seem to exist in Margaret Thatcher's England. Where these conditions are not met, rational expectations equilibrium models imply that contractionary monetary and fiscal policy actions are likely to be costly in terms of real output and unemployment.

4.2 The "Poincaré Miracle"

We have seen that extensive preconditions must obtain before rational expectations, equilibrium theories can be taken to imply that there is a costless cure to inflation, or equivalently, that the neutrality theorems of the theory can be expected closely to approximate reality. It has been argued by some that these preconditions are so stringent that they have rarely if ever been satisfied in practice, so that the example of Thatcher's England is the standard case. While this is a respectable argument, it is useful to point out that there are repeated historical episodes that seem to fit the rational expectations equilibrium model fairly well. I have recently described four such episodes, namely, the events surrounding the ends of hyperinflations in Poland, Germany, Austria, and Hungary in 1922 to 1924 [39]. Each of those countries successfully stopped drastic inflations dead in their tracks by interrelated fiscal and monetary policy changes that can be interpreted as abrupt changes in regime. The costs in foregone output were much smaller than would be suggested by modern estimates of Phillips curves and were in no sense proportional to the magnitudes of the inflations that were halted. Some readers' response to those examples has

Table 4.1
French wholesale price index (base 1913 = 100, 1913 from 1901–1910 index = 115.6)

Year	January	February	March	April	May	June
1923	386.9	421.8	424.0	414.7	406.5	408.7
1924	494.0	543.7	499.3	450.0	458.5	465.3
1925	514.4	515.0	513.5	512.8	519.8	542.6
1926	633.5	635.6	631.8	650.1	687.9	738.4
1927	621.8	631.6	641.4	636.5	628.6	622.6

July	August	September	October	November	December
406.7	413.1	423.6	420.5	442.9	458.6
481.0	476.6	485.6	497.1	503.5	507.2
556.8	557.2	555.7	572.3	605.5	632.4
836.2	769.5	786.9	751.5	683.8	626.5
619.9	617.9	600.3	587.5		

Source: League of Nations Bulletin, Haig [21, p. 448].

been that because those inflations were so spectacular, between 5,000 and 1,000,000 percent per year, the procedures undertaken to end them have few implications about the problem of ending more moderate inflations like the ones faced by industrialized countries today. The argument seems to rest on an appeal to a model in the style of Taylor [43]. It asserts that the hyperinflations had proceeded to the point where long-term nominal contracts had ceased to operate, thereby destroying the dominant source of momentum in the inflation process. The argument is then that for milder inflations, the existence of long-term nominal contracts still remains a source of momentum that will make it costly in terms of real output and unemployment to end inflation quickly by draconian changes in fiscal or monetary regime.[6]

However, in the 1920s other countries successfully used essentially the same monetary and fiscal reforms that worked in Austria, Poland, Germany, and Hungary to stabilize much milder currency depreciation.[7] One dramatic example was the stabilization of the French franc that was achieved by the government formed by Raymond Poincaré in July 1926.[8] (Tables 4.1 and 4.2 report the French wholesale price index and the dollar–franc exchange rate between 1923 and 1927.) Poincaré formed his government at a time when it was universally recognized that "the country was in trouble again, and all political parties except the Socialists and Communists gathered behind Poincaré. Five former premiers joined his

Table 4.2
Dollar Exchange in Paris

	1923	1924	1925	1926	1927
January	15.57	21.74	18.49	26.77	25.32
February	16.45	25.57	19.38	27.49	25.55
March	15.23	18.32	19.06	28.65	25.54
April	14.84	15.45	19.20	30.15	25.53
May	15.15	18.80	19.83	30.60	25.53
June	16.32	18.88	21.56	34.93	25.54
July	16.84	19.86	21.11	41.15	25.56
August	17.65	18.48	21.30	35.12	25.51
September	16.15	18.96	21.12	35.66	25.48
October	17.19	19.13	23.92	32.52	25.47
November	18.51	18.82	26.09	28.11	25.43
December	19.59	18.56	26.90	25.25	25.40

Note: Averages of daily rates for final weeks of each month, francs per dollar.

government. There was a political truce," Shirer [41, 163]. For some time there had been broad consensus both about the principal economic factors that had caused the depreciation of the franc—persistent government deficits and the consequent pressure to monetize government debt—and the general features required to stabilize the franc—increased taxes and reduced government expenditures sufficient to balance the budget, together with firm limits on the amount of government debt monetized by the Bank of France. For several years a political struggle had been waged over *whose* taxes would be raised, with the monied interests in the country resisting efforts to raise taxes on them.[9] The accession to power of Poincaré in 1926 settled that issue in a fashion acceptable to the country's monied interests.

France financed its effort in World War I by borrowing at home and abroad, mainly in the United States. After the war France continued to run substantial government deficits. That it did so was partly rationalized by the expectation that "Germany will pay" for the French deficits. Under the Treaty of Versailles, Germany was obligated to pay massive reparations, which the French used partly to finance the reconstruction of territories devastated during the war. However, neither the total amount to be paid, nor the payment schedule was fixed by the treaty. Instead, these were to be determined by the Reparations Commission, and in the event were subject to continuous revision and renegotiation. The uncertain character of these claims complicated the public finances of both Germany and the countries that were owed reparations by Germany.[10] With the collapse of the German mark during 1923 and the relief from reparations provided Germany under the Dawes plan in 1924, it became clear that France could not continue to expect that German reparations would be sufficient to redeem the French government's debt. From that time on the franc depreciated, and the domestic price level rose, as table 4.2 shows.[11] The big financial question for French governments was how much of its outstanding debt would be paid off or honored by channeling increased tax revenues to bondholders, and how much would be defaulted on through depreciation of the franc.

The period from 1924 through July 1926 was marked by political instability and a rapid succession of governments and finance ministers in "the waltz of the portfolios." There were repeated and unsuccessful attempts to deal with the increasing difficulties associated with refinancing the massive government debt as it gradually became due. The controversy was tainted by scandal as it was revealed that the government under Herriot had cooperated in an accounting subterfuge that concealed the fact that the Bank of France had exceeded the legal limit on the amount of its note issue that could be used to purchase government bonds. The period was also characterized by a massive flight of French capital abroad, partly an anxiety reaction to some of the tax proposals under discussion, such as a capital levy, and partly a reaction to the deteriorating prospects for the returns of franc-denominated assets.

Raymond Poincaré was a fiscal conservative, who had raised taxes while Prime Minister in 1924 and was known to advocate a balanced budget and France's return to gold. In 1926 he served as his own Finance Minister. As soon as he assumed control of the government, and even before his program was enacted by the legislature, the franc recovered, and inflation stopped. Under Poincaré taxes were raised with an eye toward assuring persistent balanced or surplus government budgets. Some direct tax rates were actually reduced, including the highest rate for the general income tax, from 60 to 30 percent, and the rates of inheritance and estate taxes. However, indirect taxes were raised markedly. The government was authorized to raise all specific taxes up to six times their prewar rates, and decrees were issued implementing this authority.[12] Customs duties were raised, and postal rates increased, as were taxes on passenger and freight rail service and on autos. The basic income tax rates were also raised, for example, from 12 to 18 percent on income from land and securities and from 7.2 to 12 percent on labor income. A once-and-for-all tax of 7 percent on the first sale of real estate or a business, a kind of capital levy, was also imposed.

There was also established an independent special fund to pay off outstanding government debt, administered by the Caisse d'Amortissement, a newly created agency independent of the Treasury and with its own earmarked revenues from the tobacco monopoly, the total receipts from the inheritance and estate taxes, and the new 7 percent tax on first sale of real estate and businesses.

As the figures in tables 4.1 and 4.2 show, these measures resulted in a sudden recovery of the franc and a cessation of inflation. The franc was permitted by the French authorities to appreciate from July until December, at which time France de facto returned to the gold standard. The appreciation of the franc was accompanied by open-market purchases of foreign assets by the French monetary authority as French citizens repatriated capital in response to Poincaré's policies. While Poincaré himself had wished to restore the franc to its prewar par, it was decided to halt the appreciation of the franc in December 1926 and de facto to return to gold at that rate. This amounted to an 80 percent depreciation of the franc from its prewar par. This magnitude indicates the substantial extent to which France had financed the war by issuing bonds to its citizens on which it largely eventually defaulted. This is to be contrasted with the situation in England, which returned to the prewar par in 1925, thereby indicating an intention not to default on its long-term debt. However, the French did not default as thoroughly as did the Austrians or the Germans.[13]

The stabilization of the French franc was followed by several years of high prosperity. The French stabilization thus seems to fit the predictions of the rational expectations equilibrium approach. To the extent that it does fit, one reason is probably the high degree of political and intellectual consensus that prevailed at the time. It should be remembered that the French stabilization occurred after a variety of neighboring countries had successfully stabilized by resorting to the same budgetary principles that France eventually applied. At the time there was widespread professional consensus about the general budgetary situation that would have to prevail in order for the franc to be stabilized in the absence of exchange controls. Shirer indicates the degree of political consensus when he reports that "Frenchmen became obsessed with the idea that the 'Poincaré franc,' shrunk though it was, must never again be devalued lest they be ruined anew," Shirer [41, 166].

The French stabilized the franc by de facto returning to the gold standard. This amounted to standing ready to convert the debt of the French government into gold on specified terms, such as on demand for currency. In order to make a domestic currency freely convertible into gold, or into any foreign money for that matter, it is necessary that the government run a fiscal policy capable of supporting its promise to convert its debt. What backs the promise is not only the valuable stocks of gold, physical assets, and private claims that the government holds but also the intention to set future taxes high enough relative to government expenditures.

This method of stabilizing a currency remains available to a small country today, even though the world is no longer on the gold standard. One country, call it the domestic country, can obtain a domestic rate of inflation no greater than, and even less than that of a large foreign country to whose currency it pegs its own currency.[14] To support this policy requires that the domestic country abstain from, or at least much restrict the extent to which it resorts to inflationary finance. Indeed, the domestic government collects seigniorage only to the extent that it engages in clever devices such as holding its reserves of the foreign currency denominated assets in the form of interest-bearing assets, while at the same time adopting legal restrictions and fostering institutions that prompt its own residents to hold currency and other zero or low nominal interest assets. It is possible for a domestic government actually to experience a lower rate of inflation than the country to which it pegs its currency if it sets things up so that government and private institutions back their monetary liabilities with interest-bearing foreign-denominated assets and also pass the interest returns to their depositors. In so doing, the government completely abstains from using inflationary finance and provides domestic residents with a higher real rate of return on "money"— a lower rate of inflation than is experienced by residents of the foreign country who happen to be holding currency and other zero nominal rate of interest assets.[15]

As we turn our attention to Mrs. Thatcher's actions, it is useful to keep in mind a number of characteristics of the French financial crisis of 1926 and the subsequent salvation of the franc by Poincaré:

1. The extent to which the large interest-bearing French government debt created during the war and the reconstruction period became more

and more difficult to refinance, thereby generating increasing pressures for its eventual monetization. This pressure eventually led to fraudulent accounting practices by the Bank of France and a scandal that brought down a government. The forces underlying these events are pertinent in Britain and elsewhere today in estimating the likely consequences and even the very feasibility of policies that propose to combat inflation with restrictive monetary policies alone, while at the same time permitting substantial government deficits to continue.

2. The manner in which France stabilized by pegging the franc to a foreign currency and adopting changes in tax and expenditure laws that delivered the prospective budget surpluses needed to support that peg without exchange controls. A similar course was available to Britain in 1979, but it did not choose to follow it.

3. The sense in which the preconditions for a successful and relatively costless stabilization along the rational expectations equilibrium model were met in France in 1926. Whether these preconditions are met is in large part a consequence of historical circumstance. However, it is also perhaps partly a function of the particular lines along which a stabilization is sought. For example, it is arguable that pegging to a foreign currency is a policy that is relatively easier to support and make credible by concrete actions, since it is possible to hook the domestic country's price expectations virtually instantaneously on to the presumably exogenous price expectations process in the foreign country.

4. The fact that France chose to stabilize at a value that was widely believed to undervalue the franc. To this the French prosperity of the late 1920s has often been partly ascribed.[16] This is to be contrasted with the situation in England today, where contemporary monetary and fiscal policies have permitted a substantial appreciation of the pound, with consequent depressing influences on export industries.

4.3 The British Experience

Tables 4.3 through 4.12 report statistics that summarize the recent behavior of United Kingdom aggregates. Since Mrs. Thatcher took office in June 1979, much of the news has been bad. Real GNP has declined; industrial production, especially in manufacturing, has fallen precipi-

Table 4.3
GDP at factor cost and final expenditures on goods and services at market prices (£ million, current prices)

	(1) GDP at current prices based on expenditure data	(2) GDP at 1975 prices based on expenditure data	Implicit price deflator 1975 = 100 (column 1 divided by column 2 × 100)	GDP at market prices	Consumers' expenditure
1970	43,532	85,402	50.97	51,065	31,778
1971	49,442	87,572	56.46	57,291	35,599
1972	55,276	88,719	62.30	63,390	40,183
1973	64,258	95,506	67.28	72,936	47,759
1974	74,414	94,527	78.72	82,879	52,849
1975	93,954	93,954	100.00	104,413	64,424
1976	111,245	97,971	113.55	124,330	74,751
1977	126,111	98,993	127.39	143,064	85,474
1978	144,442	101,929	141.71	164,034	98,395
1979	163,647	102,563	159.56	189,702	114,805

General government final consumption	Gross domestic fixed capital formation	Value of physical increase in stocks and work in progress	Exports of goods and services	Imports of goods and services	Taxes on expenditure	Subsidies
8,991	9,470	421	11,551	11,146	8,417	884
10,250	10,517	158	12,960	12,193	8,788	939
11,675	11,606	44	13,653	13,771	9,627	1,153
13,380	14,238	1,448	17,124	19,013	10,121	1,443
16,609	16,867	1,304	22,985	27,375	11,469	3,004
23,074	20,417	−1,534	27,011	28,979	14,162	3,703
26,779	23,599	864	35,211	36,874	16,553	3,468
26,209	25,739	1,860	43,352	42,570	20,252	3,299
32,934	26,695	1,070	47,442	45,502	23,253	3,661
38,316	33,646	2,760	54,676	54,501	30,361	4,306

Table 4.4
Exchange, price, and balance

	Current balance (million £)	Exchange rate ($/£)	Retail price (1975 = 100)	
			Index	Percentage increase on one year earlier
1970	+779	2.396	54.2	6.4
1971	+1,076	2.444	59.3	9.4
1972	+189	2.502	63.6	7.1
1973	−1,056	2.453	69.4	9.2
1974	−3,380	2.340	80.5	16.1
1975	−1,674	2.220	100.0	24.2
1976	−1,060	1.805	116.5	16.5
1977	−206	1.746	135.0	15.8
1978	+707	1.920	146.2	8.3
1979	−1,630	2.122	165.8	13.4
1980	−2,737	2.328	195.6	18.0
1976 1	+106	1.998	110.9	22.5
2	−352	1.805	114.9	16.0
3	−436	1.766	117.6	13.7
4	−378	1.651	123.0	15.0
1977 1	−362	1.714	129.2	16.5
2	−431	1.719	134.9	17.4
3	+307	1.735	137.0	16.5
4	+280	1.813	139.0	13.0
1978 1	−194	1.928	141.4	9.5
2	+417	1.835	145.3	7.6
3	+87	1.932	147.8	7.9
4	+397	1.984	150.3	8.1
1979 1	−692	2.016	155.0	9.6
2	−192	2.081	160.7	10.6
3	−189	2.234	171.4	16.0
4	−557	2.157	176.2	17.3
1980 1	+70	2.254	184.6	19.1
2	−88	2.286	195.3	21.5
3	+870	2.382	199.4	16.4
4	+1,885	2.387	203.2	15.3
1981 Jan.	+1,042	2.405	205.7	13.0
Feb.	+614	2.294	207.6	12.5

Table 4.5
Output and unemployment

DP (at 1975 factor cost, million £, seasonally adjusted)		Industrial production (1975 = 100, seasonally adjusted)		Unemploy-ment rate
		All industries	Manufacturing	
1970	85,402	99.7	98.0	2.4
1971	87,572	99.8	97.5	3.1
1972	88,719	102.0	100.0	3.4
1973	95,506	109.5	108.4	2.4
1974	94,527	105.1	106.6	2.3
1975	93,954	100.0	100.0	3.6
1976	97,971	102.0	101.5	4.9
1977	98,993	105.9	103.0	5.2
1978	101,929	109.8	103.9	5.2
1979	102,973	112.6	104.2	5.0
1976 1	24,486	100.4	99.4	5.1
2	24,156	101.8	101.7	5.3
3	24,518	101.4	101.6	5.4
4	24,811	104.4	103.2	n.a.
1977 1	24,397	106.2	104.5	5.5
2	24,660	105.5	102.5	5.6
3	24,677	105.9	102.7	5.8
4	25,259	106.1	102.4	5.9
1978 1	25,156	107.6	102.9	5.8
2	25,602	110.6	104.5	5.8
3	25,507	111.0	104.9	5.7
4	25,664	110.0	103,1	5.4
1979 1	25,175	110.1	102.3	5.6
2	26,287	115.0	107.3	5.4
3	25,655	112.7	103.2	5.2
4	25,856	112.6	104.2	5.3
1980 1	25,596	110.0	100.0	5.7
2	25,445	106.6	96.8	6.2
3	24,991	102.9	93.3	7.0
4		100.2	89.1	8.4

Table 4.6
Gross domestic fixed capital formation by sector

	Total	Private sector	General government	Public corporations
1969	18,954	10,390	5,385	3,201
1970	19,460	10,685	5,475	3,316
1971	19,743	11,099	5,297	3,334
1972	19,823	11,776	5,076	2,932
1973	21,195	12,267	5,793	3,135
1974	20,616	11,641	5,418	3,557
1975	20,417	11,530	4,974	3,913
1976	20,636	11,811	4,786	4,039
1977	20,089	12,438	3,964	3,687
1978	20,802	13,793	3,520	3,489
1979	20,506	13,761	3,352	3,393
1975 1	5,112	2,916	1,239	957
2	5,086	2,846	1,306	934
3	5,178	2,986	1,165	1,027
4	5,041	2,782	1,264	995
1976 1	5,226	2,844	1,280	1,102
2	5,158	2,920	1,226	1,012
3	5,203	3,097	1,156	950
4	5,049	2,950	1,124	975
1977 1	4,883	2,892	1,079	912
2	5,065	3,149	988	928
3	4,997	3,119	953	925
4	5,144	3,278	944	922
1978 1	5,287	3,493	938	856
2	5,282	3,499	899	894
3	5,136	3,401	868	867
4	5,097	3,400	825	872
1979 1	4,998	3,318	818	862
2	5,052	3,401	820	831
3	5,182	3,436	882	864
4	5,274	3,606	832	836
1980 1	5,169	3,547	765	857
2	5,058	3,429	741	888
3	4,923	3,357	719	847
4				

Table 4.7
Money Supply in the United Kingdom (£ million: amounts outstanding)

At end period	M1 seasonally adjusted	Sterling M3 seasonally adjusted	M3 seasonally adjusted
1970 1	8,640	16,000	16,450
2	8,920	16,460	16,980
3	9,020	16,830	17,350
4	9,420	17,300	17,810
1971 1	9,820	18,020	18,510
2	9,900	18,270	18,780
3	10,210	18,670	19,180
4	10,310	19,530	19,960
1972 1	11,200	21,140	21,670
2	11,680	22,480	23,090
3	11,750	23,320	23,970
4	12,240	24,720	25,520
1973 1	12,280	26,290	27,390
2	13,130	27,650	28,720
3	12,660	29,620	30,940
4	13,040	31,450	32,880
1974 1	12,870	32,730	34,520
2	13,370	32,810	34,940
3	13,510	33,490	35,940
4	14,330	34,610	37,100
1975 1	14,880	35,560	38,120
2	16,080	35,840	38,100
3	16,770	37,030	39,780
4	17,070	36,920	40,010
1976 1	17,940	37,960	41,160
2	18,530	33,790	42,210
3	19,100	40,300	44,310
4	18,980	40,380	44,470
1977 1	19,540	40,720	45,070
2	20,530	41,740	46,220
3	22,020	42,990	47,390
4	23,180	44,540	48,950
1978 1	24,350	46,880	51,480
2	25,090	48,230	53,260
3	26,010	49,560	54,480
4	27,020	51,310	56,350
1979 1	27,580	52,370	57,150
2	28,250	54,380	59,290
3	28,950	56,210	61,040
4	29,460	57,830	63,270
1980 1	29,370	59,250	65,110
2	30,110	62,570	68,140
3	29,780	65,340	71,200
4	30,520	68,350	74,870

Table 4.8
General government receipts and expenditure (£ million)

	Receipts		Expenditure	
	Taxes national insurance, etc., contributions	Trading income, rent, interest, etc.	Goods and services	
			Final consumption	Gross domestic capital formation
1975	38,547	4,439	23,074	5,064
1976	44,724	5,223	26,779	5,483
1977	51,008	5,909	29,209	4,935
1978	56,704	6,488	32,934	4,741
1979	68,053	7,353	38,316	5,239
1977 1	12,700	1,527	7,040	1,565
2	12,371	1,371	7,257	1,007
3	12,822	1,697	7,368	1,171
4	13,115	1,314	7,544	1,192
1978 1	14,116	1,720	7,972	1,483
2	13,539	1,512	8,073	962
3	13,897	1,702	8,252	1,145
4	15,152	1,554	8,637	1,151
1979 1	16,032	1,917	8,875	1,500
2	16,387	1,722	9,316	1,023
3	17,250	1,962	9,896	1,356
4	18,384	1,752	10,229	1,360
1980 1	20,845	2,045	10,872	1,700
2	18,713	2,136	11,656	1,144
3	21,811	2,157	12,386	1,415
4				

Note: An article describing the new presentation of government income and expenditure was published in the March 1977 issue of *Economic Trends*.
[a] Net lending to public corporations, private sector and overseas; cash expenditure on company securities, etc. (net).

Expenditure

Current and capital transfers

Current grants and subsidies	Capital transfers	Debt interest	Net lending, etc.[a]	Total
14,353	1,196	4,211	3,755	51,653
17,015	1,435	5,394	2,365	58,471
19,502	1,537	6,373	251	61,807
23,239	2,027	7,224	1,687	71,852
27,348	1,901	8,829	3,273	84,906
4,742	470	1,832	433	16,082
4,833	363	1,314	−178	14,596
4,847	328	1,747	88	15,549
5,080	376	1,480	−92	15,580
5,658	693	1,995	74	17,875
5,725	413	1,455	439	17,067
5,783	442	1,951	729	18,302
6,073	479	1,823	445	18,608
6,522	504	2,330	554	20,285
6,855	454	1,877	670	20,195
6,617	443	2,523	1,054	21,889
7,354	500	2,099	995	22,537
7,747	576	3,149	152	24,196
8,145	521	2,209	1,444	25,119
8,075	618	3,299	1,185	26,978

Table 4.9
Financial transactions of the public sector (£ million)

	Financial deficit			Net lending, etc., to private sector and overseas	Total
	Total	General government	Public corporations		
1971	300	−786	1,086	620	920
1972	1,547	804	743	558	2,105
1973	2,764	1,997	767	880	3,644
1974	4,695	3,165	1,530	1,697	6,392
1975	7,705	4,912	2,793	1,833	9,538
1976	8,413	6,159	2,254	1,286	9,699
1977	5,868	4,639	1,229	126	5,994
1978	8,048	6,973	1,075	467	8,515
1979	8,344	6,227	2,117	432	8,776
1979 1	2,329	1,782	547	167	2,496
2	1,823	1,416	407	224	2,047
3	2,636	1,623	1,013	104	2,740
4	1,556	1,406	150	−63	1,493
1980 1	1,700	1,226	474	−128	1,572
2	3,543	2,646	897	490	4,033

Receipts

Public sector borrowing requirement

Financial transactions (net receipts)	Total	Contributions by central government	Contributions by local authorities	Contributions by public corporations	Seasonally adjusted total
−483	1,403	637	676	90	1,403
55	2,050	1,600	514	−64	2,050
−547	4,191	2,331	1,348	512	4,191
−41	6,433	3,523	2,161	749	6,433
−946	10,484	8,345	1,629	510	10,484
572	9,127	6,786	1,103	1,238	9,127
−1	5,995	4,469	183	1,343	5,995
184	8,331	8,371	659	−699	8,331
−3,788	12,564	10,396	1,732	436	12,564
1,031	1,465	247	1,003	215	2,117
−1,298	3,345	3,797	−267	−185	3,006
−1,085	3,825	2,842	666	317	3,893
−2,436	3,929	3,510	330	89	3,548
2,771	−1,199	−1,950	1,397	−646	131
−802	4,835	4,587	574	−326	4,122

Table 4.10
Net purchases (+) or sales (−) of government debt, by maturity

		Classification by maturity				
	Total stocks	Redemptions and conversions	Up to 1 year	Over 1 and up to 5 years	Over 5 and up to 15 years	Over 15 years and undated
Financial years						
1975/76	+4,159	−735	−1,120	+2,196	+1,008	+2,810
1976/77	+6,290	−703	−1,402	+2,600	+817	+4,978
1977/78	+6,684	−672	−2,259	+2,931	+2,826	+3,858
1978/79	+6,256	−404	+1,098	+1,994	+1,441	+4,323
1979/80	+8,977	−1,133	−2,068	+2,333	+2,905	+6,940
Quarter ended						
1978 Sept.	+793	−151	−364	+257	+154	+897
Dec.	+1,288	−16	−57	+2	+802	+557
1979 Mar.	+2,254	234	324	+824	+486	+1,502
June	+2,732	−1	−314	+358	+1,159	+1,530
Sept.	+2,648	−403	−932	+1,062	+496	+2,425
Dec.	+2,511	−431	−178	+159	+1,317	+1,644
1980 Mar.	+1,086	−298	−644	+754	−67	+1,341
June	+3,377	−544	−574	+1,358	+943	+2,194
Sept.	+3,186	−19	−136	−261	+3,130	+472
Dec.	+3,055	−263	−734	+1,186	+1,425	+1,441

Table 4.11
Calculated redemption yields of government bonds percent per annum

	Short-dated (5 years)	Medium-dated (10 years)	Long-dated (20 years)
Last working days			
1980 Oct.	13.15	13.29	13.15
Nov.	12.97	13.43	13.35
Dec.	13.30	13.89	13.80
1981 Jan.	13.21	13.86	13.86
Feb.	13.00	13.84	13.94
Mondays			
1980 Oct. 20	13.07	13.33	13.23
Oct. 27	12.93	13.07	12.95
Nov. 3	13.29	13.40	13.24
Nov. 10	13.38	13.53	13.35
Nov. 17	13.11	13.26	13.10
Nov. 24	13.03	13.22	13.08
Dec. 1	12.95	13.34	13.26
Dec. 8	13.04	13.44	13.34
Dec. 15	13.62	14.08	13.94
Dec. 22	13.18	13.79	13.70
Dec. 29	13.28	13.88	13.80
1981 Jan. 5	13.19	13.89	13.85
Jan. 12	13.38	14.06	14.02
Jan. 19	13.30	14.05	14.06
Jan. 26	13.29	13.95	13.95
Feb. 2	13.19	13.83	13.83
Feb. 9	13.29	13.89	13.90
Feb. 16	13.24	13.92	13.94
Feb. 23	12.97	13.83	13.93
Mar. 2	13.03	13.87	13.97
Mar. 9	13.15	13.95	14.03
Mar. 16	12.85	13.59	13.63

Table 4.12
Interest rates, security prices and yields percentage rate

	Last Friday		Last working day		Average of working days
	Bank of England's minimum lending rate to the market	Treasury bill yield	Euro-dollar 3-month rate	Building Societies Association recommended rate on shares	British government securities: long-dated (20 years)
1969	8	7.80	10.07	5.00	9.05
1970	7	6.93	6.57	5.00	9.25
1971	5	4.46	5.75	5.00	8.90
1972	9	8.48	5.91	5.25	8.97
1973	13	12.82	10.19	7.50	10.78
1974	11.50	11.30	10.07	7.50	14.77
1975	11.25	10.93	5.88	7.00	14.39
1976	14.25	13.98	5.07	7.80	14.43
1977	7	6.39	7.19	6.00	12.73
1978	12.50	11.91	11.69	8.00	12.47
1979	17	16.49	14.50	10.50	12.99
1980	14	13.45	17.75	10.50	

tously; the unemployment rate has climbed from around 5 percent in June 1979 to over 10 percent in March, to attain its highest level since the 1930s. Meanwhile inflation in the retail price index accelerated for the first year of Thatcher's administration, though in the last nine months it has receded markedly so that the inflation rate in the United Kingdom during this more recent period was actually less than it was in the United States. The pound sterling rose vis-à-vis the U.S. dollar, from 2.11 $/£ in June 1979 to 2.40 $/£ in January 1981, while the balance of payments in current account swung toward surplus. Interest rates rose to very high levels.

Recent economic events in Britain have been well summarized in recent papers by Meltzer [30] and in the Morgan Guaranty Trust Survey [31]. I refer the reader to those sources for many interesting details and will devote most of my space to highlighting and interpreting a few of the facts from the viewpoint of rational expectations macroeconomics.

4.4 Mrs. Thatcher's Plan

A hallmark of Mrs. Thatcher's publicly announced economic strategy is gradualism. For the most part her government did not propose to execute any abrupt or discontinuous changes in aggregate government variables such as tax collections, government expenditures, or the money supply. Instead, the Conservatives proposed to carry out a preannounced and gradual tightening of monetary and fiscal policy over a five-year period. These intended goals were embodied in the "medium-term financial strategy" (MTFS) the new government announced in 1979. The plan included the following elements:

1. A gradual reduction in the rate of growth of the money supply over a five-year period. The monetary aggregate that was chosen as the monetary instrument variable was "sterling M3" or "£M3" which corresponds to currency plus sterling denominated demand and time deposits of United Kingdom commercial banks. The initial plan called for £M3 to grow annually at a 9 percent rate in 1980–81, with its rate of growth gradually to decline to 6 percent by 1983–84.

2. A reduction in the real value of government spending within four years to a level 5 percent less than the level in 1979–80.

3. A public sector borrowing requirement (PSBR) of £8.5 billion in 1979–80, and £7 billion in 1980–81, (both in 1978–79 prices). Even these borrowing requirements, reduced though they were from those projected under the previous Labor Government's policies, represent deficits that as a ratio to GNP are several times those experienced in the United States.

Other elements of the government's plan were executed immediately. These included reductions in marginal income tax rates ranging from 33 to 30 percent for the lowest brackets to from 83 to 60 percent for the highest brackets, and substantial increases in the taxes on consumption, most notably a substantial increase in the Value-Added Tax (VAT). This change in tax structure was made with an eye toward increasing the rate of saving. In addition, in October 1979, exchange controls were removed, so that for the first time since World War II, residents of Britain were permitted freely to invest abroad. The government committed itself to flexible exchange rates with neither current nor capital account exchange controls, nor substantial government open market operations in foreign assets designed to peg or influence the exchange rate. In line with the theme of deregulation, the government permitted the Special Depository Regulations, widely known as the "corset" to expire. These regulations had directly limited the extent to which the banks could increase their interest-bearing deposits. The corset represented an attempt to influence directly the £M3 aggregate and was widely and correctly believed to distort the interpretation of the £M3 figures, as depositors moved into close substitutes for £M3 in response to the restrictions.

In its conception, and even more so in its execution, the plan incorporates central aspects of monetarism. The key monetarist plank is embodied in the use of gradual reductions in a measure of the money supply, sterling M3, as the central vehicle for reducing the rate of inflation. These reductions in the money supply are recommended despite very large planned budget deficits, planned deficits that in the actual event have been overrun. A keystone of monetarist doctrine is that even in the face of persistent government deficits, by managing the money supply properly the government can avoid inflation.[17] Referring to England's recent experience, Allan Meltzer has recently put the case as follows: "Excess public spending, larger than expected budget deficits and the growth of money in excess of targets are related problems. The relation would disappear if the central bank changed its operating procedures and permitted market rates to fluctuate as much as is required to control money. The excess deficit would than be financed by domestic saving or by foreigners, but money growth and inflation would fall."[18]

There are various possible interpretations of this argument, not all equally credible. In one rational expectations interpretation, by restricting itself now and forever to a binding "k-percent growth rule"[19] for the monetary base, the government effectively limits the extent to which it will collect seigniorage by resorting to inflationary finance now and in the future. Under rational expectations, current government budget deficits—expenditures net of both explicit taxes and seigniorage—must be balanced by prospective government surpluses in the future. That is, additional government bonds will be valued according to the same principles that give bonds of private corporations value: their real prospective returns. Ultimately, these prospective returns are represented by the government's willingness to tax highly enough in the future. On this view a k-percent rule for the monetary base plays a similar role as a gold standard rule, in the sense that it places a limit on the time path of real government deficits. Both the k-percent rule and the gold standard rule in effect require that, if the government is to sell its debt, the expected present value of the current and prospective government surpluses must be positive. Each rule permits the government to run deficits, even a number of deficits in succession, but these deficits must be accompanied by prospects that eventually the government budget will turn to surplus in sufficient amount to outweigh the deficits. This interpretation of the k-percent rule is one that is compatible with the Barro-Ricardo result about the equivalence of bond and tax financing.[20] In this interpretation a k-percent rule is not compatible with an everlasting government deficit but only with a deficit that is temporary in the appropriate sense.

In my view the preceding interpretation of the relationship of a k-percent rule to the budget deficit is the correct one. As with most rational expectations lines of thought, that interpretation emphasizes the dynamic or intertemporal features of the process, and the constraints that a k-percent rule requires on the future time path of the government deficit.

There is an alternative, and I believe defective view, that seems to assert that a k-percent rule is compatible with a more or less permanent deficit. This view is based on reasoning from standard Keynesian or monetarist models without rational expectations. Versions of those models exist in which the government can control inflation by sticking to a k-percent rule for the monetary base given an unrestricted path for the deficit.[21]

The preceding argument raises questions about the credibility of an announced plan to lower the monetary growth rate and to move to a k-percent rule, while simultaneously projecting substantial government budget deficits for the several years in the immediate future. The doubtful credibility of such a plan stems from the fact that a large permanent real government deficit is simply incompatible with a k-percent rule for the monetary base. A minimal requirement that a plan be credible is that it be feasible in the first place. As we have argued, a restrictive k-percent rule for the base and a permanent and large government deficit just aren't feasible. On this view, in order that the current British plan be viewed as credible, it is necessary that the large prospective government deficits over the next several years be counterbalanced by prospective surpluses farther down the line. It is difficult to point to much either in current legislation or, equally important, in the general British political climate that could objectively support such an outlook. On this view, the large government deficits that have accompanied the government's medium-term financial strategy raise serious questions about whether the plan has the logical coherence that is necessary for the plan to be credible to the public.

Samuel Brittan has recently drawn attention to a closely related issue. At the same time that the government has touted its determination to bring inflation permanently down through monetary restraint, the substantial government deficits have been financed by issuing large amounts of nonindexed long-term government debt at nominal yields to maturity ranging between 13 and 14 percent. Attention is directed to tables 4.10 and 4.11. Table 4.10 indicates the substantial extent to which the government has been financing its deficit by selling additional long-term government debt. Thus in financial year 1979–80 most of the additional government debt was over fifteen years in maturity. Now if the government were actually to deliver on its hope permanently to reduce the inflation rate, it would imply substantial increases in the real value of the long-term government debt and the real value of the interest payments on the debt. For example, investors who purchased debt at nominal rates of 14 percent while expecting average inflation of 12 percent and a real return of 2 percent would experience ex post real yields higher than 2 percent, precisely to the extent to which realized inflation falls short of the 12 percent inflation rate that they had expected.[22] For the same reason, but in the other direction, governments in the past have sometimes given way to the temptation to default on part of their interest-bearing government debt by causing inflation to occur at a higher rate than was anticipated at the time that the debt was sold.[23] This same incentive confronts the government now and raises suspicions about the current and future governments' commitment permanently to lower the inflation rate. According to this argument a government intent on eradicating inflation has a strong incentive to finance its deficit and refinance its outstanding debt by issuing indexed government bonds. This would isolate it from any increase in the real value of the burden of the debt once inflation is lowered. This the British government has not done to any significant extent.

For advocates of "Irving Fisher's effect," table 4.11 contains an important piece of evidence about the public credibility of Mrs. Thatcher's plan for reducing inflation over the longer run. The term structure of interest rates on government bonds is high and fairly flat, suggesting that the market expects the continuation of high inflation rates on a sustained basis.

As emphasized earlier, in the rational expectations view, these matters of coherence and credibility are very important in determining the likely effects of a program on real variables such as output and employment. If a program is constructed in a fashion that makes private agents believe that its execution is uncertain, then, even if preannounced, restrictive monetary policy actions can easily produce substantial reductions in output and employment.

4.5 The Outcome of the Plan So Far

Having described the government's anti-inflation plan and some possible reservations about it, I shall now proceed briefly to describe how events have actually unfolded. First, sterling M3 has exceeded its target range, despite the fact of a restrictive minimum lending rate (MLR) and a basically tight open-market stance. For example, the fiscal year 1980–81 target range for £M3 of 7 to 11 percent per year is to be compared with the annual rate of increase in £M3 of 21 percent between February 1980 and February 1981. During the same time period, sterling M1—currency plus demand deposits—increased by only 8 percent. Despite the overshooting of £M3, British interest rates have been very high, making many commentators of Keynesian inclination believe that monetary policy is very tight. Second, the public sector borrowing requirement has overrun its target. The 1980–81 PSBR had been forecast in the government's 1980 budget as £8$\frac{1}{2}$ billion, or 4.5 percent of GDP, while it is now expected to be around £13.5 billion, or 6 percent of GDP. I shall comment in turn on the overshooting of each of these targets.

Overshooting the £M3 Target

There have been several reactions to the overshooting of the £M3 target.[24] One has been to argue that, since the overshooting reflects mainly a response to removal of the distorting effect of the corset, it does not indicate a failure to pursue a tight monetary policy. As evidence in support of this position, the relatively slow growth of £M1 is often cited. Another response has been to criticize the Bank of England's operating procedures for focusing too heavily on interest rates as an intermediate instrument. Allan Meltzer [30] takes this line in arguing that by pegging interest rates, the British monetary authority necessarily gave up direct control over monetary aggregates and allowed them to be market determined.

The analytics of using monetary aggregates as opposed to interest rates as the monetary instrument have been characterized in Martin Bailey's book [2] and in papers by William Poole [34] and John Kareken [24]. The case for superiority of a particular monetary aggregate over a particular interest rate depends on the demand schedule for that monetary aggregate being less uncertain than is the aggregate demand schedule expressed as a function of that particular interest rate. Other things equal, factors that contribute to uncertainty about the demand for a given monetary aggregate diminish the relative merit of using that aggregate as the monetary instrument.

This analytical argument is quite pertinent in evaluating the controversy about the overshooting of the £M3 target (and also about the appropriate monetary instrument for the United States in 1981). The removal of the corset and the dismantling of exchange controls at the outset of Mrs. Thatcher's administration presumably shifted the demands for a whole host of assets in historically unprecedented and uncertain ways. Regardless of the possible merits of the case for relaxing these controls, it seems clear that for some time after they are relaxed the interpretation of a variety of monetary aggregates becomes more uncertain and difficult than it had been. During such periods the case for using an interest rate rather than a monetary aggregate as the monetary instrument becomes substantially strengthened. It is ironic that both in the United Kingdom and the United States the accession of monetarists to a dominant influence over policy has coincided with substantial revisions in the structure of financial regulations which at least temporarily cloud the meaning of the particular monetary aggregates they favor controlling.[25] It seems to me that it is a defensible view that, despite their own problems of interpretation, the high nominal interest rates in Britain over the last year have more appropriately signaled the stance of monetary policy than any particular monetary aggregate.[26]

The Government Deficit

I now turn to discuss the behavior of the public sector borrowing requirement, which so far has exceeded the government's target by so much that the government has moved to correct the situation by raising taxes.

The 1980–81 PSBR which has been forecast by the government to be £8.5 billion or 4.5 percent of GDP, appears to be coming in at £13.5 billion or 6 percent of GDP. In the March 1981 budget the Chancellor of the Exchequer, Sir Geoffrey Howe, announced a number of tax increases designed to reduce the prospective PSBR for 1981–82 to about £10.5 billion. Without those additional tax measures the government estimated that the 1981–82 PSBR would have been about £14.5 billion. The new revenue-raising measures included increases in the excise taxes on drink, tobacco, gasoline, diesel road fuel, cigarette lighters, matches, and road vehicles. The extent to which income tax payments were indexed against inflation was reduced. A Supplementary Petroleum Duty on North Sea oil and gas was announced, which together with adjustments in the Petroleum Revenue Tax is expected to yield about £1 billion. The Chancellor also announced a once-and-for-all tax on low-interest bank deposits that is expected to yield £.4 billion in 1981–82.[27] The government announced these tax increases because it has become increasingly aware of the threat that a persistent and large government deficit sooner or later poses to an anti-inflation policy based on monetary restraint.

Before considering the nature of the British deficit in more detail, it helps to remember a few analytical principles about government finance. In interpreting reported figures on the government's budget deficit, it is useful to keep in mind the hypothetical distinction between current account and capital account budgets and their deficits. A pure current account expenditure is for a service or perfectly perishable good that gives rise to no government-owned asset that will produce things of value in the future. A pure capital account expenditure is a purchase of a durable asset that gives the government command of a prospective future stream of returns, collected, for example, through user charges, whose present value is greater than or equal to the present cost of acquiring the asset. A pure capital account budget would count as revenues the interest and other user charges collected on government-owned assets, while expenditures would be the purchases of capital assets. By these definitions government debt issued on capital account is self-liquidating and fully backed by the user charges that are earmarked to pay it off. Government debt issued to finance a pure capital account deficit is thus not a claim on the general tax revenues that the government collects through sales and income taxation. The principles of classical economic theory condone government deficits on capital account. The idea is that certain government capital projects are worthwhile on cost-benefit grounds and that it is reasonable to finance them by levying taxes on the people who receive the benefits throughout the time the benefits accrue. In short, so far as capital account deficits are concerned, a government is in a sense like a firm, it being wise to borrow to finance worthwhile long-lived projects with taxes and other user charges whose stream over time matches the time profile of the benefits.

A deficit on current account is very different because it is not self-liquidating. The classical economic doctrine was, first, that the current account budget should always be balanced and, second, on those extraordinary occasions such as wars when it could not be balanced, that a current account budget deficit should be financed by long-term debt and a plan to run current account surpluses in the future sufficiently large to retire the debt. Thus a current account deficit, should it be unavoidable, was to be financed by earmarking some future general tax revenues for the purpose of retiring the debt.

It is no coincidence that these classical doctrines about government finance were developed at a time when England and other leading economic powers were on the gold standard, each government promising to convert its currency and other government debt into gold on certain specified conditions. To make good on that promise, a government had to back its debt with sufficiently large and sufficiently probable prospective government surpluses denominated in gold. Deficits on capital account did not threaten a government's adherence to a gold standard, while deficits on current account did. The force of a gold standard was to cause the government to back its debt and to refrain from raising revenues from seigniorage.

Under contemporary monetary institutions in which currency is inconvertible or fiat, governments have access to seigniorage as an additional means of raising government revenues. (Whether the additional freedom this gives government is helpful is very controversial both among theorists and practical people.) When a government finances its long-term debt without indexing repayment to the price level, the freedom to expand government demand debt and longer-term debt without the limits imposed by adherence to the gold standard gives the government a wide range of options about if, when, and to what extent to default on its long-term debt by monetizing it and depreciating its real value.[28]

Under a fiat money regime the extent to which a current account deficit is inflationary depends on the extent to which private agents believe that the government will ultimately finance it by monetization. For example, the Ricardo-Barro doctrine about the irrelevance of the current taxation-debt-issuing choice assumes that the government refrains from monetizing the debt and in effect binds itself to a classical financial policy. Under that policy current real government deficits are not inflationary because they are accompanied by expectations of future government surpluses. The additional real government debt is backed by prospective real tax revenues. However, as Bryant and Wallace [9] have emphasized, in a policy regime where the current deficit is eventually monetized in some proportion, a current account deficit is inflationary. In some models it is more inflationary, the larger the proportion of it that is eventually monetized and the sooner the monetization occurs. In those models the precise dynamics by which the prospect of future monetization of the debt influences inflation rates depends on the detailed specification of the demand functions for assets, in particular, on how responsive they are to the expected rate of return on currency. It can readily happen, for example, as under a demand function for money like Phillip Cagan's [11], that *current* rates of inflation respond positively to the prospect of *future* increases in money brought about by eventual monetization of government debt; see Sargent and Wallace [38].

Although it seems not to have been something that Keynes himself would have advocated, the widespread adoption of Keynesian ideas about fiscal policy after World War II has been accompanied by abandonment of the classical public budgeting and accounting procedures at the level of national governments (although not at the level of state and local governments in the United States). For example, in the United Kingdom the nationalized industries do not float their own debt. Instead, they borrow from the National Loan Board, which in turn borrows by issuing government debt. This arrangement is one that departs from or at least obscures the earmarking of revenues from particular projects to back a given bond issue. Moreover the recent history of public finances in the United Kingdom displays little sensitivity to the distinction between capital and current account so, for example, as table 4.6 and figure 4.1 show, capital formation by the general government and nationalized industries has stagnated or actually fallen. Further, as table 4.9 shows, while general government final consumption and current grants and subsidies have risen substantially in recent years, and have continued

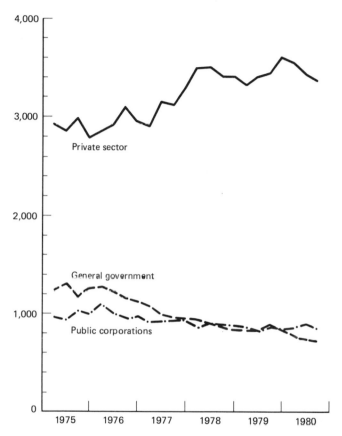

Figure 4.1
Gross domestic fixed capital formation (millions of Pounds, 1975 prices seasonally adjusted)

to rise under Mrs. Thatcher, capital expenditures have not. Under both Mrs. Thatcher's government and the previous Labor Government, belt tightening has fallen largely on public sector investment items. According to the classic canons of public finance that we alluded to earlier, this structure of expenditure cuts is perverse from the viewpoint of anti-inflationary policy.

The failure of Mrs. Thatcher's government to control public expenditures has been widely commented upon and will receive only brief mention here. Mrs. Thatcher has been criticized for a number of what are essentially tactical errors, for example, in her stance toward pay for public employees. Her early decision to stand by the Conservative Party's campaign pledge to honor the recommendations of the Clegg Commission, which the Labor Government instituted to establish pay standards for civil servants comparable to those in the private sector, resulted in earnings increases for civil servants of 24.5 percent between 1979III and 1980III. Thatcher responded, albeit belatedly to that criticism, by eventually abolishing the Clegg Commission in the fall of 1980. Since that time, the government has announced the adoption of a cash limit system, which essentially creates a total wages fund with which the government intends to confront a given public sector union or collection of unions. The idea is to force the unions to take into account a trade-off between wage rates and the number of public sector employees. A problem is that such cash limits have been breached in the past and have already been breached by Thatcher in the coal miners' settlement.

4.6 North Sea Oil and the Pound Sterling

In the late 1970s the magnitude of Britain's prospective revenues from North Sea oil became clearer and coincided with a simultaneous appreciation of the pound sterling from 1.65 U.S.$/£ in 1975IV to 2.39$/£ in 1980IV, and a swing of the current account balance of payments from a deficit toward surplus. The fact that Great Britain moved from being a net importer to being a net exporter of petroleum helped swing the current account into surplus. Some observers have attributed the strength of the pound to Britain's claim on North Sea oil and its contribution in swinging the current account toward surplus. However, few macroeconomic models imply that there is any direct connection between possessing oil and having a strong currency. There is an indirect connection, namely, that North Sea oil is heavily taxed and thus contributes to prospective government revenues, thereby tending to diminish the government deficit. Revenues from the taxation of North Sea oil are substantial and are expected to grow over time. The 1981 budget forecasts revenues from all taxes on oil (in 1979–80 prices) of £3.25 billion in 1980–81, £4.50 billion in 1981–82, £4.75 billion in 1982–83, and £5.25 billion in 1983–84. These revenues are a substantial fraction of the current government deficit of £13.5 billion. However, most macroeconomic theories assert that only the total deficit and how it is financed influence inflation and the international value of the pound. So long as total prospective government deficits remain as large as they are, it is difficult to subscribe to the view that the United Kingdom's possession of oil strengthens the pound. As a scrap of empirical evidence supporting this judgment, it has been observed that Norway is in a similar situation to England vis-à-vis North Sea oil and that neither has its currency appreciated internationally nor has it experienced the severe depression of industry that England has. One explanation for the difference appears to be that Norway has embarked on a looser monetary policy than has England.

Another popular explanation for the strong pound is that OPEC countries have begun to diversify their overseas investments by holding assets denominated in a variety of foreign currencies and that this has resulted in an increased preference for pound-denominated assets. This factor is probably part of the explanation but is not the dominant force leading to a strong pound.

Probably the most plausible explanation for the emergence of a strong pound builds on the "overshooting" idea of Dornbusch and has the advantage that it simultaneously explains other aspects of the current situation including high British interest rates and depressed British output and employment.[29] Dornbusch modeled a small country under the following assumptions: (1) The domestic price level has some sort of stickiness. Either domestic prices are exogenous, as in one of Dornbusch's original formulations [12], or there is a Taylor-like long-term contracting mechanism, as in a later contribution by Dornbusch [13], or there are information discrepancies à la Lucas and Phelps that prevent domestic prices from adjusting instantaneously to certain classes of random events, as in the setup of Nasser Saidi [36]. Which of these devices is resorted to makes an important difference, as we shall see. (2) There is assumed to be perfect international capital mobility in high yielding assets. This implies that the interest parity condition must hold. The interest parity condition states that the domestic interest rate must equal the foreign rate of interest minus the expected rate of appreciation of the domestic currency. Thus, letting r_{jt} be the domestic nominal interest rate on j period bonds, r_{jt}^* be the foreign nominal interest rate on j-period bonds, e_t be the exchange rate or foreign price of domestic money, measured in foreign currency per unit of domestic currency, and $E_t \ln e_{t+j}$ be the logarithm of the exchange rate expected as of time t to prevail at time $t + j$, the interest parity condition is

$$r_{jt} = r_{jt}^* - \frac{1}{j}\{E_t \ln e_{t+j} - \ln e_t\}.$$

The interest parity condition insures that foreigners can attain the same nominal rate of return, in terms of their own currency, by investing in the domestic country as by investing elsewhere. (3) The market for domestic currency and other "money" is assumed to be isolated internationally in the sense that the real rate of return on domestic money is permitted to be strictly dominated by other assets, including domestic and foreign bonds and equities and maybe also foreign currencies. What is crucial for the results is that there be some restriction on the scope of international currency substitution, most formulations ruling out any currency substitution at all. Notice the asymmetry between the assumption of integrated world bond and equities markets but nationalistic markets for currencies. The demand for domestic real balances is assumed to vary inversely with the domestic nominal interest rate, and directly with domestic real output, in the standard way. (4) The demand for domestic real output depends, among other things, inversely on the domestic real rate of interest and on the "real exchange rate" or terms of trade. Thus, letting p be the domestic price level measured in pounds per British good, p^* the foreign price level measured in dollars per U.S. good, and e the exchange rate measured in dollars per pound, the "real exchange rate" is defined as ep/p^*. Thus, given p and p^*, an increase in e decreases the demand for British output, since it raises the relative price of British goods in terms of U.S. goods. (5) While the domestic price level is to some extent sticky, the exchange rate and domestic interest rate are perfectly flexible instantaneously. (6) The foreign price level and interest rate are exogenous to events in the domestic country, the operational meaning of the small-country assumption. (7) Expectations are rational.

Given these assumptions, consider a situation where the British monetary authority undertakes a restrictive monetary action. Because of price level stickiness, the initial effect is to drive the domestic interest rate upward. But the upward tendency in the domestic interest rate threatens to disturb the interest parity condition and to create a capital inflow. To maintain interest parity in the face of less than perfectly flexible prices, the entire expected exchange rate path must adjust to generate an expected path of subsequent depreciation of the pound sufficient to offset the higher British interest rate. For this to happen, the exchange rate e must first jump upward to a higher level than before the restrictive monetary action, from which higher level it gradually falls in order to generate the rational expectations of a depreciating pound needed to maintain interest parity. Thus the immediate effect of the restrictive monetary action is to cause the exchange rate initially to appreciate suddenly and subsequently to depreciate gradually. However, since the domestic price level is somewhat sticky, the initial effect of the appreciated pound is to raise the real exchange rate ep/p^*, and so to reduce the demand for British goods. This effect reinforces the effect on demand of the higher real domestic interest rate and leads to a recession along standard Keynesian lines of insufficient aggregate demand.

This sequence of events depends on there being some source of price stickiness that prevents the domestic labor market from clearing. Had domestic prices and wages been assumed perfectly flexible, the response to a downward movement in the domestic money supply would have been very different than that described here. In particular, under flexible prices equilibrium is restored by a drop in the domestic price p proportional to the drop in the money supply, together with an off-setting increase in the exchange rate just sufficient to leave the real exchange rate ep/p^* unaltered. No changes in the domestic interest rate or output are needed to restore equilibrium. A version of classical neutrality occurs in these models under flexible domestic prices.

Versions of the model such as Saidi's that rest on limited information and temporary confusion to provide price stickiness, or a Phillips curve, exhibit an interesting mixture of the responses under sticky prices and under perfectly flexible prices. In particular, with respect to monetary disturbances that were perfectly predictable given private agents' information and understanding in the past, the system responds exactly as if prices were perfectly flexible: there are no real effects, the domestic price level and the exchange rate adjusting just enough to off-set the disturbance while leaving domestic real output and employment unaltered. However, with respect to monetary disturbances that are not predictable, given agents' information and understanding, the system responds qualitatively in the same fashion as described when prices are sticky.

Each of these variants of the Dornbusch model works in explaining the broad features of recent British experience, including high nominal interest rates, a strong pound sterling, and depressed industry. However, the different versions of the model support different interpretations and perhaps also policy recommendations.[30] On the one hand, according to the models that rely on momentum or long-term contracts to generate domestic price inflexibility, the response to restrictive monetary actions will be qualitatively similar whether or not those actions were foreseen by private agents. Such versions of the model could explain events even on the interpretation that Mrs. Thatcher's restrictive actions represent execution of a once-and-for-all regime change that is widely believed and irreversible. On the other hand, according to versions of the model like Saidi's that rely solely on information limitations to induce a Phillips curve, the events must be interpreted as reflecting the perceived temporary and reversible nature of the restrictive monetary actions that the government has undertaken.

Explanations along Dornbusch's line seem to be the best ones available for simultaneously explaining the strong pound, depressed British industry, and persistent British inflation. However, the recent literature on currency substitution makes it clear that this argument is delicate in that it depends on a demand function for domestic currency that permits domestic currency to be dominated in rate of return by large and variable amounts by foreign currencies and other assets. As several researchers have emphasized, there are incentives for international currency substitution that threaten the temporal stability of the demand schedule for domestic currency and the durability of the preceding class of explanations.[31] The literature on currency substitution points toward a problem that may loom on the horizon for British policy. That literature predicts that a country that runs much larger persistent deficits than its neighbors and that monetizes a large fraction of them will require the imposition of international currency controls if it is to support its currency internationally.[32] The models analyzed in the currency substitution literature thus indicate that high and persistent government deficits are over the long haul incompatible with permanent abstention from exchange controls. While it might take some time for these forces to break through various frictions, they will acquire strength and create problems precisely to the extent that large budget deficits loom in the future. It is certainly arguable that only temporarily can a tight monetary policy delay the operation of these forces, à la Dornbusch, in the face of large, persistent government deficits.

4.7 Conclusion

The theoretical doctrines and the historical evidence described in this chapter provide little reason for being optimistic about the efficacy of a plan for gradual monetary restraint which is simultaneously soft on the government deficit. Gradualism invites speculation about future reversals, or U-turns, in policy. Large contemporary government deficits unaccompanied by concrete prospects for future government surpluses promote realistic doubts about whether monetary restraint must be abandoned sooner or later to help finance the deficit. Such doubts not only call into question the likelihood that the plan can succeed in reducing inflation permanently but also can induce high real costs in terms of depressed industry and lengthened unemployment in response to what may be viewed as only temporary downward movements in nominal aggregate demand due to the monetary restraint.

These considerations are pertinent in assessing the state of the United Kingdom's economy today and the situation facing the French in the 1920s. They are also pertinent in evaluating the wisdom of passing Kemp-Roth in the United States while simultaneously planning to implement a tight k-percent monetary rule.

If we are bent on reducing inflation, then by consulting both our theoretical imaginations and history, we can find methods that improve on gradualist monetary restraint in the face of large government deficits. That is why it behooves us to recall Poincaré and his contemporaries even as we think about Thatcher.[33]

Notes

I am exceptionally indebted to David Beers for educating me about recent economic events in the United Kingdom. Conversations with Rudiger Dornbusch and Neil Wallace have also been very helpful. This chapter was written in May 1981. No substantive revisions have been made since except for a theoretical clarification of John Taylor's model.

1. For example, see Otto Eckstein [14].

2. For example, see Lucas [25], Barro [3], Sargent and Wallace [37], and McCallum [29].

3. Robert Barro [5] has pointed out that after a change in policy regime, it can happen that it is in the interests of neither party to enforce some long-term contracts of the Taylor-Fischer variety that had been agreed upon before the regime change. Presumably such contracts would never be enforced.

4. Leland Yeager [44, 472] summarizes British postwar macroeconomic policy as follows: "The rapid reversibility of British policy ... has been almost comical at times. Balance-of-payments troubles have brought a variety of *ad hoc* responses, including two devaluations and one abandonment of exchange rate pegging, the selective Employment Tax of 1966, the import surcharge of 1964, the import deposit scheme of 1968, the tightening and loosening of various exchange controls on current and capital transactions, and various attempts at wage and price control, as well as turnarounds in domestic financial policy. Reliance on

such expedients creates chances of improper timing, of anticipatory private actions, of overshooting the mark, and of intensified instability as a result."

5. It goes without saying that the "credibility" that is essential under the rational expectations theory cannot be manipulated by promises or government announcements.

6. Rudiger Dornbusch made this argument in oral comments on my earlier paper [39].

7. The reader is referred to the accounts of post-World War I stabilizations in Brown [8] and Young [45]. For example, the Italian stabilization might as easily have served as our example as the French one. Brown [8, 431] quotes Count Volpi's account of the important aspects of the plan that the Italian government used to stabilize the lira:

1. Balancing of the national budget.

2. Consolidation of war debts.

3. Unification of the note issue and its concentration in the hands of the Bank of Italy.

4. Progressive and more efficient utilization of Italian resources and raw materials.

5. Gradual deflation in currency and in credit.

6. Consolidation of the floating debt and reorganization in the Treasury Department.

7. Regulation of the influx of foreign capital into Italian industry.

8. Reorganization in the whole field of production, and readjustment of taxes with a view to increased industrial efficiency.

9. Gradual amortization of the domestic debt.

10. Defense of the Treasury surplus by the reduction of state expenditures.

Count Volpi was the "architect of Italy's return to gold."

8. Interesting accounts of the "Poincaré miracle" appear in Shirer [41], Yeager [44], Alpert [1], Haig [21], and Rogers [35].

9. William Shirer [41] describes this struggle.

10. Another element of uncertainty was injected by the substantial war debts owed the United States, coupled with the French belief that the United States should not insist that these be repaid.

11. For accounts of the effects of war debts and reparations on the public finances and currencies in Europe after World War I, see Yeager [44] and Alpert [1].

12. See Haig [21, 163].

13. The strength and endurance of French politicians' resolve not to repeat such a default was indicated by the fact that France was the last of the major countries to devalue its currency in terms of gold in the 1930s: France devalued in 1936, while England did so in 1931 and the United States in 1933.

14. Stanley Fischer [17] provides a more complete discussion of this issue and the other issues described in this paragraph. Bryant and Wallace [9] discuss optimal seigniorage from the viewpoint of price discrimination. They describe setups in which a government can find it worthwhile to issue an array of debt with differing yields, tailored to segments of the market with differing interest elasticities of demand for government debt. Applying their idea to the issue in the present discussion, setups can be imagined where the domestic country arranges to hold high-yielding foreign government debt and where it is in the interests of both the foreign and the domestic country to permit the domestic country to back its monetary liabilities by the higher-yielding foreign government debt rather than the lower-yielding debt.

15. Bilson [7] describes a scheme of this sort that can lead to a positive real return on government issued or privately issued "currency" through a process of deflation.

16. For example, see Yeager [44] or Alpert [1].

17. See Friedman [18, 19, 20].

18. See Meltzer [30].

19. Presumably, a rule in which k is a small number.

20. See Barro [6].

21. In the literature it has been pointed out that such a k-percent rule implies an explosive path for the government interest-bearing debt. As Bennett McCallum [28] has pointed out, depending on the precise specification of the model, that fact may or may not imply that other variables in the model that are of interest are unstable.

22. The recent issue of indexed bonds in England sold at a real rate of interest of about 2 percent.

23. This issue was central to the struggle for the post-World War I stabilizations.

24. From the technical viewpoint of controlling monetary aggregates, the banking and financial intermediary systems in the United Kingdom differ in important respects from those in the United States. First, in the United Kingdom banking is more concentrated, there being five main "Clearing Banks." Second, in the British assets eligible to meet the 12.5 percent reserve requirement include all of the following interest-bearing assets: money at call from discount houses, treasury bills and other short-term government securities, local authority paper, corporate tax anticipation certificates, and bills of exchange. Notice that some of these assets are evidences of government indebtedness, while others are private debts. Since demand deposits do not bear interest in the United Kingdom, vis-à-vis the U.S. system, this system of reserve requirements tends to increase the banking system's share of seigniorage revenues relative to that of the government. On the other side of this issue, currency is a higher proportion of £M1 in the United Kingdom than in the United States. Third, the building societies (the analogue of savings and loan institutions in the United States) have long issued mortgages with variable maturities and variable rates of interest both linked to the general level of market interest rates. Therefore in the United Kingdom high interest rates do not produce the disintermediation from saving institutions that is so troublesome for the conduct of monetary policy in the United States. Fourth, partly as a result of the third feature, there is no analogue of Regulation Q in the United Kingdom, and small savers have access to a variety of instruments yielding close to market rates, as for example, Building Society shares. This fact also explains the absence of money market funds in the United Kingdom. Fifth, the Bank of England does not lend directly to the clearing banks but instead operates a discount window for the discount houses that make markets and hold portfolios of short-term government and private securities. The minimum lending rate, formerly known as the bank rate, applies to the Bank of England's loans to the discount houses.

25. I have in mind the Monetary Control Act.

26. As in the United States, in the United Kingdom there is a bewildering variety of monetary aggregates. The main ones are £M1, £M3, £M3, PSL 1 (Public Sector Liquidity number 1), and PSL 2. The variety of aggregates is spawned by the vagueness of "means of payments" as a category setting off one class of assets as "money." See Sargent and Wallace [40].

27. Recall the remarks in note 24 about the way in which seigniorage is allocated between the banks and the government under the British system of reserve requirements.

28. This was the choice that French politicians consciously faced and struggled with from 1919 to 1926 and that politicians also face today, although perhaps less consciously.

29. See Dornbusch [12, 13]. Buiter and Miller [10] argue that Dornbusch's idea explains contemporary observations in the United Kingdom.

30. One popular policy recommendation stemming from the momentum version of the model is to impose inward capital controls, for example, an interest equalization tax on the yields of British securities held by foreigners. Such a tax is presumed to weaken the pound and stimulate aggregate demand and real domestic output. See Buiter and Miller [10].

31. Kareken and Wallace [23] propound a model with an extreme amount of currency substitution.

32. See Kareken and Wallace [23].

33. Economists have begun devoting more attention to devising ways of reducing the costs of winding down inflation. For example, Jeffrey Shaefer and Axel Leijonhufvud have recently described a kind of dynamic currency reform scheme that aims to eradicate the costs of eliminating inflation that are due to long-term contracts. To illustrate their scheme, suppose that up to date t, the monetary and fiscal policy regime and the other random processes that influence inflation have been such as to make it rational for private agents to expect that future prices will follow some given path $\hat{p}(t + j)$, $j \geq 0$, where the expected price level $\hat{p}(t + j)$ is measured as usual in units of green dollars at time $t + j$ per good at time $(t + j)$. For example, if a constant rate of inflation of π is expected, then $\hat{p}(t + j) = (1 + \pi)^j p(t)$, where $p(t)$ is the actual price level at t. If these price expectations are built into long-term contracts that have been entered into t and earlier, and so form a legacy that influences actual prices and quantities at times $t + j$, then the act of bringing inflation to a sudden halt will cause substantial redistributions across traders. To the extent that actual prices turn out to be less than those expected at the time that the contracts were negotiated, real output and unemployment will be adversely affected.

The idea of Shaefer and Leijonhufvud is to circumvent these costs by carrying out an imaginative kind of currency reform. The government passes a law at date t that states that all contracts that call for payment of y dollars at date $t + j$ can be discharged by paying only $yp(t)/\hat{p}(t + j)$ dollars. Thus, in the constant expected inflation case, dollars due at $(t + j)$ are paid off at only $1/(1 + \pi)^j$ on the dollar. More important, the government successfully commits itself to run a fiscal and monetary policy that implies a stable price level so that the actual price $p(t + j) = p(t)$ for all $j \geq 1$. With a constant actual price path of $p(t + j) = p(t)$, and the new debt conversion law, both sides of all contracts end up being just as well off as if the debt conversion law had not been enacted and prices had risen as expected, $p(t + j) = \hat{p}(t + j)$. Thus the debt conversion law is crafted to neutralize the real effects of the monetary and fiscal policies needed to support a zero inflation price path. It is as if the government announces that it is calling in all the green-colored currency and issuing new blue-colored currency on the following terms: green dollars will be converted into blue dollars at par at time t, and subsequently the green dollar price of a blue dollar is $\hat{p}(t + j)/p(t)$.

References

1. Alpert, Paul. *Twentieth Century Economic History of Europe.* Henry Schuman, New York, 1951.

2. Bailey, Martin. *National Income and the Price Level.* 2nd ed. McGraw-Hill, New York, 1970, pp. 175–186.

3. Barro, Robert J. "Rational Expectations and the Role of Monetary Policy." *Journal of Monetary Economics* 2 (January 1976): 1–32.

4. Barro, Robert J. "Unanticipated Money Growth and Unemployment in the United states." *American Economic Review* 67 (March 1977): 101–115.

5. Barro, Robert J. "Long Term Contracting, Sticky Prices, and Monetary Policy." *Journal of Monetary Economics* (July 1977): 265–285.

6. Barro, Robert J. "Are Government Bonds Net Wealth?" *Journal of Political Economy* (November/December 1974): 1095–1118.

7. Bilson, John. A Proposal for Monetary Reform. Unpublished manuscript. Hoover Institution, 1980.

8. Brown, William Adams, Jr. *The International Gold Standard Reinterpreted, 1914–1934.* Vol. 1. National Bureau of Economic Research, New York, 1940.

9. Bryant, John and Neil Wallace. "A Suggestion for Further Simplifying the Theory of Money." Staff Report no. 62. Federal Reserve Bank of Minneapolis, 1980.

10. Buiter, Willem, and Marcus Miller. "Monetary Policy and International Competitiveness." Unpublished manuscript. October 1980.

11. Cagan, Phillip. "The Monetary Dynamics of Hyperinflation." In *Studies in the Quantity Theory of Money*, M. Friedman, ed. University of Chicago Press, Chicago.

12. Dornbusch, Rudiger. "Expectations and Exchange Rate Dynamics," *Journal of Political Economy* 84 (1976): 1161–1176.

13. Dornbusch, Rudiger. *Open Economy Macroeconomics.* Basic Books, New York, 1980, chapter 9.

14. Eckstein, Otto. *Core Inflation,* forthcoming.

15. "The 1981 Budget." *Economic Progress Report*, no. 131, March 1981. Published by the Treasury.

16. *Economic Trends.* Central Statistical Office, Her Majesty's Stationary Office, 1981.

17. Fischer, Stanley. Seigniorage and the Case for a National Money. Unpublished manuscript. Massachusetts Institute of Technology, Cambridge, 1981.

18. Friedman, Milton. "A Theoretical Framework for Monetary Analysis." *Journal of Political Economy* 78 (March/April 1970): 193–238.

19. Friedman, Milton. "A Monetary Theory of Nominal Income." *Journal of Political Economy* 79 (March/April 1971): 323–337.

20. Friedman, Milton. "Comments on the Critics." *Journal of Political Economy* 80 (September/October 1972): 906–950.

21. Haig, Robert Murray. *The Public Finances of Post-War France.* Columbia University Press, New York, 1929.

22. Kareken, John H., and Neil Wallace. Samuelson's Consumption-Specific Fiat Monies. Unpublished manuscript. Federal Reserve Bank of Minneapolis, July 1978.

23. Kareken, John H., and Neil Wallace. "On the Indeterminacy of Equilibrium Exchange Rates." *Quarterly Journal of Economics* 96 (May 1981): 207–222.

24. Kareken, John H. "The Optimum Monetary Instrument Variable." *Journal of Money, Credit, and Banking* 2 (August 1970): 385–390.

25. Lucas, Robert E., Jr. "Expectations and the Neutrality of Money." *Journal of Economic Theory* 4 (April 1972): 102–124.

26. Lucas, Robert E., Jr. "Some International Evidence on Output-Inflation Tradeoffs," *American Economic Review* 58 (1973): 326–334.

27. Lucas, Robert E., Jr. "An Equilibrium Model of the Business Cycle," *Journal of Political Economy* 83 (December 1975): 1113–1144.

28. McCallum, Bennett T. "On Macroeconomic Instability from a Monetarist Policy Rule," *Ecomonics Letters* 1 (1973): 121–124.

29. McCallum, Bennet T. "The Current State of the Policy-Ineffectiveness Debate." *American Economic Review*, Papers and Proceedings, 1979.

30. Meltzer, Allan. Tests of Inflation Theories from the British Laboratory. Unpublished manuscript. Carnegie-Mellon University, February 1981.

31. Thatcherism: A Mid-Term Review. Morgan Guaranty Trust Company, February 1981.

32. Phelps, Edmund S. "The New Microeconomics in Employment and Inflation Theory." In *Microeconomic Foundations of Employment and Inflation Theory*. Norton, New York, 1970.

33. Phelps, Edmund S., and John B. Taylor. "Stabilizing Powers of Monetary Policy under Rational Expectations." *Journal of Political Economy* 85 (February 1977): 163–190.

34. Poole, William. "Optimal Choice of Monetary Policy Instruments in a Simple Stochastic Marco Model." *Quarterly Journal of Economics* (May 1970): 197–216.

35. Rogers, James Harvey. *The Process of Inflation in France, 1914–1927*. Columbia University Press, New York, 1929.

36. Saidi, Nasser H. "Fluctuating Exchange Rates and the International Transmission of Economic Disturbances." *Journal of Money, Credit, and Banking* 12 (November 1980, part 1).

37. Sargent, Thomas J., and Neil Wallace. "Rational Expectations and the Theory of Economic Policy." *Journal of Monetary Economics* 2 (April 1976): 169–183.

38. Sargent, Thomas J., and Neil Wallace. The Limits of Contemporary Monetary Policy. Unpublished manuscript. Summer 1981.

39. Sargent, Thomas J. "The Ends of Four Big Inflations." In *Inflation*, ed. by R. E. Hall. University of Chicago Press, Chicago, 1983.

40. Sargent, Thomas J., and Neil Wallace. The Real Bills Doctrine vs. the Quantity Theory: A Reconsideration. *Journal of Political Economy* 90 (December 1982): 1212–1236.

41. Shirer, William L. *The Collapse of the Third Republic: An Inquiry into the Fall of France in 1940*. Simon and Schuster, New York, 1969.

42. Taylor, John B. "Staggered Wage Setting in a Macro Model." *American Economic Review*, Papers and Proceedings, 1979, pp. 108–118.

43. Taylor, John B. "Estimation and Control of a Macroeconomic Model with Rational Expectations." *Econometrica* 47 (September 1979): 1267–1286.

44. Yeager, Leland B. *International Monetary Relations: Theory, History, and Policy*. 2nd ed. Harper and Row, New York, 1976.

45. Young, John Parke. *European Currency and Finance*. Vols. 1 and 2. Printed for the use of the Senate Commission of Gold and Silver Inquiry. Government Printing Office, Washington, D.C., 1925.

46. *Bank of England Quarterly Bulletin*, 1981.

II Indexation Experience

5 Indexation: Current Theory and the Brazilian Experience

Mario Henrique Simonsen

5.1 The Policy-Maker's Contention

Indexation is a natural and appealing device to counter general price level uncertainties. It was proposed in 1807 by an English writer on money, John Wheatley, and was enthusiastically supported by at least two great economists of the past, Alfred Marshall and Irving Fisher. From the theoretical viewpoint, if the possible states of nature differed only with respect to the general price level, all the Arrow-Debreu contingent claims would be equivalent to fully indexed contracts.

The success of widespread indexation is open to controversy. In the absence of regulatory impediments, high and variable inflation rates pave the way for endogenous indexation as a risk-sharing device in medium- and long-term contracts. Comprehensive indexation schemes for wages, bonds, and taxes have been adopted by a number of countries, including Brazil, in order to minimize the welfare losses caused by chronic and uncertain inflation rates, and they proved to be reasonably successful in this direction. Yet most policy-makers object to indexation on the grounds that it is an inflation-perpetuating mechanism. This incidentally explains why a number of countries have abandoned their experiments with mandatory wage indexation.

Recent economic literature suggests that wage indexation aggravates the instability of the general price level. This result was originally derived by Jo Anna Gray and Stanley Fischer under the following assumptions: (1) the alternative to indexation is nominal wage contracting on the basis of rational expectations; (2) labor contracts determine a wage base, which may be subject to full, fractional, or no indexation at all and which is kept unchanged throughout the contract period; (3) employment is determined by the ex post labor demand curve, after uncertainties are realized. A Keynesian disposition is clearly perceived in the Gray-Fischer description of the labor markets, at least as long as the real wage-employment equilibrium falls to the left of the labor supply curve. Some complications arise when supply and demand shocks move this equilibrium to the right of the labor supply schedule, since modern societies cannot force people to work. Yet these complications can be solved by a contract adjustment function that prevents the unemployment rate from falling below some critical limit and keeps the substance of the Gray-Fischer findings.

An extended version of the Gray-Fischer model will be presented in section 5.2. It confirms all the original conclusions on the effects of wage indexation, and it also shows that any arrangement that weakens some existing drag on price changes, such as the indexation of income and capital gains taxes and the indexation of public bonds, increases the sensitivity of the general price level to any type of shock. Much of this extended version was inspired by the following passage in the *General Theory of Employment*, where Keynes presented his penetrating views on the effects of wage indexation:

If, as in Australia, an attempt were made to fix real wages by legislation, there would be a certain level of employment corresponding to that level of real wages; and the actual level of employment would, in a closed system, oscillate violently between that level and no employment at all, according as the rate of investment was or was not below the rate compatible with that level; whilst prices would be in unstable equilibrium when investment was at the critical level, racing to zero whenever investment was below it, and to infinity whenever it was above it. The element of stability would have to be found, if at all, in the factors controlling the quantity of money being so determined that there always existed some level of money-wages at which the quantity of money would be such as to establish a relation between the rate of interest and the marginal efficiency of capital which would maintain investment at the critical level. In this event employment would be constant (at the level appropriate to the legal real wage) with money-wages and prices fluctuating rapidly in the degree just necessary to maintain this rate of investment at the appropriate figure. In the actual case of Australia, the escape was found, partly of course in the inevitable inefficacy of the legislation to achieve its object, and partly in Australia not being a closed system, so that the level of money-wages was itself a determinant of foreign investment and hence of total investment, whilst the terms of trade were an important influence on real wages. (p. 269)

The first part of the Keynesian analysis seems a little confusing. If both the real wage rate and the investment level are exogenously given, there is no way to reconcile the two different employment-output equilibria. In the second part, however, in the discussion about the investment level made sensitive to the interest rate, the theory Keynes advances is one of the main conclusions of the Gray-Fischer model: wage indexation protects employment and output against demand shocks, but at the cost of increased price instability. He also showed that fixed exchange rates in an open indexed economy dampen the price fluctuations in two different directions. First, they introduce an exogenous component in the consumer price index which lowers the indexation parameter in terms of the GNP deflator. This is equivalent to substituting fractional for full indexation. Second, they make the current account balance a decreasing function of the domestic price level, thus introducing, through the external component of aggregate demand, a drag on domestic price changes. Of course by modern standards the Keynesian analysis of the macroeconomic effects of wage indexation is incomplete. It says nothing about supply shocks, and it fails to distinguish the real interest rate, which affects investment, from the nominal one, which acts on money demand.

The Gray-Fischer results, important as they may be, hardly support the policy-maker's contention that indexation is an inflation-perpetuating mechanism and that even in the absence of shocks widespread escalator clauses produce sticky inflation rates. The stickiness argument of course does not preclude the eventual effectiveness of a tight monetary policy. Rather, it suggests that indexation makes inflation harder to fight because of worsened price-output trade-offs.

An extended version of the Gray-Fischer model comes exactly to the opposite conclusion, however, one that was announced by Milton Friedman in a challenging essay published in 1974. In the absence of shocks, widespread indexation arrangements ease the side effects of anti-inflationary policies since price expectations are phased out from medium- and long-term contracts. Full-wage indexation transforms the short-run Phillips curve into a vertical straight line, thus eliminating any output loss caused by tight monetary policies. It might involve a substantial social cost by overexposing output and employment to supply shocks. It might even produce an unemployment disaster if the real wages are settled at an excessively high level and if the invisible hand is not quick enough in correcting labor market disequilibria. Yet a vertical Phillips curve in the short run can be due to anything but sticky inflation rates.

Thus the question remains how to reconcile the Gray-Fischer results with the policy-maker's contention. One possible explanation is that indexation reduces the political will to fight inflation because it minimizes the welfare losses caused by price instability, at least in the absence of adverse supply shocks. Yet the weakened political motivation could still work if anti-inflationary policies became painless, as they would be with a vertical short-term Phillips curve. A more promising possibility is based on the assumption that, when associating indexation with inflation rigidity, policy-makers have in mind lagged escalator clauses.

Keynes in chapter 19 of the *General Theory of Employment*, Friedman's argument in favor of widespread escalator clauses, the Gray-Fischer model, and most recent studies on indexation conceive of a type of labor contract that makes the real wage independent of the general price level. This is what one should call perfect indexation. The usual type of indexed wage contract found in real life, however, is based on a staggered rule: nominal wages are adjusted at regular intervals of time (such as every six months) according to the inflation rate of the previous period.

Lagged indexing of course does not make real wages invariant to the general price level. Since nominal wages are kept fixed for a certain period of time, the general price level behavior during that time interval is a key determinant of their purchasing power. Thus the possibility of accommodating output and employment through short-term demand policies, which was ruled out in the models of perfect wage indexation, is again reopened by the price adjustment lag, as it is associated with the indexation lag.

A model of lagged wage indexation is developed in section 5.3. It assumes rational expectations, but it leads to a Phillips relation formally equivalent to the one that would be generated by adaptive inflationary expectations. Moreover it shows that mandatory indexation might produce highly unfavorable inflation-output trade-offs in the short run. The conclusions strongly support the policy-makers' views on the effects of widespread wage indexation.

One may ask what is the rationale for staggered indexation arrangements of the type described here, which after all represent nothing but perfect indexation plus a cheating mechanism. The answer is partly to be found in the inevitable information lag and partly in the fact that perfectly indexed labor contracts are often Pareto inefficient.

The first part of the explanation stresses a very important point: in a perfectly indexed labor contract nominal wages should be made proportional to the consumer price index of the payday. And, as long as a minimum time period (for example, one month) is required to compute the price indexes and transfer their results to the payrolls, indexation can never be perfect.

Yet one can easily imagine a number of practical arrangements that come closer to perfect indexation than the information lag argument. One could, for instance, substitute fixed inflation rate thresholds for the fixed time intervals, such as nominal wages adjusted to inflation after every percentage increase in the consumer price index. Basically, however, there is no serious reason why perfectly indexed labor contracts should even be desired. As will be shown in section 5.4 in terms of the Azariadis framework, efficient wage contracts should be fully indexed but with an adjustment mechanism for supply shocks. But moral hazard and practical measurement problems make this type of contract very hard to implement, especially because the supply shocks should be measured at the individual firm level. This appears as an incentive for some apparently imperfect indexation arrangements, such as fractional indexation or lagged escalator clauses.

Whatever the reason may be, the fact is that lagged wage indexation at fixed time intervals has been practiced by a number of countries, including Brazil, and therefore this policy alternative deserves a careful analysis. The Brazilian experience since 1965 is described in section 5.5.

Tax indexation will be discussed in section 5.6. From the outset it presents a theoretical disadvantage, namely, it eliminates a drag on unanticipated price changes, thus contributing to increased price instability. Yet it is defensible from the welfare point of view and usually inevitable in face of high and persistent inflation rates. The Brazilian experience is extremely interesting, although the income tax has never been properly indexed.

Bond indexation and other forms of escalator clauses will be discussed in section 5.7 in connection with the Brazilian case. The concluding remarks of section 5.8 stress the following basic points: (1) lagged wage indexation is neither better nor worse than perfect indexation, but it is surely quite different; (2) mandatory wage indexation may in fact create inflation rigidities, as usually contended by policy-makers, and, if indexation comes close to its perfect version, it may lead to persistent unemployment; (3) it is impossible for government to be out of the indexation process, since taxes and public bonds may be involved in it yet, apart from that, some laissez faire with escalator clauses seems quite advisable.

5.2 An Extended Gray-Fischer Model

Let us analyze the effects of perfect wage indexation using a simple macro-economic model of the Fischer-Gray type.

The supply side of the economy will be described by a markup price equation and by a wage-adjustment rule. The price equation is

$$p_t = n_t + w_t + f_t - v_t, \tag{5.1}$$

where p_t, n_t, w_t, and f_t are the logs of the general price level, the labor input per unit output, the nominal wage, and the markup factor and v_t is a random walk supply shock:

$$v_t = v_{t-1} + u_t, \tag{5.2}$$

$$E_{t-1}u_t = 0. \tag{5.3}$$

The expectation, E_{t-1}, is conditional on information available at the end of period $t-1$. The markup factor is sensitive to the output gap:

$$f_t = f + \mu h_t, \quad f, \mu > 0, \tag{5.4}$$

where

$$h_t = y_t - \hat{y}_t, \tag{5.5}$$

with y_t and $\hat{y}_t$ indicating the logs of actual and full-employment real output.

Unanticipated supply shocks may shift labor productivity and full-employment output. This effect is summarized

$$(I - E_{t-1})\hat{y}_t = cu_t, \quad c \geq 0, \tag{5.6}$$

where I stands for the identity operator.[1]

The nominal wage adjustment rule will be postulated as:

$$w_t - w_{t-1} = \alpha(p_t - p_{t-1}) + (1 - \alpha)(E_{t-1}p_t - p_{t-1}) + (n_{t-1} - n_t) + F(h_t), \tag{5.7}$$

where α stands for the indexation degree. Equation (5.7) should be interpreted as follows:

1. Nominal wage adjustments depend on price changes, productivity gains, and the unemployment level.

2. With an indexation degree α the nominal wage adjustment for price changes is divided into two components: a fraction α of the log of the nominal wage is adjustment according to the actual inflation rate $p_t - p_{t-1}$ and the remainder $1 - \alpha$ according to rational inflationary expectations.

3. Labor productivity gains $(n_{t-1} - n_t)$ are fully transferred to nominal wage.

4. Besides price changes and productivity gains, nominal wage adjustments are affected by the unemployment rate, or equivalently, by the output gap. This effect is introduced in equation (5.7) by the component

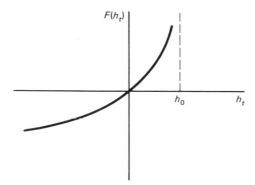

Figure 5.1
The nonlinear Phillips curve

$F(h_t)$ which should be an increasing and strictly convex function of h_t, such that $F(0) = 0$, as described in figure 5.1. For some positive h_0, $F(h_t)$ should tend to infinity, since the unemployment rate can never fall to zero.

The nominal wage adjustment equation (5.7) is somewhat similar to the one adopted by Stanley Fischer in 1977. It implicitly refers to lifetime labor contracts, since it links the nominal wage of each period to its preceding level. Lifetime contracts involve a number of implicit contingent clauses, including the response of nominal wages to unemployment rates, and this is the reason for the adjustment function $F(h_t)$. Since it is strictly convex, tending to infinity when h_t approaches some critical limit h_0, it serves a very useful purpose: it prevents the real wage-employment equilibrium from falling too much to the right of the labor supply curve, the threatening nightmare in the Gray-Fischer model.

Whenever necessary, in order to solve rational expectations equations, we shall approximate $F(h_t)$ by its slope at the origin:

$$F(h_t) = \beta h_t. \tag{5.8}$$

For small deviations of output from its full-employment level, β can be taken as a measure of short-term wage flexibility. A neoclassical approach, along the lines of Barro and Liviatan assumes $\beta = \infty$, transforming $F(h_t)$ into a vertical line through the origin: wages adjust immediately to full-employment equilibrium. Absolute rigidity corresponds to $\beta = 0$. Wage regulations are effective as long as they change the adjustment function $F(h_t)$. We shall assume that mandatory indexation schemes deter market flexibility and lower β. This is in fact the difference between voluntary and mandatory indexation arrangements.

Reasonable as it may be, equation (5.7) can be criticized as an ad hoc wage rule. Unfortunately it can only be avoided if a deus ex machina is brought on stage: a Walrasian auctioneer who clears the labor market at the beginning of each period, before uncertainties are realized, and who suddenly disappears from earth until a new round of labor contracts are to be signed. This is a key underlying assumption of the Gray model. The choice is a question of judgment, and I prefer to stay with equation (5.7).

But let us turn back to the supply side of our model. Taking the first differences of equation (5.1) and combining the result with equations (5.2) and (5.4) and with the wage adjustment rule (5.7) yields

$$(1 - \alpha)(I - E_{t-1})p_t = F(h_t) + \mu(h_t - h_{t-1}) - u_t, \tag{5.9}$$

which is our Phillips relation. Whenever necessary, it will be replaced by the linear approximation

$$(1 - \alpha)(I - E_{t-1})p_t = (\beta + \mu)h_t - \mu h_{t-1} - u_t. \tag{5.10}$$

In the absence of shocks rational expectations are equivalent to perfect foresight, and equation (5.9) is reduced to

$$F(h_t) + \mu(h_t - h_{t-1}) = 0.$$

Except in the case of absolute rigidity ($F(h_t) = 0$), h_t converges to zero: in the absence of shocks the economy approaches its full-employment equilibrium. Yet, because of the strict convexity of $F(h_t)$, prosperity is dissipated more quickly than a recession. When shocks are introduced, this asymmetry leads to a stochastic bias toward unemployment, a Keynesian touch in our model not grasped by linear approximation. In fact, applying the E_{t-1} operator to both sides of equation (5.9) and using Jensen's inequality,

$$F(E_{t-1}h_t) + \mu E_{t-1}h_t \leq E_{t-1}F(h_t) + \mu E_{t-1}h_t = \mu h_{t-1}.$$

Assuming full employment in the previous period ($h_{t-1} = 0$), this equation yields $E_{t-1}h_t \leq 0$.

For small deviations of output from full employment, the linear approximation (5.10) to the Phillips relation leads to

$$E_{t-1}h_t = \frac{\mu}{\beta + \mu}h_{t-1}, \tag{5.11}$$

a result that is independent of the indexation degree and that stresses the importance of the β/μ ratio in quickly phasing out the deviations of output from full-employment equilibrium. The formula makes an important point against any regulation that lowers β, such as mandatory indexation.

The demand side of the model will be described by the log-linear IS and LM relations:

$$y_t = C_t - D(r_t - E_{t-1}(p_{t+1} - p_t)) - Hp_t + e_{1t}, \tag{5.12}$$

$$m_t - p_t + G + e_{2t} = Ly_t - Br_t, \tag{5.13}$$

where m_t stands for the log of the money supply and r_t for the nominal interest rate. In the IS equation (5.12), e_{1t} indicates the real demand shock, D is assumed to be a positive, and H is a nonnegative constant. The term D takes care of the real interest rate effects on aggregate demand, and H reflects the price change drags that might be introduced by fixed exchange rates, by a nonindexed income tax, and so on. Of course a positive H cannot be sustained in a chronic inflation environment. In the portfolio balance equation (5.13) L and B are positive constants, and e_{2t} the monetary shock.

Let us now analyze the effects of the wage indexation degree on output, prices, and on the gap. The parameter α has no effect on the anticipated components $E_{t-1}y_t$, $E_{t-1}p_t$, and $E_{t-1}h_t$, since it does not appear in equation (5.11) nor in the demand equations of the model and can only affect the unexpected components of the endogenous variables.[2] Applying the operator $I - E_{t-1}$ to equations (5.10), (5.12), and (5.13) and using (5.6), we obtain

$$(I - E_{t-1})y_t = \frac{(1-\alpha)(e_t + \eta_t) + K(1 + (\beta + \mu)c)u_t}{A(1-\alpha) + K(\beta + \mu)}, \tag{5.14a}$$

$$(I - E_{t-1})h_t = \frac{(1-\alpha)(e_t + \eta_t) + (K - A(1-\alpha)c)u_t}{A(1-\alpha) + K(\beta + \mu)}, \tag{5.14b}$$

$$(I - E_{t-1})p_t = \frac{(\beta + \mu)(e_t + \eta_t) - A(1 + (\beta + \mu)c)u_t}{A(1-\alpha) + K(\beta + \mu)}, \tag{5.14c}$$

where

$$\eta_t = (I - E_{t-1})m_t \tag{5.15}$$

indicates the unanticipated increase in the log of the money supply and where

$$A = L + \frac{B}{D}, \tag{5.16a}$$

$$K = 1 + \frac{BH}{D}, \tag{5.16b}$$

$$e_t = e_{2t} + \left(\frac{B}{D}\right)e_{1t}. \tag{5.16c}$$

Assuming u_t, e_t, and η_t to be uncorrelated, the conditional variances of y_t, h_t, and p_t are derived directly from equations (5.14a), (5.14b) and (5.14c). Equation (5.14a) shows that increased indexation protects output against demand shocks and monetary surprises but overexposes it to supply shocks, a well-known Gray-Fischer result. In fact full indexation would completely offset the effects of monetary surprises and demand shocks on output. As far as those shocks are concerned, equation (5.14b) leads exactly to the same conclusions as to the effects of the wage indexation degree on employment. The difference between the effects on output and employment results from supply shocks, which can shift the full-employment output equilibrium. Equation (5.14b) concludes that, even if shocks were limited to the supply side of the economy, a certain indexation degree could still be desirable in order to minimize employment fluctuations. This is a well-known result of Jo Anna Gray's model on optimal indexation. Finally, equation (5.14c) shows that wage indexation increases price instability in face of either type of shock or error.

In the absence of supply shocks, equations (5.14a) and (5.14b) support the Friedman argument in favor of widespread indexation as a way to ease the side effects of anti-inflationary policies. Such side effects result from expectational errors on the future course of monetary policy (even if expectations are rational) and can be modeled by a negative η_t in the preceding equations. Full indexation ($\alpha = 1$) would make the Phillips relation (5.10) a vertical straight line even in the short run, thus eliminating any temporary inflation-output trade-off.

The comments by Keynes on the effects of wage indexation in Australia can be easily explained by a adaptation of equation (5.14c). Keynes was just concerned with the real demand shocks resulting from private investment fluctuations so that, in his context, $\eta_t = e_{2t} = 0$. With an income elasticity L of the demand for money equal to one, equation (5.14c) reduces to

$$(I - E_{t-1})p_t = \frac{B(\beta + \mu)}{(B + D)(1 - \alpha) + (D + BH)(\beta + \mu)} e_{1t}. \qquad (5.17)$$

In the absence of price drags ($H = 0$) and with fully indexed wages ($\alpha = 1$), prices would fluctuate according to

$$(I - E_{t-1})p_t = \frac{B}{D} e_{1t}.$$

This represents exacerbated price instability under the conditions described in the general theory of employment: extreme volatility of private investment, interest rate elastic demand for money (high B), and slow response of investments to interest rate changes (low D). The Australian escapes, quoted by Keynes, were basically two (besides the ineffectiveness of the legislation), and both associated with fixed exchange rates: fractional instead of full indexation and the current account drag on price changes, described by the coefficient H of equation (5.17).

5.3 Lagged Indexation

Let us now analyze the effects of lagged indexation. In the usual arrangement described in section 5.1, nominal wages are adjusted at fixed intervals of time (such as six months) according to the inflation rate of the previous period: wages are corrected for inflation with a time lag. In a simplified version, if the indexation degree is equal to one, if there are no productivity gains, and if the economy is kept at full employment so that $F(h_t) = 0$, wages are adjusted according to the formula

$$w_t - w_{t-1} = p_{t-1} - p_{t-2}. \qquad (5.18)$$

This equation assumes that all nominal wages are adjusted at the beginning of each period and that prices move by steps, remaining unchanged throughout the period, as in figure 5.2. In most practical cases the wage adjustment interval is long enough to introduce two further

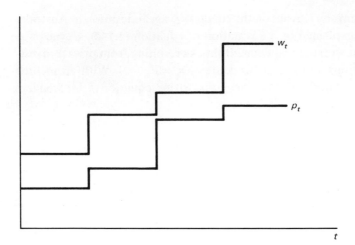

Figure 5.2
Stepwise increases of wages and prices

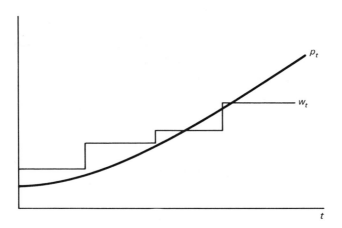

Figure 5.3
Smooth price adjustment

complications. First, price movements are better described by a continuous curve, as in figure 5.3. As a result real wages vary continuously
as long as their nominal level is kept unchanged. Second, different labor
groups have their nominal wages adjusted in different months, so that
the nominal wage staircases overlap. Yet equation (5.18) keeps the
substance of the problem of lagged indexation: real wages decline whenever the inflation rate accelerates, and vice versa. It can be shown moreover that, even if prices move up continuosly and wage adjustment dates
do not coincide, equation (5.18) provides a satisfactory approximation
to the average wage adjustment rule, with an appropriately calculated
time lag.

With a lagged indexation degree equal to α, equation (5.7) should be
replaced by

$$w_t - w_{t-1} = \alpha(p_{t-1} - p_{t-2}) + (1 - \alpha)(E_{t-1}\,p_t - p_{t-1})$$

$$+ (n_{t-1} - n_t) + F(h_t). \tag{5.7a}$$

Nominal wage adjustments for price changes are divided into two
components: the backward looking $\alpha(p_{t-1} - p_{t-2})$ and the forward
looking $(1 - \alpha)(E_{t-1}\,p_t - p_{t-1})$. A similar wage-adjustment rule was
derived by John Taylor in his model of monetary accommodation with
staggered wages. Substituting βh_t for $F(h_t)$, equation (5.7a) leads to the
Phillips relation:

$$p_t - p_{t-1} = \alpha(p_{t-1} - p_{t-2}) + (1 - \alpha)(E_{t-1}\,p_t - p_{t-1})$$

$$+ (\beta + \mu)h_t - \mu h_{t-1} - u_t. \tag{5.10a}$$

In the extended Gray-Fischer model it was shown that the wage
indexation degree did not affect the conditional expectations of the price,
output, and employment levels but did affect their unanticipated components. If lagged is substituted for perfect indexation, one is led to the
opposite conclusion. In fact, applying the $I - E_{t-1}$ operator to both
sides of equation (5.10a) yields

$$(I - E_{t-1})p_t = (\beta + \mu)(I - E_{t-1})h_t - u_t.$$

The result is independent of α and can be derived from the Phillips
relation (5.10) of the preceding section if $\alpha = 0$. In conclusion, with any
degree of lagged indexation, equations (5.14a), (5.14b), and (5.14c) hold
with $\alpha = 0$, that is, as if there were no perfect indexation at all. This is

not a surprising result since in wage equation (5.7a) both the imperfectly indexed part of the wage increase and the rational expectations component are based on elements of the existing information set.

The trouble now comes with the expected inflation-output trade-offs. Applying the E_{t-1} operator to equation (5.10a) yields

$$\alpha(E_{t-1}p_t - p_{t-1}) = \alpha(p_{t-1} - p_{t-2}) + (\beta + \mu)E_{t-1}h_t - \mu h_{t-1}. \tag{5.19}$$

In the absence of shocks, and if $\pi_t = p_t - p_{t-1}$ stands for the inflation rate in period t, equation (5.19) reduces to

$$\alpha(\pi_t - \pi_{t-1}) = (\beta + \mu)h_t - \mu h_{t-1}. \tag{5.20}$$

This is a standard Phillips relation with no shocks and with adaptative expectations on the inflation rate. Inflation can only be brought down at the cost of some temporary unemployment, and in order to reduce the inflation rate by 1 percent, the required output loss L can be measured by

$$L = \frac{\alpha}{\beta}.$$

This result obviously supports the policy-maker's contention that indexation (in its lagged and not in its perfect version) is an inflation-perpetuating mechanism. The contention is basically directed to mandatory wage indexation which makes $\alpha = 1$, and which, as noted in the preceding section, yields a low β. Because of the worsened short-term trade-offs, and because life is made easier even with lagged indexation than with no escalator clauses at all, the political will to fight inflation is considerably reduced. This is why accommodating demand policies, which can be effective with the Phillips relation (5.10a), are so often adopted by countries where wages are indexed by law. If $\alpha = 1$, and if the accommodating policies manage to keep full employment in every period, the inflation rate described by equation (5.10a) becomes a random walk $\pi_t = \pi_{t-1} - u_t$.

Since perfect indexation has a virtue that is completely absent in its lagged version (it makes inflation easier to fight), one might be tempted to recommend a drastic shortening of the nominal wage-adjustment interval in order to come as close as possible to the Gray-Fischer model. Policy-makers strongly object to this idea, which in fact can be toxic medicine, except if the wage basis is properly revised downward. Let us explain why.

Let us assume full lagged indexation ($\alpha = 1$), no productivity gains, and an accommodating monetary policy that manages to keep the economy at full employment. Equation (5.18) is equivalent to

$$w_t - p_{t-1} = w_0,$$

where w_0 indicates the log of the contractual wage basis. Now let us assume that $\tilde{w}_0 < w_0$ is the full-employment real wage level. In the absence of shocks accomodating policies require an inflation rate measured by

$$\pi_t = p_t - p_{t-1} = w_0 - \tilde{w}_0.$$

This is the yearly rate of inflation produced by the accommodating policies if nominal wages are adjusted every twelve months. It becomes the quarterly rate of inflation if w_0 is not reduced and if the monetary correction period is shortened to three months.

5.4 Wage Indexation and Efficient Labor Contracts

The foregoing analysis was only concerned with the macroeconomic effects of wage indexation. It made some important points against mandatory escalator clauses, because, when perfect, they could create persistent unemployment and, when imperfect, they might lead to inflation rigidities. Yet the fundamental question is still to be answered: To what extent is wage indexation desirable from a welfare point of view?

Wage indexation can be understood as a form of risk sharing between workers and firms. It only covers one type of risk—unanticipated changes in the general price level—and thus is a highly incomplete insurance scheme. It is simple enough, however, to be enforceable without the costs of describing and checking all the possible states of nature in the Arrow-Debreu model of general equilibrium under uncertainty.

To discuss the relationship between indexation and Pareto efficiency in the labor market, one must define what is a feasible labor contract. It is impossible, to avoid some discretion in such a definition. On the one hand, because of transaction costs and moral hazard, the possibility range should be narrower than the one described by the Arrow-Debreu contingent claims; on the other hand, it should be large enough to take into account risk aversion by economic agents, the basic reason why escalator clauses are entered into contracts. As a compromise solution the following discussion will be based on the Azariadis model of labor contracts. It involves at least two strong hypotheses: homogeneous expectations and a Japanese-type loyalty between firms and workers seldom found in the western world. Throughout the following discussion we shall assume that labor contracts are written according to the following hypotheses of Azariadis:

1. An enforceable labor contract extends for T periods. In each period m different states of nature may occur, with stationary probabilities g_1, $g_2, \ldots, g_m$.

2. Expectations about contingencies are homogeneous across the firm and its workers.

3. The firm recruits N workers and undertakes to employ N_s randomly chosen among them $(N_s \leq N)$, at the real wage W_s, in every period in which the state of nature s occurs $(s = 1, \ldots, m)$.

4. No worker can contract his services with more than one firm, and firms are not allowed to employ individuals who were not assigned to them in the labor contract. Any possibility of default is ruled out.

5. There are only full time jobs.

Let us indicate by $m_s f(N_s)$ the net real revenue of the firm, and hence by $R_s = m_s f(N_s) - W_s N_s$ its real profit in the state of nature s; $f(N_s)$ is assumed to be concave and nondecreasing in N_s and m_s represents the supply shock that may result from a proportional displacement of the production function or from a change in relative prices. The firm will be assumed to be either risk averse or risk neutral with a utility function $F(R)$, where R indicates its real profit. Its expected utility will be given by

$$EF = \sum_{s=1}^{m} g_s F(R_s) = \sum_{s=1}^{m} g_s F(m_s f(N_s) - W_s N_s). \qquad (5.21)$$

All workers are assumed risk averse with the same utility function $V(Y, L)$, where Y indicates the individual real income, and L the leisure time per period. Since only full-time jobs are offered by the firms, there are only two possible values for L: L_0 for the unemployed and L_1 for the employed one $(L_1 < L_0)$. Every worker is assumed to receive a capital income Y_0 and an unemployment compensation W_0 is paid by the government. (Of course the possibilities $Y_0 = 0$ and $W_0 = 0$ are not ruled out.) This is to say that the utility of the unemployed individual in any state of nature is given by $V(Y_0 + W_0, L_0)$, moving to $V(Y_0 + W_s, L_1)$ when employed which is the state of nature s.

Since the origin of a von Neumann-Morgenstern utility scale can be arbitrarily chosen, we shall take the utility of the unemployed individual $V(Y_0 + W_0, L_0) = 0$ and define $U(W_s) = V(Y_0 + W_s, L_1)$. $U(W_s)$ is the utility of the employed worker in state of nature s. Since the probability of being hired by the firm in that state is equal to N_s/N and since the utility of the unemployed is equal to zero, the expected utility of the individual in state of nature s is given by $N_s U(W_s)/N$, and his expected utility when the labor contract is signed is indicated by

$$EU = \sum_{s=1}^{m} g_s \frac{N_s}{N} U(W_s). \tag{5.22}$$

We shall assume $U(W)$ to be twice differentiable, with $U'(W) > 0$ (because of nonsatiation) and $U''(W) < 0$ (because of risk aversion). A similar assumption will be made for the firm's utility function, except that now $F''(R) \leq 0$, since the firm may be either risk averse or risk neutral.

Let us indicate by U_0 the expected utility offered to the individuals by a competitive labor market. The problem of the firm is to choose the wage-employment plan $(W_1, W_2, \ldots, W_m)$, $(N, N_1, N_2, \ldots, N_m)$ that maximizes EF subject to $EU \geq U_0$. For any given employment program $(N, N_1, \ldots, N_m)$ the Kuhn-Tucker theorem yields

$$\frac{F'(R_1)}{U'(W_1)} = \frac{F'(R_2)}{U'(W_2)} = \cdots = \frac{F'(R_m)}{U'(W_m)} = \lambda. \tag{5.23}$$

This is the well-known Arrow-Borch condition, according to which the ratio of the marginal utilities of the contracting parties should be independent of the state of nature in an efficient risk-sharing scheme.

In two cases full indexation is the outcome of efficient wage contracting: (1) when the firm is risk neutral; (2) when the firm is risk averse but shocks are purely nominal. If the firm is risk neutral, the marginal utility of its income is a constant. Hence, by the Arrow-Borch condition, $U'(W_s)$ should be invariant to the state of nature. Since, because of risk aversion, $U'(W)$ is a decreasing function of W, the result (5.23) implies full wage indexation, that is, W_s should be independent of the state of nature.

If firms are risk averse but shocks are purely nominal, then $m_s = 1$ for every state of nature. Let us assume that $(W_1, \ldots, W_m), (N, N_1, \ldots, N_m)$ is a wage-employment program where real wages and employment are not invariant to the state of nature. We shall prove that this program is dominated by one with invariant wages $\overline{W}$ and employment $\overline{N}$, where

$$\overline{N} = \sum_{s=1}^{m} g_s N_s,$$
$$\overline{N}\overline{W} = \sum_{s=1}^{m} g_s W_s N_s.$$

In fact, since both the firm's utility function and its production function are concave and nondecreasing,

$$EF = \sum_{s=1}^{m} g_s F(f(N_s) - W_s N_s) \le F(f(\overline{N}) - \overline{W}\overline{N}).$$

Let us now observe that

$$\overline{N} \le N,$$

and that because of strict concavity in the worker's utility function

$$\sum_{s=1}^{m} g_s N_s U(W_s) \le \overline{N} U(\overline{W}).$$

Since wages and employment are not uniform in the initial program, at least one of these inequalities must hold with strict sign. Hence

$$EU = \sum_{s=1}^{m} \frac{N_s}{N} U(W_s) < U(\overline{W}).$$

Summing up, if shocks are purely nominal, the firm's expected utility will not decrease, and the workers utility will increase if wages and employment are made invariant to the state of nature at $\overline{W}$ and $\overline{N}$. This, once again, implies full-wage indexation.

The latter result is by no means surprising. To say that shocks are purely nominal is equivalent to assuming that states of nature just differ by the choice of the price units. In this very special case, full indexation of all contracts solves the Arrow-Debreu model with uncertainty.

With supply shocks and risk averse firms, full-wage indexation ceases to be efficient, since a constant W_s now violates the Arrow-Borch condition. All we can now derive from equation (5.23) is that real wages should be an increasing function of the firm's real profits. A plausible additional assumption is that firms are relatively less risk averse than their workers, in the Arrow-Pratt sense:

$$A_F = -\frac{RF''(R)}{F'(R)} < \frac{WU''(W)}{U'(W)} = A_W.$$

Differentiation of the Arrow-Borch condition yields

$$A_F \frac{dR}{R} = A_W \frac{dW}{W},$$

which means that real wages should change in the same direction, although proportionally less than the firm's real profits. Since firms are usually risk averse and since the world is crowded with supply shocks, the foregoing analysis suggests that mandatory indexation is not desirable from the welfare point of view. An important question is whether a scheme exists that can be imposed by law and that will automatically produce efficient labor contracts.

An idea that has found a number of supporters is perfect indexation with an adjustment for supply shocks. In practice, the idea would be implemented as follows: First, nominal wages would be adjusted for inflation whenever prices increased to the trigger point, that is, after every x percent increase in the appropriate price index. As previously discussed, this arrangement would lead to a closer approximation to perfect indexation than the staggered escalator clauses of section 5.3. Second, price increases would be measured by a consumer price index corrected for supply shocks—for indirect tax increases, for changes in terms of trade, for the impact of unfavorable crops, and so on.

The Gray-Fischer model supports this arrangement: assuming full indexation ($\alpha = 1$) and substituting $p_t + v_t$ for p_t in wage equation (5.7), the Phillips relation (5.9) reads as follows:

$$F(h_t) + \mu(h_t - h_{t-1}) = 0.$$

This is a deterministic difference equation: the output gap is insensitive to shocks and converges to zero.

Summing up, if full-wage indexation is imposed by law, it works much better with an adjustment of the price indexes for supply shocks than with a simple consumer price index. There is no indication, however, that such a rigid scheme leads to Pareto-efficient labor contracts. The Arrow-Borch equation (5.23) can be interpreted as saying that wages should be fully indexed with adjustments for supply shocks. Shocks really should be measured at the microeconomic level that encompasses the firm's relative price positions, but the microeconomic measurement of supply shocks is

Table 5.1
Minimum wage for Rio de Janeiro, 1952–1965

Readjustment month	Minimum wages (old cruzeiros per month)	Increase over previous levels (percent)	Cost of living increase since previous adjustment (percent)
January 1952	1,200	—	—
July 1954	2,400	100.0	54.4
August 1956	3,800	58.3	51.4
January 1959	6,000	57.7	47.8
October 1960	9,600	60.0	70.0
October 1961	13,400	40.0	42.2
January 1963	21,000	56.3	67.1
February 1964	42,000	100.0	109.5
March 1965	66,000	57.1	90.3

too much a nightmare to be included as an explicit clause of any feasible labor contract.

5.5 Wage Indexation in Brazil

Wage indexation was never practiced in Brazil before 1965. Nominal wages were frequently adjusted because of the soaring inflation rates, but automatic escalator clauses were never included in labor contracts. Minimum wage levels, which were decreed by the federal government, were increased nine times from 1952 to 1965, but at irregular intervals of time and price increases, as shown in table 5.1

Wage indexation laws were introduced in 1965, and basically for a period of time they were intended to act as incomes policy tools. The 1965 wage law was changed in 1968 and 1974 and then in late 1979 was replaced by a completely different indexation scheme. From 1965 through 1979 wage laws had a binding effect in all collective wage negotiations, leaving no degree of freedom for the employers or the employees. The market could only work over and above the wage formula in individual negotiations, not below.

The wage laws of 1965, 1968, and 1974 established that nominal wages should be fixed for periods of twelve months. We shall indicate by w_t the log of the nominal wage in year t, by p_t the log of the (geometric) average cost of living in year t, and by $\tilde{p}_t$ the log of the cost of living index at the end of year t. The use of year here constitutes any twelve-month period. Obviously, none of the wage laws referred to logarithms, although their authors had them clearly in mind.

The 1965 wage law established that nominal wages should be adjusted so that, taking into account the expected inflation rate, their average purchasing power would be equal to the average real wage of the past twenty-four months, plus a productivity gain z_t:

$$w_t - p_t^e = 0.5(w_{t-1} - p_{t-1} + w_{t-2} - p_{t-2}) + z_t, \tag{5.24}$$

where p_t^e stands for the expected average cost of living index in year t. It was calculated as

$$p_t^e = \tilde{p}_{t-1} + 0.5\pi_t^e, \tag{5.25}$$

where

$$\pi_t^e = \tilde{p}_t^e \quad \tilde{p}_{t-1} \tag{5.26}$$

indicated the anticipated inflation rate for the twelve-month period during which the nominal wage would be kept unchanged. Thus the 1965 wage formula actually read

$$w_t = 0.5(w_{t-1} + \tilde{p}_{t-1} - p_{t-1}) + 0.5(w_{t-2} + \tilde{p}_{t-1} - p_{t-2}) + 0.5\pi_t^e + z_t.$$

$$\tag{5.27}$$

From a technical standpoint the formula was a rational expectation staggered wage determination rule, and not an indexation scheme. It became an incomes policy device because both the productivity gain and the expected rate of inflation were decreed by the government, leaving no room for collective bargaining or strikes. Parties were not even free to choose the cost of living index for the calculation of the past real wages but were obliged to use the consumer price index calculated by the Ministry of Labor. (This was in fact a minor point, since the use of other available price indexes would make no significant difference.)

Except for market adjustments in individual negotiations which were never prohibited by the government, the 1965 wage formula would actually squeeze the real wages whenever the future inflation rates were underestimated by the authorities. The problem was felt in 1965, 1966, and 1967, when the cost of living increased 45.5, 41.2, and 24.1 percent, respectively, compared to prospective inflation rates of 25, 10, and 15 percent. In fact the average real wage in the manufacturing industry declined 24.8 percent between 1964 and 1967. This was partly due to the weakened position of the labor unions and partly the result of the indirect tax increases, subsidy cuts, and rent and administered prices defreezes. The combination of the wage formula with tight monetary and fiscal policies produced sound anti-inflationary results: the inflation rate, which soared to 91.8 percent in 1964, fell to 24.3 percent in 1967. Inflation-output trade-offs were not particularly adverse. A recession was experienced in 1965, when industrial production declined 4.7 percent, but the recovery was already achieved in 1966, with industrial growth of 9.8 percent. Moreover the road was paved for a seven-year period of accelerated growth and declining inflation.

Public complaints against the squeeze led the government to revise the wage adjustment rule in 1968. According to the new law, nominal wages in the previous twelve months should enter into the formula not by their actual values but by those that would have prevailed if inflation rates had been properly foreseen. Summing up, the 1968 formula read as

$$w_t = 0.5(\hat{w}_{t-1} + \tilde{p}_{t-1} - p_{t-1}) + 0.5(w_{t-2} + \tilde{p}_{t-1} - p_{t-2}) + 0.5\pi_t^e + z_t,$$

$$(5.28)$$

where

$$\hat{w}_{t-1} = w_{t-1} + 0.5(\tilde{p}_{t-1} - \tilde{p}_{t-2} - \pi_{t-1}^e). \tag{5.29}$$

Oddly enough, very few people realized that the new wage formula only corrected half-way the inflation underestimation, that of year $t-1$ but not that of year $t-2$, so that, on average, real wages would still be squeezed by one-fourth of the unanticipated cost of living increase. Also very few people remarked that the productivity coefficient z_t should refer to an eighteen-month and not to a twelve-month period. In any case the formula was in force until December 1974. It did not survive by its own merits but for three other reasons: (1) inflation rates were not considerably underestimated from 1968 through 1973; one-fourth of the underestimated rate, which lay in the range of 1 to 2 percentage points, was largely offset by the productivity gain so that, in practice, a system of staggered wage indexation was institutionalized; (2) since the economy was growing at exceptionally high rates, individual negotiations were able to raise the wages substantially above the official adjustment rules, especially those of skilled workers; (3) a tough political regime, which was introduced on December 13, 1968, when the Institutional Act 5 was enacted, quickly discouraged the emerging labor movement.

Inflation rates leaped from 15.7 percent in 1973 to 33.8 percent in 1974, making up for repressed inflation in 1973 but also responding to a 47 percent increase in the money supply during 1973 and to the oil shock and world inflation. The inflationary outburst brought into discussion the shortcomings of the 1968 wage rule, and a new one was enacted. Accordingly, as of January 1, 1975, wage adjustments were calculated by the formula:

$$w_t = \tilde{p}_{t-1} + (w_{t-1} - p_{t-1}) + 0.5\pi_t^e + 0.5(\tilde{p}_{t-1} - \tilde{p}_{t-2} - \pi_{t-1}^e) + z_t, \quad (5.30)$$

which referred the real wage basis to the previous twelve months (instead of the previous twenty-four months) and which introduced full compensation for past inflation underestimation. The government decided that the expected inflation rate should enter into the formula at the highly idealized figure of 15 percent a year, so that π_t^e and π_{t-1}^e were duly canceled. Moreover with $p_{t-1} \cong 0.5(\tilde{p}_{t-1} + \tilde{p}_{t-2})$ the wage formula practically corresponded to

$$w_t = w_{t-1} + \tilde{p}_{t-1} - \tilde{p}_{t-2} + z_t, \qquad (5.31)$$

which is a simple lagged indexation rule for twelve-month intervals. From July 1976 to July 1979 the productivity coefficients were corrected for supply shocks, which was equivalent to adjusting the price indexes for those shocks.

Summing up, from 1968 through 1979 Brazil lived with a system of lagged wage indexation at regular twelve-month intervals. According to the model developed in section 5.3, the Phillips relation should behave as if expectations were adaptive, and accommodating policies would transform the inflation rate into a random walk. A number of empirical studies, by Cardoso, Lemgruber, Simonsen, and other Brazilian economists support such hypotheses.

A completely different wage indexation law was enacted in October 1979. It still combines indexation plus productivity, but three major changes were introduced. First, the nominal wage adjustment interval was reduced from twelve to six months, with no downward revision of the real wage basis. Second, the productivity coefficient, which was formerly determined by the government and often adjusted for supply shocks, is now freely bargained between employers and employees. As a result the indexation rule sets a floor but no ceiling to collective wage negotiations and is no longer used as an incomes policy instrument. Third, the indexation degree was made a function of the wage level, in minimum wage units. Up to three minimum wage overindexations were introduced, since nominal wages must be increased 1.1 times the cost of living increase (plus productivity). Full marginal indexation applies to the 3-to-10 minimum-wage brackets, and fractional indexation to higher wages. The law was amended in late 1980, and the marginal indexation degree is now 0.8 in the 10-to-15 minimum-wage brackets, 0.5 from 15-to-20 minimum wages, and 0 after 20 minimum wages.

According to our model in section 5.3, the reduction of the wage-adjustment interval with no downward revision of the real wage basis should lead either to massive unemployment or to a sudden leap in the inflation rate. From 1976 through mid-1979, when nominal wages were adjusted once a year, the inflation rates were kept in the range of 40 to 45 percent a year. Since later 1979 this became the six-month inflation rate. Also, according to our theory, the wage law should produce highly unfavorable inflation-output trade-offs. The performance of the Brazilian economy in 1981 appears to give strong support to that hypothesis. After an uninspired experiment with supply economics which started in late 1979 and went through 1980, the government decided to move back to the orthodoxy track in early 1981. Interest rate controls were abolished, and a tight monetary policy was implemented. As a result the country experienced its first major industrial recession since 1965: industrial production declined 9.6 percent. Yet the yield in terms of inflation deceleration was rather unimpressive: the inflation rate, which reached its 110 percent historical peak in 1980, only declined to 95 percent in 1981, and optimistic forecasts for 1982 still remain in the 80 to 90 percent a year range. Of course trade-offs were much more favorable in 1965, when a milder industrial recession allowed inflation to decline from 92 to 34 percent.

The indexation arithmetic of the present law has a quite extraordinary implication. Leaving productivity gains aside, the only wage level that corresponds to full indexation is 11.5 minimum wages. All salaries below 11.5 minimum wages are overindexed, and all the ones above that level underindexed. Thus, if the real minimum wage were kept constant, if productivity gains were absent, and if the market actually behaved according to the law, all individual labor incomes would converge to 11.5

minimum wages, the faster the higher inflation rate. The same conclusion would hold if a uniform productivity increase was accrued to all wages, including the minimum wage.

According to some government officials, the law is intended to improve income distribution in the country. Of course this is a highly questionable proposition. Opponents to the law, who now include some important members of the government, argue that there is no logic in an income distribution policy that is confined to wage-earners and that depends on inflation rates. They also stress the cost-pushing effect of the 10 percent overindexation factor in the lower-wage bracket, which cannot be offset by the fractional indexation of the higher wages, given the existing wage pyramid. They finally remember that the market can always bypass the law. After all, the highly paid workers who are not protected by the law are sheltered by the competition in the labor market. And firms may lay off unskilled workers and hire cheaper substitutes.

5.6 Tax Indexation

Fiscal policy is intended to maximize some social welfare function. Of course the efficacy of the existing fiscal systems in achieving this objective is highly controversial. In any case there are strong reasons to believe that chronic inflation can only damage the welfare properties of a tax system designed to work in a stable price environment:

1. The total tax burden, as well as its distribution among economic agents, is made a function of the general price level. This is the result of fixed nominal brackets for progressive income taxes; of inevitable time lags in some tax payments; and, occasionally, of the existence of specific indirect taxes.

2. The failure of the tax legislation to distinguish nominal from real interest rates introduces a real fiscal transfer from lenders to borrowers. In the absence of usury ceilings the market will largely offset this transfer by an appropriate increase in nominal interest rates. Yet distortions may arise because of unanticipated inflation and because the marginal income tax rate is not the same for all economic agents.

3. Inflation partly transforms nominal capital gains taxes into real transaction taxes.

4. In the same line a real tax on the replacement of fixed assets is introduced by inflation, as long as depreciation allowances are calculated on the basis of nominal historical costs.

5. Inflation depreciates the purchasing power of cash holdings, an effect not taken into account by conventional income tax systems.

Tax indexation in inflationary economies is usually introduced in steps. The first, which represents the most elementary type of fiscal indexation and is already practiced by most countries, is the substitution of ad valorem for specific taxes. In Brazil this action was taken in the mid-fifties.

The second step, a more controversial one, is the indexation of the personal income tax brackets. It is a highly popular issue, since it affects many people. It can be defended from the welfare point of view, but it eliminates a fiscal drag on inflation rates. It also makes life with inflation less uncomfortable, and as such it may weaken the political will to fight inflation. The strength of the opposing arguments depends very much on the actual inflation rate. Violent and continuous price increases make the discussion somewhat sterile since, in practice, only two alternatives are left, indexation or the very frequent revision of the nominal income tax brackets. Otherwise, minimum wage earners would be shifted in a few years to the upper tax limit. In the case of Brazil personal income tax brackets were linked to the minimum wage in 1961. This indexation rule was changed in late 1964, and since then income tax brackets are annually revised according to an ad hoc price index determined by the Ministry of Finance.

Further steps are the indexation of tax debts, the monetary correction of the capital gains taxes, the fiscal distinction between nominal and real interest rates (both as the lender's revenue and as the borrower's expenditure), and the calculation of the depreciation allowances on an inflation-adjusted basis. In the case of Brazil these forms of tax indexation were introduced in 1964. In a more advanced step, inflationary accounting is made mandatory for all corporations, and profits are taxed according to the inflation corrected results.

Oddly enough a major loophole still exists in the Brazilian tax indexation system. Income taxes on the earnings of a calendar year are only due in the following calendar year, and there is no monetary correction for the interim period. This is to say that the real tax burden is a decreasing function of the inflation rate: the upper personal income tax rate of 55 percent is actually reduced to 39.3 percent if inflation runs at 40 percent a year, and to 27.5 percent if the annual inflation rate leaps to 100 percent. Shorter tax payment lags with no indexation for the interim period also exist in the case of excise taxes, varying from one to six months. In fact the present system was structured when the inflation rate was steadily sustained in the neighborhood of 40 percent annually. It was kept unchanged when the inflation rate soared to a three-digit figure with a very unfavorable impact on the federal budget.

The transition from the conventional to an indexed tax system involves a tax reform. The macroeconomic effects of tax indexation partly depend on the contents of such tax reform and partly on the subsequent management of the monetary policy.

It is often argued that tax indexation is inflationary since it deprives the government of some important sources of revenue, such as the taxes on purely nominal capital gains and on the replacement of fixed assets. This is a precautionary but not a convincing argument, since the tax reform should simultaneously introduce tax indexation and adjust the tax rates so as to keep the expected fiscal revenue at the desired levels. A stronger point is that indexation substantially reduces the fiscal drag on unanticipated price changes. In fact the fiscal drag would be eliminated completely if taxes, budgetary expenditures, and public debt were all fully indexed. This is an important argument that deserves a careful analysis.

Perfect tax indexation has one single impact in the extended Gray-Fischer model of section 5.2: it reduces the price drag coefficient H in the aggregate demand (IS) equation (5.12). As a result prices would become more sensitive to all types of shocks. And, except if wages are fully indexed, output and employment would show increased vulnerability to demand shocks and unanticipated changes of the money supply.

In one case fiscal indexation could produce a disaster: if the Central Bank, instead of controlling the money supply, decided to peg the nominal interest rate. The disaster already imminent in the absence of tax indexation would be precipitated by the insistence of the monetary authority on controlling what should be an endogenous variable, as recognized long ago by Wicksell. In fact some sort of economic stability can only be reconciled with nominal interest rate controls if drags on price changes, such as the ones produced by fixed exchange rates and nonindexed tax structures, are extremely strong. If in equations (5.10) and (5.12) of the extended Gray-Fischer model the nominal interest rate is taken as the exogenous variable (equation 5.13 can be left aside since it now only serves to determine another endogenous variable, namely, the money supply), a unique price equilibrium will be found, if and only if

$$\lim_{n \to \infty} \left(\frac{1}{1+H} \right)^n E_{t-1} p_{t+n} = 0. \tag{5.32}$$

This condition can only be expected to be fulfilled if $H > 0$, that is, if price drags are operative. In that case

$$(I - E_{t-1})y_t = \frac{(1 - \alpha)e_{1t} + H(1 + (\beta + \mu)c)u_t}{H(\beta + \mu) + (1 - \alpha)},$$

$$(I - E_{t-1})p_t = \frac{(\beta + \mu)e_{1t} - (1 + (\beta + \mu)c)u_t}{H(\beta + \mu) + (1 - \alpha)}.$$

If the wage indexation degree is close to one and price drags are weak, prices will oscillate violently. This clearly shows that widespread escalator clauses cannot be reconciled with interest rate controls.

5.7 Bond Indexation and Other Escalator Clause Arrangements in Brazil

Until 1964 escalator clauses were illegal in Brazil. Usury law, which was then in force, established a nominal interest rate ceiling of 12 percent a year. Since annual inflation rates soared from 11 percent in 1952 to 92 percent in 1964, bond markets were doomed. Government deficits were then fully financed by money creation. Mortgage and long-term loans were only supplied in very limited amounts by a few government agencies, borrowers being usually selected by political criteria.

In the late fifties a number of escapes were found to the usury ceilings. Commercial banks, who were then funded by demand deposits, were permitted to charge front fees which were not considered part of the interest rates as well as to require compensating balances from borrowers. Courts decided that, if a bond was quoted on the stock exchange with a discount from its face value, such discount did not infringe the usury law. The latter escape encouraged the development of a market for short-term acceptances and commercial paper in the early sixties. Yet, because of price uncertainties, and because escalator clauses were prohibited, a market for medium- and long-term bonds did not emerge.

In fact until 1964 the government often tried to impose money illusion by law. Tenancy laws virtually froze nominal rents, by indefinitely extending rent contracts after their maturities, at the option of the tenant. Public utility profits and depreciation allowances were limited, by law, to fixed percentages of the historical cruzeiro net asset values. The proliferation of bottlenecks was the natural outcome of this set of regulations. A collapse was avoided only because the government invested heavily in public utilities and because subsidized loans were massively extended to the privately owned public utility companies.

A widespread indexation system was introduced in Brazil in 1964. Besides the already discussed arrangements for wages and taxes, escalator clauses were adopted for public and private bonds, time deposits, rents, and public utility rates. To a certain extent, the indexation system also includes the crawling peg exchange rate.

Indexed treasury bonds (ORTNs) were created in July 1964. Their face value was formerly adjusted every quarter, but lately every month. Except in 1973, 1980, and 1981, the nominal value of the ORTN has always been determined by a three-month moving average of the general wholesale price index of the Getulio Vargas Foundation. For a number of years the face value V_t of the ORTN in month t was determined by the formula

$$V_t = K(P_{t-4} + P_{t-5} + P_{t-6}), \tag{5.33}$$

with K indicating a constant and P_{t-i} the wholesale price index for month $t - i$. Lately, since the Getulio Vargas became able to produce each month's index in the first ten days of the following month, lags have been reduced, and the following chain rule was substituted for formula (5.33):

$$\frac{V_t}{V_{t-1}} = \frac{P_{t-2} + P_{t-3} + P_{t-4}}{P_{t-3} + P_{t-4} + P_{t-5}}. \tag{5.34}$$

In July 1975 it was suggested by former Minister of Finance Octavio Bulhões that indexation rules should exclude the effects of supply shocks. For some months the Getulio Vargas Foundation attempted to produce a series of wholesale price indexes where supply shocks were duly offset (the so-called "accident correction"). The idea was technically sound and was implemented for an interim period, but calculations proved to be rather difficult and discretionary. Thus in July 1976 the accidentality was put aside, and a new chain rule was adopted for the monthly correction of the nominal value of the ORTN:

$$\frac{V_t}{V_{t-1}} = 0.8 \frac{P_{t-2} + P_{t-3} + P_{t-4}}{P_{t-3} + P_{t-4} + P_{t-5}} + 0.2033. \tag{5.35}$$

Since $0.2033 = 0.2(1.15)^{1/12}$, the formula actually meant fractional indexation whenever the inflation rate exceeded 15 percent a year, presumably on account of systematically adverse supply shocks. For an annual inflation rate of 40 percent, indexation would be reduced to approximately 35 percent, and so on.

In late 1979 formula (5.35) was coupled with substantial discounts for accidentality, so that the ORTN adjustment lagged 30 percentage points behind the actual inflation rate. For 1980 the monetary correction of the ORTN was prefixed, at 50 percent at the beginning of the year and later changed to 54 percent. This was less than half of the actual inflation rate, and such a procedure not only discouraged savings but undermined confidence in the system. A similar, although less distorted arrangement, had been adopted in 1973, when the government persistently stuck to a 12 percent annual inflation rate target. Since the beginning of 1981 the ORTN adjustments have been following some ad hoc rule never made explicit by the government. The accumulated results, however, are closely in line with the actual inflation rate.

Saving accounts and mortgages are indexed according to the ORTNs, except that the nominal adjustments are made on a quarterly rather than monthly basis. Private indexed bonds are also adjusted according to the ORTNs (other escalator clause arrangements are not permitted by law). Fixed nominal interest rate bonds compete with the indexed bonds for maturities up to approximately eighteen months. Of course, because of price uncertainties, a market for long-term nominal bonds does not exist.

Fiscal debts are also indexed along with the ORTNs. Until 1978 fixed assets were adjusted once a year, according to the annual averages of the wholesale price index. Since 1978 they have been quarterly adjusted with the ORTN. Public utility profits and depreciations are calculated, since 1964, on the basis of their corrected asset values.

From August 1968 to December 1979 foreign exchange rates were indirectly indexed by minidevaluations of the cruzeiro. As a basic guideline, the dollar/cruzeiro rate was changed by small percentages, and at short and irregular intervals of time (10 to 50 days) according to the inflation rate differential between Brazil and the United States. Domestic inflation, for this purpose, was measured by the industrial wholesale price index, which appropriately reflected changes in costs of manufactured exports. Slight adjustments were superimposed on this basic rule, taking into account a number of factors, namely, (1) the fluctuations of the dollar relative to other major currencies, (2) the inflation rate differentials between the major OECD countries, (3) changes in the terms of trade, and (4) balance-of-payments problems. On December 7, 1979, the tradition was broken by a 30 percent devaluation of the cruzeiro, and for 1980 the increase in the dollar/cruzeiro rate was predetermined at 45 percent and later adjusted to 50 percent. A return to the traditional minidevaluation rules was announced at the beginning of 1981.

Rents have been subject to various indexation rules. In 1964, law 4494 established two regimes of rent adjustments, one for so-called new rents, those under contract as well as those to be contracted, another for the so-called old rents. The latter were the result of the previously mentioned tenancy laws, which indefinitely extended rent contracts after their maturities. Rent adjustments in new contracts follow the minimum wage increase. The same rule has applied to the old rents, combined with a catch-up increase intended to phase out, in a ten-year period, the real gap accumulated in the past. In 1967 free choice of escalator clauses was authorized in new rent contracts. Since 1979 rent payments can be adjusted only once a year, proportionally to the change of the ORTN.

From a technical standpoint the Brazilian indexation system is open to a number of criticisms. Wage indexation, besides being lagged at fixed intervals of time, is extremely rigid, and now follows the strange arithmetic described in section 5.5. Tax indexation left a major loophole in the tax payment lags not subject to monetary correction. Other forms of indexing are excessively tied to the ORTN, whose ruling can be changed at any moment by the Minister of Finance, independent of congressional approval. Despite all these shortcomings life with inflation is now easier, and the allocation of resources appears to be less distorted than in the early sixties when indexation was illegal.

5.8 Concluding Remarks

Risk aversion and price uncertainties cannot be phased out by a government decree. Whenever they are combined, a potential develops for some sort of indexation arrangements. Legal obstacles to escalator clauses can only damage market efficiency, the first victim usually being the market for long-term bonds.

Only in a very few special circumstances, are fully indexed contracts Pareto efficient. Hence, from the welfare point of view, there is no reason why indexation should be made mandatory. In fact governments should avoid extreme positions, neither impede nor force escalator clause arrangements.

The effects of indexation greatly depend on how escalator clauses are introduced in contracts. In recent times two types of arrangements have been widely adopted for wages: the trigger point system, where wages are nominally adjusted whenever the inflation rate accumulates to a certain percentage figure and lagged indexation, according to which nominal wages are adjusted at regular time intervals in proportion to the past inflation rate. Lagged indexation still appears to be the most frequently adopted, although it makes real wages sensitive to changes in the inflation rate. The trigger point system comes much closer to perfect indexation. Lagged indexation has been the arrangement experienced in Brazil.

Perfect indexation eliminates inflation-output trade-offs, even in the short term. As a result it is frequently considered an anti-inflationary device. Nonetheless, as policy-makers should be made to understand, accommodating demand policies become fully ineffective if wages are perfectly indexed.

An important point is to be made against mandatory wage indexation. Perfect indexation may overexpose output and employment to supply shocks, as well as increase the sensitivity of the general price level to any type of shock and to monetary noises. The result may be persistent unemployment if markets do not quickly deviate from indexation rules in response to fluctuations in the unemployment rate. The problem is particularly serious for countries that need to improve their current account positions in the balance of payments.

Lagged wage indexation is much less dangerous as far as unemployment is concerned, since it provides an emergency outlet for monetary accommodating policies. Yet it may produce highly unfavorable output-inflation trade-offs in the short run when market flexibility is deterred by rigid indexation schemes, such as those imposed by law. As a result of accommodating policies and of staggered indexation rigidities, inflation may follow a random walk, as it apparently did in Brazil since 1968.

Tax indexation may appear inevitable when inflation rates exceed a certain level. This may be defensible from the welfare point of view, but tax indexation should not be introduced without a comprehensive tax reform since it deprives the government of taxes from purely nominal gains.

Adverse supply shocks are the nightmare of widespread indexation arrangements. The effects may be minimized by monetary corrections based on price indexes that exclude the impacts of indirect tax increases, of exchanges in trade, and of highly unfavorable crops.

Widespread indexation eliminates most conventional drags on price changes. It should therefore be accompanied by a careful monetary policy that tries to keep the money supply on target. Interest rate controls in an indexed economy can easily lead to an inflationary disaster.

Notes

The author is indebted to Rudiger Dornbusch for his fruitful comments on the preliminary version of this chapter.

1. Equations (5.1) to (5.6) are consistent with both the hypothesis of oligopolistic price determination and the assumption of perfectly competitive product markets. In the latter case they can be derived from a log-linear aggregate production function combined with a log-linear labor supply curve.

2. In order to avoid the possibility of multiple rational expectations equilibria the following transversality condition is postulated:

$$\lim_{n \to \infty} \left(\frac{B}{B + K} \right)^n E_{t-1} p_{t+n} = 0.$$

References

Azariadis, C. 1976. "On the Incidence of Unemployment." *Review of Economic Studies* 115–126.

Azariadis, C. 1978. "Escalator Clauses and the Allocation of Cyclical Risks." *Journal of Economic Theory* 18: 119–155.

Barro, R. J. 1977 "Long Term Contracting, Sticky Prices and Monetary Policy." *Journal of Monetary Economics* 3: 305–316.

Baumgarten A. L., Jr. 1981. A aritmética perversa da política salarial. Mimeographed Fundação Getulio Vargas.

Bernstein, E. 1974. *Indexing Money Payments in a Large and Prolonged Inflation*. American Enterprise Institute, Washington, D.C.

Cardoso, E. A. 1981. Indexation, Monetary Accommodation and Inflation in Brazil. Mimeographed. INPES, Rio de Janeiro.

Fischer, S. 1977. "Wage indexation and macroeconomic stability." A supplementary series to the *Journal of Monetary Economics* (1977a): 107–148.

Fischer, S. 1980. Indexing and Inflation. Mimeographed. Fundação Getulio Vargas, Rio de Janeiro.

Friedman, M. 1974. *Monetary Correction*. American Enterprise Institute, Washington, D.C.

Giersch, H. 1974. *Index Clauses and the Fight against Inflation*. American Enterprise Institute, Washington, D.C.

Gray, J. A. 1976. "Wage Indexation—A Macroeconomic Approach." *Journal of Monetary Economics* 2: 221–235.

Kafka, A. 1977. *Indexing for Inflation in Brazil*. American Enterprise Institute, Washington, D.C.

Keynes, J. M. 1936. *The General Theory of Employment, Interest and Money*. Reprint Harcourt Brace Jovanovich, New York, 1965.

Lemgruber, A. C. 1980. Real Output-Inflation Trade-offs and Rational Expectations in Brazil—Some Evidence. Mimeographed. Fundação Getulio Vargas, Rio de Janeiro.

Liviatan, N. 1981. On Equilibrium Wage Indexation and Neutrality of Indexation Policy. Mimeographed. The Hebrew University of Jerusalem.

Sargent, T. J. 1979. *Macroeconomic Theory*. Academic Press, New York.

Simonsen, M. H. 1980. Inflation and Anti-inflationary Policies in Brazil. Mimeographed. Fundação Getulio Vargas, Rio de Janeiro.

Taylor, J. 1974. "Staggered Wage Setting in a Macro Model." *American Economic Review*, Papers and proceedings, pp. 108–118.

6 Wage Indexation and Inflation: The Recent Brazilian Experience

Roberto Macedo

In November 1979 the Brazilian government adopted a semiannual wage indexation that replaced the former system of annual indexation. This change led to extensive discussion about the effects on inflation, unemployment, labor turnover, income distribution, and the balance of payments, among other issues. The discussion has been mainly directed to win public support for different viewpoints on these issues. Over the last two years, the press has been giving considerable attention to the statements issued by government authorities, politicians, economists, businessmen, and trade union leaders in favor or against different aspects of the new wage policy. Some recently published studies have already brought the debate into the economic literature.[1]

This chapter considers the impact of the new wage policy on inflation. It puts the emphasis on three points. The first is an attempt to define what is meant by "inflationary impact" of the new wage policy. The second examines institutional problems that emerged in the transition from the old policy to the new one and argues that they are very important for the analysis. The third is an attempt to show that an important inflation effect occurred during the initial stages via the aggregate demand side of the economy.

6.1 The New Wage Policy

Brazilian wage policy establishes specific rules for the collective nominal wage and salary readjustments in the private urban sector of the economy, including state enterprises organized as corporations. These readjustments are received by workers of industry groups represented by trade unions which are, in general, organized by region and by activity branch at the two-digit level of classification. Each of these groups has a base date from which the different aspects of working conditions are annually negotiated.[2] These negotiations take place between the trade unions and the employers' associations and are subject to a series of legal restrictions, and the most important subject of these negotiations is the collective wage readjustment.

The collective readjustment means that all the workers in a particular industry group, whether or not trade union members, will receive an increase of their nominal wages. This increase, expressed in terms of a rate of readjustment, must be understood as a *minimum rate to which all*

permanent workers are entitled. The firms may give increases that are
higher than those fixed by the collective readjustment and may avoid, at
least partially, the payment of this increase by resorting to a fast turnover
of their employees, if this is convenient in terms of the costs involved and
of the conditions prevailing in the labor market, which determines the
absolute value of the salaries of newly hired employees. The existing
legislation does not establish rules to define absolute wage values, as
these are agreed upon by the employer and employee at the time of
employment. Some trade unions, however, have been successful in obtaining a wage floor for their industry groups, which limits the possibility
of the employer resorting to labor turnover in order to avoid complying
with a collective wage readjustment.

In general in the short run the collective readjustment rates involve a
minimum increase which the employers usually accept rather than attempt
to carry out a major turnover of employees. Employers may also choose
not to resort to an extensive turnover because of the response of the
economy itself to changes in the system of nominal wage readjustments.
When increases or recoveries in real wages occur, the general price level
tends to rise in order to relieve the cost pressure caused by the nominal
wage increases. In this way, in real terms, the wage gain or recovery is
jeopardized, and so it is no longer necessary to resort to turnover of the
labor force. This proposition will follow from the discussion of the effects
of the new wage policy, undertaken in this chapter.

The new wage policy adopted at the end of 1979 has six important
features:[3]

1. The adoption of semiannual collective readjustments instead of the
annual readjustments of the previous policy.

2. The use of a consumer price index, the National Consumer Price Index
(INPC), as a single indexation criterion, replacing the four price components of the formula adopted, even if not in an effective way, by the
previous policy.[4]

3. The establishment of rates of readjustment differentiated by wage
levels.

4. The introduction of an additional reajustment, contingent upon the
productivity growth of each industry group, to be settled every year by
collective bargaining.

5. The publication, in the month before the date of the readjustment, of the semiannual change in the INPC which serves as its base, replacing the previous system where the official index was published in the same month in which the readjustment was due.

6. A 22 percent once-and-for-all readjustment became effective on the date the new policy went into effect, covering all the industry groups whose last collective readjustment had occurred in the period from November 1978 to April 1979, that is, for whom six or more months had passed since their last collective readjustment.

The first change deserves special attention, not only because of its importance in the analysis of the impact of the new policy on inflation but also because it emerged as a response to the political pressures that forced the new policy to be adopted. It is worth remembering that these pressures had their origin in the high inflation rates since 1974. Roughly speaking, the rate of inflation doubled in 1974, increasing from approximately 20 to 40 percent a year and thus reaching a new plateau where it remained until 1979.

If nominal wages are readjusted on an annual basis, a doubling of inflation between readjustments will lead to a lower yearly average real wage. Simple intuition suggests that, in principle, this larger decline in real wages could be avoided if the period of time between the readjustment were reduced in the same proportion by which the rate of inflation has increased. This is equivalent to saying that if the rate of inflation doubles, and the period between readjustments is reduced by half, the average level of real wages could be maintained. In this case readjustments would be made semiannually rather than annually.

This line of reasoning is illustrated by figure 6.1a. Its shows what happens to the average real wage when there is an annual readjustment and the inflation rate doubles. Part b shows that the average real wage is maintained by adopting semiannual readjustments.[5]

These observations serve to illustrate, first, that it is possible to identify a relationship between the adoption of semiannual readjustments and the phenomenon of the observed doubling of the inflation rate, as described here. Since the idea of semiannual indexation was already discussed in government circles well before 1979, it can be seen that one of the objectives of the new policy was to correct a problem that emerged five years before. But this would only be successful if it were possible to keep

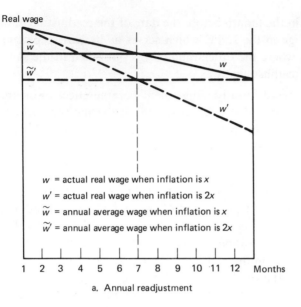

a. Annual readjustment

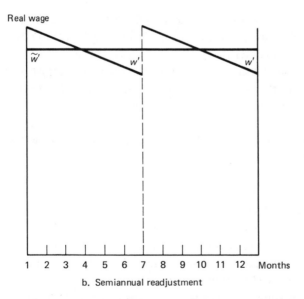

b. Semiannual readjustment

Figure 6.1
Effect of changes in the rate of inflation and in the time interval between wage
readjustments on the annual average real wage. The inflation rate doubles, from x to $2x$.
(a) When the rate of inflation increases from x to $2x$, the real wage loss over the year is
doubled. (b) When inflation is $2x$ and a semiannual readjustment is given, this maintains
the annual average real wage of the period when inflation was x.

Table 6.1
Marginal rates of readjustment for different wage sizes as established by wage policy

Class ($i = 1, \ldots, 5$)	Wage to be readjusted (w), in units of w_m	Marginal rate of readjustment, in units of V_6 (semi-annual rate of change of the INPC)
1	$w \leq 3w_m$	1.1
2	$3w_m < w \leq 10w_m$	1.0
3	$10w_m < w \leq 15w_m$	0.8
4	$15w_m < w \leq 20w_m$	0.5
5	$w > 20w_m$	0

Source: Law No. 6886, of 12/10/80. This law changed the original marginal rates of the new wage policy (Law No. 6708, of 10/30/79), which were only three: the same of the first two classes mentioned here and a marginal rate of 0.8 for the wages over $10w_m$.

inflation at the plateau it had reached by the time the new policy was decided, that is, around 40 percent a year. In figure 6.1b it can be noted that the average real wage can only be protected from inflation if the latter is maintained at $2x$ after the introduction of the semiannual readjustment.

The adoption of rates of readjustment differentiated by wage levels allows higher increases for lower wages without upsetting the ranks of the wage hierarchy. To meet this objective, the new policy established the rule that the higher the wage rate, the lower the *marginal* rate of readjustment. The wage to be readjusted is divided into parts according to a scale running from lower to higher values, and the marginal rate of readjustment applied to these parts diminishes as the wage reaches higher levels on the scale. This scale is defined in units of the highest regional minimum wage (w_m) in effect in the country.

Table 6.1 shows the marginal rates of readjustment. Since the readjustments are based on the semiannual rate of change of the INPC, which is shown as V_6, the marginal rates in the table are defined in units of V_6.[6]

The whole method of semiannual readjustments differentiated by wage levels may be summarized in the single formula (6.1) which shows the readjustment rates applied to wages as they reach the different levels listed in table 6.1:

$$r_{ijt} = V_6[w(1.1k_1 + k_2 + 0.8k_3 + 0.5k_4)$$
$$+ w_m(0.3k_2 + 2.3k_3 + 6.8k_4 + 16.8k_5)]/w \tag{6.1}$$

where

r_{ijt} = semiannual rate of readjustment to be applied to the wage in the class i, of industry group j, starting in month t,

$V_6 = (\text{INPC}_{t-2}/\text{INPC}_{t-8}) - 1$ is the semiannual rate of change in the INPC (the government announces in the month $t-1$ the semiannual rate up to the month $t-2$, which is applied to the readjustments due in the month t),

w = nominal wage to be readjusted,
w_m = value of the highest regional minimum wage,

k_i = 1 for the wage class i which includes the value of $w(i = 1, \ldots, 5$; see table 6.1) and 0 otherwise.

Equation (6.1) works as follows: if $i = 1$, $r_{1jt} = 1.1V_6$; if $i = 2$, $r_{2jt} = V_6(w + 0.3w_m)/w$, and the term $(w + 0.3w)$ emerges after simplifying $1.1(3w_m) + 1.0(w - 3w_m)$, if $i = 3$, $r_{3jt} = V_6(0.8w + 2.3w_m)/w$, and the term $(0.8w + 2.3w_m)$ emerges after simplifying $1.1(3w_m) + 1.0(10w - 3w_m) + 0.8(w - 10w_m)$; and so on.

As noted by equation (6.1), the wage policy implies the transformation of w into another value, w^*, which will receive the whole readjustment denoted by V_6:

$$r_{ijt} = \frac{V_6 w^*}{w}, \tag{6.2}$$

where w^* is the term in brackets, on the right-hand side of (6.1).

Equation (6.2) indicates that the different marginal rates in table 6.1 will lead to an average rate of readjustment of a given nominal wage. This average rate will be a proportion of V_6, the coefficient of proportionality being given by w^*/w. By varying w from 1 to 20 units of w_m, table 6.2 gives the values of w^*/w obtained by applying equation (6.1). Notice how the average readjustment, calculated as a proportion of V_6, diminishes as the nominal wage goes up.

This policy of differentiated readjustments is also shown in figure 6.2. It presents the relationship between w^* and w, which can be obtained from

Table 6.2
Values of w and w^*/w for w varying between 1 and 20 units of w_m

w	w^*/w
1	1.1
2	1.1
3	1.1
4	1.075
5	1.06
6	1.05
7	1.043
8	1.038
9	1.034
10	1.03
11	1.009
12	0.992
13	0.977
14	0.965
15	0.954
16	0.925
17	0.9
18	0.878
19	0.858
20	0.84

table 6.1 or equation (6.1). In the figure the original framework of the wage policy, which imposes different marginal rates of readjustment, can be also presented as being one that transforms the nominal wage to be readjusted into another which receives the whole rate of readjustment given by V_6. This transformation is denoted by $w^* = f(w)$, which for comparative purposes is shown together with the line where $w^* = w$.

Equation (6.1) or figure 6.2 also permits one to conclude that the wage policy imposes an upper limit on the transformed wage, that is, $w^* \leq 16.8w_m$, and that the value $11.5w_m$ defines the limit where the semiannual readjustments pass from being higher to lower and then equal to V_6 at this limit.[7]

For what follows, the most important implication of this policy of different marginal rates of readjustment is that its impact on the wage costs of firms will depend on their wage structures. For wage structures where low wages are predominant, the wage cost pressures emerging from the wage policy will be stronger.

On the base date itself, that is, once a year, besides the readjustment

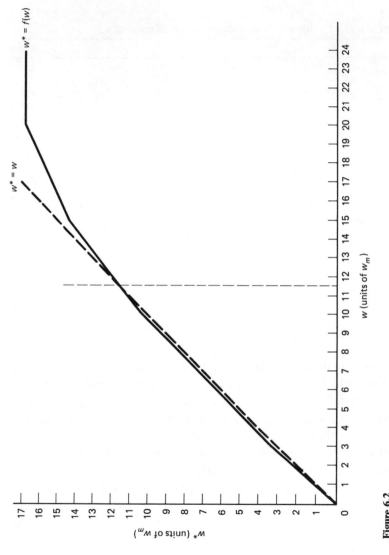

Figure 6.2
Adjustment of the actual wage (w) into a wage w^* which receives full indexation

calculated by equation (6.1), an additional readjustment will be applied to the readjusted wage. It represents the estimate of the annual rate of growth of the productivity of each industry group. That is, on the base date of each industry group the total readjustment will be given by:

$$r_{ij(t\,=\,\text{base date})} = (1 + r_{ijt})(1 + m_j) - 1, \tag{6.3}$$

where m_j is the estimate of the annual rate of growth of productivity of industry group j.

Up to now the description of the changes introduced by the new wage policy has covered four of the changes listed at the beginning of this chapter. In addition the government designed special readjustments for the transition period and moved the publication of wage readjustments to be made one month earlier than had been the case. The whole set of changes will now be used to analyse the inflationary impact of the new wage policy.

6.2 The Impact on Inflation

The impact of the new wage policy on inflation will be discussed here in terms of three specific questions: (1) Was the new policy a major factor behind the inflationary outburst which became clear in 1979? (2) Given this outburst, did the new wage policy serve to accelerate it still further? (3) If yes, what was the nature of the impact? Did it converge to a higher rate of inflation or did it have an explosive effect, leading to increasingly higher rates of inflation?

Beginning with the first question, table 6.3 shows data on the Brazilian inflation since 1977, in terms of the annual rate of the change of the General Price Index of the Getulio Vargas Foundation, calculated quarterly, together with other data which will be discussed later. The figures from 1977 to 1978 illustrate the 40 percent plateau we referred to previously. These data show that inflation clearly worsened during the second half of 1979 but that increasing rates of inflation began in the second half of 1978. Rapidly rising inflation seems to have begun during the third quarter of 1979 when the steady increase in inflation sharply accelerated, breaking through the 40 percent upper bound of the previous period.

As the new wage policy was established only in November, one can conclude that it was not the initial cause of the increase in inflation unless the increase in the third quarter of 1979 could be attributed to inflationary

Table 6.3
Annual rate of change, on quarterly basis: general and agricultural price indexes, price of regular gasoline and bank credit to the private sector

Year-quarter	General Price Index	Bank credit to the private sector	Price of regular gasoline	Wholesale price index of agricultural products
1977–I	46.4	52.8	40.8	35.7
II	46.7	50.7	65.2	43.8
III	40.3	48.9	38.6	43.4
IV	38.6	50.6	40.2	39.5
1978–I	37.1	50.6	36.2	40.1
II	36.0	46.2	21.7	39.1
III	39.9	49.6	30.2	46.6
IV	41.3	48.1	33.3	56.3
1979–I	43.7	51.9	34.6	54.9
II	45.8	50.4	34.6	52.9
III	53.0	56.2	42.4	65.1
IV	69.5	68.1	108.7	80.2

Source of raw data: *Conjuntura Econômica, Bulletin of the Central Bank of Brazil*, Resolutions of the National Petroleum Council.

expectations arising from the knowledge that the government had decided to adopt a new policy and that it was the subject of a message sent to the National Congress. This is not unlikely although very difficult to prove. But if one assumes that such a phenomenon had occurred, one can discuss its importance in determining the rate of inflation in the third quarter of 1979, in the light of an examination of the other factors that influenced that rate.

By doing so, one can distinguish the role of the three elements generally regarded as being responsible for the strong inflationary forces in mid-1979 or even before. What is even more important is the fact that they had manifested themselves before the new wage policy went into effect. These three elements were the expansion of bank credit to the private sector, the large petroleum price increases, and the weak performance of the agricultural sector, particularly poor in 1978 to 1979. It is worth remembering that the expansion of credit that occurred in 1979 was fed in large part by the government's agricultural credit policy, which was spurred on by the vision of the so-called Great Harvest in the following year. To accomplish this, the government made wide use of credit financed by issuing more currency. It should be noted that the major part of the financing of agriculture is concentrated in the third and fourth quarters of each year.

When faced with these three factors, whose movements are confirmed by the other columns included in table 6.3, one may conclude that it is difficult to attribute the acceleration of inflation of mid-1979 to the new wage policy. Moreover one could state that this acceleration, made more dramatic by the breaking of the 40 percent plateau, would have occurred quite independently of the changes introduced by the new wage policy.

We can now move to the second question, which considers the possible inflationary character of the policy. Inflation is regarded here in a non-orthodox manner as a process where workers and businessmen attempt to recover or increase levels of earnings already attained in the past and where the government transfers income to itself and/or to other groups in society. The process may start in various ways. Worthy of special attention are external factors such as the petroleum price increases or the rise in agricultural prices due to bad harvests. Both phenomena could have had an important role in breaking through the previous inflation rate plateau. With the increase in the prices of petroleum and of agricultural products, leading to higher raw material costs, this would mean a reduction in profit margins of the firms, if the prices of their products were maintained at a fixed level. As a result they would try to pass on their cost increases to prices in order to maintain their profit margins.

It is acknowledged that the money supply plays a role that to a large extent is accommodating and expanding in a way that sanctions higher prices as the result of a greater demand for liquidity. But it may also be an agent that contributes directly to the process, particularly if, as in the Brazilian case, the money supply is closely linked to the expenditure and credit policies followed by the government.

In this context the situation in the third quarter of 1979 could be outlined as follows: new cost pressures are combined with expansion of money supply, stimulating a new phase of accelerating inflation. It is clear that this is a simplified picture, both from the theoretical and empirical points of view, but I am convinced that it captures the essence of the process, needed for the analysis that follows.

In order to include the wage policy in this picture, one must emphasize the aspects that are particularly relevant for analytical purposes. The first is the adoption of the more frequent, semiannual readjustments, as described by figure 6.1. This point is usually emphasized in the existing

Table 6.4
Industry groups, base dates, and month of the first semiannual readjustment

Industry groups with last base date in	Month of the first semi annual readjustment
November 1978	November 1979 (two semiannual readjustments)
December 1978 to May 1979	November 1979
June 1979	December 1979
July 1979	January 1980
August 1979	February 1980
September 1979	March 1980
October 1979	April 1980

Source: Article 15, Law No. 6708 of 10/30/79.

analyses which, however, neglect the procedure the government used to move to the new policy from the previous system of annual readjustments. In November 1979, when the semiannual readjustments were introduced, the industry groups that had their base date between November 1978 and April 1979 had already gone seven or more months since their last collective readjustment. For these groups the law established a readjustment of 22 percent on November 1, 1979, with the purpose of putting them roughly in the same position of the groups with base date in May 1979, which would immediately receive the semiannual readjustment in accord with the new law.[8]

Table 6.4 shows, for the industry groups with base date in each of the months of the year preceding the implementation of the new law, the months when they received their first semiannual readjustment.

This transition procedure is essential if one is to understand fully the nature of the inflationary pressures generated during these periods. It is necessary to remember what happened when the old policy was in effect. When a new annual rate of readjustment was decreed by the government every month, the index was only applied to the industry groups whose base date coincided with that month. Assuming a uniform distribution of the value of payrolls covered by the policy over the twelve monthly base dates, this means only 1/12 of this value being readjusted every month. Using the same assumption, one can get an idea of the initial impact of the new wage policy by considering that in November 1979, apart from the 1/12 of the total wages that received an annual readjustment (or two semiannual readjustments at the same time), another 6/12 received a semiannual readjustment. The proportion of total wages that received a readjustment in that month was around four times larger in terms of annual rates (1/12 on an annual basis plus 6/12 on a semiannual basis) than under the previous system.

In an attempt to find a measure that better reflects the nature of the official readjustments taking into account their coverage, an Index of the Coverage of the Readjustments the Wage Policy (ICRPS) was constructed. The index was built as follows: (1) it is monthly and takes as its point of reference the month of December 1977; (2) it assumes that in the same month the total value of the wages covered by the policy is divided into 12 equal parts; (3) it further assumes that each of these parts corresponds to industry groups, with the first part corresponding to groups with base dates in January, the second to those with base dates in February, and so on; (4) from January 1978 the official rates of readjustment began to be applied to these 12 simulated payrolls taken as a base, the first being readjusted by the January rate, the second by the February rate, and so on; (5) up to October 1979 the readjustments made in this fashion were of an annual nature, becoming semiannual in November 1979; (6) in that month the readjustments were made in such way as to include those established for the transition from the old to the new policy, as indicated in table 6.4; (7) an increase in productivity of 4 percent per year, corresponding to an estimate of the rate which on average has actually been applied, was added to the readjustments due annually on the base date; (8) for each month the ICRPS is given by the sum of the 12 parts readjusted by this process, divided by the sum of the same parts at their initial values in December 1977, this last sum being made equal to 100.

The index obtained in this way represents the simulation of the nominal payroll covering all workers affected by the policy, with groups of them having readjustments at different times. Since under the new policy the readjustment is differentiated by wage class, the ICRPS can be calculated on different assumptions with respect to the total impact of the differentiated readjustments on the payroll as a whole.[9] ICRPS (1), (2), and (3) shown in table 6.5 were therefore calculated using coefficients of impact equal to 1.1, 1.0, and 0.9, respectively, multiplied by the semiannual rates of change of the INPC applied in the readjustments.

These indexes are given in the table in the form of monthly calculated annual rates of change, in order to compare them with the rates issued by the government and shown in column (a). The ICRPS calculated in this

Table 6.5
Annual rates of readjustment of the wage policy and of the change in the ICRPS, by different criteria of impact on the payrolls of the firms (percent rates)

Year-month	Official readjustments (a)[a]	ICRPS (1)[b]	ICRPS (2)[c]	ICRPS (3)[d]
1979–1	43.0	40.74	40.74	40.74
2	44.0	41.23	41.23	41.23
3	44.0	41.69	41.69	41.69
4	44.0	42.13	42.13	42.13
5	44.0	42.54	42.54	42.54
6	44.0	43.00	43.00	43.00
7	44.0	43.36	43.36	43.36
8	44.0	43.58	43.58	43.58
9	46.0	43.90	43.90	43.90
10	50.0	44.50	44.50	44.50
11	54.5	62.50	61.88	61.27
12	56.4	65.77	64.53	63.29
1980–1	62.5	70.12	68.05	65.99
2	69.2	74.90	72.70	69.73
3	71.9	80.57	77.67	73.78
4	70.7	86.01	82.23	77.50
5	74.3	91.31	86.48	80.78
6	75.6	96.25	90.44	83.82
7	82.2	103.18	96.17	88.40
8	86.4	109.21	101.30	92.46
9	88.1	114.77	105.85	96.00
10	88.0	119.90	109.94	99.13
11	87.1	101.66	92.31	82.25
12	91.0	104.43	94.71	84.35
1981–1	95.6	107.42	97.31	86.61
2	95.3	109.94	98.98	88.07
3	95.0	111.51	100.19	89.15
4	97.7	113.33	101.81	90.58
5	98.7	115.40	103.63	92.17
6	101.0	117.19	105.20	93.53
7	104.1	119.12	106.87	94.99
8	103.9	120.87	108.44	96.36

Source of raw data: Ministry of Labor and Foundation Brazilian Institute of Geography and Statistics (IBGE).
[a] The semiannual rates were converted to annual rates. For the period November 1979 to April 1980 the annual rates were obtained by combining the semiannual INPC change with a rate of 22 percent in the previous semester to account for the fixed readjustment given in the transition from the old policy to the new. The official rates of readjustment of the old policy (in effect until October 1979) include the rate of productivity growth estimated by the government.
[b] ICRPS obtained by multiplying the INPC rate by 1.1 and applying a 4 percent rate of productivity growth on the annual readjustment due on the base date.
[c] The same procedure described in (1) was adopted, except that the INPC rate was multiplied by 1.0.
[d] The same procedure described in (1) was adopted, except that the INPC rate was multiplied by 0.9.

way allows us to estimate the potential impact of official readjustments on the total nominal wages covered by the legislation, both in the period governed by the old policy and in that governed by the new. In the latter case it is important to point out that the indexes reflect practically all the characteristics of the new wage policy, that is, the switch to semiannual readjustments, the adoption of the INPC, the readjustments of the phase of transition, and the readjustments differentiated by wage size. Therefore it is useful to compare the differences between the two policies in terms of their impact on nominal wages.

The data in table 6.5 clearly show that the government rates, taken in isolation, give a unrealistic idea of their impact on nominal wages. It should be noted that the differences between the official rates and the various ICRPS rates do not derive only from the adoption of different criteria for estimating the impact of the readjustments differentiated by wage size. In the case of ICRPS (2) the INPC has been multiplied by 1.0, and the differences between the annual rates produced by this index and the official rates continue to be large. They cannot be explained either by productivity growth rate of 4 percent incorporated into ICRPS (2). From an analytical standpoint it is important to point out the discontinuity of the annual rates given by the ICRPS in two important occasions: in November 1979 and November 1980. In the first case the rates increase substantially, which is essentially the result of the 22 percent readjustment adopted in the transition from the old to the new policy, as mentioned earlier. As to the falling ICRPS annual rates for the month of November 1980, they indicate that for that month the rates refer to a base that was substantially higher than previously.

Even in the case of the ICRPS (3), where the INPC is multiplied by 0.9, its rates are higher than the official rates for the whole period between November 1979 and October 1980. In short, the discontinuity of rates in this period derives from the fact that, as compared to the previous period, there is a semiannual readjustment mechanism instead of an annual one, plus the 22 percent readjustment given in November 1979; after October 1980 the rates refer to a comparison being made between two periods where the semiannual readjustments prevail and the impact of the adoption of the latter is thus reduced in terms of annual rates.

In figure 6.3 the ICRPS (2) is shown with annual rates on the left axis and with absolute values on the right axis, allowing a clearer view of the phenomenon described. The large increase of the rates of readjustment in

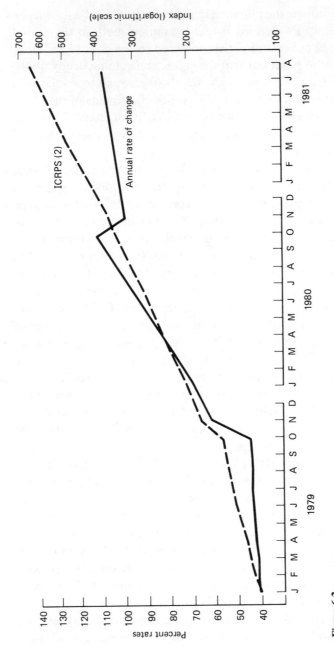

Figure 6.3
ICRPS(2) and its annual rate of change, January 1979–August 1981

November 1979 is clear, as well as the higher rates of readjustment from then on, as compared to the previous period.[10]

Having demonstrated that the transition from the old policy to the new implied a sudden nominal wage increase in November 1979, it is important to note that the three ICRPS predict a rate of increase ranging from 14.6 to 15.5 percent in that *month*, when compared to the previous one. In the same month several price indexes show rates of increase ranging from 4.0 to 6.0 percent.[11] This confirms that there really was an attempt to increase or recuperate previously attained real wage levels.

Let us now return to the discussion of the inflationary impact of the new wage policy, in terms of whether it has contributed to an inflation rate higher than those previously being observed. To answer this question, two aspects must be considered: (1) the cost push elements of the new wage policy working within the price-setting mechanisms on the supply side and (2) its effects on aggregate demand, emerging from expected increases in the real income of the workers affected by the policy.

As for the cost push element, the impetus given to the inflationary process in the third quarter of 1979 could be linked, even if only partially, to the shocks brought about by the increase in the price of petroleum and of agricultural products, which led businessmen to increase prices in order to maintain their profit margins. To these shocks we can add the cost push elements of the new wage policy, then there is an additional increase in nominal costs leading to attempts to transfer it to prices.

Taking into account that the objective of the new policy was to increase real wages and that this could not be achieved if the costs of the new policy were to be passed on to prices, one would imagine that the government would prevent this by using price controls. We tried to find out whether the legislation that implemented the new policy or the CIP (the government's price control board) took any initiative in this direction.

The legislation of the new wage policy does not mention the passing through to prices of the wage readjustments expressed by equation (6.1), and thus one may conclude that it does not forbid it. The law mentions only the productivity coefficient and says that the respective wage readjustment cannot be absorbed by higher prices, "except with the CIP's permission."[12] For various reasons I do not believe that the passing through to prices has been prevented even this case.[13] However, it is in the readjustment described by equation (6.1) that the worst occurs. Being a semiannual readjustment, it is the most frequent one, and it is by far the largest portion of the nominal wage readjustments established by the policy.

Let us assume that the objective of the new policy was to prevent the fall of the annual average real wage. In order to achieve this objective, it would be necessary not to pass on the semiannual readjustment due in the seventh month from the base date. The law neglected this point reflecting an ambiguity between its objectives and the means employed to achieve them. The government's own price control agency, instead of preventing the passing on of the new wage costs, explicitly laid down rules that even facilitated the process of passing on wage costs. Twelve days after the new policy was in effect, a CIP resolution, signed by the Minister of Planning, determined the routine procedures for petitions to transfer to prices the readjustments made in accordance with equation (6.1) as well as those linked to the transition from the old to the new policy.[14]

It is certainly amazing that the new wage policy not only neglected mechanisms to ensure the fulfilment of its objectives but that some government bodies seemed to act against them. However, we are not arguing that the strategy to be followed should have been one of strict price controls, an issue that will be discussed later.

Still considering the attempt to pass on costs and that nothing prevented it, the inflationary impact of the new policy is not limited merely to the question of passing on wage costs to prices. The data previously presented in table 6.3 show in the fourth quarter of 1979 a new inflationary wave, already identified in the previous quarter. Several elements contributed to this, but the expansion in bank credit and the increase in the prices of gasoline and of wholesale food products must be emphasized.[15] As for those elements not included in table 6.3, the maxi-devaluation of 30 percent in the exchange rate in December is also important along with the cost pressure of the new wage policy, working in the fashion described earlier.

Concerning the impact of the new wage policy, its influence is not only felt in the costs, putting pressure on profit margins and leading to price increases supported by the accommodative behavior of the government sector. From the Keynesian standpoint, it is also important to take into account its impact on aggregate demand. For the worker the nominal wage increases meant, though only in temporary terms, an increase or recovery of real purchasing power. If we assume that the expectation of higher inflation rates was not widespread among workers, it follows that the introduction of the new wage policy led to a recovery or gain expected to be maintained in the future. It must also be added that the wage policy moved up by a month the release of the monthly readjustment rate, and this also may have contributed to an increase in the difference between the expected and actual real wages, with the first being higher than the second.[16]

Another important consideration is that the new policy was introduced in the month of November, when part of the "thirteenth monthly wage" is paid. Its initial impact quickly reached the month of December, when the last part of the "thirteenth monthly wage" is due. Moreover this coincided with Christmas and New Years when people tend to spend more. All these factors lead to the proposition that for the worker the new wage policy must have led to a recovery or expansion of real income levels reached in the past and to an overestimation of real income in the future. Both effects occurred in a period of high propensity to spend and thus led to an increase in aggregate demand of the economy which was already suffering inflationary pressures from other sources.

The aggregate demand effect is in accordance with data available concerning the performance of the economy at the end of 1979 and during 1980. Brazilian GDP increased by 8 percent in 1980, the highest rate since 1976.[17] Employment also increased, and this is reflected, for example, in the fact that the industrial employment in the greater São Paulo region increased by 2.7 percent between December 1979 and December 1980.[18]

It would be overly hasty to attribute the 1980 performance of the economy only to the effects of the wage policy. Other aspects of the government economic policy must be emphasized. In 1980 this policy controlled the interest rate and fixed in advance the "indexation" affecting government bonds and savings accounts, bringing it to a level that turned out to be approximately half the observed inflation rate in 1980. This caused the real interest rates to fall together with the return from the savings accounts, acting as an incentive for business expenditures and consumer spending.

More detailed information shows that the role of the wage policy can be identified on the side of aggregate demand. In figure 6.4 data referring to the Brazilian electro-electronic industry sales of household appliances are shown. These data are presented as annual growth rates of monthly sales and of the accumulated sales index and cover the period from January 1979 to June 1981. There is a large sales growth in the first six

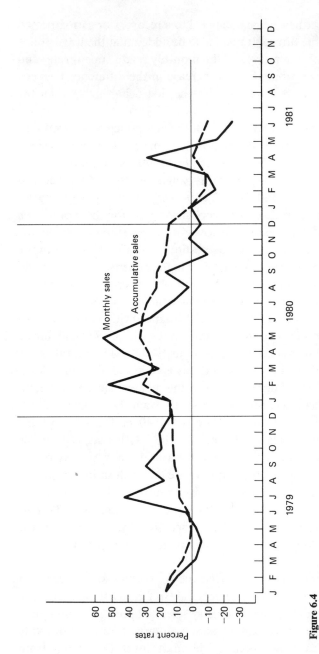

Figure 6.4
Annual rate of change of household appliance sales in Brazil's electric-electronic
industry. (Source: National Association of the Electric-Electronic Machinery Industry)

months of 1980 which, from our point of view, is linked to the stock replacement demand of retailers, intensified by the higher volume of sales registered at the end of 1979 as well as by the increased consumer demand in the first two quarters of 1980.

This intensification of sales in the first semester is contrary to the typical seasonal pattern of sales of durable consumer goods, as expressed in figure 6.4 by the sales performance in 1979; the highest levels are generally reached in the second half of the year as production and sales perk up in order to cope with the increased demand that occurs at the end of the year. The decrease in sales shown in figure 6.4 for the second half of 1980 can also be linked to the role of the wage policy, insofar as its effects on wage growth expectations and on the effective growth or recovery of real wages tended to disappear as inflation accelerated from the beginning to the end of 1980. Given that inflation almost doubled in the period between the adoption of the new policy and the end of 1980, a new recovery or increase in real wages, or rising expectations of an increase, would have required, in broad terms, a quarterly indexation.[19]

Thus there was an inflationary impact provoked by the introduction of a policy that has served to increase the inflation rates in the context of an inflationary spurt whose origins can be attributed to other causes. It is worth saying that the new wage policy did not affect the salaries of civil and the military servants, who continued to receive only annual readjustments, and it also did not directly influence workers whose employment relationships are not constrained by legal regulations in the rural areas and in the so-called urban informal sector. This observation is important since otherwise one would tend to overestimate the inflationary potential of the new wage policy.

The third and last question to be asked is, Was the impact of the new wage policy explosive in the sense of leading to increasingly higher inflation rates? The answer is, No, and it covers three aspects of the subject.

The reduction of the time interval between the readjustments and the regulations covering the transition led to cost pressures which in turn were absorbed by the passing on of these costs to prices. This again reduced average real wages in the period between two readjustments and the cost pressures ceased to occur from the moment the real wages reached the levels they attained prior to the new policy. On the side of aggregate demand, the rise in prices tended to absorb the initial expansion by reducing disposable real income of consumers and by reducing their expenditures in the face of expectations of rising income that did not materialize. As a result the inflationary impact of the new wage policy would be a convergent one: it led to a rate of inflation higher than that which would be observed in its absence, but it did not imply a continuous increase in the rate of inflation.

The same reasoning may be applied to a second aspect of the question, that is, the readjustment coefficient labeled productivity growth. In terms of the new policy this coefficient is not included in the rates of readjustment released by the government, which covers only the inflation indexation component of the readjustment. In the discussion of the relation between the new wage policy and inflation, this coefficient is frequently mentioned as having an inflationary impact of an explosive nature, given that, in terms of equation (6.3), it is being applied to a wage that has already undergone indexation and so would tend to amplify the effect of the latter.

Behind this proposition we find again the idea of nominal wage costs being transferred to prices. If the productivity growth coefficient added to equation (6.1) is not realistic, an attempt to pass it on to prices will be made (even if the coefficient is realistic, such an attempt is also conceivable if firms try to retain all productivity gains, and nothing precludes this from happening). But it should be remembered that if such an attempt is made its impact will occur with a lag and will be again of a converging nature. A "productivity growth" of, say, 4 percent, was applied in the first month of the new wage policy only to the industry groups having a base date in that month. Within the assumptions adopted to formulate the various ICRPS, this 4 percent would be reduced to approximately 0.3 percent on the total wages covered by the policy in the month of November 1979. In fact the whole 4 percent would be transferred to prices only after a year had passed. If the estimate for the growth of productivity was to be maintained at this level, from this point the passing on would always be stable at 4 percent per year, and, in terms of annual rates, it cannot be said that would lead to increasingly higher inflation rates. To sum up, the passing on of the full 4 percent would only have happened after a year, and this level would have been maintained from then on.

The third issue is that of the readjustments differentiated by wage size. Their result is a readjustment of the total wage bill which is above or below the INPC. At the upper extreme, it would be 10 percent above the INPC if the firms were to apply to all their employees the readjustment given to those who receive up to 3 minimum wages. But this would be an extreme case; in practice we do not know what has been the reaction of the firms when facing the government rules, either in terms of readjustments of the total payroll or of the passing on of the differentiated readjustments to the consumers. If one supposes that the readjustment is transferred to prices, the question will depend on the firms' wage structures and how they are changed by the wage policy.

This question has already been partially analyzed by Camargo (1980). His analysis takes into account data for the wage structure of the firms affected by the policy. Given the existing wage structure, he verifies that in large firms the indexation of wages should lead to payrolls being readjusted by a rate below that of change in the INPC. He argues that large firms play a leading role in the price setting in the market and concludes that after its initial impact the wage policy would lead to a slowing down effect on the rates of inflation.[20] Camargo does not take into account the possibility that his conclusion could be nullified by the firms' attempt to pass on the rate of "productivity growth" as well as additional nominal wage costs emerging from an attempt to maintain the existing wage hierarchy in absolute terms, giving to the whole wage structure a readjustment equal to that received by the workers at the bottom of the wage scale. However, after Camargo's analysis, the wage policy reduced still further the marginal rates of readjustment given to the highest wages. [21] Moreover some surveys have shown that in recent months the firms are following the wage policy more closely in terms of complying with the lower rates it establishes for the higher wages.[22]

Given these factors, the conclusion put forward by Camargo sounds plausible. Taking also in account the other two aspects discussed, it is difficult to identify an explosive impact of the new wage policy on inflation. It should also be noted that in recent months the inflation rates have been falling. This confirms this proposition or at least the conclusion that, if the effect was explosive, it ceased to be so or became less intensive, as it is by itself not capable of maintaining increasingly high inflation rates.[23]

6.3 Concluding Comments

Our conclusion is that the new wage policy, through its influence on costs and aggregate demand, was *one* of the factors causing Brazil's inflation to rise from an annual level of 40 percent to the rates around 100 percent of late 1980 and 1981. But it was neither the initial cause of this inflationary spurt nor the only one that added to it. The inflationary effect of the new wage policy could be less important, were it not for the absence of mechanisms to avoid, even partially, the transfer of its nominal wage increases to prices. On the other hand, after its impact was felt, the wage policy cannot be held responsible for further accelerating the inflationary process, but in fact this acceleration is no longer taking place. This follows from our conclusion that the role of the wage policy was to increase the rate of inflation to a point where its effects on real wages and aggregate demand were absorbed by price increases emerging from these effects as well as from other causes.

The new wage policy was not the initial nor the only cause of the accelerated inflation from the third quarter of 1979. From all that has been written and is known about the Brazilian inflation, it is evident that the wage policy played a smaller role than the whole set of other government policies, with all its errors and mistakes in determining the level and nature of government spending, the ways of financing it and in the execution of its monetary and credit policies was well as those related to the external sector.

In retrospect, seen from another perspective, the experience of the wage policy reflects the difficulty of the Brazilian economy in absorbing the shocks that affect the internal and external terms of trade. The increase in the price of petroleum, which has been the most important external shock, brings about a fall in the real income as a whole which leads to the problem of how to distribute the loss among groups in the society. The new wage policy can be seen as an attempt to protect the workers from this type of shock but with only a transitory effect. Conceived to correct, five years later, the fall in real wages emerging from the shock of 1973–74, its objectives have been frustrated because inflation went up again. Today inflation is higher, and real wage rates are not being preserved by the new wage policy. Unemployment, too, has served to nullify what was gained or not lost as a result of the new policy.

If the government had imposed rigid price controls when the policy was introduced, this would have been equivalent to transferring the loss in real income to businessmen. It is difficult to believe that abuses were not committed in the process of transferring to prices the costs of the new policy. However, to believe that everything could have been solved by strict price controls would be equivalent to suggesting a basic change in the rules of the capitalistic game. Within these rules the lessons learned from the more rapid indexation of wages, which is the cornerstone of the new policy, show that attempts to maintain the worker's wages in real terms through more rapid readjustments of nominal wages are blocked by the difficulties emerging from the passing on of these readjustments to prices and by the ambiguity of the government policies that lead to a sanction of higher prices in the absence of price controls or to adopting other policies that accelerate inflation and therefore nullify the effect of the more rapid readjustments of nominal wages. What we can see is therefore an impasse in the process of distribution of the losses from external shocks, a process also complicated by the problems that the government adds on its own initiative when managing the other components of its economic policy.

More recently, the government has attacked the problems of inflation and external deficit by restrictive monetary and fiscal policies, bringing protests from workers and businessmen. From the point of view of the government policy-makers, the process of absorbing the external shocks would be easier if the new wage policy were abandoned, and the policy of annual readjustments reinstated. However, it is difficult to do this in the present climate of "political liberalization," because such actions would be directly hostile toward workers who are now counted as potential voters. Indirectly, the outcome is different: higher inflation has eroded the gains or the recovery of losses brought about by the new wage policy and unemployment increases as a result of the monetary and fiscal policies.

In the end despite the climate of liberalization the political framework has neither the institutions nor the attitudes that could lead to a political solution to the problem. By this we mean an agreement by which workers would accept changes in wage policy in exchange for political power and/or advantages in taxes or public spending.

Notes

A first version of this paper was presented in the "Debate on the Wage Policy", sponsored by the "São Paulo Association of Economists", in August 1981, in São Paulo. The author thanks Paulo Vieira da Cunha, José Serra, José Paulo Chahad, and Rudiger Dornbush for their comments and suggestions.

1. See Camargo (1980), Lopes and Resende (1980), and Silva (1981).

2. For example, there is the Bank Employees Trade Union, covering the states of São Paulo and Mato Grosso, whose base date is September 1st every year.

3. See text of Law No. 6708 of 10/30/78.

4. These four components were (1) an index designed to reconstitute the average real wage of the last twelve months, (2) an index adding half of the inflation expected for the following twelve months, (3) a component for the correction of the error embodied in the estimation of expected rate of inflation in the previous readjustment, and (4) an index for adjusting wages to changes in the foreign and domestic (urban/rural) terms of trade. Although all these price elements, plus the annual rate of change of the productivity of the economy, were included in the formula, there is evidence that it has been applied on an ad hoc basis. During the period from February to August 1979, for example, the formula always issued the same readjustment rate of 44 percent. It is difficult to believe that a formula with all these components would always issue precisely the same value during seven months. See Simonsen (1982) for additional details of the earlier rules.

5. The situation described in figure 6.1 a and b must be taken as a case where the inflation rates (geometric) x and $2x$ are constant during the year while the real wage is measured on a logarithmic scale.

6. A more precise definition of v_6 will be presented shortly.

7. In figure 6.2 this is the value for w for which $f(w) = w$.

8. During the period from February to August 1979, the annual rates of readjustment of the old system were fixed at 44 percent. It was at the end of this period that the decision of changing the policy was adopted and the law prepared, the 22 percent meaning half of the annual rate of readjustments then given. However, inflation went up while the law was in Congress, and as a result the industrial groups with base date in May 1979 received a 26.6 percent readjustment in November, higher than that obtained by the industrial groups with base dates before May.

9. As mentioned in section 6.1, this impact will depend on the firms' wage structure.

10. Only the ICRPS (2) is shown in figure 6.3. The idea is to emphasize its sudden jump in November 1979, due to the transition from old to new policy. The 22 percent readjustment that followed from the transition covered wages regardless of size, and table 6.4 shows that in that month the differences between the three ICRPS are minor.

11. The INPC grew 5.8 percent, the General Price Index, 5.6 percent, the Wholesale Price Index of the manufacturing sector, 4.0 percent and the Cost of Living Index (FIPE) in São Paulo, 4.7 percent. The contrast is more marked if it is taken into account that, on the basis of the argument that follows, these price changes must have already incorporated part of the wage readjustment of the same month.

12. Paragraph 4 of article 11 of Law No. 6708, of 10/30/79.

13. The coverage of the CIP is limited, and even where it comes into force, its efficacy is doubtful. The idea that wages must follow the increase in productivity of the workers is questionable: for example, it ceases to hold when the supply of labor is infinitely elastic. Apart from this it is doubtful whether the estimates of the productivity coefficient correspond to any real rise in productivity.

14. Resolution CIP No. 130 of 11/12/79 published on the "Union's Official Daily" of 11/16/79, pp. 17057–17058.

15. It should be remembered that a strong increase also affected the price of diesel fuel. Its price passed from Cr$5.80 to Cr$12.00, that is, 107 percent between the end of June and the end of November 1979.

16. This brings to the discussion the only one of the five characteristics of the new wage policy, described in section 6.1, that thus far has been left out of the analysis.

17. Central Bank of Brazil, *Annual Report—1980*, p. 23.

18. According to the employment index of the Federation of Industries of the State of São Paulo (FIESP). This increase in employment was concentrated on the first two quarters: between December 1979 and June 1980, the rate of increase in employment was 3.0 percent.

19. In the fourth quarter of 1979 the monthly calculated annual rates of inflation, measured by the General Price Index, averaged 69 percent; in the fourth quarter of 1980 the same average reached 111 percent. The General Price Index is published by *Conjuntura Econômica*.

20. Camargo (1980, section 3, pp. 982–998).

21. See the observation in table 6.1 which describes the change in the marginal rates of readjustment.

22. According to articles published in *Exame*, dated 5/6/81 and 8/12/81, based on research carried out in various firms involved in the hiring of executives.

23. Taking the average rate calculated according to the procedures described in note 20, it can be seen that this rate fell from 120 to 110 percent from the second to third quarter of 1981.

References

1. Camargo, José M. "A Nova Política Salarial, Distribuição de Rendas e Inflação," *Pesquisa e Planejamento Econômico* 10 (December 1980): 971–1000.

2. Lopes, Francisco L., and André L. Resende. Sobre as Causas da Recente Aceleração Inflacionária. Discussion Paper no. 6. Catholic University of Rio de Janeiro, Department of Economics, October, 1980. Mimeographed.

3. Silva, Adroaldo M. "Inflação e a Experiência Brasileira." *Revista de Economia Política* 1 (July–December 1981): 57–81. See also the discussion of this paper contained in the same journal: 1 (October–December 1981): 116–153.

7 A View of Current European Indexation Experiences

Michael Emerson

The conference organizers gave me the somewhat intriguing task of re-counting European indexation experience under the billing "unresolved issues, promises, and skepticism." I have tried to find some of each to offer, mainly related to current policy issues.

7.1 Unresolved Issues

The first, old unresolved issue is, Does indexation produce high inflation? Or, is it neutral?

Within the European Community we have a cross section of ten rather comparable economies, but with an almost complete range of indexation regimes and a fairly wide range of inflation experiences—from 4.5 percent in Germany to some 20 percent in Italy and Greece.

There is no *prima facie* correlation in Europe between the extent of wage indexation and the rate of inflation. In the no-indexation camp we find Germany and the UK, respectively, the least and until recently one of the most inflationary of member countries. In the full and rapid index-ation camp, where there are adjustments every two points of the index, or every three months, we find Belgium and Italy, who are, respectively, at the low and high ends of the inflation spectrum. In the middle we have countries with heavily qualified or limited systems of wage indexation:

• France, where it concerns mainly the minimum wage.

• The Netherlands, where indirect taxes are excluded from the index, and pauses in indexation adjustments are negotiated from time to time in the interests of real wage adjustment.

• Denmark, which is similar to the Netherlands, except that energy products have also been taken out of the index.

• Ireland and Greece, where the recent tradition has been for negotiations to be reopened if a threshold rate of inflation is passed by the end of the contract year. Latest developments in 1981 suggest a weakening of this wage-price linkage in Ireland, but an intensification of the index link in Greece following formation of the Papandreou government.

These middle countries also range from the most stable to the most inflationary countries in an apparently random way.

This is a very agnostic beginning, perhaps one that supports the view that indexation is neutral toward inflation. However, my own interpretation of the evidence, going more deeply but also more casually into the evidence, would be to steer somewhat on the more worried side of neutrality, to the effect that indexation practices may be more actively and positively associated with inflation rates. For this I would advance two types of perhaps second-order evidence.

First, the timely or untimely change of indexation regimes may be clearly associated with some episodes in which a country's relative inflation worsened or improved. There have been some blunders. For example, the UK for the first and only short time in its history introduced a wage indexation threshold in 1973 just when the first oil shock was arriving. But in the last two years, we have seen more positive results in the Netherlands where the inflation rate has stayed close to the German inflation rate and disconnected itself from the rising Belgian inflation rate because of a substantial allowance made for the second oil shock in its indexation practice. Belgium and the Netherlands had, incidentally, been following very similar monetary policies until the October 1981 realignment of exchange rates in the European Monetary System, when the Belgian franc dropped 5.5 percent against both the DM and the florin.

Second, there is a clear and seemingly significant correlation between the extent of income indexation and public finance deficits. This is the case of Belgium and Italy, both with rapid and rather comprehensive wage indexation and 10 percent of GDP or more deficits in the budget, although their inflation rates are very different. Ireland, Greece, and Denmark also have very high public finance deficits and rather a substantial degree of income indexation. The connection here would be identified in national tendencies, in both public and private sectors, to settle for something less than rigor in their economic affairs, that is, to fail to adjust promptly when trends risk becoming unstable or unviable for the medium run: on the one hand, to fail to accept real wage realities in the light of supply shocks and competitiveness criteria and, on the other, to fail to constrain the public sector's appetite for resources. A further clue is found in examining some of these countries' external positions. At present Belgium and Denmark, in the high indexation, high public deficit, but low inflation camp, have large balance of payments deficits of 7 and 3.5 percent of GDP, respectively. One may diagnose some degree of suppressed inflation in these countries. The exchange rates are defended with extremely high real interest rates because it is correctly realised that, if they devalued, in the presence of indexation mechanisms, inflation would accelerate fast. Thus adjusting for some suppressed inflation, held back by the monetary authorities, the cross-country correlation between indexation and inflation might improve a bit, although the causality remains rather unclear.

Another unresolved issue is whether to even out the relative degree of indexation, as between wage incomes and financial assets. There is some movement in Europe in favor of less complete wage indexation and more extensive financial asset indexation, starting from a more privileged situation for wage earners. Concern for the adequacy of savings and for the equity position of the small saver are being translated into limited issues of indexed or floating rate bonds for small savers in some countries, such as the UK and France. A political problem is that it may be difficult to ask trade unions to moderate their traditional "rights" in wage indexation, while increasing indexation opportunities for savers. I have the impression that many economists in Europe would tend to favor a more balanced set of regimes on the relative degree of indexation, as between wages and financial assets. The logical case for a government really determined to reduce its inflation rate by issuing indexed bonds is rather strong, with or without indexation.

7.2 Promises

I have two promises. Both are in the realm of certainties, rather than the "promised land."

The first is that if you pursue a very high degree of rapid wage indexation in an economic environment frequently subject to violent, world wide macro economic shocks, you will run into trouble. Beware of the language in some of the theoretical papers submitted to this conference that speak of "optimal or perfect indexation" as that which enables us to prevent so-called "disturbances" from affecting output and employment. The authors, if I understand them rightly, are not actually advocating "optimal indexation" in the normative or practical policy sense, if for no other reason than that they consider wage indexation to be wholly outside the domain of official policy. In Europe it is widely considered to be an urgent and practical issue how to reconcile wage indexation with the needs to make major real economic adjustments, for example, (1) with respect to oil price shocks costing, say, as in 1979–80, 4 percent of national income, or (2) a devaluation against the dollar, as in 1980–81, representing for Europe a similar impact on the terms of trade as the oil shock, or (3) the need for financial policy in some countries to increase taxes that may be in the index by large amounts such as several points of GDP. In these conditions, one has, I would argue, to choose either to adjust promptly indexation practices to accommodate the real needs, or to adjust just the same, but a little later on, with an extra dose of inflation and probably more unemployment too.

This first promise is really applicable to all open economies. My second promise is more specifically European. If one is also trying to create a regional monetary bloc, as we are in the European Monetary System, then there are further constraints to respect. Such a group of countries must surely adapt its habits before a lethal mixture of highly diverse indexation practices, international shocks, and integrationist monetary ambitions explodes in the form of intolerable unemployment differences or substantial exchange rate instability.

This is why in 1981 the Commission (which is the proposer of EEC policies and its executive body) addressed a public communication to member states on the principles of indexation in the Community. Europe has to make some choices. The commission's recommended choice, which is still at this stage only a proposal, is at three levels:

1. The Commission advocates as a medium- and long-run objective for the European Monetary System the defense of nominal values. The Community has to converge on some model, and one may consider that the German model looks more convincing than some kind of European average practice.

2. But, as the next thing to do, it is not proposed to abolish indexation, or even to condemn it. The contribution of indexation mechanisms to social and economic kinds of stability in several countries is appreciated, but on certain conditions.

3. Thus the Commission proposed a selection of techniques to prevent indexation from impeding either real economic adjustments or a downward convergence of inflation rates. The techniques may be listed as follows:

- exclusion of indirect taxes from the index,
- as also terms of trade, oil price, and devaluation effects,

- delays in adjustments (not more than twice a year),
- use of a European average inflation norm in the inflation countries,
- ad hoc suppression of some adjustment, without suppressing the system.

Some of these techniques are evidently more or less substitutes for others; moreover the range of techniques is intended to fit the diversity of circumstances and traditions of individual countries, while retaining a common philosophy.

7.3 Skepticism

If I have to find place for skepticism, then it would be over how far, or quickly such principles may be freely taken up by the social partners and negotiated through into changes in existing habits.

It is also sometimes suggested that the time taken to renegotiate the system may be longer than some of the ills we have to defend against. It is now, for example, getting a bit late in the day to limit the indexation pass-through of the second oil shock or even the 1980–81 dollar shock. If these two factors are now for a few years likely to stabilize or even turn around, some would argue now in favor of staying put and hoping that indexation will help decrease inflation. One may recall that Italy's inflation came down from 21 percent in 1974 to 13 percent in 1978, when the terms of trade turned to the advantage of the industrialised countries. But these considerations do not dissolve the fact that much of Europe still has large real wage adjustment and unemployment problems to solve—which cannot be solved in conditions of near-perfect indexation of labor costs.

But if one admits an uncertainty prospect for some European countries to change, it is not for lack of efforts to adjust extreme practices in the directions proposed by the commission, such as in Belgium and Italy. In these and several other countries, indexation issues are in the forefront of election campaigns, government programs, and negotiations between government and the social partners. There is no consensus in Europe in favor of following the Israeli model toward achieving perfection in the indexation of incomes, taxation, and financial markets, and so to live, hopefully not too uncomfortably, in a high inflation steady state. The risks of a high inflation state not being steady are judged in Europe to be high: there is deep skepticism here, whether Israel is, in this respect, the promised land.

To give some idea of current movements in Europe, a new Belgian government in early December 1981 proposed a 3 percent nominal wage increase for 1982, implying a significant real wage cut and some adjustment of past indexation habits; the Italian trade unions agreed very recently for the first time to limit wage income increases to 16 percent target fixed ex ante for 1982 (with inflation currently running at 20 percent), on the condition that the government made fiscal concessions, but which are not at present accepted. The Danish government has moved to exclude energy products and indirect taxes from the wage index. The Dutch government proposes, against a background of intermittent incomes policy intervention in the past, that the unions forego an indexation adjustment in 1982.

So, maybe some things are changing, but we are not yet sure. Meanwhile, the European Monetary System has had to learn to negotiate fairly frequent exchange rate parity realignments, which may be disappointing compared to some initial hopes for inflation convergence. But these have been kept to a controlled minimum. Erratic and overshooting movements of exchange rates within the countries of the European Community have been largely eliminated, and so also the ravages that an interaction between free-floating and diverse indexation practices could inflict on a densely interdependent group of industrialised economies.

Postscript, 24 January 1983

In 1982, the year since the Rio de Janeiro conference, there have been developments in wage indexation practices in several European countries, along the lines of the recommendations of the Commission of the European Communities. Broadly speaking, the past year saw a convergence of wage bargaining practices in Europe with the traditional "extreme indexers" moving toward a more qualified practice (Belgium, Italy) and some more intermediate cases moving more categorically in a de-indexation direction (Denmark, Netherlands).

For *Belgium*, 1983 is the second year of limited compensation for price rises. A Royal Decree recently maintained the system of fixed money payments, based on indexation of the minimum wage, in force for a further period of two fixed payments after which percentage indexation will be restored, subject to a revision of the index and a reduction in frequency of adjustments. In *Denmark* automatic wage adjustments were abolished in October 1982 until January 1985, while in the *Netherlands* a wage freeze was instituted in the public sector and negotiations are in progress in the private sector for the conversion of the January 1983 cost of living adjustment into an adjustment in working time. Finally in *Italy* the *scala mobile* will be modified in February 1983 to cut by 15 percent compensation for each point of the index and to exclude increases in value-added tax from the index. No compensation will be given for a rise in the dollar against EEC currencies if inflation exceeds the agreed target of 13 percent in 1983 and 10 percent in 1984.

Appendix A: Principal Characteristics of Systems for the Indexation of Incomes of Member States of the European Community[3]

The services of the European Commission have made a comparison of the principal characteristics of the systems in force in the member states in May 1981. The results are summarized in the thirteen tables that follow.

Three member states (Germany, the UK, and Greece) have no formal system for indexing incomes, in particular wages and salaries. The situation in the other states differs widely, ranging from the indexation of the minimum wage only (France) or the occasional introduction, into wage agreements, of cost-of-living adjustments (Ireland), to generally applied indexation (Italy, the Benelux countries, and Denmark).

In recent years the system has evolved toward greater flexibility. In three countries (Denmark, the Netherlands, and Luxembourg) changes have been made to take account of the difficulties of the economic situation; they concern either the extent to which incomes are adjusted to the rise in prices or the time taken to make these adjustments.

In Denmark the regulating price index, based on consumer prices, has since 1963 ceased to include the impact of indirect taxes and subsidies. As part of a set of important measures aimed at reducing the increase in costs and the balance of payments deficit, the indexation system, and particularly its base, was modified from 1 January 1980. As shown by table 7.5, energy products were withdrawn from the regulating price index. The wage adjustments planned for 1 March 1980 were also canceled.[1] The Netherlands took a similar measure in 1981, cutting the January compensation by 2 percent (see table 7.9). In line with the government's

Table 7.1
General characteristics

Belgium	The system is considered a major element in peaceful labor relations, an extremely automatic, rapid, and very rigid mechanism.
Denmark	The system's main characteristic is its egalitarian application (flat rate per hour, whatever the remuneration). On the whole, it is neither too rigid nor too automatic.
Federal Republic of Germany	Collective wage agreements are freely negotiated, but changes in the cost of living are taken into account, as an important factor.
Greece	No automatic indexation. Nonetheless, the government sets guidelines for wage and salary increases, which take account of previous price increases. A proposal for a form of indexation of wages and salaries is currently being studied.
France	Although the indexation of other wages is not lawful (order of December 1958), adjustments to the SMIC have always had a knock-on effect, though with some delay, throughout the wage structure.
Ireland	Different forms of partial indexation have figured in five of the last nine National Agreements. Under the present National Understanding there is no direct application of indexation (see table 7.2).
Italy	The system is considered an important factor in peaceful labor relations. The lower the wage level, the greater the "protection" of purchasing power, since the cost of living allowance consists of a single flat-rate sum (Lit 2 389 for wage and salary earners). It is estimated that on average a 1 percent price rise produces an 0.7 percent increase in the average wage in industry.
Luxembourg	Uniform and automatic system, of average speed but with rigid framework.
Netherlands	System of average speed. Its characteristic, for the public sector and social security benefits, is that it forms part of a wider adjustment consisting of the application of the increase in private wages and salaries (agreed wages and salaries) to officials' salaries and social security benefits.
United Kingdom	There is no formal system of indexation of earned incomes.

Table 7.2
Elements of income covered

Belgium	All elements of private and public sector wages and salaries.
Denmark	All elements of public and most elements of private sector wages and salaries.
France	Statutory minimum wage (SMIC) since 1970 (hourly wage).
Ireland	In the period August 1980 to November 1981 there exists a National Understanding between the trade unions and employers (including the government) on the level of basic pay increases. This agreement did not provide for automatic indexation but only a commitment to reconvene the "Employer Labor Conference" if the increase in the Consumer Price Index between mid-May 1980 and mid-February 1981 exceeded 10 percent. While the index increased by 12.7 percent over the relevant period, no compensation was paid under this provision.
Italy	Virtually all wages and salaries. Flat rate sum in absolute value.
Luxembourg	All elements in private and public sector wages and salaries.
Netherlands	Almost all elements in private and public sector wages and salaries (the public sector "follows" the private sector).
Federal Republic of Germany, Greece, United Kingdom	None.

objective of stabilizing real wages the July 1980 wage compensation had already been replaced by a flat-rate payment.[2] Lastly, in the Grand Duchy of Luxembourg, it was decided, at the end of June 1981, to suspend the "advance adjustment" equivalent to 1.5 percent of the wage and to introduce a one-month delay in applying indexation (see tables 7.3 and 7.4).

Italy is moving in the opposite direction. After the introduction of certain exceptions to the indexation system in 1977 (see table 7.9), the frequency of sliding scale adjustments in the public sector was made quarterly with effect from March 1980 (see table 7.7), and the pensions system was adapted from the beginning of 1981 (revision every four months, see table 7.10).

Table 7.3
Frequency of adjustment

Belgium	In most cases one month after the index reaches the trigger point.
Denmark	1 March (April) and 1 September (October) for the private (public) sector on the basis of the January (average of period November–January) and July (average of period May–July) quarterly regulating price indexes.
Italy	Every three months for wages and salaries (February–May–August–November). Based on the movement of the index between the periods November–January, February–April, May–July, and August–October.
Luxembourg	The month in which the average of the last six months of the index reaches the trigger point. Following the tripartite agreement concluded on 21 May 1981 in the steel industry, a law passed on 26 June 1981 provides for the introduction of a delay of one month for all sectors.
Netherlands	Half-yearly (January and July) on the basis of the rise in the ad hoc index between April and October (for the January adjustment) or between October and April (for the July adjustment).
Federal Republic of Germany, Greece, France, Ireland, United Kingdom	None.

Table 7.4
Adjustments

Belgium	In the public sector and in most private sector cases, 2 percent adjustment for each 2 percent rise in the index.
Denmark	Nominal amounts of DKR 0.9 per hour for each rise of 3 percentage points in the regulating price index.
France	2 percent of the cost of living.
Italy	A cost-of-living allowance is granted for a rise of at least one absolute point in the index.
Luxembourg	Fixed adjustment of 2.5 percent for each 2.5 percent rise in the trigger point. The 1.5 percent advance adjustment is suspended, for all sectors, in accordance with the tripartite agreement concluded in the steel industry and pursuant to a law passed on 26 June 1981.
Netherlands	Adjustment generally proportional to the percent rise in the ad hoc index.
Federal Republic of Germany, Greece, Ireland, United Kingdom	None.

Table 7.5
Index used

Belgium	Consumer price index, no element excluded.
Denmark	The regulating price index is based on consumer prices, minus the impact of indirect taxes and subsidies. Using this basis of a monthly index, quarterly averages of three-month periods are established (January as average for November, December, January, etc.); the January and July values being used as a reference.
France	Consumer price index for urban households whose head is a wage or salary earner.
Ireland	On occasions where agreements included indexation clauses, the index used was the general consumer price index, base mid-November 1975 = 100.
Italy	Special index (*Indice sindacale del costo della vita*), August–October 1974 = 100. Standard consumption of four-person household. Concentrates on consumer products (especially in the food sector). The price of petrol is not included, but the price of energy products is, with a small weight.
Luxembourg	Weighted index of consumer prices, no element excluded.
Netherlands	Household consumer price index, minus the impact of changes in indirect taxes and with a lower weighting for health care costs.
Federal Republic of Germany, Greece, United Kingdom	None.

Table 7.6
Legal force of provisions

Belgium	In public sector, single national clause pursuant to the law, in private sector, agreed by economic sector (wage agreements).
Denmark	For all earned incomes, collective agreement. However, the index is calculated in pursuance of legal provisions.
France	1970 Law on the statutory minimum wage.
Ireland	National voluntary agreement.
Italy	Legal force, like all general contractual provisions concerning agreed minimum wages.
Luxembourg	In public sector, pursuant to legal provisions. In private sector, (a) minimum social wage pursuant to the law (obligatory clause for all collective agreements); (b) collective agreements for others.
Netherlands	Contractual (collective agreements). However, the half-yearly adjustment of the statutory minimum wage is imposed by law.
Federal Republic of Germany, Greece, United Kingdom	None.

Table 7.7
Indexation clauses

Belgium	In public sector, general clause pursuant to the law; in private sector, clauses other than those mentioned under 4 (ranging from 1 to 2.5 percent according to economic sector).
Denmark	Clauses in collective agreements, legal provisions and private contracts.
France	National regulations.
Ireland	When indexation clauses have formed part of national agreements no distinction between the public and private sectors has been drawn.
Italy	A standardization process was started in 1975 and completed when the sliding scale in the public sector was put on a quarterly basis (March 1980).
Luxembourg	In public sector, general legal provision; in private sector, clauses contained in collective agreements.
Netherlands	Various clauses in collective agreements.
Federal Republic of Germany, Greece, United Kingdom	None.

Table 7.8
Number of wage and salary earners concerned

Belgium	Almost all wage and salary earners, some 77 percent of the labor force.
Denmark	Nearly all wage and salary earners, some 85 percent of the labor force.
France	Around 800,000 (September 1979), or under 4 percent of the labor force.
Ireland	Most wage and salary earners.
Italy	Virtually all wage and salary earners. But in certain regions, especially the south, and in small firms the system is not always observed (*economia sommersa*).
Luxembourg	Almost all wage and salary earners, some 85 percent of the labor force.
Netherlands	Almost all wage and salary earners, some 82 percent of the labor force.
Federal Republic of Germany, Greece, United Kingdom	None.

Table 7.9
Exceptions to the indexation rules

Belgium	From 1 April to 31 December 1976, indexation of wages and salaries in excess of BFr 40 250 was suspended.
Denmark	There have been many exceptions in the past, the latest from January 1980 include (a) the two installments due in respect of the March 1980 adjustment were canceled, (b) the adjustment due September 1980 was reduced from DKR 0.9 to DKR 0.6 in order to exclude the effects of the devaluation in November 1979.
France	The general system is that the indexing of wages is prohibited except for the cases explicitly provided for by law (SMIG from 1952 to 1970; SMIC from 1970).
Ireland	Not applicable.
Italy	Since 31 January 1977, the sliding scale no longer applies to severance grants or to production bonuses. (See also table 7.7 concerning the sliding scale in the public sector being put on a quarterly basis from March 1980.)
Netherlands	Exceptions have been made in the past. They are made pursuant to the law on wages (*Wet op de loonvorming*); thus the July 1980 compensation was replaced by a flat rate payment (HFl 26, with HFl 36 for minimum wages); the January 1981 compensation was cut by 2 percent. The indexation of tax scales can be limited to 80 percent of the rise in prices.
Federal Republic of Germany, Greece, Luxembourg, United Kingdom	None.

Table 7.10
Indexation of social security benefits: old age and disability pensions

Belgium	Social security benefits in lieu of remuneration follow the indexation of public sector pay. Automatic adjustment of pensions by 2 percent when the consumer price index varies by the same percentage in relation to the preceding index. Rates of pensions are adapted in line with the evolution of the general standard of living by fixing an annual adjustment coefficient for increases or flat rate adjustment via an allowance.
Denmark	Social pensions are indexed (each rise of 3 percentage points releases an installment equivalent to the percentage rise of the index) on 1 April and 1 October. The maximum allowances for sickness and maternity leave are indexed according to the same method, but by a fixed amount (see table 7.4) of 36 DKR per week.
Federal Republic of Germany	Adjustment to economic situation by automatic incidence of general basic earnings when the amount of the pension to be paid is fixed, and by adjustment of current pensions.
Greece	No automatic indexation.
France	Pensions are adjusted every six months (with effect from 1 January and 1 July) by statutory instrument fixing the coefficient of increase.
Ireland	Pensions normally increased once a year.
Italy	From the beginning of 1981 pensions are adjusted, by decree, every four months (instead of every six months, as previously). (The adjustment consists of a flat-rate amount—LIT 1.910 for each percentage point rise in the index—plus a percentage.)
Luxembourg	The majority of social security benefits in lieu of remuneration follow the indexation of public sector pay.
Netherlands	Social security benefits in lieu of remuneration follow private sector wages (adjustment on 1 January and 1 July) with a six-month time lag.
United Kingdom	Retirement pensions and other social security benefits are increased in November each year in line with the rate of inflation foreseen at the time of the preceding spring budget. In some cases this increase is a matter of custom and practice; in others it is a legal requirement.

Table 7.11
Indexation of social security benefits for employment injuries and occupational
diseases

Belgium	Adjustment for annuities which for specified categories of invalidity rates do not reach a specific sum. The adjustment is equal to the difference between the annuity and the said sum. These sums are fixed by royal decree and are pegged and adjusted annually but, in other cases, adjusted annually with indexation.
Denmark	Automatic adjustment twice a year according to change in the regulating index. In addition basic allowances are adjusted once a year in line with the change in wages.
Federal Republic of Germany	Annual adjustment by decree according to changes in wage levels.
Greece	None.
France	Annual adjustments on 1 January and 1 July, by decree fixing the coefficient of increase.
Ireland	Benefits are normally increased once a year.
Italy	Automatic regular adjustments linked to changes in industrial earnings during the preceding three years.
Luxembourg	Adjustment by regulation (at least every five years) according to changes in wage level (at present wage level of 1977). The sums adjusted by this means are pegged to the cost-of-living index. No monthly payment can be made on a basis below the minimum reference levels for the first month in which it is payable.
Netherlands	There is no special insurance for employment injuries and occupational diseases: these risks are normally covered by sickness insurance (benefits in cash and in kind), incapacity for work (invalidity) insurance, and survivors' insurance.
United Kingdom	All long-term benefits are adjusted by legislation in line with the general level of prices.

Table 7.12
Indexation of tax scales

Belgium	In principle, personal tax scales are not indexed.
Denmark	Personal tax scales and allowances are indexed with a one-year time lag (for 1982 scales, on the April 1981 increase over April 1980 in the regulating price index).
France	The income tax scale is revised annually (partial indexation).
Ireland	No systematic indexation; adjustment linked to changes in the level of prices.
Luxembourg	Personal tax scales are pegged to the same index but by annual reference (scale of year t pegged to the rise in the index for July of year $t-1$ over July of year $t-2$); if the rise in prices is under 5 percent, adjustment of the scales is not compulsory.
Netherlands	Income tax and wage tax scales are generally indexed pursuant to the law (*inflatiecorrectie*).
United Kingdom	Personal allowances, the bands for higher rates of income tax, and the threshold for the investment income surcharge are automatically adjusted each year in line with the retail price index, unless Parliament decides otherwise, as it did in respect of the financial year 1981–82. Excise duties are usually adjusted at the beginning of each tax year, unless Parliament decides otherwise.
Federal Republic of Germany, Greece, Italy	None.

Table 7.13
Other application of indexation

Belgium	Certain professional fees are indexed nonautomatically, pursuant to special provisions or agreements. Since 1976, the maximum rate of rent increase has been fixed each year after taking into account the rise in prices.
Denmark	Maximum unemployment benefits are indexed by a fixed amount of 36 DKR per week.
France	Commercial leases and certain rents are pegged to the cost of construction index.
Italy	Rents are adjusted annually on the basis of the ad hoc index and as a percentage.
Federal Republic of Germany, Greece, Ireland, Luxembourg, Netherlands, United Kingdom	None.

Appendix B: Commission Communication to the Council on the Principles of Indexation in the European Community[4]

1. In its Annual Report on the economic situation, the Commission proposed to the Council that mechanisms for indexing nominal incomes should be "used with sufficient flexibility or limitations to avoid passing on, into wages, unavoidable terms-of-trade losses, and to allow other necessary adjustments in income distribution or tax structure without causing extra inflation."

The Council adopted this text in its decision of 15 December 1980.

2. The European Council discussed the question during its meeting at Maastricht on 23 and 24 March 1981. The Presidency concluded as follows: "High and divergent inflation rates are a threat both to the prospects of growth and to the economic and monetary cohesion of the Community. In this context the European Council also discussed the effects caused by rigid systems of indexation of incomes and expressed the opinion that an adjustment of such mechanisms should be considered."

3. Beginning from these discussions and guidelines, the Commission presents below various elements and conclusions aimed at preparing the discussions.

4. Firstly, the analysis should be considered in the light of two general remarks:

—the first concerns the way in which existing indexation mechanisms in various Member States contribute to the settlement of pay issues. This suggests that any changes in these systems should be made only with caution and with a full understanding of its implications. Thus the essential objective should be to adjust existing mechanisms so as to remedy their main disadvantages;

—the second concerns the fact that, in practice, the consequences of an indexation system greatly depend on how the mechanism in question operates: how general it is, the definition and content of the price index used, the degree and frequency of compensation, what categories of prices and incomes are indexed.

5. An automatic or semi-automatic link between the cost of living and wages or other prices or incomes—which exists at present in a number of Member States—may form a serious obstacle to efforts to correct an underlying balance-of-payments disequilibrium, to improve the produc-

tion structure of an economy, or to measures designed lastingly to reduce inflation. In particular:

—where the economy in question suffers an inflationary shock which has nothing to do with the relative shares of wages and profits—such as a rise in the price of oil—automatic indexation extends the inflationary process and blocks adjustments required by changes in relative prices;

—where the exchange rate is modified to correct an external imbalance, an automatic link gravely hampers the adjustment process and thus tends to keep the economy in its position of imbalance;

—where, for budget policy reasons, the authorities wish to increase taxes or social security contributions (with a short-term effect on prices) automatic indexation pushes up wage costs, at the same time fuelling domestic inflation and damaging competitiveness.

Thus, by making adaptations in cost and price structures more difficult, an automatic link between prices and wages can endanger the viability of existing jobs as well as increase obstacles to the creation of new jobs.

6. Furthermore, indexation mechanisms represent a considerable danger that divergences within the European Monetary System will be prolonged since such mechanisms may help to preserve inflation differentials and distort relative costs. In a country seeking—by the use of budgetary and monetary policy measures—to keep the exchange rate within margins of fluctuation, unlimited indexation also results in purchasing power compensation, thus weakening the ability of economic policy to tackle the necessary adjustments.

7. At present, Belgium, Luxembourg and Italy are the only Member States to have a very developed and rapid system of linking a consumer price index on the one hand to hourly wages (and other prices) on the other hand. In Denmark, indexation is semi-annual on the basis of a special index which excludes the effects of rises in indirect taxes and the price of energy products. In the Netherlands indexation is also semi-annual on the basis of a special index which excludes indirect tax increases and gives a reduced weight to medical services. In the other Member States, to the extent that it exists at all, automatic indexation is limited. In France automatic indexation is limited. In France, automatic indexation applies only to the statutory minimum wage (SMIC), but this is principally a low-income protection measure; in the Federal Republic of Germany, indexation is illegal. However, in Greece and Ireland the last collective wage

agreements provide for compensation should the rise in consumer prices go above a certain threshold (20% and 10% respectively).

8. In view of the need to improve employment prospects in the Community by strengthening competitiveness, making a flexible adjustment to the new economic situation, substantially slowing down inflation, and reducing the extent to which prices and costs diverge, and in view also of the need to reduce budget deficits and balance-of-payments disequilibria, the Commission suggests that the Council adopt a recommendation relating to indexation practices:

(i) in the Member States in which the principle of wage indexation is accepted, the basis for indexation should be a price index adapted in such a way as to prevent price increase factors outside corporate control from working through to wage costs; the regulation index ought thus to exclude the impact of any changes in indirect taxes and certain public service prices such as public transport and medical service charges; where the rise in prices is attributable to a deterioration in the terms of trade due, for example, to a rise in important raw material prices or to a depreciation of the currency, the impact of these factors ought to be excluded from indexation;

(ii) in order to prevent temporary fluctuations in consumer prices from being permanently incorporated into wage costs, giving a further boost to the prices and incomes spiral, wage adjustments should be implemented with a delay and should number no more than two a year;

(iii) where the inflation rate is appreciably above the Community average and the indexation principle widely applied, the aim should be to limit the degree of indexation to an agreed rate, for example, the Community average inflation rate, so that the upward movement of prices and costs is gradually slowed down and exchange rates become more stable;

(iv) a simple and temporary technique for adapting to an inflationary shock could be to forego entirely a certain number of indexation adjustments.

9. These principles should also apply to other types of income such as the fees of the liberal professions and rents, where they are indexed to consumer prices.

10. The recommendation ought to be addressed to the social partners in the Member States concerned so that they can undertake negotiations

with a view to making rapid changes in the existing indexation mechanisms.

11. Looking ahead to the institutional phase of the European Monetary System, the Commission considers it vital for the Community to clarify the monetary principles of the European economy. In this regard, the European economy must move towards a system which adopts as its basic objective the defence of the nominal value for its use in contracts and transactions and for the denomination of monetary and financial assets.

12. In the light of the discussions which will take place on the basis of this communication, the Commission will present a draft recommendation implementing the principles set out in paragraphs 8 and 9.

Notes

Director, Macroeconomic Analyses and Policies, Directorate General for Economic and Financial Affairs, Commission of the European Communities. These remarks are made in a personal capacity, and do not necessarily reflect the views of any institution. Factual information is annexed in a document on the "Principal Characteristics of Systems for the Indexation of Incomes in the Member States of the European Communities," and the Commission's policy position is also annexed in a "Commission Communication to the Council on the principles of indexation in the Community."

1. For details of incomes policy in Denmark, see *European Economy*, 8 (March 1981): 45–46.

2. See *European Economy*, 8 (March 1981): 82.

3. Working Document, Commission of the European Communities, Directorate-General for Economic and Financial Affairs, (May 1981).

4. Commission Communication to the Council, Brussels July 23, 1981. Reproduced from *European Economy*, 10 (November 1981).

III Indexation and Assets Markets

8 On the Relevance or Irrelevance of Public Financial Policy: Indexation, Price Rigidities, and Optimal Monetary Policies

J. E. Stiglitz

8.1 Introduction

Does it make any difference whether or not the government issues indexed bonds? Few governments have in fact issued such bonds, despite repeated calls from distinguished economists for them to do so. Is the failure to issue these bonds an example of lack of innovativeness of government officials? What difference would such bonds make to the equilibrium of the economy?

This question is part of a much broader question, of the effect of alternative public financial policies. The effect of any single policy, such as the issuance of indexed bonds, cannot be analyzed in isolation from the other aspects of public financial policy. Moreover the effect of any change in government policy today cannot be assessed without specifying, at the same time, future governmental policies (or perhaps more accurately, specifying the beliefs of economic agents concerning those future government policies). Finally, it is our contention that a central aspect of public financial policy is the intertemporal (intergenerational) distribution of income and risk bearing which it generates.

In the absence of these intergenerational distribution effects, public financial policy is irrelevant. In section 8.2 we show that an increase in government debt (whether indexed or not), an exchange of an indexed bond for a nonindexed bond, or an exchange of a short-term bond for a long-term bond (which corresponds in our model to an open market operation), has neither real nor financial effects. The first result—on the irrelevance of government deficits—we have referred to as the Say's law of government deficits (Stiglitz 1982): an increase in the supply of government bonds gives rise to an equal increase in the demand for government bonds.

These results are in marked contrast to those suggested, for instance, by the standard portfolio theories. In those models an increase in the supply of one kind of financial asset and a decrease in the supply of another will have real effects: the risk properties of these different financial assets are different, and because of risk aversion individuals will want to diversify their portfolios among the different assets. A change in the supply of different assets necessitates a change in the equilibrium prices, and these changes in equilibrium prices have real consequences (say, for the pattern and level of investment). Our analysis differs from these models in that they fail to take into account the implicit liability associated with government bonds, and the change in that liability with a change in the level or form of government bonds. When there are no intergenerational distribution effects of public financial policy, and when individuals do take their future tax liabilities into account, then it turns out that public financial policy, including the issuance of indexed bonds, is irrelevant.[1]

The more relevant case, however, is that where public financial policy has an effect on the intergenerational distribution of income. The literature on money and growth in the late 1960s emphasized this role of debt policy.[2] As such, the effects of debt policy cannot be analyzed separately from those of social security and tax policy, as noted by Atkinson-Stiglitz (1980). These studies, however, analyzed public financial policy in a completely nonstochastic framework. When there is variability in the productivity of labor and capital, then public financial policy has an additional role: it is concerned not only with controlling the optimal rate of capital accumulation but also with the sharing of risks among members of different generations. This notion appears in earlier discussions of the burden of the debt. Could the generation alive at the time of World War II manage to shift the burden of paying for that war to future generations, by financing the war by means of debt? For a period the consensus, at least of textbook writers, was no: the resources foregone during the war were spent at that time. As long as we "owe the debt to ourselves" (we do not finance the war through borrowing abroad), how we finance it cannot make a difference. The view taken here is that the burden of the war can indeed be shared with succeeding generations, and this sharing is implemented through public financial policies, including social security and debt policy. Though we will not address the question of how the costs of a particular event, such as a major war, should be shared among different generations, we will address the question of how public financial policy can be used to smooth out the variability in intergenerational welfare induced by variability in the productivity of labor and capital.

In the context of a life cycle model, where public financial policy affects the intertemporal distribution of welfare, public financial policy does, in general, matter. Some kinds of public financial policies have financial effects (affect price levels) but have no real effects. We discuss two important instances. First, an increase in the rate of interest paid on government bonds, with the ensuing deficits financed by the issuance of additional bonds, has no real effects. Second, if all members alive in one generation were identical, any intertemporal distribution of welfare that was desired could be attained through the use of a single financial asset; thus, adding additional financial assets—such as indexed bonds—makes no difference. Again, indexed bonds serve no function.

More generally, changes in public financial policies have real effects. For instance, when there are more than one type of individual alive in a given generation, then issuing indexed bonds can have a real effect, even if there is a complete set of intragenerational risk markets.

Once it is recognized that public financial policy matters, it becomes important to ascertain the effects of alternative policies. Although the characterization of the first-best policies, for any stochastic structure of general interest, is beyond the scope of this chapter, we present some preliminary results comparing the welfare effects of three simple rules. The first attempts to keep prices constant, the second attempts to keep the value of real debt constant, and the third keeps the level of debt constant (this corresponds, in our model, to the Friedman rule of a constant growth in the money supply, since, in our model, we have no exogenous sources of growth).

Our analysis suggests that a policy of holding the value of the out-standing debt constant may be preferable to the other two. An outsider, not knowing that the government was following a policy aimed at maintaining a constant value of the outstanding debt, might be misled by the empirical observation that in such an economy the price level moves in proportion to debt into believing that the level of debt determined the price level; in fact both are responding to the exogenous shocks which the economy is experiencing.

For reasons that we detail later, for most of the analysis we assume a single short-term government financial asset, which normally is interest bearing. We focus on the role of government debt as a store of value, ignoring its potential role as a medium of exchange. In section 8.4 we show how the analysis can easily be modified to incorporate explicitly non-interest-bearing government debt (money); if anything, the transactions demand for money strengthens our earlier results on the relevance of public financial policy.

Up to this point the models we use are all neoclassical, assuming full employment of labor and capital. Yet one of the more important functions of public financial policy, as it is usually conceived, is to affect the level of national income and employment. Recent theoretical work using models of rational expectations has questioned the ability of the government to use financial policy to affect the level of national income (other than by adding noise, making it more difficult for economic agents to distinguish real shocks from monetary shocks, and as a result making it more difficult for economic agents to respond efficiently to changed circumstances).[3] In our neoclassical models we assume rational expectations and symmetric information; yet alternative financial policies do have an effect, both on the level of capital accumulation and on the labor supply (through the income effects associated with the intertemporal distribution of income).[4]

In section 8.5 we show that public financial policy may be even more effective if wages and prices are not perfectly flexible, so that there is not full employment. Again, we postulate rational expectations. This result reemphasizes the result noted by others (see, for example, Taylor 1980, Neary and Stiglitz 1983) that the conclusion of the rational expectations models concerning the inefficacy of government policy does not depend so much on the expectational assumptions as on other features of the model, in particular, the assumptions concerning wage and price flexibility.

Before beginning the formal analysis, two remarks may be helpful. First, we limit ourselves throughout to public financial policies; real government expenditures are assumed to remain constant (at each date and in each state). Second, the question is sometimes posed, what can the government do that the private sector cannot do—or at least undo? There is a simple answer here: the government can enforce intergenerational redistributions. And there is, in the life cycle model, an implicit market failure. Individuals in one generation cannot trade with those of another generation; in particular, they cannot engage in the sharing of risks. (Of necessity, then, the set of Arrow-Debreu contingent claims markets must be incomplete.) The government provides a mechanism by which this kind of risk sharing can occur.[5]

For most of the analysis, we focus our attention on a model in which all individuals within a generation are identical; for those who are alive and can trade with each other, we assume that there are perfect markets.

8.2 Three General Irrelevance Theorems

In this section we prove three very general theorems, establishing the irrelevance of a wide class of government financial policies. We establish the results in the context of a simple model of an economy with overlapping generations and a constant population. Following the proof of the first irrelevance theorem, we comment on the implications of this result for an economy with a single infinitely lived generation.

The model

Each generation lives for three periods; individuals work in the first two, and live off their savings in the third. (Later we shall consider a simplification where individuals live for only two periods.) We thus write the utility function of an individual born at time t:

$$U_t = U(c_{1t}, c_{2t}, c_{3t}, L_{1t}, L_{2t}), \tag{8.1}$$

where

c_{it} = the tth generation's consumption in the ith period of their life,

L_{it} = the tth generation's labor supply in the ith period of their life.

For simplicity, we assume that the wage that an old individual receives is the same as the wage that a young person receives; both are random variables which are exogenously determined.[6]

We assume that the government can impose age-specific lump sum taxes but that all individuals within a generation must be treated the same.[7] For the moment we assume that all individuals within a generation are identical, and hence this constraint is of no consequence; later, when we assume that there are different individuals within a generation, this constraint will have some real consequences. We denote the lump sum tax imposed on the tth generation in the ith period of its life by T_{it}. (T_{it} may be negative, that is, the government may provide a lump sum subsidy; thus a social security payment corresponds to $T_{3t} < 0$.)

Individuals take their aftertax income and either consume it or invest it. There are three classes of securities in which they can invest:

1. Capital (equity), the return to which is a random variable, $\tilde{\eta}$.

2. Government securities. We shall distinguish several government securities:

• A short-term bond. In this model we shall assume that there is a single nonindexed short-term government bond and that it is (or at least may be) interest bearing. It may be thought of as interest-bearing money. The price of this bond in terms of consumption goods is denoted by v, and $p = 1/v$ is the price level. The real return on holding a short-term bond purchased at time t with a nominal rate of i_t is[8]

$$\frac{(1 + i_t)\tilde{v}_{t+1}}{v_t} - 1 \equiv \tilde{\rho}_t. \tag{8.2}$$

Even though the nominal interest is known, the real return on short-term bonds is risky, because the price level next period is unknown.

• Short-term indexed bonds. These specify a real rate of return, r_{1t}. In other words, the nominal payment $\tilde{i}$ is whatever it must be so that[9]

$$\frac{v_{t+1}(1 + \tilde{i}_t)}{q_{1t}} - 1 = r_{1t},$$

where q_{1t} is the price, in terms of consumption goods, of a short-term indexed bond at date t.

• Long-term bonds. For simplicity, we shall only consider here perpetuities, with a fixed interest payment i per bond. (Other long-term bonds may be easily introduced into the model.) The real return on long-term bonds is a random variable, because the price at which the bond can be sold, q_{2t}, is uncertain. We denote the real rate of return by $\tilde{r}_{2t}$:

$$\frac{\tilde{q}_{2t+1} + v_{t+1}\check{i}}{q_{2t}} - 1 = r_{2t}.$$

The aggregate supply of the short-term bonds is denoted by B. The aggregate supply of short-term indexed bonds is denoted by D_1 and of long-term bonds by D_2; the price of short-term indexed bonds in terms of consumption goods is denoted by q_1, and that of long-term bonds q_2.[10] The holdings of the young (those in the first periods of their life) of the jth security are denoted by $D_{1\,jt}$, and those of the old (those in the second period of their life) by $D_{2\,jt}$.

3. Exchange securities. These are trades between individuals both living over two periods (thus in our model, where all individuals within a generation are identical, they are trades between the young and the middle aged); the jth exchange security promises to pay $e_j(\theta)$ the second period if state θ occurs, and costs Z_j the first period.[11] Because the payment and prices are state dependent, it makes no difference at this level of generality whether we denominate the payments in consumption goods or in dollars (short-term bonds). It is more convenient to denominate them in terms of consumption goods. An exchange security which pays $e(\theta)$ in terms of

consumption goods pays $e(\theta)p(\theta)$ in terms of dollars. (An Arrow-Debreu security is one that pays in only one state of nature; in all other states $e(\theta) = 0$.) An indexed loan (ignoring the possibility of default) has the property that $e(\theta) = $ constant for all θ. An unindexed loan has the property that $e(\theta)$ varies inversely with $p(\theta)$. N_{1jt} is the quantity of the jth exchange security purchased by the young at time t; N_{2jt} is the quantity purchased by the middle aged.

The Individual's Budget Constraints The individual maximizes his expected utility subject to his budget constraints:

1. His wage income the first year of his life is either consumed, invested, or paid to the government in lump sum taxes:

$$w_t L_{1t} = c_{1t} + A_{1t} + T_{1t}, \tag{8.3a}$$

where w_t is the real wage at t and A_{1t} is his asset holdings the first period of his life, which consist of capital, government securities, or exchange securities. Thus

$$A_{1t} = K_{1t} + v_t B_{1t} + \sum_{j=1}^{2} q_{jt} D_{1jt} + \sum_{j} Z_{jt} N_{1jt}, \tag{8.3b}$$

where B_{1t} is the holdings of short-term bonds by the young and K_{1t} is their holdings of capital.

2. At the beginning of the second period his portfolio is worth

$$W_{2t} \equiv (1 + \eta_t)K_{1t} + v_t(1 + \rho_t)B_{1t} + \sum_{j=1}^{2} (1 + r_{jt})q_{jt}D_{1jt} + \sum_{j} e_{jt} N_{1jt}. \tag{8.3c}$$

This, plus his wage income, is either consumed, invested, or paid out in taxes:

$$W_{2t} + w_{t+1} L_{2t} = c_{2t} + A_{2t} + T_{2t}, \tag{8.3d}$$

where again, his asset holdings consist of capital (K_{2t+1}), government securities (B_{2t+1}), or exchange securities:

$$A_{2t} = K_{2t+1} + v_{t+1} B_{2t+1} + \sum_{j=1}^{2} q_{jt+1} D_{2jt+1} + \sum_{j} Z_{jt+1} N_{2jt+1}. \tag{8.3e}$$

3. In the third period of his life he consumes his savings less any taxes (plus any social security receipts):

$$c_{3t} = (1 + \eta_{t+1})K_{2t+1} + v_{t+1}(1 + \rho_{t+1})B_{2t+1}$$

$$+ \sum_{j=1}^{2} (1 + r_{jt+1})q_{jt+1}D_{2jt+1}$$

$$+ \sum_{j} e_{jt+1}N_{2jt+1} - T_{3t} \equiv W_{3t} - T_{3t}. \tag{8.3f}$$

We can thus derive the individual's consumption functions and demand for asset equations. These are of the form

$$y_1 = y_{1t}(w_t, T_{1t}; \tilde{X}_t, \tilde{X}_{t+1}; \tilde{w}_{t+1}; \tilde{T}_{2t}, \tilde{T}_{3t}),$$

$$y_2 = y_{2t}(w_{t+1}, T_{2t}; W_{2t}; \tilde{X}_{t+1}; \tilde{T}_{3t}),$$

where

$$y_1 \equiv \{c_{1t}, L_{1t}, K_{1t}, v_t B_{1t}, \{q_{jt}D_{1jt}\}, \{Z_{jt}N_{1jt}\}\},$$

$$y_2 \equiv \{c_{2t}, L_{2t}, K_{2t+1}, v_{t+1}B_{2t+1}, \{q_{jt}D_{2jt}\}, \{Z_{jt}N_{2jt}\},$$

$$\{q_{jt+1}D_{2jt+1}\}, \{Z_{jt+1}N_{2jt+1}\}\},$$

and

$$X_t \equiv \{\tilde{\eta}_t, r_{1t}, \tilde{r}_{2t}, \{e_{jt}\}\},$$

and where W_{2t} is defined by (8.3d), and c_{3t} is given by (8.3f). Consumption, labor, and portfolio decisions depend on wealth and the joint probability distribution of future wages, returns on assets, and taxes.[12]

The Government's Budget Constraint and the National Income Identities
Each period the government makes decisions concerning its expenditure, G, the supply of bonds of various sorts, the interest rate which it will pay, and the taxes it will impose. It must do this within its budget constraint, which says that its expenditures (including interest payments) must be equal to its receipts (taxes plus issue of new debt).

It is easiest if we first express the budget constraint in terms of dollars and then rewrite it using our consumption numeraire. Since government expenditures, G_t, and taxes

$$T_t = T_{1t} + T_{2t-1} + T_{3t-2}$$

are both expressed in real terms, the dollar deficit of the government is

$$p_{t+1}[G_{t+1} - T_{t+1}] + i_t B_t + \tilde{i}_t D_{1t} + i D_{2t}$$

which must be financed by new debt,

$$B_{t+1} - B_t + p_{t+1} \sum_{j=1}^{2} q_{jt+1}(D_{jt+1} - D_{jt}).$$

Dividing through by p_{t+1} and rearranging terms, we arrive at the real budget constraint

$$G_{t+1} - T_{t+1} = v_{t+1}B_{t+1} - (1 + i_t)v_{t+1}B_t + \sum_{j=1}^{2} q_{jt+1}(D_{jt+1} - D_{jt})$$

$$- v_{t+1}(\check{\imath}_t D_{1t} + \check{\imath}_t D_{2t})$$

$$= v_{t+1}B_{t+1} - (1 + \rho_t)v_t B_t + \sum_{j=1}^{2} (q_{jt+1}D_{jt+1} - (1 + r_{jt})q_{jt}D_{jt})$$

$$(8.4)$$

where we have made use of (8.2).

Market Equilibrium Market equilibrium requires that the demand for each kind of government security add up to its supply, and that the net demand for exchange securities be zero:[13]

$$B_{1t} + B_{2t} - B_t, \tag{8.5a}$$

$$D_{1jt} + D_{2jt} = D_{jt}, \quad j = 1, 2, \tag{8.5b}$$

$$N_{1jt} + N_{2jt} = 0. \tag{8.5c}$$

Walras's law assures us that, if each individual's budget constraint is satisfied, and the government's budget constraint is also satisfied, then the national income constraint is satisfied:

$$\underbrace{c_{1t} + c_{2t-1} + c_{3t-2}}_{\text{Consumption}} + \underbrace{K_t - K_{t-1}}_{\text{Investment}} = \underbrace{w_t(L_{1t} + L_{2t-1})}_{\substack{\text{Wage} \\ \text{income}}} + \underbrace{\eta_{t-1}K_{t-1}}_{\substack{\text{Capital} \\ \text{income}}},$$

where K_t is the aggregate capital stock,

$$K_{1t} + K_{2t} = K_t. \tag{8.7}$$

In formulating their consumption-investment strategy, individuals must form expectations about the joint probability distribution of future wage rates, taxes, and returns on different securities. A rational expectations equilibrium is one where those subjective probability distributions (conditional on whatever is observable at the time the expectations are formed) correspond to the conditional probability distributions actually generated in the equilibrium.

Neutrality Propositions

There are two classes of neutrality propositions, those that establish that a particular perturbation in the financial policy of the government has no real effects *and* no effects on the level of prices, and those that establish that a particular perturbation in the financial policy of the government has no real effects but has effects on the level of prices. (The classical proposition concerning the neutrality of money was of the second kind; it asserted that doubling the money supplied doubled the price level but had no further real effects on the economy.)

The First Irrelevance Theorem (Say's Law of Government Deficits)

An increase in short-term government debt, with the proceeds used to finance a reduction in lump sum taxes on the young or middle aged, followed by a decrease in the government debt, financed by an increase in taxes of the middle aged and the aged (in proportion to the reduction in taxes which they experienced the previous period) has neither real nor financial effects. An increase in the supply of government bonds gives rise to an exactly equal and offsetting increase in the demand for government bonds, provided that there are no intergenerational distributional consequences of the government policy.

Assume we are initially in an equilibrium, denoted by

$$\{y_{1t}^*, y_{2t-1}^*, c_{3t-2}^*, P_t^*, \phi_t^*\},$$

where $P_t \equiv (v_t, \{q_{jt}\}, \{Z_{jt}\})$ is the vector of prices, and $\phi_t^* \equiv (B_t^*, \{D_{jt}^*\},$ $T_{1t}^*, T_{2t-1}^*, T_{3t-2}^*, \{N_{jt}\})$ is the corresponding vector of government debt and taxes and private securities. Then the first irrelevance theorem is concerned with the following change in government policy: at $\hat{t}$, the government increases B_i by an amount ΔB_i, and generates thereby a surplus $v_i \Delta B_i$ which it distributes to the young and the middle aged, so that

$$\Delta T_{1i} + \Delta T_{2i-1} = -v_i \Delta B_i, \tag{8.8}$$

where ΔT denotes the change in the lump sum tax liability.

Then next period it returns the debt to its original level. To do this, it must raise additional taxes, in the amount of (measured in consumption good numeraire)

$$(1 + i_i)v_{i+1}\Delta B_i.$$

It does this by levying lump sum taxes on the middle aged and the aged in proportion to their previous tax reduction, so

$$\frac{\Delta T_{1i}}{\Delta T_{2i}} = \frac{\Delta T_{2i-1}}{\Delta T_{3i-1}}. \tag{8.9}$$

Thus, if a fraction α of the tax revenues the first period went to the young

$$\Delta T_{1i} = -\alpha v_i \Delta B_i, \tag{8.10a}$$

then later they pay the same fraction of the subsequent increases in taxes

$$\Delta T_{2i} = -\alpha(1 + i_i)v_{i+1}\Delta B_i. \tag{8.10b}$$

To establish the result, we first will show that if prices remain unchanged, then the feasible consumption sets remain unchanged. If the feasible consumption sets remain unchanged, then clearly each individual will choose the same consumption plan as in the initial situation. We will then establish that when they do this, the demand for all assets (including the demand for short-term government bonds) equals the supply of all assets, and all markets clear.

To see that, if prices remain unchanged, the set of feasible consumption plans remain unchanged, denote by a single caret a feasible consumption investment strategy in the initial situation, and by a double caret one in the new situation. Let

$$\hat{\hat{c}}_{it} = \hat{c}_{it}; \hat{\hat{L}}_{it} = \hat{L}_{it}, \qquad \text{all } i, t, \tag{8.11a}$$

$$\hat{\hat{N}}_{ijt} = \hat{N}_{ijt}, \qquad \text{all } i, j, t, \tag{8.11b}$$

$$\hat{\hat{D}}_{ijt} = \hat{D}_{ijt}, \qquad \text{all } i, j, t, \tag{8.11c}$$

$$\hat{\hat{B}}_{1i} = \hat{B}_{1i}\left(1 + \frac{\Delta T_{1i}}{v_i}\right) \qquad t = \hat{\imath}, \tag{8.11d}$$

$$\hat{\hat{B}}_{2i} = \hat{B}_{2i}\left(1 + \frac{\Delta T_{2i-1}}{v_i}\right) \qquad t = \hat{\imath},$$

$$\hat{\hat{B}}_{it} = \hat{B}_{it}, \qquad \text{all } i, t \text{ except } i = 1, 2 \text{ and } t = \hat{\imath}.$$

Individuals do exactly what they would have done in the initial situation, except that those whose tax liability is reduced spend their extra income to purchase short-term (unindexed) government bonds.

Direct substitution into the budget constraints, (8.3a) through (8.3f), makes it clear that, if the first set of consumption-investment plans is feasible in the initial situation, the second set of consumption-investment plans is feasible in the new situation.

The reason for this can be easily seen. The bonds that the young have purchased with the extra revenues they receive the first period increase their assets the next period by the amount

$$v_{t+1}(1 + i_{t+1})\Delta T_1 = v_{t+1}(1 + i_{t+1})\alpha\Delta B.$$

But this is exactly equal to their increased tax liability, which is given by (8.10b).

This establishes that individuals can do as well under the new public financial policy as under the old. Exactly the same arguments can be used to establish that any consumption sequence that is feasible under the new public financial policy is feasible in the original situation. Thus the two consumption opportunity sets are identical.[14]

Since the consumption opportunity sets are identical, it is clear that, if individuals chose the values of variables with single carets in the initial situation, they will choose the values with double carets in the new situation. We now need only check that markets all clear.

Since the demand for all securities except short-term bonds has remained unchanged, if the demand for each kind of security equals the supply in the initial situation, it does in the new situation.

Similarly for all consumption and capital goods. By Walras's law, if all but one market clears, the last market must clear, thus establishing that the values with double carets do represent an equilibrium.

It may be useful, however, to examine in somewhat greater detail the market for short-term bonds.

From (8.11d), the total increase in the demand for short-term bonds the $\hat{t}$ period is

$$\frac{\Delta T_{1i} + \Delta T_{2i-1}}{v_i},$$

which is just equal to the increase in the supply of bonds, using (8.8). Hence the demand for short-term bonds is equal to the supply of short-term bonds: the increase in government debt has given rise to an exactly equal and offsetting increase in the demand for bonds.

Several comments are in order. First, if all of the proceeds of the increased debt went to reduce the tax liabilities of the young, the reduction in the debt could have occurred either the next or the following period; the reduction in the debt would have to be financed, of course, by a levy on the same generation (the middle aged, if done the period immediately following the increased deficit; the aged, if done the following period). More generally, if each generation lives for n periods, the deficit need not be reduced until n periods later. All that is required for the validity of the irrelevance theorem is that there be no intergenerational redistribution; that is, those who benefit from the increased deficit, through lower taxes, must be the same ones who pay for the subsequent reduction in the government debt (and who pay for the interest in the intervening periods). By the same token, as we shall emphasize in the next section, whenever there are intergenerational redistributions effected through the deficit policy, then public financial policy is not irrelevant; it has real effects.

It is important to observe that the individual, when he decides to buy the additional short-term bonds, does not know the real return on these bonds; there is uncertainty about the price level. He does not spend the increase in his purchasing power, made possible by the reduction in his lump sum taxes, in a balanced way, keeping, say, the relative proportions of safe and risky assets (capital, indexed bonds, long -term bonds, short-term unindexed bonds) unchanged. The individual knows that there is risk associated with his tax liabilities in the future, and he chooses his portfolio to take this risk into account. When he does this, it turns out that he increases his demand for the securities that have increased in supply by exactly the amount that they have increased in supply.

Arguments analogous to those presented for changes in the short-term bond supply can be made for changes in the supply of other bonds. Rather than repeat the argument, we consider next the consequences of a change in the structure of the public debt.

The Second Irrelevance Theorem

A temporary change in the structure of the government debt has no real or financial effects, provided it is accompanied with the appropriate lump sum taxes/subsidies to avoid the change having any distributive effects. The change in the structure of the debt this period means of course that its interest obligations next period will be altered and this necessitates some change, either in taxes or in debt.

The perturbation in public financial policy considered in the second irrelevance theorem can be easily described. We increase, say, the supply of indexed bonds and decrease the supply of short-term (unindexed) bonds in such a way as to leave the government budget constraint still satisfied. Thus, denoting the change in the supply of indexed bonds by ΔD_{1t} and the change in the supply of short-term (unindexed) bonds by ΔB_t, we require

$$q_{1i}\Delta D_{1i} + v_i\Delta B_i = 0, \quad \Delta D_{1i} > 0, \quad \Delta B_i < 0. \tag{8.12}$$

In the next period the increase in indexed bonds gives rise to additional interest payments of $\tilde{i}\Delta D_{1i}$, while the decrease in (unindexed) short-term bonds reduces interest payments by $i\Delta B_i$. Since we are concerned with temporary changes in the structure of the government debt, we assume that in the next period the government decides to reduce the indexed bonds by the amount that it had increased them the previous period and increase the (unindexed) short-term bonds by the amount it had reduced them the previous period. (The analysis for the case where the return to the ex ante structure of the government debt is postponed follows along similar lines.)

This gives rise to a deficit (or surplus) in the government budget. To finance this deficit, we impose a lump sum tax on the middle aged and the aged. The exact pattern of the imposition of this tax makes no difference. All that is required is that the individuals know the preceding period what fraction of the tax burden they will bear:

$$\Delta T_{2i} = \alpha[(1 + i)v_{i+1}\Delta B_i + q_{1i+1}\Delta D_{1i} + \tilde{i}v_{i+1}\Delta D_{1i}], \tag{8.13}$$

$$\Delta T_{3i-1} = (1 - \alpha)[(1 + i)v_{i+1}\Delta B_i + q_{1i+1}\Delta D_{1i} + \tilde{i}v_{i+1}\Delta D_{1i}]. \tag{8.14}$$

To see that such a perturbation in public financial policy has no effects, we again assume that all prices remain unchanged. We then show that individuals' consumption opportunity sets are completely unaffected. Hence they will choose the same point in the consumption opportunity set as they chose in the initial equilibrium. We then show that, when this point in the consumption opportunity set is chosen, the demand for all securities—including those whose supply has changed—equals the supply. The change in the structure of the government debt has given rise to an exactly offsetting change in the demand for different financial instruments.

To see that the consumption opportunity set remains unchanged, we again use a single caret to denote values of variables in the initial situation, and double carets to denote values of variables in the new situation. Let

$$\hat{\hat{c}}_{it} = \hat{c}_{it}, \quad \hat{\hat{L}}_{it} = \hat{L}_{it}, \qquad \text{all } i, t, \tag{8.15a}$$

$$\hat{\hat{N}}_{ijt} = \hat{N}_{ijt}, \qquad \text{all } i, j, t, \tag{8.15b}$$

$$\hat{\hat{D}}_{ijt} = \hat{D}_{ijt}, \qquad \text{all } i, j, t \text{ except } j = 1 \text{ and } t = \hat{t}, \tag{8.15c}$$

$$\hat{\hat{B}}_{1t} = \hat{B}_{1\hat{t}} + \alpha \Delta B_{\hat{t}}, \tag{8.15d}$$

$$\hat{\hat{B}}_{2\hat{t}} = \hat{B}_{2\hat{t}} + (1 - \alpha) \Delta B_{\hat{t}},$$

$$\hat{\hat{D}}_{1\hat{t}} = \hat{D}_{1\hat{t}} + \alpha \Delta D_{\hat{t}},$$

$$\hat{\hat{D}}_{2\hat{t}} = \hat{D}_{2\hat{t}} + (1 - \alpha) \Delta D_{\hat{t}}.$$

To check that such a policy is feasible, first, observe that at time $\hat{t}$ the increased expenditures on indexed bonds less the decreased expenditures on (unindexed) short-term bonds adds up, for the young, to

$$\alpha[v_t \Delta B_t + q_{1t} \Delta D_t],$$

which, by (8.12) is identically zero. Similarly for the middle aged. Second, notice that with the perturbation in their portfolios "corrected" in the next period, the change in the wealth of the young in the second period of their life is

$$\alpha[(1 + i)v_{\hat{t}+1} \Delta B_{\hat{t}} + q_{1\hat{t}+1} \Delta D_{1\hat{t}} + \tilde{w}_{\hat{t}+1} \Delta D_{1\hat{t}}],$$

exactly enough to pay off the extra tax liabilities they will face (equation 8.14a) (similarly for the middle aged turned aged). Thus this change in portfolio leaves them in a position to pay their extra tax liabilities without affecting their consumption at all.

To complete the argument that the consumption opportunity sets are identical, we must again show that any point feasible with the new public financial policy was feasible under the original public financial policy. This follows by exactly parallel arguments. (Again, we need to point out that the two consumption opportunity sets will be equivalent if there are no binding nonnegativity constraints. Since it may be more difficult for individuals to issue indexed bonds or perpetuities than to issue short-term bonds, nonnegativity constraints may be more relevant here than in the previous case.)

Since the consumption opportunity sets are the same, if the individual chooses the careted values of variables in the original situation, he will choose the double-careted values in the new situation.

The total increase in the demand for indexed bonds at time $\hat{t}$ is

$$\alpha\Delta D_{1i} + (1 - \alpha)\Delta D_{1i} = \Delta D_{1i},$$

the increase in the supply of indexed bonds, while the total decrease in the demand for short-term (unindexed) bonds is

$$\alpha\Delta B_i + (1 - \alpha)\Delta B_i = \Delta B_i,$$

just equal to the decrease in the supply. Since the demand for all other securities (and for all commodities) remains unchanged, if in the initial situation all securities and goods markets cleared, they do in the new situation.

This result has an important implication. It means that changes in the number of indexed bonds have no consequences, either real or financial. Only if the issuance of indexed bonds opens up trading opportunities for individuals who are alive contemporaneously over two periods to exchange risks which they otherwise could not, can the provision of indexed bonds by the government have any real effects. It is obvious that a sufficient condition for the government provision of indexed bonds to have no real effects is that there be a complete set of securities at date t whose payoffs are contingent on the state at $t + 1$ (a condition far weaker than a complete set of Arrow-Debreu securities markets). An alternative sufficient condition is that the private market provide an indexed bond (or that there exists a linear combination of securities that provides a safe real return).

A third set of circumstances in which the public provision of indexed bonds does not matter, even when such bonds are not provided in the private market, are those in which, were there an exchange market for indexed bonds, there would be no trade in them. In such situations we say that an indexed bond market is redundant.[15] A sufficient condition for the redundancy of the indexed bond market is that individuals be risk neutral.[16]

It should be equally obvious that, in general, if for some inexplicable reason an indexed bond (or its equivalent) were not provided in the exchange market, and such a security is not redundant, then the government provision of this security will have real effects. Provided the government has sufficient flexibility in its imposition of lump sum taxes and subsidies, the provision of these indexed bonds will be a Pareto improvement.

The Third Irrelevance Theorem

An increase in the nominal interest rate on short-term (unindexed) government bonds financed by an increase in the supply of short-term bonds has financial but no real effects. The price level, (v) changes, and consequently the price of other securities relative to the short-term bond changes; but the price of these other securities relative to consumption goods remains unchanged.

Assume the government increases the interest rate on short-term bonds outstanding at date t from $\hat{\imath}_t$ to $\hat{\hat{\imath}}_t$. This generates a deficit the next period of $(\Delta i_t)B_t$, where

$$\Delta l_t = \hat{l}_t - i_t.$$

Now we assume that the real return on all securities remains unchanged, $q_{j\tau+1}(j = 1, 2)$, all τ is unchanged, v_t remains unchanged, and the real value of government debt at all subsequent dates is unchanged;

$$\hat{\hat{v}}_t \hat{\hat{B}}_t \equiv \hat{v}_t \hat{B}_\tau. \tag{8.16}$$

It is immediate from (8.4) that under these conditions the government's budget constraint is satisfied now if it was satisfied originally. Since, from the structure of the demand functions individuals' real demands for securities at all dates (e.g., $v_\tau B_{i\tau}$) are a function only of real returns, taxes, and wages (all of which remain unchanged), real demands are unchanged. Since by hypothesis real supplies are unchanged, if demand equalled supply initially, it still does. Note that for $\tilde{\rho}_\tau$ to remain unchanged, (from equation 8.2)

$$\frac{v_\tau + 1}{v_\tau}$$

must remain unchanged, for $\tau \geq t + 1$. This, together with our earlier result (8.16 and 8.17), implies that an increase in the interest rate at time t increases prices (decreases v) at all subsequent dates proportionately and increases the supply of bonds in proportion to the decrease in the price of short-term bonds (v).

It immediately follows that any sequence of changes in the interest rate paid on short-term bonds has no real effects.

Combinations of Policies

The three irrelevance propositions can be combined to consider a variety
of financial policies of the government which can be viewed as combinations of the three policies considered. Thus, if the government decides to
issue indexed bonds at time t, to be retired at time $t + 1$, then, provided
the appropriate lump sum taxes are imposed to offset any distributional
consequences, the policy has neither real nor financial (price) effects.[17]
Such a change can be decomposed into two steps. The government issues
short-term unindexed bonds, with the proceeds used to reduce lump sum
taxes on the young or middle aged. By the first irrelevance theorem such
a change has neither real nor financial consequences. Then the government
temporarily exchanges the increase in the short-term unindexed bonds
for short-term indexed bonds, again imposing taxes (the next period) on
the (then) middle aged and old to finance the deficit that will result. By
the second irrelevance theorem such a change has no real or financial
consequences.

As a second example, suppose that the government simultaneously
increases the supply of short-term bonds and increases the interest rate
it pays on these bonds (perhaps because it mistakenly believes that it
must in order to sell the increased supply of these bonds). Assume that
at the same time it increases the supply of bonds it announces that it will
shortly retire the additional bonds, in such a way as to have no intergenerational distributional effects. Then such a change can be thought of
as a combination of a temporary increase in the supply of short-term
bonds (which, by the first irrelevance theorem, has no effects) and an
increase in the interest rate (which, by the third irrelevance theorem, has
no real effects but does increase the rate of inflation).

An Alternative Interpretation

Note that, if individuals believe that the rate of inflation is going to be
higher as a result of the increase in the supply of short-term bonds, then
equilibrium can be restored (and their beliefs confirmed), provided the
interest rate the government pays rises in accord with their expectations.

To put it another way, though we have presented the analysis as if the
government sets the interest rate on government bonds, we could have
phrased the analysis in a slightly different way; rather than announcing
interest rates the government will pay at different dates in different contingencies, we could have announced the corresponding bond supplies, and

let the market determine the interest rates that are consistent with equilibrium. (This way of looking at the matter has a slightly greater sense of realism, since the interest rates on short-term bonds are determined in competitive auction markets, in response to government announcements concerning the supply of bonds.)

8.3 The Relevance of Public Financial Policy

In general, any financial policy other than those presented in the preceding section will have both real and financial effects. Public financial policy is not irrelevant. Since public financial policy matters, it is important to ask what are the relative merits of alternative financial policies. The objective of this and the next section is to show that financial policy is relevant and to provide some insights into the consequences of alternative policies.

To do this, we simplify the general model presented in the preceding section. We assume individuals live for only two periods (which eliminates the possibility of exchange securities), working only in the first.[18]

We illustrate our general proposition about the relevance of public financial policy by considering the kind of financial policy discussed in the *first irrelevance theorem*. The government increases its debt at one date, t_1, with the proceeds distributed as lump sum payments (either to the young or the old), and at some later date, t_2, reduces the debt. To do this, it again raises taxes. The dates t_1 and t_2 are sufficiently far apart that quite different generations are involved; there are intertemporal redistribution effects. (In intervening periods it increases the short-term bond supply to pay the additional interest costs.) The question is, Under what conditions will the change in debt policy have no real effects, for instance, on the rate of capital accumulation?[19]

There is one special case that may be helpful in developing our intuition as to why public financial policy is, in general, relevant. Assume that there is no risk, and bonds and capital are thus perfect substitutes. Clearly, they must yield the same return. This in turn implies that, if the change in debt policy is to have no effect, the price level in the new equilibrium must be the same as the price level in the old equilibrium at every date t. But this implies that the real supply of bonds must have increased in the period $t_1 < t < t_2$. But for those generations between t_1 and t_2, neither their taxes nor wages are changed, and thus their savings must remain unchanged at each date.[20] But if savings are unchanged, while real debt is increased, capital accumulation must be decreased. It is impossible for financial policy not to matter.

Similarly, if the real debt remained unchanged (so v_t changes inversely to B_t), at $t_1 - 1$ individuals would recognize that the return to holding bonds will be lower for the next period as a result of the increased debt.[21] But this would decrease their demand for bonds. Market equilibrium at $t_1 - 1$ would then require that bond prices change at that date. Yet, since the real bond supply at that date is altered, this would have real effects, for instance, on capital accumulation.

Exactly parallel arguments hold if there is uncertainty, so that debt and capital are not perfect substitutes. To see this most vividly, we restrict ourselves to policies that leave i_t unchanged as well as the mean real return to short-term bonds (so that the mean rate of inflation also remains unchanged).[22] The government announces that at some date $t + 1$ in the future it will alter the financial policy from what it had previously planned. It will increase the short-term debt in some state and decrease it in another. (In all other states and dates financial policy is unchanged.) Moreover the surplus (deficit) thus generated will be distributed to the young of the $t + 1$ generation. We show that, unless the marginal utility of income in the two states is identical (the individual is risk neutral), such a policy has real effects.

If we simplify our general model and assume that the individual has a separable utility function of the form

$$U_1(c_1, L) + U_2(c_2),$$

and for notational simplicity we assume the government only issues short-term bonds (there are no long-term or indexed bonds), then we can write the tth generation's first-order condition for the optimal investment portfolio:

$$EU_2'[(1 + \eta_t)K_t + (1 + \rho_t)B_t - T_{2t}](\rho_t - \eta_t) = 0 \qquad (8.18)$$

(where, it will be recalled, η_t is the real return on capital).

We shall consider two cases. In the first the price of bonds at $t + 1$ changes in the two states, so ρ_t changes. Then the individual's portfolio condition (8.18) will still be satisfied if and only if [23]

$$\Delta\{U_2'^a[c_2^a](\rho_t^a - \eta_t^a)\} + \Delta\{U_2'^b[c_2^b](\rho_t^b - \eta_t^b)\} = 0 \qquad (8.19)$$

(where the superscripts a and b denote the two states with altered prices). Recalling our hypothesis that the mean return is the same, this implies for a small change in ρ_t that[24]

$$B_t U_2''^a[\rho_t^a - \eta_t^a] + U_2'^a = B_t U_2''^b[\rho_t^b - \eta_t^b] + U_2'^b. \tag{8.20}$$

This will not, in general, be satisfied, except if $U'' = 0$, that is, the individual is risk neutral.

Assume, on the other hand, that the price of bonds at $t + 1$ does not change. The increase in the supply of bonds results in an increase in the demand for bonds by the young (because of the lump sum transfer payment made to the young with the proceeds of the bonds), but the increase in the demand for bonds will be less than the increase in supply, provided only that first period consumption and equities are normal. (That is, we require that a decrease in the lump sum taxes by $\Delta T_{1t+1} = -v\Delta B_{t+1}$ lead to an increase in the real demand for short-term bonds by an amount less than ΔT_{1t+1}, a natural assumption.)

Hence, except under the strong and unrealistic hypothesis of risk neutrality, a mean inflation preserving change in financial policy has real effects.

Financial Policy and Intergenerational Risk Sharing

In the preceding section we established that, except under the special conditions specified in theorems 1 through 3, public financial policy has important redistributive consequences, and whenever public financial policy has intergenerational redistributive consequences, public financial policy matters. The level of capital accumulation, for instance, will depend on public financial policy.

Different public financial policies will have different implications for how the risks faced by society are shared among different generations. The intergenerational redistributions to which variations in debt policy give rise can be used to provide a kind of insurance which the market cannot provide (since members of one generation cannot make contracts with members of another generation, except through the government). The intertemporal distribution of risk is presumably one of the objectives of a well-designed social security program; as we have asserted before, it is impossible to separate out debt policy from social security. All public financial policies must be examined together.

Thus, if the present generation is lucky, and experiences, say, a high wage or a high return on capital, it can share this "luck" with other generations. In return, generations which have particularly bad luck (say, a low wage), can be partially compensated by an increase in social security payments to the elder individuals in that generation. (It should be clear that this insurance argument involves no altruism, and thus is distinctly different from the considerations which motivate intergenerational transfers of income based on children's welfare entering parents' utility functions.)

In this section we shall show how different financial policies give rise to different stochastic processes for prices (and the other relevant variables in the economy), and how, as a result, different financial policies affect the extent to which intertemporal risks are shared among different generations.

We shall consider three polar policies: the first and simplest keeps the real value of debt vB, fixed; the second keeps the price level, v, fixed and has the debt supply change by whatever amount is necessary to ensure that; and the third keeps the debt fixed (and corresponds to the Friedman rule for an economy of no growth).

There is a widespread belief that the last rule is the best rule. Variations in the debt (money supply) lead to variability in the level of economic activity and make it difficult for firms to distinguish variations in demand arising from variations in, say, tastes (real changes in the economy) from variations in demand arising from monetary disturbances. In the simple model developed in this chapter, these beliefs are shown to be incorrect. A constant supply of government debt (or money) forces individuals to absorb a considerable amount of risk which could be shared better (among different generations) by alternative financial policies. Thus, if the next generation has a high wage, this leads to a high demand for assets in general, including financial assets. As a result the value of government bonds (relative to goods) increases. Conversely, if the next generation has a low wage, the demand for financial assets is reduced, and the price of bonds (relative to consumption goods) is reduced. Some of the consequences of variations in the $t + 1$ generation's wages are effectively borne by the members of the t generation. This, we will see, is also true of the other financial policies we consider. The issue is thus not whether one policy or another eliminates risk, rather which of the simple policies being considered is most effective in sharing the risks among different generations. We shall show that for the model investigated here, the policy of a constant real debt is preferable to the other two policies.

Constant Real Money Supply This is the easiest policy to analyze. To generate a constant real money supply, the government imposes a lump sum tax on the young, used to retire the government debt, whenever the wage exceeds $\bar{w}$, the mean wage, and conversely when the wage is less than $\bar{w}$.[25] For simplicity, we set $i_t = 0$ for all t. Thus the government sets

$$-\Delta B = \frac{w_t - \bar{w}}{v_t}. \tag{8.21}$$

As a result the net income (after paying lump sum taxes) of each generation is constant, at $\bar{w}$. Notice that this implies that the debt follows a random walk. Since $Bv = k$,

$$\frac{\Delta B}{B_t} = -\frac{w_t - \bar{w}}{v_t B_t} = -\frac{w_t - \bar{w}}{k}.$$

Moreover

$$\frac{v_{t+1}}{v_t} = \frac{v_{t+1} B_t}{v_t B_t} = \frac{v_{t+1} B_{t+1} + v_{t+1} \Delta B}{v_t B_t} = 1 - \frac{w_{t+1} - \bar{w}}{k}.$$

The probability distribution of the return to debt is the same every period, and hence, since income (after tax) is the same, the real demand for government debt is indeed fixed.

One might be tempted in this situation to say that the change in debt (government deficits) causes the change in prices, but this would be misleading. The exogenous event in the model is the level of wages; government policy adjusts to the change in wages in such a way that prices move proportionately to debt. Nevertheless, prices would change, as we have emphasized, even in the absence of a change in the debt supply.

The variability of consumption may be easily calculated. Since real income is fixed the first period, there is no variability in c_1. A given fraction of income, s, will be saved, and of this, a particular fraction α will be invested in capital and the remainder in government bonds.[26] Thus

$$c_{2t} = s\bar{w}[\alpha(1 + \eta_t) + (1 - \alpha)(1 + \rho_t)]$$

$$= s\bar{w}\left[\alpha(1 + \eta_t) + (1 - \alpha)\frac{v_{t+1}}{v_t}\right]$$

$$= s\bar{w}\left[\alpha(1 + \eta_t) + (1 - \alpha)\left(1 - \frac{w_{t+1} - \bar{w}}{k}\right)\right].$$

Note that consumption in the second period of the tth generation individual depends not on his own wages but on those working when he is old. The higher their wages, the greater his consumption. We can now calculate

$$\operatorname{var} c_{2t} = s^2 \bar{w}^2 \left[\alpha^2 \operatorname{var} \eta + (1-\alpha)^2 \frac{\operatorname{var} w}{k^2} \right] \tag{8.23}$$

$$= s^2 \bar{w}^2 \alpha^2 \operatorname{var} \eta + \operatorname{var} w$$

(since $Bv = (1-\alpha)s\bar{w} = k$). There is an alternative way of calculating the variance of c_{2t}. Since c_{1t} and K are fixed, the variance of c_{2t} is simply the variance of national income.

$$\operatorname{var} c_{2t} = \operatorname{var} w + K^2 \operatorname{var} \eta. \tag{8.24}$$

Constant Price Level Assume the government adjusts the deficit every period in such a way as to keep the price level constant. It uses the proceeds (finances the deficit) with a lump sum distribution to (tax upon) the aged. The individual saves a fraction s of his first-period income, and of this he invests a fraction α in capital and the remaining in debt.[27] We allow s to be a function of w, $s(w)$. Without loss of generality, let $p = v = 1$ for all t. For the demand for government bonds to equal the supply, we require that

$$s(\tilde{w}_t)(1-\alpha)\tilde{w}_t = \tilde{B}_t. \tag{8.25}$$

It immediately follows from the government's budget constraint that, if the changes in debt are offset by changes in payments to the aged,

$$-T_{2t} = B_{t+1} - B_t - i_t B_t$$

$$= (1-\alpha)\left[s(w_{t+1})w_{t+1} - s(w_t)w_t\right] - i_t B_t, \tag{8.26}$$

and hence

$$c_{1t} = (1 - s_t)\tilde{w}_t, \tag{8.27a}$$

$$c_{2t} = s_t \alpha \tilde{w}_t (1 + \eta_t) + (1-\alpha)s_{t+1} w_{t+1}$$

$$= K_t(1 + \eta_t) + w_{t+1} s_{t+1}(1 - \alpha) \tag{8.27b}$$

(from the national income identities). Now there is variability in the individual's income in both the first and second periods of his life, and his consumption the second period depends both on his wage and the wage the next period. For small variances, we can calculate the variance of c_{1t} and c_{2t} in a straightforward manner:

$$\text{var } c_{1t} = \text{var} (1 - s(w))w \approx (1 - s - s'\bar{w})^2 \text{ var } w, \qquad (8.28a)$$

$$\text{var } c_{2t} \approx (1 - \alpha)^2 (s + s'\bar{w})^2 \text{ var } w + \bar{K}^2 \text{ var } \eta + (1 + \bar{\eta})^2 \text{ var } K$$

$$= (s + s'\bar{w})^2 (\alpha^2 (1 + \bar{\eta})^2 + (1 - \alpha)^2) \text{ var } w + (\alpha sw)^2 \text{ var } \eta. \quad (8.28b)$$

Suppose the government chooses i (the rate of return on government debt) in such a way as to make the average value of K the same as it is in the situation with a constant real debt. Since $\bar{K}$ is the same, and average income of the young is the same in this regime as in the previous, $s\alpha$ must be the same. We postulate that α is the same, implying that the average values of c_{1t} and c_{2t} are the same. But while the variance of c_1 is higher with the constant price rule, the variance of c_2 may be higher or lower with the constant real debt rule. (Compare equations 8.23 and 8.28.)

Consider first the limiting case with $s = 1$. Then straightforward calculations show that the variance of c_{2t} is lower with the constant real debt policy, provided only that

$$1 + \bar{\eta} > \frac{\sqrt{1 - (1 - \alpha)^2}}{\alpha}.$$

If government debt constitutes 15 percent of individuals' savings, this implies that the policy of a constant real debt is unambiguously preferable, provided the mean real return on capital exceeds 16 percent.

More general comparisons require a specification of the utility function. Assume we have a utility function of the form

$$U = U(c_1) + \frac{U(c_2)}{1 + \delta}.$$

Then the loss in welfare from the consumption variability can be approximated by assuming $U''(c_1)/U'(c_1) \approx U''(c_2)/U'(c_2)$ (which will be true if $\bar{\eta} \approx \delta$ and var η is small):

$$\frac{a}{2} \left[\text{var } c_{1t} + \frac{1}{1 + \delta} \text{var } c_{2t} \right] \approx \frac{a}{2} \left[\text{var } w \left\{ (1 - s - s'\bar{w})^2 \right. \right.$$

$$+ \frac{(s + s'\bar{w})^2 ((1 - \alpha)^2 + \alpha^2 (1 + \bar{\eta})^2)}{1 + \delta} \right\}$$

$$\left. + \frac{\bar{K}^2 \text{ var } \eta}{1 + \delta} \right],$$

where $a = -U''/U'$, the Arrow-Pratt measure of absolute risk aversion. This should be contrasted with the loss of welfare in the preceding case. The loss of welfare is greater with a policy of a constant price level than with a policy of a constant real debt, under even weaker conditions than those derived for $s = 1$.[28]

Constant Nominal Money Supply   Though purportedly the "simplest" policy, it is not the simplest policy to analyze. The probability distribution of the return to bonds will not be the same at each date, and hence, even if the utility functions have constant elasticity, the demand for bonds will not be a constant proportion of savings. To see this most simply, assume there are two equally like states with wages w_1 and w_2. Assume then the probability distribution of the return to capital is the same in both. Let $s = 1$ (individuals get no enjoyment out of consumption the first period of their lives). Equilibrium is characterized by a value of v^a, K^a, v^b, and K^b, satisfying

$$EU'[K^a(1 + \eta) + v^a(1 + i)B][(1 + i) - (1 + \eta)] + EU'(K^a(1 + \eta)$$

$$+ v^b(1 + i)B)\left[(1 + i)\frac{v^b}{v^a} - (1 + \eta)\right] = 0,$$

$$EU'[K^b(1 + \eta) + v^a(1 + i)B]\left[\frac{v^a}{v^b}(1 + i) - (1 + \eta)\right] + EU'[K^b(1 + \eta)$$

$$+ v^b(1 + i)B][(1 + i) - (1 + \eta)] = 0, \tag{8.29}$$

$$K^a + v^a B = w^a,$$

$$K^b + v^b B = w^b.$$

In the good state the demand for bonds is high because savings are high. However, if the economy moves to a poor state next period, there will be a fall in the value of bonds. Hence, although individuals normally invest more in bonds in the good state, as a proportion of savings, they invest less. Thus K_t is more variable than w_t; c takes on four values, depending on the "state": if c^{ij} is consumption in state j, assuming that the process state was i, then

$$c^{aa} = (w^a - v^a B)(1 + \eta) + (1 + i)Bv^a,$$

$$c^{ab} = (w^a - v^a B)(1 + \eta) + (1 + i)v^b B, \tag{8.30}$$

$$c^{bb} = (w^b - v^b B)(1 + \eta) + (1 + i)Bv^b,$$

$$c^{ba} = (w^b - v^b B)(1 + \eta) + (1 + i)v^a B.$$

Since

$$\operatorname{var} c = (1 + \bar{\eta})^2 [\operatorname{var} w + B^2 \operatorname{var} v - 2B \operatorname{cov}(w, \mathrm{v})]$$

$$+ (1 + i)^2 B^2 \operatorname{var} v + \bar{K}^2 \operatorname{var}(1 + \eta)$$

$$+ 2(1 + i)B(1 + \bar{\eta})[\operatorname{cov}(w, v) - B \operatorname{var} v]$$

$$= (1 + \bar{\eta})^2 \operatorname{var} w + (i - \bar{\eta})^2 B^2 \operatorname{var} v$$

$$+ \bar{K}^2 \operatorname{var} \eta + 2(1 + \bar{\eta})B(i - \bar{\eta}) \operatorname{cov}(w, v),$$

and since $\operatorname{cov}(w, v) > 0$, $\operatorname{var} v > 0$, it is clear that the policy of a constant debt, B, induces a greater variance in consumption than does the policy of constant real money supply, provided $i \geq \bar{\eta}$.

In this section, we have compared three alternative, simple financial policies. None of these policies are, however, optimal. In Stiglitz (1982) I show how the optimal intertemporal distribution of welfare can in fact be implemented through the appropriate set of public financial policies. I also show that, to implement the optimal financial policy, one needs only to have sufficient flexibility in the structure of social security payments and a single public financial instrument; additional bonds (including indexed government securities) make no difference. However, if there are restrictions on the extent to which social security payments (taxes) may vary from year to year, then additional financial instruments are necessary in order to implement the optimal intertemporal distribution of welfare.[29]

8.4 Monetary and Debt Policy

Thus far I have assumed that there is a single interest-bearing financial asset, which presumably can be used for transactions purposes as well as a store of value. Recent developments in monetary institutions (interest-bearing checking accounts) make this assumption not as unreasonable as it might have seemed a decade or so ago. How important is it that until recently demand deposits did not earn interest? Will the widespread use of CMA accounts have a fundamental effect on the structure of the economy? Is it plausible that what remains of noninterest-bearing financial assets—cash and currency used to pay those taxi cabs who still do not take Visa cards or checks—will be the central determinant of economic behavior that monetarists have claimed in the past?

These questions cannot be settled by theoretical arguments. Theoretical analyses can establish whether the presence of a noninterest-bearing financial asset used to facilitate transactions has qualitative effects; they cannot, however, assess the quantitative importance of any effects noted.

If there were only one financial asset, noninterest-bearing money, our analysis would be completely unaffected. We established earlier that corresponding to any equilibrium, with a particular interest rate at each date, and a particular level of prices at each date, there were an infinity of equivalent (in a real sense) equilibria, which differed in the interest rate they paid and in the price level. Among the set of equilibria is one with the nominal interest rate equal to zero.

However, if there are two financial assets, one noninterest bearing while the other yields a return, it is obvious that, if the former asset is to be held by anyone, it must have some property that makes it more attractive (at the same yield) than the interest-bearing asset. It is conventionally postulated that the noninterest-bearing financial asset can be more readily used for transactions purposes. We write the demand function for money as

$$M_t^d = M(p_t, p_{t+1}, \ldots; w_t, w_{t+1}, \ldots; i_t, i_{t+1}, \ldots;$$

$$\eta_t, \eta_{t+1}, \ldots; I_t, I_{t+1}, \ldots; T_t, T_{t+1}, \ldots). \tag{8.31}$$

The demand for money is a function of prices at date t and at all subsequent dates; the yield on interest-bearing assets at date t and at all subsequent dates; the yield on equities at date t and at all subsequent dates; taxes and transfers at date t and at all subsequent dates; and the levels of real income at date I_t, at date t, and at all subsequent dates.

Two properties of this demand function should be noted. First, the level of income appears explicitly to remind us of the transactions motive for holding money, but it should be emphasized that this is probably not an adequate reduced form representation. For instance, changes in tax or debt policy may induce changes in the sets of transactions that occur. These generate changes in the demand for money which are quite distinct from the change that they might induce in real income. Similarly, changes in risk will not only have a direct effect on portfolio composition but also may have an effect on the transactions demand for money. Since our main objective is to argue that the introduction of a second noninterest-bearing asset implies that government financial policy will not be neutral, the oversimplified version of the demand for money which we will employ will suffice for our present purposes.

Second, we postulate that the demand for money is homogeneous of degree one in all prices. Increasing prices at all dates leaves unchanged the return on money and is simply a change in units. This is of course well known. But it should also be noted that the demand for money is not homogeneous of degree one in the current price. Changing the current price does increase the transactions demand for money, but, if subsequent prices remain unchanged, the real return on money is reduced. Thus the "asset" demand for money will, in general, decrease. There may of course be some special specifications of utility functions and transactions technology for which the return on money does not affect its demand, but for which the only determinant of the demand for money (besides the level of income) is the opportunity cost associated with holding the noninterest-bearing asset (money) rather than the interest-bearing financial asset (i_t).

Under further restrictions we might be able to derive a demand function for money in which the entire impact of future events (taxes, interest rates, yields on equities) on the demand for money could be summarized in, say, a wealth variable. We could then write down a demand function for money

$$\frac{M_t^d}{p_t} = M^d(I_t, i_t; W_t), \tag{8.32}$$

which is of the kind conventionally seen in undergraduate texts. It is important to emphasize, however, that a large number of not clearly articulated assumptions had to be introduced into the analysis to reduce the general demand function for money down to the simple form postulated in equation (8.32).

Consider now the impact of an open market operation which entails the government exchanging a bond at t_1 for money, which it will subsequently undo at a later date t_2. We focus our attention on an economy with infinitely lived individuals, to avoid the intertemporal distribution issues raised earlier. We wish to show that such a change will, in general, have real effects on the economy.

Assume that it has no real impact, that is, real incomes and real returns are unchanged. This necessitates that the price level at time t increase proportionately (so real holdings of money remain unchanged; otherwise, real expenditures on transactions would change). The price level needs to change proportionately not only at t_1 but at all dates between

t_1 and t_2. This in turn implies that, if the real return to holding bonds is to be unchanged at t_1 and t_2, i_{t_1} and i_{t_2} must change to offset the change in the rate of change in prices. But a change in i_{t_1} and i_{t_2} will, in general, generate a change in the demand for money. Only if demand for money is invarant to the financial opportunity cost of holding money (the demand for money is interest inelastic) will it be neutral. This is of course what monetarists have assumed all along. The question is, Is there any reasonable specification of utility functions and transactions technoloies that generates this? One can of course write down models with the individual needing a fixed amount of money to engage in each transaction. But such models really do little more than assume what is to be proved. The recent innovations in financial institutions (CMA accounts) suggest that significant changes in the opportunity cost of holding money will indeed result in significant changes in the amount of noninterest-bearing financial assets individuals are willing to hold for transactions purposes.[30]

We have ignored so far the possibility that there is another financial asset, produced in the private sector, that can be a substitute, for transactions purposes, for the noninterest-bearing government financial asset. For simplicity, let us assume it is a perfect substitute. For both of these assets to be held, it must yield a return of zero. The return to the suppliers of this asset is thus i_t. Assume they have a horizontal supply schedule, at i^*. Then, for an interior solution, the market equilibrium rate of interest must initially be at i^*, and must remain so after the perturbation. Assume the change in the private supply of money just offsets the change in the public supply of money so that the price level remains unchanged. But now the supply of bonds is reduced. In our earlier analysis, for any change in the supply of bonds, there was a corresponding change in the demand for bonds. This will be the case here only if money and bonds are perfect substitutes, for asset purposes, in individuals' portfolios—if individuals are indifferent about whether they receive the return on their assets directly or through savings in transactions costs. In any case there will be a real effect on the economy through the increase in resources spent on transactions cost (the private money supply). Only if the private money supply is costless to produce (so i^* is zero) will there be no impact, but then the equilibrium return on bonds will be zero.[31]

We can similarly show that an anticipated money rain (a lump sum distribution of money to individuals in the economy) will, in general, have real effects. For again, assume it does not. Then at t_1, the date of the money rain, prices must rise above what they would have been otherwise; hence the return to money has been altered. For the real return to bonds to remain unchanged, the rate of interest, i, must change. But unless the demand for money is completely interest inelastic, this will change the demand for (real) money at time t_1.[32]

If the private money supply acts as a perfect substitute for the public money supply, then it is possible that the price of money remains unchanged, and since the supply of bonds has not been altered, the bond market is still in equilibrium. Again, under these extreme assumptions, the only real affect of a money rain is on the expenditures of resources on the production of private money. Ignoring this effect, it should be recalled that in this instance the change in the money supply has had neither an inflationary effect nor a real effect.

The skeptical reader may well have misgivings about the quantitative significance of all of this. Is it not a good enough approximation to ignore the costs associated with producing money?

In macroeconomics (as in any other branch of economics) we make simplifications, idealizations, and approximations. It is not always obvious what are the most appropriate simplifications. Macroeconomics is replete with models focused on qualitative effects of phenomena whose quantitative importance is at best dubious. There are, obviously, transactions costs, and in certain situations they are significant.[33] There have been times, such as in some recent years in Italy, when the shortage of small denomination coins caused minor inconvenience. It may have had some real effects on the economy: the consumption of small candies (given in change) may have risen. Here, as elsewhere, resourceful firms and individuals should be—and are—able to find effective substitutes or to adapt their behavior to make a given money supply "go further." It seems implausible that individuals, who are presumed to be so flexible and rational in some dimensions, should be as rigid and irrational with respect to their demand for money as some naive monetarist theories seem to suggest. The adaptations of behavior may indeed not be instantaneous, and the institutional changes that facilitate the changes in behavior may take even longer. But if the discrepancy between the return to holding money and to bonds becomes significant enough, the economy will adapt, to reduce the holdings of money or to enable "money" to become interest bearing.[34]

I am thus dubious whether the real effects of monetary policy that I have analyzed in this section are of any quantitative significance. This is not to say, however, that monetary policy may not have an important effect on the economy (particularly in the short run, in the presence of short-run individual and institutional rigidities); but the major mechanism by which this may work arises not from a transactions or asset demand for money but rather from the central role of the banking system in supplying credit and the linkages between monetary policy and credit availability.[35]

8.5 Fixed Prices and Public Financial Policy

The models considered here have assumed that prices are completely flexible and that as a consequence there is always full employment. Each generation faces risks—there is variability in the productivity of labor and of capital—but there is no risk of unemployment. Much of the earlier literature on public financial policy focused on the effect of monetary and debt policy on aggregate demand and the level of employment. We can use a slight modification of the model we developed earlier to show how debt policy can be used to affect the variability in employment.

We assume that the price level is fixed; it is well known that price rigidities can give rise to unemployment equilibria. For simplicity, we specialize our model, assuming a logarithmic utility function. This implies that the savings rate is fixed at s^*.[36] Moreover, since with fixed prices financial assets are perfectly safe, the proportion of savings that the individual invests in government debt $(1 - \alpha)$ is a function only of the nominal rate of interest: $\alpha^*(i)$ is the solution to

$$E\frac{\eta - i}{\alpha(1 + \eta) + (1 - \alpha)(1 + i)} = 0. \tag{8.33}$$

We assume that the interest payments are financed by a lump-sum tax on the young. Hence, if the debt supply is fixed at $\bar{B}$, the demand for debt is given by

$$s^*(1 - \alpha))[w_t N_t - i\bar{B}] = \bar{B} \tag{8.34}$$

when N_t is the level of employment. If we assume that in equilibrium the demand for bonds must be equal to the supply (but equilibrium is consistent with the demand for labor not equaling supply), then the level of employment is given by

$$N_t = \frac{\bar{B}[1 + is^*(1 - \alpha)]}{s^*(1 - \alpha)w_t}. \tag{8.35}$$

In this highly simplified model, if the government fails to vary either the debt supply or the interest rate, then variations in the level of productivity of labor, w_t, lead to exactly offsetting variations in the level of employment.

Variations in B can be used to stabilize the level of employment. Consider the extreme case where $i = 0$. If the government varies its debt according to the difference equation

$$B_t = s^*(1 - \alpha^*)[w_t \hat{N} + B_t - B_{t-1}], \tag{8.36}$$

where $\hat{N}$ is full employment, then there will be full employment. The demand for bonds will then be

$$B_t - s^*(1 - \alpha^*)(w_t \hat{N} + B_t - B_{t-1}), \tag{8.37}$$

which will just equal the supply. This implies that

$$B_t = \frac{s(1 - \alpha)(w_t - \bar{w})N_t - (B_{t-1} - B^*)}{1 - s(1 - \alpha)}, \tag{8.38}$$

where

$$\bar{w} = Ew_t$$

and

$$B^* = s(1 - \alpha)\bar{w},$$

the equilibrium level of debt in the absence of wage variability. This is of course exactly the difference equation we analyzed earlier in our discussion of the financial policy that would sustain a constant price level (with the variations in government revenue being used to finance lump sum distributions to the young). When wages are high, the government expands the debt (an accommodating public financial policy). There is, however, a force returning the debt to its long-run equilibrium level B^*.[37]

8.6 Concluding Remarks

We have attempted to analyze the effect of government indexed bonds in the much broader context of alternative public financial policies.

Whether a change in public financial policy has any effect depends simply on whether the change has an effect on the intertemporal distribution of income. We have shown that there are some important classes of public financial policies which, when appropriately implemented, have no impact on the intergenerational distribution of welfare. Some of these policies, such as an increase in the supply of government debt or a change in the maturity structure of the government debt, have neither real nor financial effects. Others, such as an increase in the interest paid on government bonds, have financial but no real effects. Any change in public financial policy that has an effect on the intergenerational distribution of welfare—and virtually all changes in public financial policy other than those spelled out in our three basic irrelevance propositions will have an effect on the intergenerational distribution of welfare—will have important effects on the economy, for instance, on the pattern of capital accumulation.

Thus the question of the effect of government indexed bonds comes down to whether a switch from, say, unindexed to indexed government securities would have any redistributional effect. We have shown how, under certain circumstances, an increase in the supply of indexed bonds will make no difference, neither real nor financial, in the economy.

Once it is recognized that government public financial policy can have important effects on the intergenerational distribution of welfare and the sharing of risks among generations, it becomes important to ascertain the consequences of alternative policies. We have shown that, while none of the simple rules commonly discussed—keeping the debt fixed, keeping the price level fixed, or keeping the real value of the government debt fixed—is optimal, the policy of keeping the real value of the government debt fixed appears preferable to the other two policies.

Most of our analysis has been conducted under the assumption that prices are perfectly flexible and that there is a single interest-bearing short-term security, which can be used for transactions purposes. We have shown, however, that, when these assumptions are removed, the case for the relevance of public financial policy is even stronger. For instance, only in the limiting cases, where the demand for money is perfectly interest inelastic, can an open market operation have no real effects if there is no inside money. In contrast, if there is inside money, an open market operation can have no real effects only if the costs of the government supplying money are identical to the costs of the private sector producing money; but then it has no effect on the price level either.

If prices are rigid, then financial policy can serve the additional function of reducing the variability in employment, a role that was traditionally ascribed to public financial policy but has become lost in the context of the currently fashionable neoclassical models.

Two important questions still need to be addressed. First, we need to formulate a model synthesizing the two roles of public financial policy, of intergenerational risk sharing and income and employment stabilization. Second, we have assume throughout that only lump sum taxes are imposed. In that case the timing of taxes affects the intergenerational distribution of welfare, but nothing more. But when taxes are distortionary, the timing of taxes also affects the total dead weight loss imposed by the tax system. Thus, whenever the changes in financial policy we analyzed in our basic irrelevance propositions entail a change in the lump sum taxes imposed at different times, then, in general, they will have real effects. The implication of this for the optimal debt-tax structure is an important issue I hope to address on another occasion.

Notes

Research support from the National Science Foundation is gratefully acknowledged. I have benefited greatly from conversations with John Taylor, Alan Blinder, J. M. Grandmont, Stan Fischer, R. Dornbusch, Frank Hahn, Dilip Abreu, and Lennie Nakamura.

1. Our result thus extends the well-known Barro-Ricardo results to an explicitly stochastic environment. In the absence of uncertainty, all assets are perfect substitutes, and the question of the effect of public financial policy on the relative prices of different assets does not arise.

2. The original papers by Tobin (1965) and Johnson (1966) gave rise to a large literature; see, for instance, Shell, Sidrauski, and Stiglitz (1967). Although much of this literature employed ad hoc savings assumptions, the work of Sidrauski (1967) and the life cycle models of Diamond (1965) and Cass and Yaari (1967) showed how the results could be extended to models with explicit intertemporal utility-maximizing individuals.

3. Obviously, if the government has an informational advantage over the private sector, it could base its public financial policy on that information; public financial policy would thus convey information from the government to the private sector. But this is a peculiarly inefficient way of conveying information, and there is little evidence that the monetary authorities are privy to information that is not publicly available.

4. We assume throughout that the only taxes imposed are lump sum taxes; if, more realistically, we had assumed a distortionary income or wage tax, then there would be further supply effects.

5. Similar remarks can be made about the role of the government in redistribution in general. If, behind the veil of ignorance, before individuals knew the endowments with

which they were to be born they could sell enforceable insurance policies to each other, with the payoffs a function of what endowments they were presented with, or of observable variables which were a function of those endowments, then it might be argued that there would be no need for the government to take a role in redistribution. But such insurance markets do not exist, and hence the role of the government in redistribution. (This way of looking at matters has, of course, its problems: should we assume that, in the original state, the individual knows what preferences he is to be endowed with? How can we reasonably describe his behavior prior to being endowed with preferences?)

6. It would be easy to extend the model to allow the wage to depend, for instance, on the capital stock.

7. The assumption that taxes are nondistortionary is important; it implies, in particular, that what individuals are concerned about is only the present discounted value of their tax liabilities, not the timing of those liabilities. With distortionary taxes, say, on wage income, the time of the imposition of the tax is critical.

8. At the time the individual buys a short-term bond, he knows i_t, but he does not know v_{t+1}. We follow the convention of denoting a random variable with a tilde, but will drop the tilde when the context makes clear the fact that the variable in question is stochastic.

9. If we denote the state of nature at time t by θ_t, then, while the interest on short-term (unindexed) bonds is a function of θ_t, and the real return a function of θ_t and θ_{t+1}, for indexed bonds, the real return is only a function of θ_t.

10. The notation is chosen to make it clear how the analysis can be extended to additional government securities.

11. In a life cycle model with individuals living only two periods and all individuals within a generation being identical, there is no scope for exchange securities.

12. If utility functions are not intertemporally separable, then past consumption and labor decisions also are relevant.

13. In addition, we require, of course, that the demand for labor equals the supply.

14. In this analysis we have assumed that there are no borrowing limitations. More generally, since the real position of the individual is unaffected, one might argue that if in the new situation the individual is called upon to borrow more (to replicate the same pattern of consumption), he should be able to do so at the same terms as he borrowed previously. But this argument is not quite correct if there is any possibility of bankruptcy (in any of the relevant points in the consumption opportunity set). Full equivalence would require, for instance, that an individual could sell a claim on a (contingent) future lump sum payment. This is presently not possible. More generally, the considerations which are relevant here are analogous to those which arise in the case of the corporate irrelevance theorems (Stiglitz 1969, 1974).

15. Newbery and Stiglitz (1982) introduce the concept of redundant markets in their analysis of the constrained Pareto optimality of markets with rational expectations but an incomplete set of risk markets.

16. That is, individuals' utility functions are of the form $c_1 + c_2 + c_3$. If the indirect utility function corresponding to $u(c_1, c_2, c_3)$ can be written as $v(I, g_1, g_2)$, where g_1 is the intertemporal price between the first and second period, g_2 is the intertemporal price between the first and third period, and I is (the present discounted value of) lifetime income, income risk neutrality implies that $v = I\psi(g_1, g_2)$. In general, this is not sufficient to ensure the redundancy of indexed bond markets. (See Newbery and Stiglitz 1982, Stiglitz 1982.)

17. We can also make a direct argument for the irrelevance of this financial policy, as we noted earlier.

18. Thus the model we analyze here is a slight extension of that presented in Atkinson and Stiglitz (1980).

19. There is a *prima facie* case that such a change will have a real effect on the intergenerational distribution of welfare, except if there are exactly offsetting changes in private bequests, as Barro has argued. For several theoretical objections to Barro's conclusions, see Stiglitz (1982).

20. Except to the slight extent necessary to finance the interest on the additional bonds.

21. This corresponds (for our model) to the quantity theory of money: the price level is inversely proportional to the supply of outside short-term bonds (money).

22. It should be clear that our analysis extends to more general changes in public financial policy.

23. We assume the two states are equally likely. The modification for the more general case is straightforward.

24. We are making use of the assumption that the mean rate of inflation remains unaltered.

25. For simplicity, throughout this section we assume that labor supply is fixed.

26. Since net income, after taxes, is constant, and since the rate of return to bonds and equities is constant, savings rates and portfolio allocations do not change over time.

27. In contrast to the previous case, where we proved α and s constant, here we simply assume that α is constant and s a function of w.

28. We require
$$(1 - s - s'\bar{w})^2(1 + \delta) + (s + s'\bar{w})^2((1 - \alpha)^2 + \alpha^2(1 + \bar{\eta})^2) \geq 1,$$
that is,
$$(s + s'\bar{w})^2(1 + \delta) + \delta + (s + s'\bar{w})^2[1 - 2\alpha + \alpha^2 + \alpha^2(1 + 2\eta + \eta^2)] + (s + s'\bar{w}) - 2\delta(s + s'w) \geq 0.$$

While in the previous analysis of the constant real debt policy the result that the savings rate was a constant held for all utility functions, here we have simply assumed a savings function, without deriving it. The difficulty in deriving the optimal savings behavior arises from the random lump sum tax imposed on the individual in the second period of his life. Still, it is easy to show that if the distribution of w_{t+1} is either independent of w, or a function only of w_t, that s_t and α_t will simply be functions of w_t. It is possible to analyze some special cases.

1. If individuals obtain utility only from consumption in the second period, $s = 1$, α will then be a constant, provided the individual has constant relative risk aversion and the distribution of w_{t+1}/w_t is independent of t. (We thus need to assume that w_t is a random walk, though elsewhere we have assumed that the w_t are independently and identically distributed random variables.) Alternatively, if there is constant absolute risk aversion, then the demand for risky assets is a constant, so that instead of (8.25) we obtain
$$w_t - \bar{K} = B_t.$$
In this limiting case, the variance associated with the constant price rule and that associated with the constant real debt rule are identical.

2. If there is no capital—a pure consumption-loans model—then $\alpha = 0$. Then if individuals have a quadratic utility function, consumption will be a linear function of w_t, so that instead of (8.25) we obtain
$$\beta + bw_t = B_t$$
and
$$c_{1t} = (1 - b)w_t - \beta,$$
$$c_{2t} = bw_{t+1} + \beta.$$

We have limited our discussions to the case where the proceeds of the increase in the government debt are used to finance a lump sum subsidy to the aged. It is possible to show that with the alternative financial policy, of distributing the proceeds of the increased government debt to the young, it is not possible to maintain (forever) a constant price level, under plausible utility functions.

Assume first that all individuals have constant absolute risk aversion. Then the demand for capital is fixed, independent of income. Thus the variations in the debt must be large enough to accommodate the variations in income, that is, if $v_t = 1$, $i = 0$, $s = 1$

$$B_t = w_t + B_t - B_{t-1} - \bar{K}, \text{ or}$$
$$B_{t-1} = w_t - \bar{K}.$$

But since there is no way, at $t - 1$ to know w_t, this policy is not implementable: there is no policy of the form considered here that can maintain a constant price level. The reason for this is simple. Increases in the supply of debt generate an increase in demand on a dollar-for-dollar basis.

Assume, in contrast, that all individuals have constant relative risk aversion. Then

$$B_t = \{w_t + B_t - B_{t-1}\}(1 - \alpha)$$
$$= \frac{(1 - \alpha)}{\alpha}(w_t - B_{t-1})$$

and

$$K_t = \frac{\alpha}{1 - \alpha}B_t,$$

so

$$\Delta K_t = \frac{\alpha}{1 - \alpha}\Delta B_t.$$

Define $B_t^* = B_t - (1 - \alpha)\bar{w}$. Then

$$B_t^* = \frac{(1 - \alpha)(w_t - \bar{w}) - B_{t-1}^*}{\alpha}.$$

This process can best be studied by taking a continuous time approximation, which generates a process of the familiar Ornstein-Uhlenbeck form. In steady state, ΔB_t^* has zero mean and variance $\frac{1}{2}[\sigma_w^2(1 - \alpha)^2/\alpha^2]$. This ignores of course the nonnegativity constraints on K and on c. Taking these into account, it is apparent that a policy of keeping price constant is not, in the stipulated circumstances, feasible. Even before the policy breaks down, however, the variance in income to which it gives rise is likely to be greater than for the policy of constant real money supply.

29. The characterization of the optimal intergenerational scheme for risk sharing is not an easy matter. In one case we can borrow results from the theory of optimal buffer stocks to provide a fairly complete characterization. Assume that the return to capital is not random, that individuals have an inelastic labor supply, and that they only consume the second period of their lives. Assume, moreover, that w_t is i.i.d. Then the stock of resources available for consumption or investment at date t is $S_t = w_t + K_{t-1}(1 + \bar{\eta})$, where $K_t = S_t - c_t$. The optimal intertemporal consumption plan entails a rule that specifies consumption as a function of S_t. We seek that rule which maximizes $E \sum U(c_t)(1/1 + \delta)^t$ such that $K_t \geq 0$. It is known that the optimal savings rule is highly nonlinear. (See Newbery and Stiglitz 1981.) Note that none of the financial rules we have considered is of the required form.

30. Some of these changes may not be completely reversible: even if the opportunity cost declines, individuals will have discovered that they need less noninterest-bearing money than they had previously thought.

31. Neutrality can be restored if costs of the government supplying money are identical to the costs of the private sector producing money. If we assume, in contrast, that the private money supply remains unchanged, but the price level changes to keep the real money supply fixed, then we are back to our earlier analysis with no private money supply.

32. A similar observation has been made by Fischer (1979) where he details the effects of a change in the money supply for a particular parameterization of the economy.

33. Transactions costs, for instance, are often cited as explaining why the private sector (the nonbanking institutions) cannot provide a set of exchange media which are close substitutes to money. But the empirical evidence on the transactions costs associated with CMA accounts and other mutual funds suggests that this is not a plausible explanation. (See also Bryant and Wallace 1980.)

34. I made this prediction a decade ago, before the advent of NOW and CMA accounts; recent events have borne this theory out. Thus, although money and bonds are clearly not perfect substitutes (otherwise, no one would be willing to hold noninterest-bearing currency), the approximation I have employed seems at least as plausible as the alternative polar assumption that individuals' demand for money is invariant to the difference between the return to money and the return to bonds.

35. A preliminary version of this "credit" theory of monetary policy, based on considerations of imperfect information in the credit market, is set forth in Blinder and Stiglitz (1983). (See also Stiglitz and Weiss 1981, 1982.)

36. In the absence of variability in taxes the second period.

37. Note that by lowering i, it may not be possible to lower the demand for financial assets enough to restore full employment if individuals believe that there is a significant probability that $\eta < 0$ (they will make a loss on their investment in capital) (This is analogous to Keynes's liquidity trap.)

Recall in our earlier discussion of the difference equation (8.38) that the relevant nonnegativity constraints will eventually be violated. This suggests that to maintain full employment may require combining interest rate policies with policies of debt expansion.

References

Atkinson, A. B., and J. E. Stiglitz. *Lectures in Public Economics*. McGraw-Hill, New York, 1980.

Barro, R. "Are Government Bonds Net Wealth?" *Journal of Political Economy* (December 1974): 1095–1118.

Blinder, A., and J. E. Stiglitz. "Money, Credit Constraints, and Economic Activity." *American Economic Review* (May 1983): 297–302.

Bryant, J., and N. Wallace. A Suggestion for Further Simplifying the Theory of Money. Mimeographed. December 1980.

Cass, D., and M. E. Yaari. "Individual Saving, Aggregate Capital Accumulation, and Efficient Growth." In K. Shell, ed., *Essays on the Theory of Optimal Economic Growth*. The MIT Press, Cambridge, Mass., 1967.

Diamond, P. A. "National Debt in a Neoclassical Growth Model." *American Economic Review* 55 (December 1965): 1125–1150.

Fischer, S. "Anticipations and the Nonneutrality of Money." *Journal of Political Economy* (April 1979): 225–352.

Johnson, H. "The Neo-Classical One-Sector Growth Model: A Geometrical Exposition and Extension to a Monetary Economy." *Economica* 33 (August 1966): 265–287.

Neary, J. P., and J. E. Stiglitz. "Towards a Reconstruction of Keynesian Economics: Expectations and Constrained Equilibria." *Quarterly Journal of Economics*, forthcoming.

Newbery, D., and J. E. Stiglitz. "The Choice of Techniques and the Optimality of Market Equilibrium with Rational Expectations." *Journal of Political Economy* 90 (April 1982): 223–246.

Newbery, D., and J. E. Stiglitz. *The Theory of Commodity Price Stabilization.* Oxford University Press, 1981.

Shell, K., M. Sidrauski, and J. E. Stiglitz. "Capital Gains, Income, and Saving." *Review of Economic Studies* 36 (1969): 15–26.

Sidrauski, M. "Rational Choice and Patterns of Growth in a Monetary Economy." *American Economic Review* 58 (May 1967): 534–544.

Stiglitz, J. E. "A Re-examination of the Modigliani-Miller Theorem." *American Economic Review* (December 1969): 784–793.

Stiglitz, J. E. "On the Irrelevance of Corporate Financial Theory." *American Economic Review* (December 1974): 853–866.

Stiglitz, J. E. "On the Almost Neutrality of Inflation." In M. J. Flanders and A. Razin, eds., *Development in an Inflationary World.* Academic Press, New York, 1981.

Stiglitz, J. E. "On the Relevance or Irrelevance of Public Financial Policy." Mimeographed. 1982.

Stiglitz, J. E., and A. Weiss. "Credit Rationing in Markets with Imperfect Information," *American Economic Review* 71 (June 1981): 393–410.

Stiglitz, J. E., and A. Weiss. "Incentive Effects of Terminations: Applications to Credit and Labor Markets." *American Economic Review*, forthcoming.

Taylor, J. B. "Aggregate Dynamics and Staggered Contracts." *Journal of Political Economy* 88 (February 1980): 1–23.

Tobin, T. "Money and Economic Growth." *Econometrica* 33 (October 1965): 671–684.

Wallace, N. "A Modigliani-Miller Theorem for Open Market Operations." *American Economic Review* (June 1981): 267–274.

9 Welfare Aspects of Government Issue of Indexed Bonds

Stanley Fischer

Economists' discussions of the welfare aspects of government issue of indexed bonds are of less practical than intellectual interest. Governments in inflationary difficulties issue indexed bonds, and those that can avoid it, do not. It is nonetheless worth discussing whether economic analysis provides any rationale for government issue of either indexed or nominal bonds, or in general for government financial intermediation.[1]

Recent analyses of government financial intermediation suggest government issue of indexed bonds is at best irrelevant (Levhari and Liviatan 1976, Wallace, 1981) and may well be harmful (Peled, 1978). In this chapter I make two main arguments. First, there is a role for government financial intermediation to provide intergenerational risk sharing that private markets cannot—but this does not directly suggest government issue of price level indexed bonds. Second, the question of why governments do not issue indexed debt is the wrong one to ask: the more appropriate question is why governments issue nominal debt. In this context, I argue that the presumption of stability of the price level, combined with frictions that are associated with indexed debt, led to nominal debt as the standard form of government liability. As the presumption of price-level stability disappears, indexed debt is more likely to be and should be issued.

Because the chapter is directed toward government issue of indexed bonds, I do not discuss private nonissue of such bonds. That question was taken up in an earlier paper (Fischer, 1977). It would be a mistake to build too convincing a theory explaining private nonissue of indexed bonds since price-level indexed mortgages have now been introduced in the United States.[2]

9.1 Review

It is well known that many of the most distinguished of past economists, including Jevons (1875), Marshall (1925), Keynes (1927), and Fisher (1934) advocated government issue of index bonds. Jevons, Marshall, and Fisher spent more time discussing the virtues of creation of a reliable price index than those of issue of index bonds; they seem to have taken it for granted that once a reliable index was available, it would be used in both private and government transactions—unless the price level was stabilized through appropriate monetary policy.[3]

Subsequently other economists have argued for government issue of indexed bonds; few economists have shared the opposition of practical men and central bankers, though skepticism has recently become more common.

The arguments in favor are

1. Indexed bonds would provide the economy with a safe real asset it otherwise does not have, and which is needed for optimal risk sharing.

2. Monetary policy could operate more accurately if indexed bonds were introduced (Tobin 1971). Indexed bonds are seen as a closer substitute for physical capital than are other government liabilities. Monetary policy should aim to control q, the market price of installed capital; such control is more accurately achieved through changes in the quantity of indexed rather than nominal bonds.

3. Government issue of an indexed bond would (a) encourage saving and reduce inflationary pressure, and (b) encourage portfolio holders to shift away from money toward bonds, implying that deficits can be financed at a lower real rate than is possible when nominal bonds are issued (Bach and Musgrave 1941, in the context of wartime financing).

4. "... by imposing upon the government a contingent liability dependent on its failure to check inflation, the flotation of stable purchasing power bonds would exert a wholesome pressure upon Congress to adopt aggressive anti-inflationary policies" (Bach and Musgrave 1941).

5. By creating inflation, the government has systematically cheated purchasers of nominal bonds, particularly small savers. This is not desirable and would not happen if indexed bonds were made available to the public (Friedman 1974, Tobin 1971).

In this chapter I concentrate on arguments (1), (4) and (5), briefly commenting on the remaining points.

The recent skepticism about government issue of an indexed bond is based largely on a number of neutrality theorems for government finance and financial intermediation:

$N1$ (Barro 1974). Debt financing of deficits has no different effects than tax financing.

$N2$ (Levhari-Liviatan 1976). Government intermediation in indexed bonds has no real effects.

$N3$ (Wallace 1981). Open market operations between money and bonds have no real effects.

$N4$ (Peled 1978). Any efficient equilibrium attainable with indexed bonds can also be attained without them; if indexed bonds make a difference, they make things worse.

An associated meta-theorem is

$N5$. If indexed bonds were a good idea, the private sector would already have invented them.

Theorems $N1$ and $N2$ turn on the internalization of the government's budget constraint by the private sector. Thus, for instance, when the government issues index bonds in exchange for nominal bonds, it is merely changing the pattern of its contingent liabilities. These future liabilities will one way or another be paid off by the private sector, which therefore is not fundamentally in any different position than it was before. This argument assumes both types of debt were in existence before the government undertook its intermediating activities.

Theorems $N3$ and $N4$ depend on the interpretation of money as purely a store of value, the role it typically plays in overlapping generations models. When money acts only as store of value, there is little or nothing that bonds can do that money cannot, particularly when the stock of money can be adjusted to affect its real rate of return.

Assumptions other than those underlying $N1$ through $N4$ have been pursued. In particular, Helpman and Sadka (1979) derive rules for the optimal financing of the government's budget, where the choices are among taxes, bonds, and money. The choice between taxes and bonds is meaningful because it is assumed individuals maximize over a finite horizon and no lump-sum taxes are available. The choice between bonds and money is determinate because money is viewed as providing productive services that bonds do not. This notion is represented by putting money in the utility function. The Helpman-Sadka framework produces results that differ from $N1$, $N3$, and $N4$, though they do not explicitly discuss $N3$ and $N4$. Because their framework is one of certainty, they do not consider government financial intermediation.

In this chapter I first examine the question of the government's potential role as financial intermediary (argument 1) and show that the government can indeed make a positive difference by issuing securities and using its taxing power to produce appropriate patterns of returns. The difference arises from the government's ability to use taxes to enforce intergenerational risk sharing.

I then briefly discuss using an optimal tax framework, like that of Helpman-Sadka, to analyze optimal forms of government debt issue when there is uncertainty. It is in this context that the Modigliani-Miller type neutrality theorems are relevant: the framework suggests that the government will optimally run deficits or surpluses on occasion, but it does not provide any guidance to the type of debt that should be issued or bought.

To understand government issue of nominal versus indexed bonds, it is necessary to move to arguments like point (4). This chapter therefore discusses government issue of nominal and indexed debt in a context where dynamic inconsistency of government policy is possible. I conclude with a brief discussion of the remaining arguments reviewed above for government issue of indexed bonds.

9.2 Government Financial Intermediation for Intergenerational Risk Sharing

In this section I outline a simple model in which government financial intermediation makes intergenerational risk sharing possible.[4] The assumptions are those of the Samuelson (1958) overlapping generations model. To begin with, assume there is only one type of person N born each period. Each person lives two periods and has a utility function defined over consumption in the two periods. Random nonstorable endowments are received in each period.

The consumer maximizes expected utility,

$$E[U(C_1^t, C_2^{t+1})|I_t], \tag{9.1}$$

and receives endowments,

$$W_1(t) \geq 0, \quad W_2(t+1) \geq 0,$$

in the two periods of life. The distributions of the endowments are identical over time and not serially correlated, with

$$W_1(t) + W_2(t) \equiv W. \tag{9.2}$$

C_1^t is the first-period consumption of an individual born in period t; C_2^{t+1} is second-period consumption of that individual. I_t is information available in period t.

In the simplest environment all individuals within each generation are identical in tastes and endowment. There is no reason for trade among members of any one generation and nothing to trade with members of other generations. Each generation therefore consumes its endowments. For convenience, assume the utility function is separable and logarithmic, in which case

$$E[U(\ )] = \ln W_1^t + \beta E \ln W_2^{t+1} \tag{9.3}$$

is the utility of the representative individual.

Assume further that

$$\overline{W}_1 = E(W_1(t)) > \frac{W}{1 \mid \beta}, \quad \overline{W}_2 = E(W_2(t)) < \frac{\beta W}{1 \mid \beta}$$

but that with finite probability $W_1(t)$ takes on values

$$W_1(t) < \frac{W}{1 + \beta}.$$

Intragenerational Trade

Trade within a generation can take place if there are differences in tastes or endowments. For instance, if endowments are identical and the function $U(\ )$ in (1) is the same for all individuals, but rates of time preference differ, the more patient will lend to the less patient. Markets in all second period contingent commodities may exist, and each individual can be thought of as maximizing subject to a wealth constraint given by the market value of the endowment. If tastes are homothetic, and given the same $U(\ )$ functions and distributions of endowments, a single second-period composite asset can be created. But in general that will not be possible.

If the utility functions differ in risk aversion, the less risk averse will be willing at a price to destabilize their consumptions relative to the pattern of endowments in the second period, enabling the more risk averse to have a more stable pattern of consumption.

Will this intragenerational trading produce a safe real asset? A complete market equilibrium will call for a full menu of contingent commodities, with agents either buying or selling the contingent commodities in different proportions, depending on their tastes and endowments. If there is a full set of contingent commodities, then a safe real asset can be created, which will pay off one unit of consumption in each second-period state of nature.

Whether such an asset will actually be created when there is a full set of markets depends on costs of transactions. Any type of model in which there is some type of fixed cost for dealing in an asset will lead to repackaging of contingent commodities in forms that fit the excess demand patterns of consumers for second-period contingent commodities. For instance, a safe real asset is most likely to be produced if there is some notion of essential consumption, represented for example by the Stone-Geary utility function $U(C - \bar{C})$, $\bar{C} > 0$, where $U'(0)$ is infinite, and if many people have no second-period endowment at all.

If there is not a full set of contingent commodities, then invention of a safe bond changes the consumption possibilities of economic agents. Assuming that transaction costs are ultimately the reason for nonexistence of particular markets, invention of a safe real asset would again be more likely under the circumstances outlined at the end of the previous paragraph.

The role of government in a model of this type is limited, perhaps to ensuring that contracts are carried out. There might be some difficulties in this regard if, for instance, the second-period endowments are wages, and if human capital is not tradable. In that event the government ideally would want to intervene to reproduce the private sector equilibrium.[5]

Given the constraint of no intergenerational trade, the equilibrium attained in models of this type with a full set of contingent markets can be described as constrained Pareto efficient. But there may be possibilities for intergenerational trade, along grounds made familiar by Samuelson (1958).

Optimal Intergenerational Allocations

The possibilities for intergenerational trade depend on the pattern of endowments. For instance, if the desired pattern of trade always involves transfers from young to old, the introduction of money or government bonds will bring about a better equilibrium than is possible with purely intergenerational trade. The allocation is better in that every generation is made better off, so long as it is assumed that the horizon is infinite.

The assumed pattern of endowments here highlights the possibilities for intergenerational risk smoothing. Specifically, the assumption in (9.2) is that the total endowment each period is nonrandom and constant. It is only the division of the endowment between the generations that is uncertain.

Clearly, allocations are possible in which every generation has a non-random pattern of consumption over its lifetime. But direct intergenerational trade is not possible. The introduction of money will not itself solve the problem since sometimes the optimal arrangements will call for transfers from old to young, which cannot be achieved with money held by the old.

Return now to the case where tastes of all agents are identical. An optimal allocation in some sense is one where consumption in each period for each individual is certain and the allocation between young and old reflects time preference. For instance, if the utility functions are logarithmic as in (9.3), consider the solution to the following problem:

$$\max_{\{y\}} V(W, y) = \ln(W - y) + \beta \ln y, \tag{9.5}$$

which implies

$$y = \frac{\beta W}{1 + \beta} = C_2^t,$$

$$W - y = \frac{W}{1 + \beta} = C_1^t. \tag{9.6}$$

This allocation is optimal in the following sense: suppose individuals are told before knowing their first-period endowments what the probability distribution of the endowments is, and what the technical possibilities for trade are. Then they will choose this allocation.[6] This optimality criterion may be objected to on the grounds that it seems to imply prior (to their existence) agreement by economic agents on the rules of resource allocation.

The issues here are deep and not simply resolved. But the criterion is appealing because it is clear that some criterion of this type is in practice used in establishing property rights, in the sense that it is assumed the rights will be binding on agents as yet unborn and that notions of fairness are used in discussing the establishment of the rules.[7] There is certainly no presumption in most societies that anyone is free to opt out of paying taxes if benefits fall short of contributions, except in the limited sense that emigration is typically permitted.

There is need for some criterion of optimality since the allocation implied by (9.6) is not ex post a Pareto improvement for all generations. Some generation might have been lucky and had high drawings in both periods of their lives. They would lose under the allocation (9.6).

Institutional Arrangements: Can the Private Sector Do It?

How is this allocation to be achieved? There are several possibilities, all involving the use of taxes.

1. The simplest in the present model is for the government to take command of all resources and allocate them between the generations as implied by (9.6).

2. The endowments of the old could be confiscated in each period and given to the young. At the same time the first old generation could be given fiat money, as in the original consumption loans model. The old sell money to the young in exchange for goods; the allocation is the same as (9.6).

3. The government could act as a financial intermediary, each period buying the rights to the second-period endowment of the currently young and paying out to the currently old the amount that generates the resource allocation (9.6). It may also be necessary to use taxes and transfers to effect the appropriate allocation.

The first two institutional arrangements require direct government intervention. The question pursued now is whether the third set of arrangements requires any government action, or whether alternatively a private financial intermediary could produce the allocation (9.6), without a government role. The question is whether use of taxation is necessary to achieve (9.6) when financial intermediation is available. If not, a private financial intermediary could be set up that would generate zero cash flow each period, balancing its payments with its receipts. If taxes and transfers are needed, government action is necessary.

To study the operation of the financial intermediary, it is convenient to assume there is a discrete number of states of nature, indexed by j, $j = 1, \ldots, J$. Let $p_{2j}(t)$ be the price in terms of period t goods for delivery of one unit of the consumption good in state of nature j in period $(t + 1)$.

The probability of state j occurring is q_j, and q_j is constant over time. Taxes in amount $T_j(t)$ are levied on the old in state of nature j in period t, and transferred to the young. The taxes may be negative.

The currently young maximize

$$E[U(\ )] = \ln C_{1i}(t) + \beta \sum_{j=1}^{J} q_j \ln C_{2j}(t+1)$$

subject to

$$C_{1i}(t) + \sum_{j=1}^{J} p_{2j}(t) C_{2j}(t+1) = W_{1i}(t) + \sum_{j=1}^{J} p_{2j}(t)(W_{2j}(t+1) - T_j(t+1))$$

$$+ T_i(t)$$

$$\equiv Y(t).$$

In the new notation, $C_{2j}(t+1)$ is consumption by the old in state of nature j in period $(t+1)$, $W_{2j}(t+1)$ is the endowment received by the old in state of nature j in period $(t+1)$; $W_{1i}(t)$ is the endowment of the young in state of nature i in period t. It is known that state of nature i has occurred.

The optimization results in

$$C_{1i}(t) = \frac{1}{1+\beta} Y(t) \tag{9.8}$$

$$C_{2j}(t+1) = \frac{\beta}{1+\beta} \frac{q_j}{p_{2j}(t)} Y(t), \quad j = 1, \ldots, J. \tag{9.9}$$

To attain the optimal allocation (9.6), it is necessary that

$$C_{1i}(t) = \frac{W}{1+\beta} \tag{9.10}$$

$$C_{2j}(t-1) \equiv \frac{\beta}{1+\beta} W, \quad j = 1, \ldots, J. \tag{9.11}$$

From (9.8) and (9.10),

$$Y(t) = W. \tag{9.12}$$

From (9.12), (9.9), and (9.11),

$$p_{2j}(t) = q_j. \tag{9.13}$$

Table 9.1
Resource flows to the financial intermediary

Inflows		Outflows	
Endowments of the old	$W_2(t)$	$\overline{W}_2$	Purchase of endowment of current young
Purchases of index bonds by current young	$B(t)$	$B(t-1)$	Payments to holders of index bonds (currently old)
		$T(t)$	Net transfers to the young

Thus actuarially fair prices should be charged for contingent commodities.

Using (9.13), we return to (9.12) to obtain

$$T_i(t) + W_{1i}(\quad) + \sum_{j=1}^{J} q_j(W_{2j}(t+1) - T_j(t+1)) = W,$$

or

$$T_i(t) + W_{1i}(t) = \overline{W}_1 + \sum_{j=1}^{J} q_j T_j(t+1). \tag{9.14}$$

On the right-hand side of (9.14), we have a term which is the expected value of second-period taxation of the old. Assuming taxes are only state and not time dependent,

$$T_i + W_{1i} = \overline{W}_1 + \overline{T} \tag{9.14$'$}$$

where $\overline{T}$ is the expected value of second-period taxation.

From (9.14)$'$ it is clear that the optimal allocation can be achieved for more than one value of $\overline{T}$. It is natural to set $\overline{T}$ to zero, in which case

$$T_i = \overline{W}_1 - W_{1i}, \quad i = 1, \ldots, J. \tag{9.14$''$}$$

Thus the financial intermediation scheme cannot operate without use of taxes and transfers, though it can operate with expected taxes equal to zero.

Given the result that contingent commodity prices are, in the optimal allocation, actuarially fair, we can describe the operations of the financial intermediary quite simply. Its resource flows are shown in table 9.1. Each period it buys the second-period endowments of the current young at their expected value, as prescribed by (9.13). It also pays out claims owned by the current old. These can be thought of as indexed bonds, paying the same amount in each state of nature. Resource inflows come from the endowments of the current old, which were purchased last period, and from sales of index bonds to the current young. Any excess of inflow over outflow is handled by making a distribution to the young; alternatively, any excess outflow is paid for by taxing the young.

It is worth noting that the financial intermediation solves two allocational difficulties. First, the intermediation makes intergenerational risk-sharing possible. Second, the government makes it possible for each generation to choose the optimal time profile of consumption. The first function can be performed without the second being satisfied. For instance, suppose that both generations alive at the same time can contract before their endowments are revealed. They will in general want to trade in contingent commodities. But such trading will still leave further gains from intergenerational trade, in that, given the pattern of endowments described by (9.4), each generation would likely want the opportunity of saving in the first period.

Dynamics of the Financial Intermediary

The financial intermediation scheme can be instituted in a period when the division of resources between the generations is about average, and in this case will make the first period old better off and raise the ex ante expected utility of all subsequent generations. For example, again using the logarithmic utility function (9.3), consider the introduction of the scheme in period t, with purchase by the government of the rights to $W_2(t + 1)$, for which it pays $\overline{W}_2$. It sells to the young an amount of bonds $B(t)$ implied by

$$\max_{\{B(t)\}} \ln (W_1(t) + \overline{W}_2 - B(t)) + \beta \ln B(t), \tag{9.15}$$

or

$$B(t) = \frac{\beta}{1 + \beta}(W_1(t) + \overline{W}_2). \tag{9.16}$$

The goverment's net resource flow in period t is

$$B(t) - \overline{W}_2 = \frac{1}{1 + \beta}[\beta W_1(t) - \overline{W}_2]. \tag{9.17}$$

If $W_1(t)$ is equal to $\overline{W}_1$ or close to that level $\Big[$ see assumption (9.4) that $\overline{W}_1 > \dfrac{\beta}{1+\beta} W \Big]$, the scheme generates a first-period surplus that can be given to the old.

The dynamics of first-period consumption are given by

$$C_1^{t+j} = \frac{W}{1+\beta} + \frac{(-\beta)^j}{1+\beta}(W_1(t) - \overline{W}_1). \tag{9.18}$$

This converges to (9.6). Provided $W_1(t)$ is close to $\overline{W}_1$, the scheme increases the ex ante expected utility of all generations. However, if the scheme were started when the first generation had very high $W_1(t)$, there would be a large demand for bonds. The next generation would accordingly have low first-period consumption and could therefore be made worse off, in an expected utility sense, by the introduction of the scheme.

Choosing among the Schemes

At the present level of abstraction there is nothing to choose between these schemes. Additional elements would have to be included in the model to make the choice determinate. If there are differences in tastes, and if the government cannot discriminate between economic agents, then the direct allocation method (1) is less likely to be optimal. The difficulty is that the total amount allocated to the young generation may be wrong. There will subsequently be trading within that generation, but there is no mechanism for them to trade with other generations. Neither of mechanisms (2) nor (3) suffers from this particular difficulty.

Choice between (2) and (3) requires more explicit modeling of the effects of taxation of second-period endowments (in 2) as compared with purchase of the endowment (as in 3). If the endowments are lump sum, as so far assumed, there is again no basis for choice. However, we might assume that the endowments represent, for example, labor income and that labor supply responds to wages. In that case the imposition of taxes under scheme (2) in general distorts the labor supply decision. But there is similarly a severe moral hazard problem under scheme (3) where individuals have sold their labor income forward. In principle a contract could be drawn up that would specify the amounts to be worked in each state of nature; with such an agreement the optimal allocation could be attained. But if the government cannot discriminate between workers, it is difficult to see how such optimal agreements could ever be negotiated.

This is to say that it is very unlikely that there is a way of attaining the optimal allocations. There is no way the government can bring about that allocation without either buying claims on future endowments (presumably human capital) or taxing. If it is not possible for the government in effect to deal in human capital, it will have to use taxation along with security issues to improve the allocation of resources. It will in general be able to improve the allocation of resources by engaging in intergenerational transactions, but because it does not have lump-sum taxes, it cannot achieve a first best allocation.[8] And because it cannot achieve the first best solution, it will not generally be optimal to eliminate uncertainty entirely.

Aggregate Uncertainty

To this point it has been assumed that the aggregate endowment is certain, although its distribution between the generations is not. Suppose now that $W(t)$, the aggregate endowment, is uncertain. It will still be true, unless the endowments are perfectly positively correlated, that there will be risk-sharing grounds for government financial intermediation.

There are again J states of nature, $j = 1, \ldots, J$. The optimality criterion for the logarithmic utility function now becomes

$$\max_{\{C_{1i}(t),\, C_{2k}(t+1)\}} \sum_{i=1}^{J} q_i \ln C_{1i}(t) + \beta \sum_{k=1}^{J} q_k \ln C_{2k}(t+1), \qquad (9.19)$$

subject to $C_{1i}(t) + C_{2i}(t) = W_i(t)$, $i - 1, \ldots, J$, for all t. The optimal allocation specifies the consumption levels for both generations in each state of nature. It is

$$C_{1i}(t) = C_{1i} = \frac{W_i}{1+\beta}, \qquad (9.20)$$

$$C_{2i}(t) = C_{2i} = \frac{\beta W_i}{1+\beta}.$$

Here W_i is the aggregate endowment in state of nature i.

This allocation can once again be brought about through the three schemes, including government financial intermediation in scheme (3). Prices and transfers are chosen to replicate the allocation (9.20). These prices are no longer equal to the probabilities of the states of nature but in addition reflect aggregate endowment in the state of nature. The financial intermediary will no longer buy second-period endowments for an amount equal to their expected value. Nor is it natural any longer to think of the financial intermediary dealing in indexed bonds, since the amount consumed in each second-period state of nature will depend on the state and no longer be state independent.

Of course, if the intermediary chooses to provide a full menu of contingent commodities, it is possible to buy an indexed bond in the sense of a financial asset that provides a payoff that is constant. But with the postulated patterns of endowments and utility functions, there is no one who will want to consume identical amounts in each state of nature.

If the financial intermediary wants to reduce the number of assets in which it deals, the natural index to use is the aggregate amount of goods available in each state, since consumption for each individual will be proportional to the aggregate endowment in each state. This is a result of the assumption of identical homothetic tastes.

9.3 Government Financial Intermediation and Indexed Bonds

The preceding analysis establishes that there may be a role for government financial intermediation that private markets cannot provide. It demonstrates that meta-theorem $N5$ does not establish the optimality of the status quo in all situations.

But the role of government as financial intermediary has to be related to the source of the private sector's inability to provide the appropriate bundle of assets. If the government's advantage derives from its claims on future labor income, then it is likely optimal for the government to sell claims on labor income in different states. Claims on the income of capital are already tradable. The institution of social security does provide some, though nontradable, claims on future labor income.

The improvement that can be expected from financial intermediation of the type described in the previous section depends on the correlation of returns on human capital with returns on other assets. Those returns are in fact highly correlated. Further the wages earned by different generations of labor alive at the same time are also strongly correlated. No great reduction of risk for the individual should therefore be expected from optimal risk-sharing arrangements provided by the government based on its ability to tax future labor income.

The case for government financial intermediation outlined here implicitly uses, as its definition of an indexed bond, a bond that pays off the same amount of goods in each state of nature. But since there is no money and no price level, the bonds are not indexed in the conventional sense that the amount of money paid out to bondholders is related to the behavior of the price level. To discuss the issue of indexed bonds in this sense, the model has to include money and prices. I now discuss a framework that seems ideal for analyzing government financial policy in such a context.

9.4 Optimal Government Financing and Index Bonds

Consider a model in which individuals maximize over two-period lifetimes, supplying labor services, using money, and able also to save by the accumulation of capital. The government has only distorting taxes at its disposal. Potentially, any asset could serve as medium of exchange. But it is technically difficult to pay interest on securities that change hands in the day-to-day process of exchange, and for that reason there is a separate noninterest-bearing asset, money, that serves as medium of exchange. Technical innovations in the process of exchange occur randomly. This last assumption is an important one, for it means that there are specific risks associated with the return to money and that money therefore will not necessarily serve in such a model to produce exactly the same pattern of returns as real assets.

Consumers maximize an expected utility function of the form:

$$E\left\{V\left[C_1^t, C_2^{t+1}, L^t, f\left(\frac{M_{t+1}}{P_{t+1}}\varepsilon_t\right)\right]\right\}, \tag{9.21}$$

where $f(\ )$ represents the services provided by the holding of money. L is the amount of labor supplied. Random variable ε_t is a technological factor representing the ability of money to perform its utility or labor-saving services; uncertainty about future values of ε generates uncertainty about future price levels as of any given values of the remaining variables in the economy. Inclusion of real balances in the utility function is a method of ensuring a demand for money even if interest is earned on other assets.

First, return to the optimal intergenerational risk sharing with aggregate certainty model of section 9.2, omitting government and labor supply from (9.21). Suppose there is a given constant money stock. The constant money stock does not in this context generate efficient intergenerational risk sharing, since uncertainty about the rate of return on money does not provide the certain one-for-one intertemporal trade-off that society faces between consumption of the generations.

This price level uncertainty provdes a role for government in the model of section 9.2, either as issuer of an indexed bond or to conduct monetary policy. Monetary policy will consist of transfers to the old that produce price-level certainty. With money as a safe asset, there is no need for indexed bonds, provided appropriate resource transfers are made between the generations. If monetary policy cannot operate rapidly enough to stabilize the price level, money will be an unsafe asset, and there will be room for indexed bonds. Indeed the government might want to lend in nominal terms to the private sector, enabling it to hedge the risks of price-level changes. At the same time the government would continue to issue the safe or indexed bond.

Analysis of optimal government policy in such a model requires full specification of the optimal tax problem. A model of this type under certainty has already been analyzed by Helpman and Sadka (1979) who show, under the assumption of no lump-sum taxation, that the government optimally will sometimes want to use deficit financing. When uncertainty is introduced, we should think of the model in terms of contingent commodities. The optimal state-contingent taxing scheme for given patterns of government spending will involve purchases or sales of contingent commodities.

Borrowing implies merely that the government collects resources today that will be paid for by delivery of commodities in future contingencies— which commodities will be provided through taxation, money issue, or future borrowing. The positions that the government takes in various markets for contingent commodities can be viewed as determining the optimal financing of the debt. In this sense, the type of debt issued by the government matters: if it takes another position, the real equilibrium is changed.

Neutrality of Government Financial Operations

Once government positions in each market for contingent commodities have been optimally determined, the government can engage in financial intermediation by taking, at the equilibrium prices of contingent commodities, positions of zero net worth across contingent markets. For instance, it can buy contracts for future delivery of wheat and sell contracts for future delivery of corn. If the profits or losses are merely to be handed back to the private sector in a neutral way, then these further financial transactions have no real effects. For the government to return the proceeds in a neutral way, it holds constant optimally determined planned spending, taxes, and transfers within each state of nature, aside from those arising from its financial intermediation activities. Thus it disposes of its wheat by selling the wheat to the market and distributing the profits of losses—it is doing nothing except churning the market. Such financial intermediation cannot in a complete contingent market setup do any good.

What is the relationship between the public finance framework of optimal debt determination outlined above and the five neutrality theorems, $N1$ through $N5$? $N1$ does not apply because individuals maximize over only two periods and therefore cannot engage in intergenerational risk sharing. To the extent that the horizon is lengthened or effectively made infinite, more intergenerational risk sharing should be expected from within the private sector. The case for government issue of special types of debt would then depend on the absence of markets for human capital and the inability of individuals from different families to arrange smoothing that is possible through pooling of the risks of within-generation wage incomes.

There is a sense in which neutrality theorem $N2$ holds. Namely, there is under reasonable assumptions a determinate optimal pattern of government spending, taxation, and money issue in each state of nature. This optimal pattern implies net supplies of contingent commodities. It is possible to superimpose on this pattern a variety of government financial operations that have no real effects, provided the underlying real activities of the government are unaltered. But it is precisely that underlying pattern of real activities that implies the optimal pattern of government financing.

Neutrality theorem $N3$ does not hold when it is optimal to pay interest on debt and when it is technically impossible to do so on money, as shown by Helpman and Sadka. Theorem $N4$ depends on the availability of lump-sum taxes. $N5$ was discussed extensively in section 9.2.

Government Issue of Indexed Debt

In the foregoing framework optimal government policy implies a particular pattern of net supplies and demands of contingent commodities by the government. The type of securities—that is, packages of contingent commodities—issued by the government will depend, as in section 9.2, on the advantages the government has over the private sector in issuing valued securities and on the small frictions associated with the packaging of assets. For instance, if many investors have very high risk aversion and no future endowments, they would essentially want to buy only indexed bonds. Rather than require them to mix their own indexed bonds, or leaving the job for private financial institutions, it could be cheaper for the government to do so.

The framework is not, however, totally compelling, except as a way of organizing thought, for its fails to explain why governments have traditionally been assumed to have an obligation to issue safe debt. Nor does it handle the question of which markets in contingent commodities are in fact available at any time. Without knowing why markets are missing—and many are missing—we cannot in some ultimate sense pronounce on the desirability of alternative forms of government deficit finance.

9.5 Government Debt Issue: An Alternative Approach

The general presumption that government deficits should be financed by the issue of safe debt probably arises from the fear that the government is big enough to manipulate the returns on any other type of debt in a way that will be disadvantageous to the lenders. In more modern terms the issue is one of the dynamic inconsistency of policy (Kydland and Prescott 1977, Fischer 1980). Given this view, indexed debt would be the standard form of government liability, particularly since the government is exceptionally well placed to affect the inflation rate.

From this perspective the right question to ask about government debt is not why it is not indexed, but how it ever came to be nominal. One argument that may have some appeal is that the government by promising to pay off in dollars (or the currency of the country) is making the only promise it can with certainty keep, since it prints the dollars. However, nominal debt predates fiat currencies, so this cannot be the explanation.[9]

The predominance of nominal government debt in countries with relatively stable inflation histories derives from frictions associated with indexed debt. The first friction is the delay in the collection and publication of price date, which means that indexed debt is not conveniently used in short-term transactions. Second, as often pointed out, variations in relative prices imply that different price indexes are appropriate for different people and purposes: when inflation rates are reasonably predictable, there is no assurance that the appropriate real value of indexed debt is more predictable than the value of nominal debt.[10]

Once the economy has accustomed itself to using nominal debt and institutions, and given the frictions associated with indexed debt, there are costs to innovating by introducing an indexed bond, and no assurance that the social surplus from doing so is appropriable by the innovator. There is no presumption, even if there were no government advantage in the issue of indexed debt, that indexed debt would be introduced by the private sector at precisely the right time. Indeed, given a nominal tax system, there is a presumption that some government action is needed to get the process under way.

Government innovation comes when the pressures to move away from nominal contracting become strong enough: these pressures arise in part from the exhaustion of devices for enforcing cheap nominal financing of deficits. They arise also from the dissatisfaction of existing lenders to the government who have suffered from the effects of unanticipated inflation on the real value of their assets.

The notion that indexed debt is an incentive for more consistent behavior by government, point 4, as argued by Bach and Musgrave (1941), is appealing, particularly given that governments typically do not appear to behave in the ways that economists' models of optimizing governments suggest they should. However, it is interesting briefly to explore the question of whether governments should always honor past commitments. The existence of a nominal debt makes it possible for the government very cheaply to impose a capital levy (by inflating). The best of all possible worlds, if governments acted optimally, might be one in which governments had the option of imposing a capital levy in this way in emergencies, like wars. Provided there is a political cost to violating past obligations, it may be optimal to set up arrangements in which they can easily be violated.[11]

Taking this logic a step further, we note the argument by Levhari-Liviatan (1976) that the direction of the effect of past commitments on current actions is ambiguous. If, in an emergency, inflation is the first line of increased government revenue, then the existence of indexed debt may make the government response to difficulties more rather than less inflationary.

Lest these speculations obscure the main message, I repeat the argument

of this section. Given the ability of the government to affect the payoffs
that it makes on debt whose return is uncertain, the general presumption
would be that governments should finance themselves with indexed debt,
as a means of encouraging consistent behavior. The predominance of
nominal debt results from frictions associated with the use of indexed
debt and relies heavily on the presumption that price-level behavior is
reasonably predictable. Once that presumption is lost, governments will
likely have to issue indexed debt in order to finance themselves.[12]

9.6 Concluding Comments

Finally I turn to arguments (2), (3) and (5) for government issue of indexed
bonds. Argument (2), that monetary policy could more accurately affect
q if there were indexed bonds, assumes that real bonds are a closer
substitute for capital than are nominal bonds. Empirically this turns out
not to be the case. It would nonetheless be useful to know what a market
real rate of interest is and how it varies through time, and for that reason
issue of an indexed bond would be of assistance to monetary and fiscal
policy makers.[13]

Argument (3), that issue of indexed bonds would reduce the interest
cost borne by the Treasury for financing the debt, and also promote
saving, has been extensively investigated. If government debt issue is
neutral, in the sense of $N2$, then government issue of indexed bonds
would have no real effect. If the government issue of indexed debt changes
its patterns of taxation and money issue, then the effects on interest rates
and saving depend on how taxes and inflation rates are changed by the
introduction of the indexed debt. An individual with given wealth, and
given future tax payments, will be willing to hold indexed debt at a lower
real return than nominal debt if the remaining assets available are on
balance not hedges against inflation. Certainly, given the adverse effects
of inflation on equity returns, the presumption is that individuals would
be willing to hold indexed bonds at lower real rates than nominal bonds—
holding constant future tax payments. The effects of the issue of indexed
bonds on saving depend on the responses of saving and labor supply to
changes in the real interest rate, topics on which there is little empirical
knowledge.[14]

Finally, consider argument (5), that government issue of indexed bonds
is desirable on distributional grounds. In the United States the adverse

distributional consequences have been associated particularly with the U.S. savings bonds program. The ability of the government to continue obtaining financing through these instruments indicates a lack of access, for whatever reason, to higher yielding dominating assets, and strongly suggests that a part of the market would be made better off by government issue of indexed bonds, or alternatively as now proposed, floating rate notes.[15]

At the theoretical level this chapter should be viewed as an exploratory attempt to analyze the question of optimal government financial policy. Previous analyses have tended to take the types of assets to be issued by the government as given. There is as yet no satisfactory theory of what types of assets governments should issue, and such a theory may require further analysis of reasons for the absence of particular markets.

Because the anslysis is exploratory, it cannot reach any firm conclusions on the desirability or otherwise of government issue of indexed bonds. There is no strong welfare argument for government issue of an indexed bond, at the abstract level of this chapter. But nor is there a strong argument against such an issue. And the analysis certainly provides little explanation or justification for the issue of nominal bonds.

Notes

Department of Economics, MIT, and National Bureau of Economic Research. At the time this chapter was written, I was a Visiting Scholar at the Hoover Institution. This is a revised version of a paper prepared for the Conference on Indexation and Economic Stability, Funacao Getulio Vargas, Rio de Janeiro, December 16–17, 1981. I am grateful to my discussants Eduardo Modiano and Stephen Ross and to participants in seminars at MIT, Stanford, and Berkeley for comments and suggestions, to Jeffrey Miron for research assistance, and to the National Science Foundation and Hoover Institution for financial support.

1. For earlier examination of the issues, see Fischer (1975), Levhari and Liviatan (1976), and Peled (1978), as well as references cited at the end of this chapter.

2. See the *Deseret News*, September 10, 1981. I am indebted to J. Huston McCulloch for this information.

3. Eagly (1967) suggests that Jevons and Marshall advocated use of a price index in private rather than government transactions. However, reading of Jevons (1884) and Marshall (1925) supports the view outlined here. Collier (1969) and Fisher (1934) both survey the literature.

4. In chapter 8 of this volume Stiglitz independently makes very similar arguments.

5. For analysis of social security and taxation as methods of overcoming the absence of human capital markets, see the excellent paper by Merton (1981). Merton also discusses the case where the government has only distorting taxes at its disposal and cannot produce the first best allocation of resources.

6. Atkinson and Stiglitz (1980), p. 340, provide references and discussion. See also Peled (1978), who discusses the criterion under the heading Equal Treatment Pareto Optimality, referring to discussion by Muench (1977). Peled is wary of the criterion, arguing that it is not compatible with a requirement that individuals have the right to refuse to participate in a cooperative procedure if that is costly. He conjectures that whenever the optimality criterion used by economists is stronger than that used by individual agents, private equilibria are likely to be nonoptimal.

7. Robert Barro, in his summary discussion at the conference, argued that use of this criterion was incompatible with the notion that individual utility is not affected by the utility of subsequent generations. However, the criterion can be thought of as follows. Suppose an intergenerational arrangement can be introduced that will make existing generations better off. How likely are future generations to repudiate the arrangement? Future repudiation is more likely if subsequent generations see that, at the time it was introduced, the scheme was known to benefit one generation at the expense of specific future generations. But if it was reasonable to think at the time of introduction of a new set of arrangements that future generations would be benefited, the future generations are more likely to uphold the scheme. It will be seen later in this chapter that introduction of government financial intermediation between generations can satisfy this criterion, benefiting the current generation and increasing the utility expected for all future generations.

8. Bhattacharya (1981) examines a related case.

9. Nor can it seriously be believed that government debt of any type is totally safe, in light of possible revolutions, debt repudiation, and so forth.

10. Michael (1979) examines variations in consumption bundles and associated price indexes in a cross-section study.

11. Keynes, *Essays in Persuasion* (Harcourt Brace, 1932), is worth quoting: "... the benefits of a depreciating currency are not restricted to the government.... Those secular changes ... which in the past have depreciated money, assisted the new men and emancipated them from the dead hand; they benefited new wealth at the expense of old, and armed enterprise against accumulation." (p. 87) Of course he was only half serious: he concluded that it would be better to handle redistributive and inheritance problems directly rather than through (unanticipated) inflation (p. 92).

12. It is difficult to see why the Treasury should not undertake an experimental issue of indexed bonds, sold at auction. These could be discount bonds, promising payment of a given real sum on a specific future date. Tax treatment of the returns would have to be specified. The simplest arrangement would be to make the returns nontaxable. Such a bond could quite easily yield a negative real return in equilibrium.

13. This assumes reasonably that either monetary or fiscal policy decisions might optimally react to changes in the real interest rate.

14. Bhattacharya (1979) examines the theoretical arguments.

15. This argument takes the existence of the U.S. savings bonds program as given. Ronald McKinnon suggested that the program would lose its rationale if interest rate controls on financial intermediaries were lifted. In the last few years the outstanding volume of savings bonds has been falling. At the end of 1981 it was $68 billion, only about 6 percent of the value of total time and savings deposits at financial intermediaries.

References

Atkinson, Anthony, and Joseph Stiglitz. 1980. *Lectures on Public Economics.* McGraw-Hill, New York.

Bach, G. L., and R. A. Musgrave. 1941. "A Stable Purchasing Power Bond." *American Economic Review* 31 (December): 823–825.

Barro, Robert. 1974. "Are Government Bonds Net Wealth." *Journal of Political Economy* 84 (December): 1095–1117.

Bhattacharya, Sudipto. 1979. "Welfare and Savings Effects of Indexation." *Journal of Money, Credit and Banking* 11 (May): 192–201.

Bhattacharya, Sudipto. 1981. Aspects of Monetary and Banking Theory and Moral Hazard. Research Paper no. 611. Graduate School of Business, Stanford University.

Collier, Robert L. 1969. *Purchasing-Power Bonds and Other Escalated Contracts.* Buffalo Book Co., Taipei.

Eagly, Robert. 1967. "On Government Issuance of an Indexed Bond." *Public Finance* 22: 268–284.

Fischer, Stanley. 1975. "The Demand for Index Bonds." *Journal of Political Economy* (June): 509–534.

Fischer, Stanley. 1977. "On the Non-Existence of Privately Issued Index Bonds in the United States Capital Market." In *Inflation Theory and Anti-Inflation Policy*, Erik Lundberg, ed. Boulder, Colo., Westview Press. Reprinted in chapter 10, this volume.

Fischer, Stanley. 1980. "Dynamic Inconsistency and the Benevolent Dissembling Government." *Journal of Economic Dynamics and Control* 2 (February): 93–107.

Fisher, Irving. 1934. *Stable Money.* Adelphi, New York.

Friedman, Milton. 1974. "Monetary Correction." In *Essays on Inflation and Indexation.* American Enterprise Institute, Washington, D.C.

Helpman, Elhanan, and Efraim Sadka. 1979. "Optimal Financing of the Government's Budget: Taxes, Bonds or Money?" *American Economic Review* 69 (March): 152–160.

Jevons, W. Stanley. 1875. *Money and Exchange.* Appleton, New York.

Jevons, W. Stanley. 1884. *Investigations in Currency and Finance.* Macmillan, London.

Keynes, J. M. 1927. "Evidence to Committee on National Debt and Taxation." *Minutes of Evidence.* London, pp. 278, 286–287.

Kydland, F., and E. C. Prescott. 1977. "Rules Rather Than Discretion: The Inconsistency of Optimal Plans." *Journal of Political Economy* 85: 473–493.

Levhari, David, and Nissan Liviatan. 1976. "Government Intermediation in the Indexed Bonds Market." *American Economic Review* 66 (May): 186–192.

Marshall, Alfred. 1925. "Remedies for Fluctuations of General Prices." *Memorials of Alfred Marshall*, A. C. Pigou, ed. London, pp. 188–211.

Merton, Robert C. 1981. On the Role of Social Security as a Means for Efficient Risk-Bearing in an Economy Where Human Capital Is Not Tradeable. NBER Working Paper no. 473, Cambridge, Mass.

Michael, Robert T. 1979. "Variation across Households in the Rate of Inflation." *Journal of Money, Credit and Banking* 1 (February): 32–46.

Muench, Thomas J. 1977. "Efficiency in a Monetary Economy." *Journal of Economic Theory* 15: 325–344.

Peled, Dan. 1978. Government Issued Indexed Bonds—Do They Improve Matters. Unpublished manuscript. University of Minnesota.

Samuelson, Paul A. 1958. "An Exact Consumption Loans Model of Interest with or without the Social Contrivance of Money." *Journal of Political Economy* 66 (December): 467–482.

Tobin, James. 1971. "An Essay on the Principles of Debt Management." In *Essays in Economics*. Vol. 1. Markham, Chicago.

Wallace, Neil. 1981. "A Modigliani-Miller Theorem for Open-Market Operations." *American Economic Review* 71 (June): 267–274.

10 On the Nonexistence of Privately Issued Index Bonds in the U.S. Capital Market

Stanley Fischer

10.1 Introduction

"Why, if both borrower and lender benefit from them, [does] an index loan market . . . not develop spontaneously and without any government initiative?" This question, asked by Professor Arvidsson at the IEA conference on inflation in 1962, provides the major theme for the present chapter which pursues in some detail possible reasons for the nonexistence of privately issued index bonds in the United States.[1]

In an earlier paper, I used portfolio theory and the capital asset pricing model to study the demand for index bonds and some properties of equilibrium in a capital market with equity assets as well as indexed and nominal bonds [7], and in which individuals may also own (but not sell) human capital. The major conclusions of that paper are that the equilibrium relationship between the real yields on indexed and nominal bonds depends on the extent to which equity and human capital are hedges against inflation[2]—the real yield on index bonds tends to be below that on nominal bonds to the extent that real returns on equity and human capital are negatively correlated with inflation; that, in the absence of human capital and with no relative price uncertainty, all private lending and borrowing would take place through indexed bonds; and that, with human capital, both types of bonds would in general be expected to exist. I noted that the analysis did not throw much light on the nonexistence of indexed bonds in most major capital markets.

The nonexistence of privately issued index bonds in the United States is a phenomenon requiring explanation for two main reasons. First, the tying of contracts to the price level is not unknown nor even especially unusual in the United States: labor contracts, certain aspects of insurance contracts, and the prices to be paid for future delivery of manufactured products have all been tied to the price level.[3] Second, there has been no dearth of innovation in the financial area over the years, although those innovations taking the form of the issue of new types of securities by existing firms—such as the certificate of deposit and the floating rate note—have been undertaken mainly by banks.

Originally published in *Inflation Theory and Anti-Inflation Policy*, Erik Lundberg, ed. (Boulder, Colo.: Westview Press, 1977), pp. 502–518. The paper appears in its original form.

The previous paper concentrated on the demand for index bonds and equilibrium in a market composed of lifetime-utility-maximizing households. However, the most likely private issuers of index bonds are corporations. Accordingly, the emphasis in this chapter is on the supply of index bonds by firms, whose assumed motivation is the maximization of their stock market value.

It is well known that in the absence of bankruptcy and the differential tax treatment of equity returns and interest and under certain other assumptions, the Modigliani-Miller theorem [16] establishes that the value of the firm is independent of its debt structure—that is, that under the postulated conditions, there is no good reason for firms to issue one sort of debt rather than another. It is accordingly necessary to develop a rationale for the type of debt issued by a firm. Section 10.2 outlines a simple theory of the supply of bonds, based on the existence of bankruptcy costs and the tax treatment of interest as a business expense, which is used in parts of the remainder of the chapter to evaluate some arguments typically advanced to explain the nonissuance of indexed bonds by private firms [1] and [10].[4]

Section 10.3 examines the view that firms should be more willing to issue index bonds the greater the (positive) correlation of their profits with the price level and also presents evidence on the correlation of the real profits of some American corporations with the price level. Because the theory makes clear the crucial role of the tax treatment of indexed payments, section 10.4 very briefly examines the ambiguous tax status of such payments in the United States. Section 10.5 considers the argument that systematic underestimation of inflation is responsible for the nonappearance of indexed bonds. Section 10.6 reviews the argument that index bonds have not been issued because such bonds would saddle firms with open-ended obligations which nominal bonds with call-clause protection do not. Two further explanations for nonissuance of index bonds are considered: section 10.7 examines the variability of the rate of inflation over the past twenty years; section 10.8 discusses the costs of innovation and the possibility that a large-scale change in the form of debt issues would be easier to accomplish than piecemeal changes. Conclusions are contained in section 10.9. An appendix compares the variability of hypothetical profit streams for sixteen U.S. firms, constructed on the assumption that all their long-term debt issues over the period were indexed, with the variability of their actual profit streams.

10.2 The Supply of Index Bonds

The theory developed in Fischer [8] uses the capital asset pricing model [12] to examine the financing decision of a firm that has made an investment decision in period one that will produce (uncertain) real profits in period two. Real profits are assumed to have a random component that is uniformly distributed and independent of the price level and also to have a component that is correlated with the purchasing power of money (the inverse of the general price level) in period two. The purchasing power of money in turn has a simple two-point symmetric distribution and its expectation for period two is the same as its value in period one.[5]

The firm is assumed to sell claims on its second-period profits in the capital market. Two possible combinations of asset supplies by the firm are examined. In the first the firm can sell indexed bonds and equity. It promises to pay an amount W in real terms to holders of index bonds, provided its profits are at least W. Such payments are treated as business expenses. Any amount of profits not paid out to index bond holders is distributed to equity holders, after payment of taxes at rate τ. If the firm's profits are less than W, it is bankrupt. In such a case equity holders receive no payments. Certain fixed real bankruptcy costs are assumed to be incurred, and bondholders receive either zero or profits minus the bankruptcy costs, whichever is greater, in the event of bankruptcy.

The elements of the theory of the supply of index bonds are accordingly simple. The issue of bonds produces a tax advantage, but the more bonds are issued, the greater the probability of bankruptcy. Thus bonds will be issued to the point at which the tax benefit balances the expected bankruptcy costs.[6] It should be noted that in the absence of differential tax treatment of interest and profit distributions, no bonds would be issued by this firm.

In the capital asset pricing model assets issued by the firm are valued by the market on the basis of their expected return and the covariance of their returns with the market return. The market rate of return is assumed to have a random component that is distributed independently of the behavior of the firm's profits except that the market rate of return is correlated with the purchasing power of money. Empirical evidence suggests that the market rate of return in the United States is negatively correlated with unexpected changes in the price level, and it is accordingly assumed that the market return is positively correlated with the purchasing power of money [3].

The result of the optimization of stock market value by the firm is a supply function for index bonds: the supply of index bonds is positively related to the maximum profits the firm expects to earn and to the tax rate on corporate profits, and negatively related to the cost of bankruptcy. The effects of price-level uncertainty on the issue of index bonds depends on the relationship between the firm's profits and the price level on the one hand, and the market rate of return and the price level on the other; if the firm's profits are related to the price level in the opposite direction to which the market's return is related to the price level, price uncertainty increases the firm's issue of index bonds; if the correlation between the firm's profits and the price level is of the same sign as the correlation of the market return with the price level, then the firm's issue of index bonds is reduced by price-level uncertainty. Under the empirically justifiable assumption that the market return is inversely correlated with the price level [3], the firm's supply of index bonds is greater, the greater the variance of the price level, and also the greater the correlation of its profits with the price level.

In the second situation the firm is assumed to issue nominal bonds and equity, again with the aim of maximising its stock market value. A supply function for nominal bonds by the firm is derived and the optimised value of the firm when it can issue nominal bonds and equity is calculated. The optimised values of the firm under the two combinations of asset issues are compared and the following results obtained:

1. Neither type of bond—indexed or nominal—dominates the other from the viewpoint of the maximization of the firm's stock market value. There are situations where a firm issuing nominal bonds will command a greater stock market value than one issuing indexed bonds; such situations seem to require that both the market return and the firm's profits be inversely correlated with the price level. There are also situations in which stock market value is higher if the firm issues indexed rather than nominal bonds.[7]

2. Given the empirically negative relationship between the market rate of return and the price level, the greater the correlation of a firm's profits with the price level, the more likely its stock market value will be higher if it issues indexed rather than nominal bonds.

3. Increases in the variance of the price level tend to increase the relative attractiveness of issuing index bonds, at least if the effect of the price level on the market rate of return is small.

Table 10.1
Correlations of after tax interest-adjusted real profits with the price level, 1954–1973

| Firm | Correlation coefficient | | Total long-term debt outstanding 1973 ($ millions) |
	Price level residuals from (10.3)	Price level residuals from (10.4) (simple time trend)	
1. US Steel	−0.06	0.08	1,464
2. Mobil Oil	0.27	0.50	1,052
3. Union Carbide	−0.29	−0.49	940
4. Bethlehem Steel	−0.11	0.15	670
5. IBM	0.32	0.65	652
6. AT & T	−0.64	−0.83	7,594
7. Consolidated Edison	0.08	−0.01	2,843
8. Pacific G & E	−0.36	−0.30	2,677
9. Public Service G & E	0.18	−0.04	1,658
10. Tennessee Gas Transmission	−0.45	−0.12	882
11. Eastern Airlines	−0.31	−0.06	785
12. American Airlines	−0.88	−0.80	692
13. Baltimore and Ohio RR	−0.12	0.03	361
14. Sears	0.30	0.46	956
15. May Co.	−0.24	−0.51	317
16. Woolworth	−0.44	−0.62	295

Data Sources: 1. Profits: *Moody's* industrial manual
2. Debt position: *Moody's* transportation manual
Moody's public utility manual
3. CPI: BLS, unpublished data series, monthly seasonally adjusted OPI.

4. Differences in tax treatment obviously affect the type of securities issued. In particular, if indexed bond interest payments are not treated as a business expense whereas nominal bond interest payments are treated as a business expense, the latter will dominate the former which will not be issued.

10.3 The Correlation of Profits with the Price Level

The analysis outlined above established that firms are more likely to have a higher stock market value by issuing indexed rather than nominal bonds if their profits are positively correlated with the price level.

In table 10.1 we present correlation coefficients between aftertax profits with an adjustment for interest payments and the consumer price index for sixteen firms. These firms were chosen from the industrial, public utilities, transportation, and merchandising categories of the *Fortune* 500 firms for 1964. The criterion of selection was originally to be the largest five firms on the basis of long-term debt outstanding in 1964 in each category, subject to the firms existing in both 1954 and 1973. There are only three transportation firms because debt issues of many of the largest transportation firms were so numerous that the analysis of section 10.5 became too costly, and there are only three merchandising firms because these firms tended to have very little debt outstanding.

Profits for each firm were adjusted by adding back to reported net profits the computed amount of interest paid on long-term debt multiplied by one minus the corporate tax rate (state plus federal) in each year. Thus we obtained a series for each firm:

$$\pi_{it} = \pi_{it}^R + (1 - \tau_t)R_{it}, \quad i = 1, \ldots, 16, \quad t = 1954, \ldots, 1973, \qquad (10.1)$$

where π_{it} will henceforth be called aftertax profits, π_{it}^R is reported net income, and R_t is reported interest payments on long-term debt. We chose to work with aftertax profits because it was simpler to make the tax adjustment to interest than to compute comparable pre-tax profits for each firm.

Nominal aftertax profits, π_{it}, were then deflated by the consumer price index for each year, a linear time trend was fitted to the real profit series, and the deviations of real profits from the trend values were calculated.[8] Similarly, an exponential time trend was fitted to the annual average of the CPI for each of the twenty years, with a dummy being included for the low inflation years, 1959 to 1965, and the residuals from that regression were calculated. The price level regression was

$$\ln(CPI_t) = \alpha_0 + \beta_1 t + \beta_2 Dt, \qquad (10.2)$$

where

$$D = 1, \quad \text{for } t = 1959, \ldots, 1965,$$

$$= 0, \quad \text{otherwise.}$$

Equation (10.2) represents a crude estimate of the predicted path of the price level. The regression, with standard errors in parentheses, was

$$\ln(CPI_t) = 4.3330 + 0.0242t - 0.0051Dt.$$
$$\qquad\quad (0.0185) \quad (0.0014) \quad (0.0018) \qquad\qquad (10.3)$$

In addition the regression was run without the dummy variable, yielding

$$\ln (CPI_t) = 4.3116 + 0.0247t.$$
$$\qquad (0.0197)\ \ (0.0016) \qquad\qquad\qquad\qquad\qquad\qquad (10.4)$$

Table 10.1 presents the correlations of the deviations of real aftertax profits from their trend values with the deviations of the price level from its trend value, for equations (10.3) and (10.4) respectively. In each case most of the correlations are negative. The correlations for the largest debt-issuing category—the utilities—are all either negative or close to zero, with the correlation for AT&T, the largest individual borrower, being strongly negative. Table 10.1 suggests that the most likely issuers of index bonds would be Mobil Oil, IBM and Sears.

While it may be surprising that the correlation of deviations of real profits with deviations of the price level from their respective trends is negative for so many firms, the major lessons of table 10.1 are that there exists a wide diversity of behavior of profits with respect to the price level and that there are indeed firms that have a positive correlation of detrended profits with the detrended price level and that, according to the theory, might have been expected to issue index bonds.[9] We conclude that the failure of indexed bonds to appear is not due to the fact that there are no firms whose profits are positively correlated with the price level.[10]

10.4 The Tax Treatment of Interest, and Indexing to the Price of the Firm's Output

The analysis outlined in section 10.2 points to the tax treatment of interest as a major determinant of the type of security issued.[11] There is also some uncertainty about the tax treatment of indexed interest payments in the United States.[12] The ambiguity stems from the fact that the courts have used fixity of the interest rate as one criterion for justifying the deductibility of interest payments [19]. There are a number of other criteria, such as fixity of the maturity date and negotiability, all of which an indexed bond would satisfy. Since the only criterion that puts the deductibility of indexed interest in question is fixity of the interest rate, and since interest paid on floating rate notes is deductible, it would now appear that in fact a very strong case could be made that indexed interest should be treated as deductible, and that there is probably no tax obstacle to the issue of indexed interest bonds. However, it should be noted that there does not appear to be any precedent precisely covering the indexed interest case, and that the issue could only be finally resolved by rulings applied to a proposed and not a hypothetical bond issue, so that some uncertainty remains.

It is also appropriate here to consider a suggestion which has been made that firms would be more willing to issue bonds indexed to their own output price than bonds linked to the general price level. If their own output price were perfectly correlated with their profits (which is the reasoning behind the suggestion), it is easy to see that the model outlined in section 10.2 would support this argument. However, it should be noted that a firm's prices can rise because of cost increases as well as demand shifts, and thus that the correlation of a firm's prices with its profits is not likely to be perfect. Further the greater the correlation of price with profits, the more likely would it seem to be that the indexed payment on such bonds would be treated as a profit distribution. It should also be noted that, in the case of the issues of such bonds by French firms in the 1950s, indexing to the own price was a device used to circumvent a series of interpretations of a law of 1895 which was taken to forbid indexation to gold or the general price level [11] and which accordingly should not be treated as evidence confirming the view that firms would prefer to issue bonds tied to their own output price.

In brief, then, it appears that the tax treatment of indexed bonds, at least in the United States, should not deter their issue. The general uncertainty concerning the tax treatment of indexed bonds suggests that there has been little effort made to clarify their tax status. Thus it is unlikely that the tax treatment of index bonds has held back potential issues.

10.5 Expectations of Inflation and Index Bonds

The experience of the last decade has been of increasing inflation. The experience of the last two decades has also been of low real yields on bonds. It is by now well known that the average pre-tax real rate of return to the holding of United States treasury bills for the period 1954 to 1973 was 1 percent [6].

The average real yield on long-term corporate debt for our sample of sixteen firms for 1954 to 1973 was less than 2 percent. Table 10.2 presents

Table 10.2
Ratio of mean real profits with indexed interest payment to actual mean real profits,
1954–1973

Firm	Real rate	
	1 percent	2 percent
1. US Steel	1.003	0.988
2. Mobil Oil	1.001	0.995
3. Union Carbide	0.997	0.980
4. Bethlehem Steel	1.000	0.991
5. IBM	1.003	0.999
6. AT & T	0.998	0.987
7. Consolidated Edison	0.983	0.919
8. Pacific G & E	0.993	0.943
9. Public Service G & E	1.010	0.954
10. Tennessee Gas Transmission	1.027	0.982
11. Eastern Airlines	1.392	0.717
12. American Airlines	1.047	0.951
13. Baltimore and Ohio RR	1.101	0.982
14. Sears	1.005	1.000
15. May Co.	1.013	0.991
16. Woolworth	1.010	0.998

Note: Actual mean real profits for Eastern Airlines is close to zero.

the results of a calculation in which hypothetical indexed bonds were issued by the sixteen firms of the sample described in section 10.3. The long-term debt outstanding at the end of each half-year for each firm was calculated, and it was then assumed that each firm paid interest on outstanding debt equal to, in one case, 1 percent at an annual rate and, in the other, 2 percent annual, plus the realized rate of inflation over the preceding six months. Profits were calculated for each firm for each year on the basis of the hypothetical interest payments and then deflated by the CPI to yield a hypothetical real profit series. Table 10.2 shows the ratio of the mean of the calculated real profit series to the mean of actual real profits over the period 1954 to 1973. The ratios are not identical for all firms, both because the share of interest payments in profits varies among firms and because dates of debt issues vary among firms. Table 10.2 demonstrates that every firm effectively obtained bond financing at less than a 2 percent real rate over the period, and that some, including AT&T, paid less than 1 percent real.

It is tempting to conclude that the low real rate is a result of rising and therefore unexpected inflation and that, if inflation had been accurately foreseen, the real rate of interest on bonds would have exceeded 2 percent. Thus it is argued, firms have had little incentive to issue index bonds because real rates on nominal bonds have been low [10]. This argument obviously requires borrowers to have had systematically higher expectations of inflation than lenders. This argument is difficult to confirm or refute. It should, however, be recognized that expectations of inflation among lenders are not homogeneous: it is possible that there are enough lenders in the American economy who are sufficiently pessimistic about inflation to make it worthwhile for some corporation to issue an indexed bond at a low real rate [1]. Thus the expectations explanation, too, should be treated with suspicion.

10.6 The Call Provision

Corporate bonds issued in the United States typically carry a call provision by which the corporation can repay the debt on specified terms before maturity, generally after five years of its existence but ten years for utilities. Thus corporations issuing nominal bonds appear to be covered against the possibility that the nominal interest rate will fall after their debt is issued, and they are of course covered against increases in the nominal rate by virtue of the fixity of the coupon rate. Accordingly, the call clause protects the corporation from the risk that the interest rate and rate of inflation will fall.

There are three points to be made in connection with the argument that the call provision has precluded the issuance of index bonds because the corporation is covered against increases in nominal interest rates by a fixed nominal rate on its debt and decreases in nominal rates by the call clause. First, the call clause is not free [4]. It could be, though, that the issue of call-protected nominal bonds dominates index bonds from the viewpoint of the firm; the model of section 10.2 is not equipped to analyze that issue. Second, the call clause provides protection only after five or ten years, and interest rates can change a great deal in that period. Third, there is no reason why index bonds should not have similar clauses creating minimum and maximum nominal payments.

The last two points suggest strongly that the call provision is not the explanation for the nonexistence of indexed bonds.

Table 10.3
Variance of rate of inflation

Period	Inflation rate variance	Variance of inflation calculated at annual % rate
1954–73	0.3771	6.0336
1954–58	0.3346	5.3536
1959–63	0.0979	1.5664
1964–68	0.1563	2.5008
1969–73	0.2892	4.6272

10.7 The Variance of the Rate of Inflation

The analysis of section 16.2 suggested that indexed bonds would be more likely to be issued, the greater the variance of the price level. Figure 10.1 shows the time path of the CPI in the United States for 1954 to 1974 (quarterly observations) and also the inflation rate, which is defined as

$$\frac{P_t}{P_{t-1}} - 1,$$

where $t = 1953$ II to 1974 IV.

Table 10.3 presents data for the variance of the quarterly inflation rate for the four five-year subperiods of 1954 to 1973. Although it is difficult to establish an absolute measure of variability, the second column of table 10.3 provides some notion of absolute variation; it presents the variance of the rate of inflation calculated at an annual percentage rate and is generally of the same order of magnitude as the mean rates of inflation for the subperiods, except for 1954 to 1958. This variance falls as the time interval over which the inflation rate is calculated is increased.

Perhaps the best notion of the relative variability of the inflation rate is obtained by comparing its variance with that of the stock market rate of return: the variance of the inflation rate is lower by a factor of the order of one hundred than the variance of the stock market rate of return.[13] It thus appears that in terms of the uncertainties portfolio holders are accustomed to facing, inflation uncertainty is relatively trivial and insufficient to make the introduction of a new financial asset worthwhile. The costs of innovation are discussed in section 10.8.

Whatever the absolute magnitude of the variance of inflation, it is clear that the periods most favorable to the issue of index bonds were 1954 to

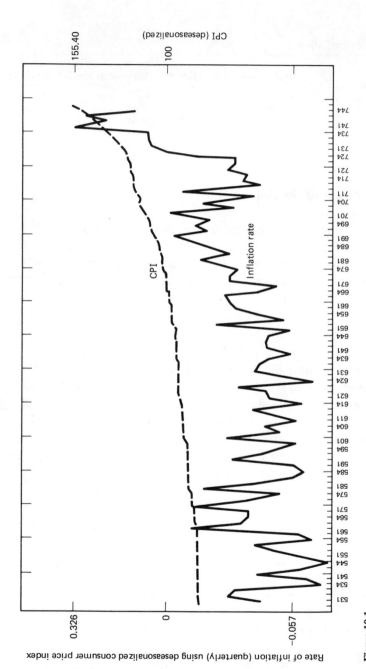

Figure 10.1
Variations of the inflation rate

1958 and 1969 to 1973. These are also of course the periods in which economists were most actively discussing indexing. Further the variance for 1970 to 1974 (11.792) considerably exceeds that for 1969 to 1973 (4.2672). Thus the recent instability of the inflation rate has created conditions substantially more favorable to the issue of index bonds than existed in the previous ten years.

10.8 The Costs of Innovation

The introduction of the floating rate note involved the issuer of the first such note in discussion and negotiation with the Federal Reserve System.[14] This resulted in modification of the terms of the note.[15] Such negotiation is an obvious cost of financial innovation. There are other costs of innovation such as the education of the public to the advantages and disadvantages of the new instrument. (Irving Fisher [9] attributed the failure of the Rand Kardex index bond to the unfamiliarity of the market with the instrument.) These costs are borne by the innovator and not by subsequent issuers.

The fact is, however, that the innovation was carried out in the case of the floating rate note. The note was aimed at the small borrower and thus the educational costs could be expected to be relatively high. Further the difficulties Citicorp encountered with the Federal Reserve System stemmed largely from the fact that the issue was regarded by financial intermediaries such as savings banks as aimed directly at their depositors.[16] It is not certain that similar interests would be affected if an indexed bond were to be issued.

In discussing innovation, it is worthwhile distinguishing financial institutions from other corporations. Financial institutions tend to carry hedged portfolios, and it is probable that they would want to innovate on both sides of their balance sheet if they innovated by issuing an indexed bond (see the model of hedging behavior by a financial intermediary in [5]). Citicorp presumably found the floating rate note more attractive than an indexed bond because its liabilities are nominal. The desire of financial intermediaries for hedging even makes a large-scale transition to indexation as feasible as the piecemeal introduction of indexation by financial intermediaries.

Nonfinancial corporations have not been particularly innovative in the types of securities they issue, and it may be that the costs of innovation for them are high. However, it is difficult to believe that the costs of educating a public, by now well aware of inflation, to understand the features of an indexed bond can be very high. Accordingly, continuance of the current levels and variability of inflation will likely make the costs of innovation for some nonfinancial corporation low enough to result in the issue of an indexed bond. Similarly, if proposals for reform of the mortgage system [15] lead to the introduction of indexed mortgages, the spread of indexation could be rapid.

10.9 Conclusions

Most of the usual explanations for the nonissuance of private indexed bonds do not in fact explain the phenomenon. There are firms whose profits are positively correlated with the price level; the tax treatment of indexed interest would probably not be adverse; the call clause provides protection to the borrower only after a lengthy period and a similar provision could in any case be applied in the case of index bonds; the costs of innovations have not prevented sophisticated innovation aimed at small lenders. There are two arguments that may have some merit. The first is that expectations of inflation by borrowers have been systematically higher than those of lenders. However, it is difficult to believe that borrowers will always expect more inflation than lenders or, for that matter, that there are not now lenders who would accept a low real rate of interest in exchange for protection against inflation. Thus this factor would not prevent the future emergence of index bonds. The second is that the variance of inflation has been low, particularly relative to the other risks incurred in the capital markets. However, this variance is now higher than it was in the 1960s, and increased instability of the inflation rate, if maintained, may well lead to the emergence of privately issued index bonds.

Appendix: The Variability of Hypothetical Profit Series for Sixteen Firms Issuing Indexed Bonds

Closely related to the question examined in section 10.3 of the correlation of a firm's detrended profits with the detrended price level, is an issue of independent interest—the stability of after-interest profits if firms were

Table 10.4
Ratio of variability of real profits with indexed interest payments to variability with
actual interest payments, 1954–1973

Firm	Rates
1. US Steel	0.918
2. Mobil Oil	0.938
3. Union Carbide	1.033
4. Bethlehem Steel	0.969
5. IBM	0.974
6. AT & T	1.050
7. Consolidated Edison	2.322
8. Pacific G & E	2.589
9. Public Service G & E	2.268
10. Tennessee Gas Transmission	0.893
11. Eastern Airlines	0.567
12. American Airlines	1.011
13. Baltimore-Ohio RR	0.721
14. Sears	0.976
15. May Co.	1.128
16. Woolworth	1.011

Note: Eastern Airlines has mean profits close to zero's, and ratio is accordingly
suspect as a measure of variability.

to issue indexed rather than nominal bonds. Table 10.4 presents the
results of comparisons of the variability of hypothetical real profit streams
where firms issued index bonds with the variability of their actual real
profit streams. The construction of the hypothetical profit series is described in section 10.5 (the real interest rate used for the construction of
the appendix was 1 percent). Each nominal profit series was deflated by
the CPI to give a real profit series.

A linear trend was then fitted to each hypothetical real profit series,
and the sum of squared residuals from that series was calculated and
divided by the square of the mean of the series to give a "coefficient of
variation" of hypothetical real profits around its trend line. An identical
procedure was applied to the time series for actual real profits, and the
corresponding "coefficient of variation" calculated.

Table 10.4 presents the ratio of the "coefficient of variation" for the
hypothetical real profit series to that for the actual real profit series. It
is seen from table 10.4 that, given the actual debt issues of firms, the
profits of the industrial firms would on the whole have been more stable
had they issued indexed debt rather than nominal debt, while profits for
the utilities would on the whole have been less stable. The reasons the

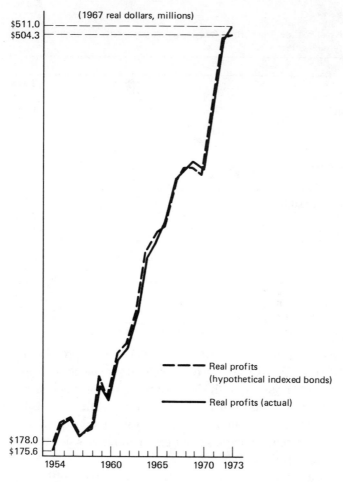

Figure 10.2
Hypothetical and actual profits, Sears, Roebuck & Co.

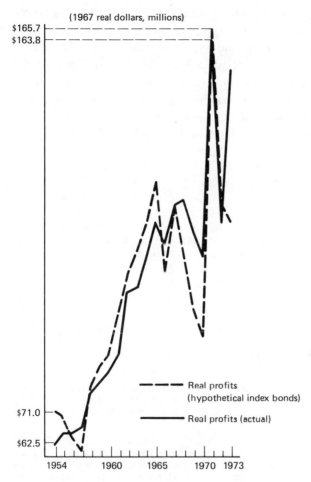

Figure 10.3
Hypothetical and actual profits, Consolidated Edison

ratios in table 10.4 are not uniformly greater (less) than unity if the corresponding correlation of table 10.1 is negative (positive) is that the variability measure is affected by the dates of issue of securities. Table 10.4 shows that a number of firms, including Mobil, IBM and Sears, would have had slightly more stable aftertax profit streams over the last twenty years had they issued index bonds rather than nominal bonds on every occasion on which they issued debt. Figures 10.2 and 10.3 show hypothetical and actual real profits for Sears and Consolidated Edison for the twenty-year period.

Notes

I am indebted to Richard Cohn, Martin Feldstein, Benjamin Friedman, Robert Merton and Stewart Myers for helpful discussions and to Olivier Blanchard and Mary Kay Plantes for excellent research assistance. Financial support from the National Science Foundation is acknowledged with thanks.

1. Arvidsson [1], p. 113. I should note that Professor Mossé, the discussant of Arvidsson's paper, was unimpressed by the question. "Opponents of index loans said that, if borrowers and lenders both wanted them, an index loan market would spring up spontaneously. This was a false argument, and needed refuting much more strongly than Professor Arvidsson had done. One might as well say that, because the government built schools for children, people did not really want their children to have schools, or they would have built schools for themselves." (From the Summary Record of the Debate, p. 402, in Hague 1962).

2. In the sense that their real returns are positively correlated with inflation.

3. The indexation of labor contracts is well documented (see, for example, Sparrough and Bolton [18]). The existence of indexation in other types of contracts is known from anecdote and personal knowledge, but the extent of such indexation has apparently not been documented.

4. The theory is developed in greater detail in Fischer [8]; the two elements of differential tax treatment of interest and dividends and bankruptcy costs are used by Kraus and Litzenberger [14] to develop a theory of optimal financial leverage in a model where there is a full set of contingent commodities. The theory developed in Fischer [8] uses the mean variance version of the capital asset pricing model to avoid assuming a full set of contingent commodities, in which case the consumer or a mutual fund could construct an index bond.

5. Since it is only uncertainty about price level that matters for the analysis, no substantive results depend on the assumption that the average purchasing power of money is not expected to change.

6. This is the essence of the view advanced by Kraus and Litzenberger [14]. This theory fails to explain the existence of bonds before the corporate income tax. Interesting papers by Jensen and Meckling [13] and Myers [17] explore the determinants of debt capacity in a longer-run perspective.

7. It should be noted that we are not here allowing the firm to issue both types of bonds simultaneously, though it is quite likely that such an option would generate a greater stock market value for the firm than the issue of only one type of bond. Our major concern, however, is to show that neither type of bond dominates the other.

8. An exponential could not be used because profits were negative for some firms in some years.

9. It is beyond the scope of this chapter to speculate on reasons for this negative correlation. One obvious "explanation" which may be forthcoming is that all the results tell us is that profits fell over the late 1960s and early 1970s when the rate of inflation was high. Since both regressions treat the inflation rate as essentially constant over specified periods, residuals will be positive in the late 1960s and early 1970s. This explanation is probably statistically correct for the cases it fits but leaves open the question of why profits fell as the rate of inflation rose.

10. Of course it is possible that the financial officers of all firms believe, despite the evidence, that their real profits are negatively correlated with the price level. Presumably, though, the evidence, if it stays firm, will eventually change such beliefs.

11. We shall not discuss the important issue of how the tax system should be adjusted for inflation but rather remain within the confines of the present U.S. tax structure.

12. In my previous paper on index bonds I stated that indexed payments would be treated as dividends, this on the basis of verbal discussion with students of the question. On further examination I now believe that indexed interest payments would be treated as interest (see Fischer [8]).

13. This point was suggested to me by Eugene Fama. See Black, Jensen, and Scholes [2] for estimates of the variance of stock market returns.

14. See Listing Application to the New York Stock Exchange, Inc., B 4337 D, July 24, 1974, by Citicorp.

15. *Wall Street Journal*, July 15, 1974, p. 4.

16. *New York Times*, July 6, 1974, p. 25.

References

1. Guy Arvidsson. "Should We Have Indexed Loans?" In D. C. Hague, ed., *Inflation. Proceedings of a Conference Held by the International Economic Association*. London: Macmillan, 1962.

2. Fisher Black, Michael C. Jensen and Myron Scholes. "The Capital Asset Pricing Model: Some Empirical Tests." In M. C. Jensen, ed., *Studies in the Theory of Capital Markets*. New York: Praeger, 1972.

3. Zvi Body. Hedging against Inflation. Unpublished Ph.D. dissertation. Massachusetts Institute of Technology, 1975.

4. Zvi Bodie and Benjamin M. Friedman. "Interest Rate Uncertainty and the Value of Bond Call Protection." *Journal of Political Economy* (February 1978): 19–44.

5. Richard Cohn and Stanley Fischer. An Analysis of Alternative Nonstandard Mortgages. Sloan School Mortgage Study Report no. 5. Massachusetts Institute of Technology, December 1974.

6. Eugene F. Fama. "Short-Term Interest Rates as Predictors of Inflation," *American Economic Review* (June 1975): 269–282.

7. Stanley Fischer. "The Demand for Index Bonds." *Journal of Political Economy* (June 1975a): 509–534.

8. Stanley Fischer. Non-Indexation in the Capital Markets. Unpublished manuscript. Massachusetts Institute of Technology, June 1975b.

9. Irving Fisher. *Stable Money*. New York: Adelphi, 1934.

10. Milton Friedman. "Monetary Correction." In Gierisch et al., *Essays on Inflation and Indexation*. Washington, D.C.: American Enterprise Institute for Public Policy Research, 1974.

11. Hamel, J. "Les Clauses d'échelle mobile et la droit monétaire francis." *Revue Economique* (March 1955): 167–184.

12. Michael C. Jensen. "The Foundations and Current State of Capital Market Theory." In M. C. Jensen, ed., *Studies in the Theory of Capital Markets*. New York: Praeger, 1972.

13. Michael C. Jensen and William H. Meckling. Theory of the Firm: Managerial Behavior, Agency Costs and Capital Structure. Unpublished manuscript. University of Rochester Graduate School of Management, New York, 1975.

14. Alan Kraus and Robert H. Litzenberger. "A State-Preference Model of Optimal Financial Leverage." *Journal of Finance* (September 1973): 911–922.

15. Donald Lessard and Franco Modigliani. "Inflation and the Housing Market: Problems and Potential Solutions." In *New Mortgage Designs for Stable Housing in an Inflationary Environment*, D. Lessard and F. Modigliani, eds. Conference series vol. 14. Federal Reserve Bank, Boston, 1975.

16. Merton Miller and Franco Modigliani. "The Cost of Capital, Corporation Finance and the Theory of Investment." *American Economic Review* (June 1958): 261–296.

17. Stewart C. Myers. A Note on the Determinants of Corporate Debt Capacity. Unpublished manuscript. London Graduate School of Business Studies, 1975.

18. Michael E. Sparrough and Lena Bolton. "Calendar of Wage Increases and Negotiations for 1972," *Monthly Labor Review* (January 1972): 3–15.

19. *Standard Federal Tax Reporter, 1974*. Vols. 3 and 4. New York: Commerce Clearing House, 1973.

11 On the Interaction between Wage and Asset Indexation

Nissan Liviatan

The idea that there exists an interaction between indexation of wages and bonds has been pointed out by various writers. The most relevant work for our purposes is the work of Blinder (1976) who claims that wage and asset indexation are substitutes. This view implies that policies designed to enhance indexation in any one of these forms will be offset to a large extent by changes in the other form of indexation. This should be borne in mind when one considers direct government intervention in wage indexation agreements or the suggestion, often made by economists, that government should index its debt.

Blinder, who uses essentially a microeconomic framework, claims that a high degree of wage indexing reduces the incentive of workers to purchase indexed bonds and of firms to issue them. In other words, as the scope of wage indexation increases, the market for indexed bonds tends to shrink. Similarly, when there exists a market for indexed bonds, there will be less incentive to index wages.

In another paper (Liviatan 1981), I tried to analyze this problem by using a general equilibrium approach and applying the principles of the Modigliani-Miller theorem. I found that, when transaction costs are ignored, the degree of wage indexation becomes indeterminate. Then it is only the *total* indexed position, in the form of wages *and* bonds, that matters. Under plausible conditions an increase in the degree of wage indexation (such as moving from partial toward full wage indexation) will lead to a reduction in the holdings of indexed bonds, which is in line with Blinder's main conclusion.

We take in this chapter a different approach. Rather than concentrate on the relation between the *degree of wage indexing* and the demand for indexed bonds. We pose the following question: Under what conditions can wage indexation be a perfect substitute for indexed bonds in the sense that there will be no incentive to develop a market for these bonds at all? The factors that can make this situation possible could reduce the economy's incentive to introduce indexed bonds.

For wage indexation to serve as a perfect substitute for indexed bonds, the basic prerequisite is that the parameter of fractional wage indexation, θ, be variable. When θ can be varied, as a part of wage contract negotiations for different groups of workers, this means that workers are in effect able to change the proportions of their indexed and nonindexed wealth.

In this sense the determination of θ is similar to the determination of an optimal portfolio of bonds. It is conceivable that under certain conditions the ability to determine θ may perform the same economic role as the indexed bonds market, provided that there exists a market for nonindexed bonds.

We shall show that the ability of θ to perform this role does not depend necessarily on the size of θ itself. In particular, it is not necessary that θ should be unitary (have full-wage indexation). The important considerations seem to be related to the uniformity of firms and of inflationary expectations and to whether or not the economy has a stock market. Uniformity of firms and expectations tends to increase the substitutability of wage for bond indexation. It will be shown, however, that, when a stock market exists, wage indexation can be a perfect substitute for bond indexation even when firms are heterogeneous.

In the real world it is not very common to introduce formally clauses of *fractional* wage indexation (raise nominal wages by some fraction of the increase in the price level) as we do in this chapter. One case where such an arrangement exists is the Israeli wage indexation scheme where the partial indexation parameter has been set for a number of years at 70 percent (it changed to 80 percent recently). Partial indexation may be introduced under various disguises. For example, it is often the case that not all the components of wages are covered by the indexation scheme. More important, however, is the length of the period elapsing between nominal wage adjustments. Lengthening this period is in a sense a reduction in the degree of indexation. These complications will not be introduced explicitly, though the various deviations from full indexation will be expressed by letting the degree of wage indexing vary.

11.1 The Model

We consider an economy with firms that produce a homogenous physical output, g, by means of production functions

$$g_i = \gamma_i \phi_i(n_i L_i), \tag{11.1}$$

where n_i is the number of workers employed by firm i, L is the number of hours worked, ϕ_i is a neoclassical production function, and γ_i is a random shift parameter with a different distribution for each firm. We start by assuming that all workers in the economy are homogeneous. The labor input relates to the beginning of the period (before uncertainty is resolved) while output comes forth only in the end of the period.

We shall denote the base (nominal) wage in firm i by V_i and the degree of wage indexation by θ_i. In general, θ and V may vary across firms, but as we shall see later, this will not be the case for the stock market economy when labor is perfectly mobile. Let π denote the value of money (the reciprocal of the price level) at the end of the period treated as a random variable, and let $\bar\pi$ be its expected value ($\bar\pi = E\pi$). We then assume that θ_i determines the real wage as follows:

Real wage $= V_i \tilde\pi_i; \; \tilde\pi_i \equiv [\theta_i \bar\pi + (1 - \theta_i)\pi]$,

where normally $0 < \theta < 1$. Thus if $\theta_i = 0$ (no indexation), then the realized real wage is $V_i \pi$ (a random variable) while under full wage indexation the real wage is fixed in real terms and given by $V_i \bar\pi$. We have partial indexation when $0 < \theta_i < 1$. It follows that the realized real profits of the firm are given by

$$X_i = \gamma_i \phi_i - n_i L_i V_i [\theta_i \bar\pi + (1 - \theta_i)\pi]. \tag{11.2}$$

Every individual may purchase (or sell) bonds in the beginning of the period. We shall denote nonindexed bonds by B^N and the nominal interest rate by i. The real value of these bonds in the end of the period is then $\pi(1 + i)B^N$. Similarly, indexed bonds (if they exist) are denoted by B^I, and the real interest rate associated with them is r (which is nonrandom).

When we deal with a stock market economy, we let every individual hold a certain fraction of the shares of any firm. Thus α_i^s will denote the fraction of the shares of firm s held by a worker employed by firm i. Similarly, α_k^s is the corresponding fraction related to nonworkers. The value of the firm, denoted by Q_s, is assumed to be maximized by the firm managers.

We also assume that every individual holds real money balances, m, which yield direct utility during the period. In addition individuals receive transfer payments from the government, t. These are random payments receivable in the end of the period, and they account for the variation in the nominal money supply in the economy.

The analysis will be conducted within the framework of a one-period model where the present period's consumption and wage payments take place in the end of the period. All the decisions are taken in the beginning of the period before uncertainty is resolved. The beginning of period price level is assumed to be predetermined.

In the beginning of the period the market determines the interest rates, the base wage rates, and the degrees of wage indexation. These solutions are based on expectations of the rate of inflation (or end-of-period prices) which will be described later.

In a stock market economy the end-of-period material wealth of a worker employed by firm i can then be expressed as

$$Y_i = L_i V_i \tilde{\pi}_i + (1 + i)\pi B_i^N + (1 + r)B_i^I + \sum_s \alpha_i^s X_s + \pi m_i + \pi t_i. \qquad (11.3)$$

The worker is faced in the beginning of the period with an asset constraint of the form

$$B_i^N + B_i^I + m_i + \sum \alpha_i^s Q_s = A_i = \text{constant}. \qquad (11.4)$$

A similar formulation applies to the wealth of nonworkers, k, except that there is no wage income. In an economy without a stock market we would omit the terms involving α from (11.3) and (11.4). In this case the firm owner's Y will include the profits X given by (11.2).

The utility functions of workers and nonworkers are given, respectively, by

$$U(Y_i, L_i, m_i); \quad U^k(Y_k, m_k); \quad U_y > 0, \; U_L < 0, \; U_m > 0. \qquad (11.5)$$

For unincorporated business firms we assume that employment conditions are determined by a contract that specifies L, V, and θ.

Such a contract is efficient in the sense of Shavell (1976), in that it requires the maximization of the expected utility of the firm owner, say, $EU^k(Y_k, m_k)$, subject to given expected utility of the workers employed, $EU(Y_i, L_i, m_i) = U_0$. It is assumed that the contract is reached when the holdings of bonds and money by the parties involved are optimally adjusted.

In a stock market economy of the type described by Diamond (1967), it is assumed that firms maximize the market value of their stock. It will be shown that the firms will not be concerned directly with V or θ but rather with the certainty equivalent of the real wage (denoted w). Given w, the workers may choose the combination of (V, θ) that maximizes their expected utility.

11.2 A Market for Indexed Bonds

When there is a market for indexed bonds, every individual determines the quantity of B^I in an optimal manner. Thus for every individual we have always the condition

$$\frac{\partial EU}{\partial B^L} = 0, \quad \text{subject to the asset constraint.} \tag{11.6}$$

This condition must be satisfied independently of the existence of a stock market. Condition (11.6) implies

$$\frac{EU_1 \pi}{EU_1} = \frac{1+r}{1+i} \tag{11.7}$$

for every individual, where U_1 denotes $\partial U/\partial Y$. (E may reflect expectation taken over a subjective probability distribution.)

The ratio on the left-hand side of (11.7) is the marginal rate of substitution between a nominal dollar receivable at the end of the period (the expected marginal utility of which is $EU_1 \pi$) and a dollar fixed in real terms receivable at the end of the period ($EU_1 = EU_1 \pi$ when $\pi \equiv 1$). Thus $EU_1 \pi/EU_1$ is the real *certainty equivalent* (as of the end of the period) of a nominal dollar receivable at the end of the period. Another way of looking at $EU_1 \pi/EU_1$ is as a weighted average of π across states of nature where the weights are the marginal utilities of Y for the individual in question. We shall accordingly use the notation $EU_1 \pi/EU_1 = \pi^*$, so the $(1+i)\pi^* = 1+r$.

The role of the markets for indexed and nonindexed bonds is to equate, through (11.7), the marginal rate of substitution of nominal for real future dollars for every individual in the economy. If no market for indexed bonds exists, there is no reason why π^* should be equal for all individuals. However, if in the absence of a market for indexed bonds we can still point out a mechanism that equates π^* for all individuals, then we may say a market (or "shadow market") for indexed bonds exists in the *economic* sense. When π^* is equal for all individuals, it is as if they have exhausted the possibilities of trade between nominal and real future dollars.

An interesting feature of an economy with indexed bonds without transaction costs, is that the degree of wage indexation (θ_i) becomes indeterminate. If the indexed part of wages, that is, $L_i V_i \pi \theta_i$, can be considered as being equivalent to indexed bonds of equal value, then clearly the distinction between these two components of indexation is immaterial. In Liviatan (1981), which is based on an economy of unincorporated business firms, I have shown that the neutrality of θ_i can be established by means of a Modigliani-Miller argument.

It can be shown that the neutrality of wage indexation holds also for the case of a stock market economy with indexed bonds.[1] Starting with an equilibrium, we can change V and θ without affecting the equilibrium, as long as the prevent value of the real wage, given by

$$\left(\frac{\theta\bar{\pi}}{1+r} + \frac{1-\theta}{1+i}\right)V, \tag{11.8}$$

is held constant. Since the considerations are similar to those discussed in my 1981 paper I shall omit the formal analysis of this point.

11.3 Wage Indexation with No Stock Market

The ability of wage indexation to be a substitute for indexed bonds depends, among other things, on the sophistication of the capital market. In order to appreciate the role of the stock market in this context it is useful to start with an economy consisting of unincorporated firms. It is assumed that there exists a market for nonindexed bonds, but there is no market for indexed bonds.

Assume for simplicity that we have only one type of homogeneous workers. Then the planned resources of firm owner i are given by

$$Y_i^f = \gamma_i\phi_i - n_iL_iV_i[\theta_i\bar{\pi} + (1-\theta_i)\pi] + (1+i)\pi(A_i^f - m_i^f) + (t_i^f + m_i^f), \tag{11.9}$$

while the resources of a worker employed by firm i are given by

$$Y_i = L_iV_i[\theta_i\bar{\pi}] + (1-\theta_i)\pi] + (1+i)\pi(A - m_i) + \pi(t + m_i), \tag{11.10}$$

where A and t do not depend on the index i because of uniformity of workers.

The efficiency of the contract requires the maximization of the firm owner's expected utility EU^{fi} subject to given values of the expected utility of the workers $EU(Y_i, L_i, m_i)$.

Let us form the Lagrangian expression

$$G_i = EU^{fi} - \mu_i(EU - U^0) \tag{11.11}$$

Differentiating (11.11) partially with respect to V_i and θ_i, we obtain

$$n_iEU^{fi}\tilde{\pi}_i + \mu_iEU_1^i\tilde{\pi}_i = 0, \tag{11.12}$$

$$n_iEU_1^{fi}(\bar{\pi} - \pi) + \mu_iEU_1^i(\bar{\pi} - \pi) = 0, \tag{11.13}$$

where we use the notation U^i for $U(Y_i, L_i, m_i)$ and where $\tilde{\pi}_i \equiv \theta_i \bar{\pi} + (1 - \theta_i)\pi$. It is easily verified that the foregoing equations imply $n_i EU_1^{fi} + \mu_i EU_1^i = 0$ which in turn implies that

$$\pi_{fi}^* = \pi_i^*, \tag{11.14}$$

that is, the owner of firm i and his employees must have the same π^*.[2]

This result has a simple explanation. When the owner and his workers negotiate the combination of V and θ, they are in fact negotiating the composition of the indexed and nonindexed components of the contract. Since this efficient contract represents a point on the "contract curve," it is only natural that the MRS between an indexed and a nonindexed future dollar should be identical for worker and employer. Thus the equalization of the MRS's between V and θ implies also the equalization of the MRS's between an indexed and a nonindexed future dollar.

It can be easily seen that the same conclusion applies to the case where the firm employs different types of workers. In this case we shall have

$$\pi_{fi}^* = \pi_{ij}^*, \quad j = 1, \ldots, J. \tag{11.15}$$

Thus within each firm we have a virtual market for indexed bonds even though such bonds do not appear explicitly.

While within each firm we have an equalization of π^*, there is at present no mechanism to equate the π_{fi}^* among firm owners.[3] Although it is true that the firms are not completely isolated because they employ homogeneous workers, this is not sufficient to ensure uniformity of π_{fi}^* if the firms are not homogeneous. The fact that workers of a given type are homogeneous means only that they will be on the same indifference curve, but they may be on different points on this curve associated with different π^*'s. It is natural to introduce at this point the stock market, which can provide the necessary link between firms in order to produce a uniform π^* across the economy.

11.4 The Stock Market Economy

For simplicity, let us begin with a case where workers do not invest in shares, so that only nonworkers ("capitalists") participate in the stock market. Let us also assume that there is only one type of (homogeneous) workers who are perfectly mobile between firms. The profits of firm i are given by

$$X_i = \gamma_i \phi_i(n_i L_i) - n_i L_i V_i[\theta_i \bar{\pi} + (1 - \theta_i)\pi] \tag{11.16}$$

and the end of period resources of capitalists and workers are given, respectively, by

$$Y_k = \sum \alpha_{ik} X_i + (1 + i)\pi B_k + \pi m_k + \pi t_k, \tag{11.17}$$

$$Y_i = L_i V_i[\theta_i \bar{\pi} + (1 - \theta_i)\pi] + (1 + i)\pi B_i + \pi m_i + \pi t, \tag{11.18}$$

with asset constraints

$$A_k = \sum \alpha_{ik} Q_i + B_k + m_k \tag{11.19}$$

$$A = B_i + m_i, \tag{11.20}$$

where Y_i denotes Y of workers employed by firm i, and Q_i is the value of the shares of firm i.

The capitalists maximize $EU^k(Y_k)$ subject to (11.17) and (11.19). The maximization with respect to α_{ik} leads to a "value-of-the firm" equation

$$(1 + i)\pi_k^* Q_i = \gamma_{ik}^* \phi_i - n_i L_i[\theta_i \bar{\pi} + (1 - \theta_i)\pi_k^*] V_i,$$

$$\gamma_{ik}^* = \frac{EU_1^k \gamma_i}{EU_1^k},$$

$$\pi_k^* = \frac{EU_1^k \pi}{EU_1^k}. \tag{11.21}$$

We shall denote the certainty equivalent of the real wage by w_i so that $(1 + i)\pi_k^* Q_i = \gamma_{ik}^* \phi_i - n_i L_i w_i.$[4]

Suppose that each firm treats its w_i as a market parameter and so do its employees. Then one can show that we shall have a labor market equilibrium where w_i, V_i, and θ_i are uniform across firms. We shall then show that another feature of the labor market equilibrium is the existence of a virtual market for indexed bonds.

The firms are assumed to maximize their market value Q_i which leads to the marginal productivity condition

$$\gamma_{ik}^* \phi_i' = w_i, \tag{11.22}$$

from which we derive a demand function for hours worked:

$$(N_i L_i)^d = D_i(w_i). \tag{11.23}$$

The worker employed by firm i maximizes $U(Y_i, L_i, m_i)$ subject to

$$w_i = V_i[\theta_i\bar{\pi} + (1 - \theta_i)\pi_k^*].$$

The maximization is carried out with respect to the set of decision variables which include L_i, V_i, θ_i. Note that the firm is indifferent to the set (θ_i, V_i) chosen by the workers as long as w_i remains constant.

Since π_k^* is uniform across firms, it follows that, for a given θ, workers will always prefer a higher V_i. In other words, workers always prefer a higher value of w. Since workers are uniform and perfectly mobile, we must have in equilibrium a *uniform* w.[5] Since the workers' U function is uniform (and does not depend on the index i), it follows that for maximization of U with respect to θ and V, given w_i must lead to uniform optimal values of θ and V across firms.

The workers' optimization, based on the parameters w and A yields a supply function for hours of work $L^s(w, A)$ which is independent of the firms. The demand of any firm for n_i is then derived by

$$\frac{(n_i L_i)^d}{L^s(w, A)} = \frac{D_i(w)}{L(w, A)} = n_i(w, A) \tag{11.24}$$

The market equilibrium value of w is then determined by

$$\sum n_i(w, A) = \bar{n}, \tag{11.25}$$

where $\bar{n}$ is the total number of workers in the economy.

The marginal rate of substitution between V and θ along a "constant w" curve, which leaves the firm indifferent, is given by

$$\left(\frac{dV}{d\theta}\right)_f = -\frac{V(\bar{\pi} - \pi_k^*)}{\theta\bar{\pi} + (1 - \theta)\pi_k^*}, \tag{11.26}$$

where π_k^* is taken by the firm as a market parameter. It can be argued that the foregoing MRS is negative since π_k^*, being the real certainty equivalent of a nominal future dollar, is ordinarily less than the expected value.

In this connection we note that in an economy with indexed bonds we have $(1 + i)\pi^* = 1 + r$. Hence, if there is a risk premium on nonindexed bonds $[(1 + i)\bar{\pi} > (1 + r)]$, we have $\bar{\pi} > \pi^*$. I have shown in Landskroner and Liviatan (1981) that the risk premium tends to be positive when the random shocks to the economy are predominantly "real" while it tends to vanish when the shocks are purely monetary. This argument is based on the assumption that expectations concerning π are formed according to

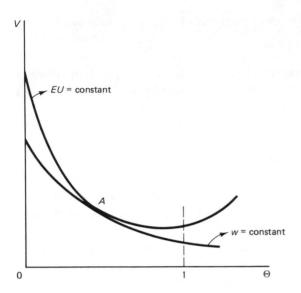

Figure 11.1
Wage indexation and expected utility

"quantity theory" equation $(m + t)\pi = ky$, where y is real output in the economy and k is the "Cambridge k." It can be shown that a similar argument can be applied to the present model. We can therefore say that when real shocks are sufficiently important then, in equilibrium, the MRS in (11.26) will be negative.

A simple calculation shows that the worker's MRS is given by

$$\left(\frac{dV}{d\theta}\right)_w = -\frac{V(\bar{\pi} - \pi_w^*)}{\theta\bar{\pi} + (1 - \theta)\pi_w^*},\tag{11.28}$$

where $\pi_w^* = EU_1\pi/EU_1$. Although (11.28) looks exactly like (11.26), there is an important difference between them. While in (11.26) the firms take π_k^* as market parameter, the value of π_w^* is endogenous in the optimization problem of the workers since U_1 is affected by the choice of (θ, V) and all the other decision variables (such as L).

The optimal choice of the worker's θ and V is illustrated in figure 11.1 by the tangency point A, where EU is maximized subject to a given w.[6] In an internal solution $(\theta > 0)$ the tangency of the curves means

$$\frac{\bar{\pi} - \pi_k^*}{\theta\bar{\pi} + (1 - \theta)\pi_k^*} = \frac{\bar{\pi} - \pi_w^*}{\theta\bar{\pi} + (1 - \theta)\pi_w^*}\tag{11.29}$$

which implies

$$\pi_k^* = \pi_w^*. \tag{11.30}$$

Since w is uniform across firms, it follows that (11.30) holds for workers in all firms throughout the economy. Hence there exists a uniform π^* for all agents which implies the existence of a virtual market for indexed bonds. This is due to the fact that the capitalists link all firms together through their investment in the stock market.

The result can be generalized in several directions. First suppose that there are many types of capitalists $k = 1, \ldots, K$. Then following the foregoing analysis for any k, we must reach conclusion (11.30). However, since π_w^* is the same regardless of k, it follows that all the π_k^* must be equal. Hence, the π^* of various capitalists are equalized despite the fact that they deal only with shares and not with indexed bonds. This is due to the fact that all capitalists participate indirectly (through their ownership in the firms) in indexation contracts between firms and workers.

If there are several types of workers ($j = 1, \ldots, J$), then (11.30) must hold for each type, that is, $\pi_k^* = \pi_{wj}^*$ for all j. Clearly, in this case w, θ, and V all vary across types of workers.

11.5 The Indexing-Spreading Effect of the Stock Market

We have seen already how the stock market can diffuse indirectly the system of indexation from workers to all shareholders. We intend to show now that the stock market may diffuse wage indexation when it is practiced only in a subgroup of the firms.

Consider a situation where some firms have wage-indexing agreements while others do not. If there were no transaction costs associated with wage indexing, this situation would not have been possible in equilibrium. The reason is that the firm that permits wage indexing can reduce its w while enabling the workers to enjoy the same expected utility as they obtain in the firms without wage indexation. If, however, transaction costs do exist, then it may be the case that some firms have lower transaction costs associated with indexing contracts than others. In the (V, θ) plane the firms without indexing will then be at $\theta = 0$, while those *with* wage indexing will be at an internal solution along the same EU of the workers.

In the foregoing situation the equality of the π^*'s given by (11.30) will apply only to the firms with wage indexing. Therefore workers employed in firms without wage indexing will in general have different π^*'s than that of the wage-indexing sector. If, however, we let workers hold shares, then the π^* of the workers in the nonindexed sector will be equated to the π^* of the workers in the indexed sector just in the same way as this result is obtained for the capitalists. Thus it is sufficient to have wage indexing in one sector of the economy in order to create a virtual market for indexed bonds in the economy as a whole.

The shortcoming of the foregoing analysis is that it ignores completely the role of transaction costs in the determination of the optimal portfolio of assets. Recent literature (see, for example, Mayshar 1979) indicates that the existence of transaction costs will limit the number of different shares held by different individuals.[7] It is clear that the larger the transaction costs involved in the optimal portfolio problem, the smaller will be the significance of the stock market in spreading indexation. Mutual Finances reduce transaction costs.

11.6 A Related "Pareto Optimum" Formulation

Let us consider now the case where all workers invest in shares and where we have wage indexing in all firms. We have seen that in this case we have a uniform π^*, which means a uniform marginal rate of substitution between real and nominal future dollars. We also have the equality of the values of the marginal products of the same factor in alternative uses, as given by (11.22). In equilibrium we also have

$$\gamma_i^* \phi_{iq}' = -\frac{EU_2^q}{EU_1^q},$$

$$i\pi^* = \frac{EU_3^h}{EU_1^h}, \quad h = \text{all } q \text{ and } k, \tag{11.31}$$

which are the conditions for efficient allocation of leisure and liquidity.

This suggests that we can formulate a related problem, as in Diamond (1967), where we have a central planner who allocates output, labor services, and transfer payments in the economy, which leads to the same efficiency conditions as stated in the preceding paragraph. This is indeed possible if we extend Diamond's model to include allocation of money balances and, in particular, if we allow the existence of two types of (zero-sum) transfer payments—real *and* nominal.[8] Nominal transfer payments are made at the end of the period, so their real value is uncertain.

In the foregoing planning problem the possibility of distinguishing between real and nominal transfers leads to the emergence of a uniform π^* in the economy—to the creation of "indexed bonds." This shows that the indexation schemes discussed in the earlier sections are efficient in the sense that no reallocation of nominal and real debt can improve everybody's welfare. This is of course a limited type of efficiency which rules out finer ways of risk allocation, such as claims conditional on states of nature specified in terms of real and nominal disturbances.

Notes

1. It is assumed that bonds are issued only by individuals.

2. This result is based on the assumption that $\overline{\Pi}$ is the same. Otherwise E may refer to subjective expectations.

3. From the maximization of G_i with respect to L_i and n_i, we obtain the marginal productivity conditions $\phi_i' \gamma_{fi}^* = V_i[\theta_i \overline{\pi} + (1 - \theta_i)\pi_{fi}^*]$ where $\gamma_{fi}^* = EU_1^{fi}\gamma_i/EU_1^{fi}$, $\pi_{fi}^* = EU_1^{fi}\pi/EU_1^{fi}$, and ϕ' is the derivative of ϕ_l. In a market equilibrium it should not pay the owner of firm i to hire a worker of firm j who has a contract characterized by (L_j, θ_j, V_j). Since the same is true for firm j, we have the following constraints:

$$V_i[\theta_i \overline{\pi} + (1 - \theta_i)\pi_{fi}^*] \leq V_j[\theta_j \overline{\pi} + (1 - \theta_j)\pi_{fi}^*],$$
$$V_j[\theta_j \overline{\pi} + (1 - \theta_j)\pi_{fj}^*] \leq V_i[\theta_i \overline{\pi} + (1 - \theta_i)\pi_{fj}^*].$$

These conditions are clearly not sufficient to enforce equality of the π_j^*'s (even if V and θ were required to be uniform across firms).

4. That is, $w_i = [\theta_i \overline{\pi} + (1 - \theta_i)\pi_k^*]V_i$

5. We can establish the uniformity of w in an alternative way. Suppose that w_i differs among firms. Specifically let $w_i > w_j$. Then firm i may offer the worker of firm j the contract L_i, θ_j, V_j (and hence also w_j). Since in firm i the $w_i = \gamma_{ik}^*\phi_i'$, we see that firm i can raise its market value while the transferred worker is no worse off. This should not be possible in equilibrium, so that $w_i = w_j$.

6. It is assumed in figure 11.1 that the workers' MRS at $\theta = 1$ is close to zero, which will lead to a solution of fractional indexation. It can be shown that this will be the case when the workers' Y consists predominantly of their wage bill.

7. On the other hand, the individual may reduce these transaction costs by investing in mutual funds.

8. It is assumed that the planner takes the inflation process itself as given, that is, he treats the transfers t (in equation 11.3), and the distribution of π as given. The additional nominal transfer payments discussed here are zero in the aggregate and may therefore be neutral with respect to the inflationary process.

References

Blinder, A. S. Indexing the Economy through Financial Intermediation. Research Memorandum no. 196. Economic Research Program, Princeton University, March 1976.

Diamond, P. "The Role of a Stock Market in a General Equilibrium Model of the Economy with Technological Uncertainty." *American Economic Review* 57 (September 1967): 759–776.

Liviatan, N. On Equilibrium Wage Indexation and Neutrality of Indexation Policy. Unpublished manuscript. July 1981.

Landskroner, Y., and Liviatan N. "Risk Premia and the Sources of Inflation." *Journal of Money, Credit and Banking* 13 (May 1981): 205–214.

Shavell, S. "Sharing Risks of Deferred Payments." *Journal of Political Economy* 84 (1976): 161–168.

12 The Effects of Government Intermediation in the Indexed Bonds Market on Consumer Behavior

David Levhari

In recent years we have witnessed quite a few innovations in financial markets. Examples of these innovations are the establishment of liquid funds and the creation of floating rate bonds. Yet despite the growing instability in the value of money, the private sector in all developed economies failed to develop a market for indexed bonds. We did witness an increasing interest in government intervention in the linked bonds market. Such an intervention has been experienced in various countries where the government provides the supply of linked bonds, but it seems that the governments of the large industrial states have not chosen to follow this practice despite the advice of well-known economists.

Various arguments have been presented in favor of government issuing linked bonds.[1] A well-known argument is that in inflationary periods the government should enable the "small investor" to maintain the real value of his savings. Another argument, which has been made recently, is that the stock of government indexed bonds issued will reduce the government's incentive to use "inflation" as a tax. We do not wish, however, to discuss these arguments, nor similar ones, since they are based essentially on some political or social conceptions. (One could argue, as an example, that indexing of the government debt makes the inflationary tax a less effective tool, and the government may be forced to inflate even more in order to acquire a given amount of real resources from the public.) Instead, we shall concentrate on a class of arguments that stresses one major aspect of the problem—that by issuing indexed bonds the government reduces the inflation risk faced by the economic agents.

It has been argued that the introduction of a risk-free asset enlarges the feasible set of the private investor and enables him to achieve a better diversification of his portfolio. In addition to this direct contribution to the welfare, it is argued that the existence of linked bonds encourages savings under inflationary conditions and reduces the tendency to make excessive investments in real estate and other physical assets. This, it is argued, will reduce the pressure on real resources of the economy and hence reduce the inflationary pressure. Advocates of linked bonds consider these properties to be desirable under inflationary conditions.

We take a critical view of these arguments for and against indexed bonds. We shall first argue that it is implicit in the foregoing approach that there be no social economic cost to the government introduction of indexed bonds. It is clear, however, that the government has to finance the interest payments on these bonds. The need to finance these payments imposes a cost on the consumers at large, a cost that may, or is likely to, abolish the benefit of the program. Thus, looking both at the costs and the benefits, one cannot argue that the introduction of such bonds necessarily improves consumer's welfare. We shall then consider the arguments that a market for linked bonds tends to encourage savings and reduce "inflationary spending" in the economy. An analysis of this proposition within the framework of a specific model supports the proposition concerning savings but is rather indeterminate concerning the effect on inflationary pressures.

In considering the merits of government intermediation, the tendency is to apply the general principle of efficiency of the competitive markets, which renders any government intervention unnecessary, in the absence of external effects. In a case of an inflationary process, however, one may consider several possible sources of external effects. One is the effect of pooling of risk which we do not consider to be significant to the type of risk involved in the inflationary process (this is explained more specifically later on). Another external effect relates to the ability of government to manipulate the value of real balances as well as consumers' expectations through the inflationary process. This is indeed a limitation of the application of laissez faire principle. We therefore have to qualify some of our foregoing conclusions in view of this limitation.

Apart from the question of whether one may apply directly the principle of laissez faire efficiency one has to take into account the specific distributional effects associated with various government methods of intermediation and financing. Accordingly, the following analysis will deal separately with governmental financing of intermediation through balanced and nonbalanced budgets. The inflationary process is at least partially created, influenced, and produced by governmental actions, and one has to take into account the ability of governments to manipulate and influence the inflationary process itself and therefore the general principle that competitive markets lead to Pareto optimality cannot be simply applied. Different rules or acts like inflationary financing and taxation will have different distributional implications.

12.1 The Model

In order to deal with these indexation problems, we need a model for individual and government behavior. For the individual, we choose a simple model based on two-period planning.[2]

Consider an individual with a two-period planning horizon who consumes a single commodity. We denote his real consumption of the commodity by c and his initial endowment by y_1. We also assume that he has an initial endowment of $\overline{M}$ nominal dollars and wishes to hold M dollars, the real value of which yields direct utility as a consumer's good. He may also hold positive or negative amounts of nonlinked or linked bonds. The dollar values of nonlinked and linked bonds are denoted by B_N and B_L, respectively. The gross nominal rates of return on a dollar invested in nonlinked and linked bonds are denoted by i and $r(p_2/p_1)$, respectively, where r is one plus the real rate of interest on linked bonds and i is one plus the interest rate.

The individual's budget constraint for the first period, in real terms is given by

$$y_1 - c + \overline{m} - m = b_N + b_L, \tag{12.1}$$

where $\overline{m} = \overline{M}/p_1$, $b_N = B_N/p_1$, and $b_L = B_L/p_1$, with p_1 being the dollar price of the commodity in the first period. Denoting by w the real value of the individual's wealth in the second period, we have

$$w = (m + ib_N)\pi + rb_L + y_2, \tag{12.2}$$

where $\pi = p_1/p_2$. Assuming p_2 (next period's price), and hence π, to be the only random variable in the system, we obtain the following expression for the expected value of w (denoted $\overline{w}$) and its variance (denoted by V_w):

$$\overline{w} = (m + ib_N)\overline{\pi} + rb_L + y_2,$$

$$V_w = (m + ib_N)^2 V_\pi, \tag{12.3}$$

where $\overline{\pi}$ and V_π denote the expected value and variance of π, respectively.

The expected utility (U) function is assumed to be based on the mean-variance approach for the second period and on separability between periods:

$$U = u(c, m) + f(\overline{w}, V_w). \tag{12.4}$$

In some of our calculations f is assumed to be quadratic:

$$f(\bar{w}, V_w) = \alpha\bar{w} - \beta(\bar{w}^2 + V_w), \tag{12.5}$$

with $\alpha, \beta > 0$ and $f_{\bar{w}} = \alpha - 2\beta\bar{w} > 0$. The individual is assumed to maximize U with respect to all the decision variables (c, m, b_N, b_L) subject to (12.1) and (12.3).

The first-order conditions with respect to the three independent variables (c, m, b_L) can be rearranged to read as follows:

$$\frac{u_c}{f_{\bar{w}}} = r, \tag{12.6}$$

$$\frac{u_m}{u_c} = \frac{i}{i-1}, \tag{12.7}$$

$$i\bar{\pi} - r = S(m + ib_N);$$

$$S = -\left(\frac{f_{V_w}}{f_{\bar{w}}}\right) V_\pi i 2 > 0. \tag{12.8}$$

The first two tangency conditions have an obvious interpretation. The last condition is $\partial U/\partial b_L = 0$, and it can be stated alternatively as

$$i\bar{\pi} - r = \frac{f_{V_w}}{f_{\bar{w}}} \frac{\partial V_w}{\partial b_L}, \tag{12.8'}$$

where $(-f_{V_w}/f_{\bar{w}})$ is the marginal rate of substitution between $\bar{w}$ and V_w, and is positive for a risk averter $(f_{\bar{w}} > 0, f_{V_w} < 0)$.

Notice that sign $(i\bar{\pi} - r) = $ sign $(m + ib_N)$. This implies that we cannot have a negative risk premium for nonlinked bonds, $i\bar{\pi} - r < 0$, because then $b_N < 0$ for everybody and no market equilibrium exists. The same is true for $i\bar{\pi} - r = 0$. The only possibility consistent with both positive and negative b_N is a positive risk premium, that is, $i\bar{\pi} - r > 0$.

12.2 The Reasons for Nonexistence of a Market for Indexed Bonds

Before we consider the need for government intermediation in the indexed bond market, we have to inquire into the problem of why no such market develops on its own. We have noted elsewhere that, while it is possible to explain a "small" market for linked bonds, it is difficult to explain its complete nonexistence.[3] The reason for this is that r is the market rate of exchange between c and $\bar{w}$. Hence, as long as the consumers' marginal rate of substitution between c and $\bar{w}$ is not identical (when no market for b_L exists), some individuals may gain by trading in b_L. A complete non-existence of market for b_L may be partially explained by imperfections in capital markets particularly if the rate paid by borrowers is different from that received by lenders. Another partial explanation along the same lines may be a different attitude by consumers toward lending and borrowing. Thus the fact that only borrowing can lead to bankruptcy may create a special aversion for borrowing. In this case the excess demand function for bonds will have a jump (or discontinuity) at the point of transition from lending to borrowing. Under these circumstances it is possible to have a situation where the supply curve for bonds is always above the demand curve so that no trading occurs.

In principle the foregoing situation is not different from the one where we have a market for b_L, but the volume of transactions in this market is very small. The question in any of these cases is why this should happen under inflationary conditions, which apparently seem to favor the establishment of markets for linked bonds. The answer to this is that the variability in the value of money associated with the inflationary period tends to reduce the supply of linked bonds at the same time that it encourages the demand for linked bonds. In particular, people (or firms) who have nonlinked incomes and assets will prefer to borrow nonindexed so as to hedge against inflationary losses on this nonindexed wealth.[4] We shall therefore assume that the smallness of the market for indexed bonds or its complete nonexistence is due to the reluctance of people to assume indexed liabilities.

12.3 The Model of Government Intermediation

We shall assume that the purpose of government intermediation in the bonds market is to increase the size of the market for indexed bonds, or to create such a market when originally it did not exist, through the supply of government indexed bonds. This is based on the presumption mentioned earlier that the private sector is reluctant to issue indexed bonds. We assume that, in order to finance its indexed borrowing, the government lends in the nonindexed market (by buying b_N). Thus the government acts as an intermediary in the capital market, borrowing indexed and lending nonindexed in order to overcome the private sector's aversion to borrow "indexed." Our purpose is to investigate the implications of this intermediation.

A common argument is that by its intermediation the government enables the individuals (or firms) to reach a better diversification of their portfolios. This would indeed be the case if the individual could ignore the government need to finance any possible losses associated with its intermediating agency. Thus suppose that originally no market for b_L exists. Then the government issues a certain value of indexed bonds B_L^*, with r set equal to $i\bar{\pi}$, and then buys an equal value of nonindexed bonds B_N^*. Let us further assume that the government agency by its actions reduces the private ownership of nonlinked bonds by B_N^*; that is, the agency essentially replaces an amount B_N^* in the hands of the lenders by giving them an equal amount B_L^* of fixed indexed bonds (with r set at $i\bar{\pi}$) and getting B_N^*, an equal amount of other individual or firm's debts, in exchange.[5] As a result all the borrowers in the economy can remain in their original situation with respect to $\bar{w}$ and V_w. As for the original lenders ($b_N > 0$), we assume that they reduce their nonindexed lending (b_N) by the same amount of their purchase of b_L.

As $r = i\bar{\pi}$, the expected $w(\bar{w})$ remain unchanged. With the variance of w,

$$V_w = (m + ib_N)^2 V_\pi,$$

one easily observes that reducing b_N (by the same amount of indexed-bond purchasing) reduces V_w. Hence the lenders can be made better off and borrowers no worse off. Thus the introduction of government indexed bonds seems to improve the overall welfare in the economy.

If, however, we take into account the need of the government to balance its accounts associated with the intermediation we shall realize that no overall improvement in welfare, such as in the foregoing example, is possible. To calculate the government profits from intermediation, notice that it pays on each dollar it borrows $r(p_2/p_1)$ (or r/π) and gets i on each dollar it lends. Thus in real second-period magnitudes the agency's profits are $B^*(i\pi - r)$, where B^* is the value of its borrowing (or lending). Let us assume first that the government balances its accounts by paying out (in the form of transfer payments) to the consumers the agency's profits when the rate of inflation is relatively low ($i\pi - r > 0$) and by taxing the consumers to finance its losses when inflation is relatively high ($i\pi - r < 0$). Thus the government operates on the principle of a balanced budget. (We shall consider later the case where the government does not adhere to this principle.) We shall assume that the amount of transfer payments received by a particular individual is independent of the amounts lent or borrowed by him. Moreover we assume that the transfer payments do not vary across individuals so that it is equal to $b^*(i\pi - r)$ where b^* is the real per capita value invested in government bonds. The individuals are assumed to be aware of the system of transfer payments associated with the intermediation. The individuals wealth constraint can then be written as

$$w = y_2 + (m + ib_N)\pi + rb_L + b^*(i\pi - r)$$
$$= y_2 + [m + i(b_N + b^*)]\pi + r(b_L - b^*). \qquad (12.9)$$

The second-period variance of wealth is

$$V_w = [m + i(b_N + b^*)]^2 V_\pi. \qquad (12.10)$$

The term $-rb^*$ is the indexed indebtedness of consumers originating from the expected taxation. This debt is equivalent to any indexed loan of size b^*. The assumption is that this debt is no different, in any respect, from indebtedness through bonds—the consumers in their behavior take into account all the future tax payments. If without the government intermediation there has been no market for indexed bonds due to some individual aversion, it is intuitively clear that the introduction of indexed bonds by the government will not improve all consumers' welfare. The cost is the simultaneous introduction of indexed indebtedness of the consumers through their future taxes.

Consider again the example discussed earlier in this section, where we show that overall welfare can be increased if government accounts are ignored. In the present case as formulated in (12.9) and (12.10) government intermediation must be reflected in V_w of the borrowers as well as lenders. In particular, if originally $m + ib_N > 0$ for the borrowers, then (12.10) shows that government intermediation will increase borrowers' V_w and hence reduce their welfare, assuming again as in the previous case $r = i\pi$. If $m + ib_N < 0$, it seems that it is still possible to increase overall welfare even under (12.9) and (12.10), since then a small increase in b^* will reduce V_w for both borrower and lender. Under closer examination, however, it seems that in a perfect competitive market (ignoring transaction costs) $m + ib_N$ cannot be negative. This is implied by the fact that borrowers and lenders may benefit by shifting to some extent from nonindexed to indexed bonds. Hence, if we assume that no market for linked bonds existed originally, it must imply $m + ib_N \geqq 0.$[6] Thus there is always an additional cost to the borrower resulting from government intermediation.

A more general way of looking at the problem is as follows. We see from (12.9) that the government intermediation is equivalent to a new allocation of b_N and b_L among individuals. Thus, if we consider an indexed obligation to pay taxes rb^* as equivalent to indexed borrowing, then we may regard $b_L + b^* = \tilde{b}_L$ as effective indexed lending. Similarly, we may consider $b_N + b^* = \tilde{b}_N$ as effective nonindexed lending. Summing over all individuals, we also have $\sum \tilde{b}_L = \sum \tilde{b}_N = 0$. Hence $\tilde{b}_L$ and $\tilde{b}_N$ represent a feasible allocation of private loans. If this allocation of loans improves the overall welfare, then the original laissez faire allocation was not Pareto-optimal (on the set of all private allocations without government intermediation), which seems to be a contradiction. In other words, the government intermediation as described here is just a reshuffle of private loans and therefore is unlikely to improve upon the competitive allocation.[7]

We argued elsewhere, using the Arrow-Lind approach (Liviatan and Levhari 1981), that there does not seem to be a case for pooling advantages resulting from government intermediation in indexed bonds.[8] According to Arrow and Lind, an intermediation company of the kind we discussed will act on the basis of expected values, reducing overall risk if at least two conditions are satisfied. First, the variation in the company's profits must be independent of the other profits or incomes of its shareholders. Second, an individual shareholder's dividend from the company should be made negligible compared with his incomes from other sources, by increasing the number of shareholders. This, however, does not seem to be the case with the problem in question. Note that the intermediating company's profits will fluctuate with the value of money and so will all the nonlinked incomes and assets of the shareholders. Thus the independence criterion is not met. Furthermore, since everybody is involved in the bond market and everybody pays taxes, we cannot make the share of an individual shareholder negligible compared with his other incomes if the company is to handle a large fraction of the loan market in the economy.

We have assumed so far that the government acts on the basis of a balanced budget. Alternatively, the government could act on the basis of an unbalanced budget, financing the agency's losses by printing new money and using its profits to reduce the money supply. Thus, when inflation is relatively high so that the agency has losses, the government will increase the money supply; on the other hand, when inflation is relatively low so that the agency has profit, the money supply will contract. It follows that the agency will increase the instability of the money supply and therefore also the value of money. Consequently, some consumers will face a reduction in welfare.

In order to see more accurately the implications of deficit financing of intermediation losses, let us use a simple quantity theory approach. Thus let us assume that the next period price level changes proportionately to the quantity of money. The quantity of money per capita in the second period is

$$\bar{M}_2 = \bar{M}_1 + p_2 g - p_2 b^*(i\pi - r), \tag{12.11}$$

where $\bar{M}_1$ represents the first period per capita money supply, g represents real government deficit (per capita) through its regular expenditures, and $-b^*(i\pi - r)$ represents the real losses per capita which are added to the money supply (as it is financed by deficit). Here inflation is endogenously determined, by real government deficit spending g. The inflation path will be induced by g through its impact on the money supply. If g is assumed to be random so will be the implied price level.

The quantity theory assumed states that

$$\frac{\bar{M}_2}{p_2} = k, \tag{12.12}$$

where k is a constant. Combining (12.11) and (12.12) and using $\pi = p_1/p_2$, we obtain

$$\pi = \frac{k - rb^* - g}{\bar{m} - ib^*}, \tag{12.13}$$

where $\bar{m} = \bar{M}_1/p_1$. The expected value and variance of π are given by

$$\bar{\pi} = \frac{k - rb^*}{\bar{m} - ib^*} + \frac{1}{ib^* - \bar{m}}\bar{g}, \tag{12.14}$$

$$V_\pi = \frac{1}{(\bar{m} - ib^*)^2} V_g. \tag{12.15}$$

We assume that $ib^* < \bar{m}$, which means that the private nonindexed liability to the government in the next period is less than the original money supply. In this case an increase in b^* leads to an increase in V_π.

Consider again the experiment described earlier where the government intermediation leaves b_N of borrowers constant (shift from private to government borrowing) and reduces lenders b_N (shift from nonindexed to indexed lending) keeping everyone's $\bar{w}$ unchanged (by setting $r = \bar{i}\pi$). The variance of second-period wealth is

$$V_w = (m + ib_N)^2 V_\pi.$$

In the case of borrowers, V_w will increase as a result of the increase in V_π (through an increase in b^*), causing a reduction of welfare. As for lenders ($b_N > 0$), b_N will decline while V_π will increase, leading to compensated changes or changes in different directions in their welfare. Consequently, some consumers will be made worse off by the government intermediation.

Of course in reality the restrictions of the foregoing experiment are too tight, and the situation is more complicated. For example, the introduction of b^* will affect not only V_π but also $\bar{\pi}$ and will have additional effects on welfare. If we calculate the difference ($\Delta\bar{\pi}$) between the value of $\bar{\pi}$ with b^* and without, we obtain after some manipulation

$$\Delta\bar{\pi} = \frac{k - rb^* - g}{\bar{m} - ib^*} - \frac{k - g}{\bar{m}} = \frac{b^*(i\bar{\pi}^* - r)}{\bar{m}}, \tag{12.16}$$

where $\bar{\pi}^*$ denotes its value with b^*. Whatever the sign of $\Delta\bar{\pi}$ (of $i\bar{\pi} - r$), it will affect different consumers in different ways. Thus if $\Delta\bar{\pi}$ is positive, it will tend to improve the lenders welfare and reduce the welfare of large borrowers as it increases the value of their real debts.

In any case, since the increase in V_π will diminish welfare for a large section of the consumers, we see that a change in the mode of operation of the agency from direct taxation to deficit financing does not change drastically the conclusions.

12.4 The Impact of Governmental Intermediation on Consumer's Portfolio and Savings

So far we have considered government intermediation from the point of view of improving the allocation of risk in the economy. There are, however, other arguments in favor of linked bonds. One such argument states that the introduction of government linked bonds tends to encourage personal savings in inflationary times. Another argument concerns the composition of savings, or of consumers' portfolios. In particular, it is argued that linked bonds tend to channel investment that would otherwise take the form of investment in real assets as a hedge against inflationary uncertainty. Thus the introduction of linked bonds enables the economy to avoid real investment which is directed to the sole purpose of inflationary hedging.

In order to analyze the foregoing arguments, we have to extend our model and include in it a physical asset that may serve as a substitute for linked bonds. We cannot ignore, however, the fact that investment in real capital has risks of its own. Let us introduce, accordingly, a physical productive commodity with a random return of the variety of "technological uncertainty." For simplicity, we take this commodity to be identical with the commodity consumed, say, wheat. The quantity of wheat held as a productive asset will be denoted by $q(q \geq 0)$, and its gross rate of return (in physical units) will be denoted by x. We assume that x is a random variable with a known distribution. The individual's w is then

$$w_N = (m + ib_N)\pi + qx + rb_L,$$

$$b_N = y - c + \bar{m} - m - q - b_L, \tag{12.17}$$

with $\bar{w}$ and V_w given by

$$\bar{w}_N = (m + ib_N)\bar{\pi} + q\bar{x} + rb_L,$$

$$V_{w_N} = (m + ib_N)^2 V_\pi + q^2 V_x + 2q(m + ib_N)\text{cov}(x, \pi). \tag{12.18}$$

We have to make some assumption about the sign of $\text{cov}(\pi, x)$, and it seems reasonable to make it nonnegative. The reason for this is that a large value of x means a high "productivity," and the high level of output tends to bring the commodity price down in the next period. As p_2 goes down π $(= p_1/p_2)$ increases, hence the tendency for $\text{cov}(x, \pi)$ to be positive. This implies that q does not act as a hedge against inflation since its return moves in the same direction as the value of money.

Although it is reasonable to assume $\text{cov}(x, \pi) > 0$, its numerical value may be so small as to be ignored. This will be the case when there is much independent variation in π, such as that originating in the quantity of money and government deficits. For simplicity of calculation, we shall usually assume $\text{cov}(x, \pi) = 0$.

Let us consider now the effect of introducing government linked bonds, by means of intermediation, when no such market exists or of enlarging the size of an existing market for linked bonds when it is considered to be too small. To analyze the effects of this policy in a framework of general equilibrium seems to be at this stage too presumptuous. We shall confine ourselves instead to a simple experiment on the micro level that may nevertheless provide some clues as to the result of the (missing) market experiment.

The individual experiment is the following. Consider a consumer who reaches his optimum with respect to the variables c, m, q, b_L, and b_N at given interest rates and prices (i, r, and p_1) and a given distribution of π (this includes the case of no market for b_L, that is, $b_L \equiv 0$). Let the optimal values of b_N and b_L be denoted by b'_N and b'_L. Let us now change the role of b_N and b_L from decision variables to parameters and change arbitrarily the composition of bonds in favor of linked bonds holding their sum constant: $b_N + b_L = b'_N + b'_L$. Clearly, the change imposed on the composition of bonds will require an adjustment in the optimal quantities of c, m, and q. Our purpose is to inquire into the nature of the changes caused by the increase in the share of linked bonds in the overall portfolio. This experiment may be considered as a method of finding out which of the variables—c, m, or q—are substitutes and which are complements of b_L as the degree of bond linkage is increased. This may provide some indication as to the effect of increasing b_L through government intermediation.

For the purpose of all our subsequent calculations we shall assume the utility function for the next period to be the special quadratic form[9]

$$f(\overline{w}, V_w) \equiv \alpha\overline{w} - \beta(\overline{w}^2 + V_w),\tag{12.19}$$

with α, $\beta > 0$ and $f_{\overline{w}} = \alpha - 2\beta\overline{w} > 0$. Our starting point may be either a nonmixed regime with b_N but no b_L or mixed regime with both kinds of bonds. The first-order condition of optimality for the two alternative regimes can then be expressed as follows, assuming $\text{cov}(x, \pi) = 0$ and an internal solution for q:

$$u_c - i\overline{\pi}f_{\overline{w}} - 2\beta V_\pi(m + ib_N) = 0,$$

$$iu_m - (i - 1)u_c = 0,$$

$$\overline{x}f_{\overline{w}} - u_c - 2\beta q V_x = 0.\tag{12.20}$$

For the mixed regime the result is

$$u_c - f_{\bar w}r = 0,$$

$$u_m - f_{\bar w}r\frac{(i-1)}{i} = 0,$$

$$f_{\bar w}(r - \bar x) + 2\beta q V_x = 0,$$

$$-f_{\bar w}(i\bar\pi - r) + i2\beta V_\pi(m + ib_N) = 0. \tag{12.21}$$

It should be noted that the third equation in (12.21) implies that $\bar x > r$, while the fourth equation implies that $i\bar\pi - r > 0$ in a market equilibrium.[10]

Suppose that consumer is in equilibrium with respect to all variables c, m, q, b_N, and b_L, where in a nonmixed regime $h_L = 0$. Taking the optimal values of b_N and b_L as parameters, let us increase b_L (possibly from zero) at the expense of b_N, that is, $db_N/db_L = -1$. We then examine the effect of this change on the remaining decision variables c, q, and m. The results of this experiment are as follows (see appendix):

$$\frac{dc}{db_L} = \{u_{mm}\bar x(i\bar\pi - r) + 2\beta[(r - i\bar x)\bar x V_\pi \quad \bar\pi V_x - iV_x V_\pi]\}\frac{2\beta}{D}, \tag{12.22}$$

$$\frac{dq}{db_L} = \{-(u_{mm} + u_{cc})\bar x(i\bar\pi - r) + u_{cc}[\bar\pi(i\bar\pi - r) + iV_\pi] - 2\beta\bar x r V_\pi\}\frac{2\beta}{D}, \tag{12.23}$$

$$\frac{dm}{db_L} = \{-u_{cc}[(i\bar\pi - r)(\bar\pi - \bar x) + iV_\pi] + 2\beta[\bar\pi V_x + iV_\pi(\bar x^2 + V_x)]\}\frac{2\beta}{D}, \tag{12.24}$$

where D is the determinant of the system and is positive by the second-order conditions.

For the mixed regime, r is the market equilibrium value and, as we have seen, must satisfy $i\bar\pi - r > 0$ and $\bar x - r > 0$—reflecting the fact that b_N and q being subject to risk must carry a positive risk premium in terms of expected returns. For the nonmixed regime, r is set by the government on its bonds. However, if everyone is allowed to purchase any amount of b_L at the given r, then market equilibrium constraints lead us again to positive risk premiums on b_N and q. It seems therefore reasonable to assume $i\bar\pi - r > 0$ and $\bar x > r > 0$.

Consider first the effect of increasing b_L (at the expense of b_N) on current consumption, c. Assuming a concave utility function, we have $u_{mm} < 0$. The sign of $r - i\bar{x}$ is negative since $\bar{x} > r$ and $i > 1$. It follows that $dc/db_L < 0$ so that more indexation in the bond market discourages current consumption and encourages saving. It is somewhat surprising that with all our simplifying assumptions we did not obtain a definite effect on q and m. Thus it is not at all clear whether the introduction of linked bonds will reduce investment in physical assets. The reason for this seems to be that not only the real value of money is subject to variation, because of π, but also the real asset, because of x. In a market equilibrium the relative return on these two assets (u_m being the return on money) is adjusted to compensate for the differences in variances, and it is not at all clear a priori which of these assets (if any) should be reduced as b_L increases. The only fact that is clear is that $m + q$ will increase since this is the counterpart of the reduction in c.

It seems, however, that in the case of m we can state on the basis of (12.24) a reasonable sufficient condition for $dm/db_L > 0$ which is[11]

$$V_\pi > (\bar{x} - \pi)\frac{(i\pi - r)}{i}. \tag{12.25}$$

The expression on the right-hand side is positive if q has a positive net productivity $\bar{x} > 1$, since then $\bar{x} - \bar{\pi} > 0$ under inflationary conditions ($\bar{\pi} < 1$). Thus, if V_π is sufficiently large, the demand for real balances will increase with b_L at the expense of $c + q$ which implies that the introduction of linked bonds has an anti-inflationary effect. Whether V_π is in fact large relative to the expression on the right-hand side is, of course, a question of empirical nature.[12]

To conclude, our experiment seems to indicate the following consequences of introducing linked bonds: a reduction in expenditures on current consumption, an indeterminate effect on investment in physical capital, and a decrease in aggregate demand for physical commodities (consumption plus capital goods), provided the variance of the value of money is sufficiently large.

12.5 Reaction to Increasing Uncertainty of Inflation

In the foregoing analysis we examined the consequences of increasing the share of linked bonds in a given inflationary setting. A different, and no less important, question is how do the alternative regimes (nonmixed and mixed) react to changes in the variance of the value of money. It is often argued that the mixed system tends to react in a better way to growing uncertainty of the value of money, as compared with the nonmixed one. For example, it is argued that in the absence of linked bonds an increase in V_π will cause a flight from money and into commodities, thus increasing inflationary pressure and leading to wasteful real investments. This tendency may be considerably mitigated when there exists a linked financial asset, such as linked bonds.

In order to examine the reaction of the alternative regimes to an increase in V_π, we differentiated the two sets of first-order conditions in (12.20) and (12.21) with respect to V_π. Differentiating (12.20), representing the nonmixed regime, we obtain, assuming $\text{cov}(x, \pi) = 0$ (see appendix),[12]

$$\frac{dc}{dV_\pi} = \frac{(2\beta i)^2 (m + i b_N) u_{mm}}{D'} [\bar{x}(\bar{x} - i\bar{\pi}) + V_x] > 0,$$

$$\text{if } V_x > \bar{x}(i\bar{\pi} - \bar{x}), \tag{12.26}$$

$$\frac{dm}{dV_\pi} = \frac{(2\beta i)^2 (m + i b_N) u_{cc}}{D'} [\bar{x}(\bar{x} - i\bar{\pi}) + V_x] > 0,$$

$$\text{if } V_x > \bar{x}(i\bar{\pi} - \bar{x}), \tag{12.27}$$

$$\frac{dq}{dV_\pi} = \frac{2\beta i(m + i b_N)}{D'} [(i - 1)^2 u_{cc} 2\beta\bar{\pi}\bar{x} + i u_{mm}(2\beta i\bar{\pi}\bar{x} - u_{cc})] > 0, \tag{12.28}$$

$$\frac{db_N}{dV_\pi} = \frac{2\beta i^2 (m + i b_N)}{D'} \{2\beta(-u_{cc})[\bar{x}(\bar{x} - \bar{\pi}) + V_x]$$

$$+ [u_{cc} - 2\beta(\bar{x}^2 + V_x)] i u_{mm} < 0, \tag{12.29}$$

$$\frac{d(c + q)}{dV_\pi} = \frac{2\beta i(m + i b_N)}{D'} \{2\beta i u_{mm}(\bar{x}^2 + V_x)$$

$$+ u_{cc}[2\beta(i - 1)^2 \bar{x}\bar{\pi} - i u_{mm}]\} > 0, \tag{12.30}$$

where $D' < 0$ is the determinant of the system of equations. It is assumed that $\bar{x} > \bar{\pi}$ since generally $\bar{x} > 1$ and in inflation $\bar{\pi} < 1$.

It can be seen that the signs of all the derivatives depend on the sign of $m + i b_N$. The intuitive explanations for the opposite reaction of those with $m + i b_N > 0$ (which includes all lenders and some of the borrowers) as compared with those with $m + ib_N < 0$ (large borrowers) can be illustrated by the following argument. Consider the effect of increasing q at the expense of b_N on the expected utility. This yields

$$\frac{\partial U}{\partial q} = f_w(\bar{x} - i\bar{\pi}) - 2if_{V_w} V_\pi(m + ib_N) + 2qf_{V_w} V_x,$$

(see appendix, equation 12.40). We see that an increase in V_π raises the marginal utility of q and therefore tends to increase q to people with $m + ib_N > 0$. Lenders reducing b_N to acquire q reduce the source of variability originating from the variability of π. While borrowers having to increase their liabilities ($|b_N|$ increases) so that the absolute value of their debts (which is the quantity relevant for determining the risk originating from π) increases. Thus acquiring an additional unit of q becomes more attractive for the lenders and less attractive for the borrowers.

Unlike the case of the mixed regime, to be discussed later, the sign of $m + ib_N$ cannot be determined for any particular individual. However, for the average individual we must have $m + ib_N > 0$ since in a market equilibrium $\sum b_N = 0$ (when summed over all individuals). In analyzing the foregoing results, we shall therefore treat $m + ib_N$ as if it were positive. The need to make this assumption reflects nevertheless a fundamental ambiguity in our results. It is possible that one may interpret this fact (that there are people with $m + ib_N > 0$ and $m + ib_N < 0$) as indicating that the overall effect of changes in V_π on our system is not very significant. One may envisage that the people with $m + ib_N < 0$ may react more strongly than people with $m + ib_N > 0$, and thus the aggregate effect of a change in V_π is not altogether clear. In the following discussion we shall assume that the consideration that $m + ib_N > 0$ is the dominant one.

The first result in equation (12.26) shows that the effect of V_π on c cannot be determined unambiguously. Current consumption will increase if and only if

$$V_x > \bar{x}(i\bar{\pi} - \bar{x}), \tag{12.31}$$

that is, if the return on the physical asset is sufficiently variable.[13] If, alternatively, the riskiness of q is small relative to nonlinked bonds, then V_x will be small and $i\bar{\pi} - \bar{x} > 0$ (reflecting a positive risk premium on b_N) which will reverse the inequality in (12.31). For the limiting case $V_x = 0$, q is a perfectly safe asset so that $i\bar{\pi} > \bar{x}$ and hence $V_x = 0 < \bar{x}(i\bar{\pi} - \bar{x})$. This is the case where q and b_L have the same properties from the point of view of the saver, and we know from our earlier discussion that for this case $i\bar\pi - \bar x > 0$. To conclude, an increase in V_π will increase c if the physical asset is sufficiently risky (so that it is not a close substitute for linked bonds), but it will decrease c if q is close in its properties to linked bonds.

The other results indicate that $dq/dV_\pi > 0$, as expected. It is also interesting to note that regardless of the sign of dc/dV_π we always have $d(c + q)/dV_\pi > 0$, that is, an increase in V_π creates an excess demand for physical commodities in general. One may be tempted to think that this implies an increase in the current price level. However, the latter effect must also depend on the developments in the money market. Thus the calculation in (12.26) shows that $dm/dV_\pi > 0$ if V_x is large—if (12.31) holds. In this case there will be no "flight from money" since the alternative asset, q, is also very risky. Since the increased demand for money is a potentially deflationary factor, it follows that, when (12.31) holds, we cannot be sure as to whether an increase in V_π is inflationary. If, however, V_x is sufficiently small, then we have both an increase in the overall demand for commodities and a decrease in the demand for money which guarantees the inflationary nature of increased V_π in the nonmixed regime. Note, however, that in the latter case the demand for c will increase, which may result in a small overall effect in the commodity market.

In the case of the mixed regime we know that $i\bar\pi - r > 0$, and hence $m + ib_N > 0$ for everybody, so that at least this source of ambiguity is removed. We also know that $\bar x > r$. Differentiating the first-order condition in (12.21) with respect to V_π, we obtain (see appendix):

$$\frac{dc}{dV_\pi} = \frac{2\beta i(m + ib_N)}{D''}u_{mm}(2\beta)^2 V_x r(i\bar\pi - r) < 0, \tag{12.32}$$

$$\frac{dq}{dV_\pi} = \frac{2\beta i(m + ib_N)}{D''}2\beta u_{cc}u_{mm}(r - \bar x)(r - i\bar\pi) > 0, \tag{12.33}$$

$$\frac{dm}{dV_\pi} = \frac{2\beta i(m + ib_N)}{D''}(2\beta)^2 u_{cc}\frac{(i - 1)}{i}r(i\bar\pi - r)V_x < 0, \tag{12.34}$$

$$\frac{db_L}{dV_\pi} = \frac{2\beta i(m + ib_N)}{D''}\{u_{cc}u_{mm}(-2\beta)[(\bar x - i\bar\pi)(r - \bar x) - V_x]$$

$$- (2\beta)^2\frac{(i - 1)^2}{i}\bar\pi r V_x u_{cc} - (2\beta)^2 i\bar\pi r V_x u_{mm}\}, \tag{12.35}$$

$$\frac{db_N}{dV_\pi} = \frac{2\beta i(m + ib_N)}{D''}\{-u_{cc}u_{mm}2\beta[(r - \bar{x})^2 + V_x]$$

$$+ u_{cc}(2\beta)^2\frac{(i-1)}{i}rV_x(r - \bar{\pi}) + u_{mm}r^2(2\beta)^2V_x\} < 0, \qquad (12.36)$$

where $D'' > 0$ is the determinant of the equation system.

It can be seen that, unlike in the nonmixed regime, dc/dV_π is now unambiguously negative. This seems to support the hypothesis that the mixed regime is more favorable to saving when V_π increases. We also see that the investment in q increases under both regimes. However the effect of V_π on $c + q$ is ambiguous, in contrast to the result for the nonmixed case. This seems to indicate that the overall pressure on the commodity market is less definite in the mixed case, again in line with the popular hypothesis. However, in order to consider the inflationary pressure, we must also look at the demand for money which by (12.34) is unambiguously reduced as V_π increases. This is potentially a source of inflationary pressure. Thus q and m tend to increase inflationary pressure while c tends to reduce it.

On the whole it seems that the qualitative differences in the reaction to the two regimes to an increase in V_π are not clear-cut, especially with respect to the resulting inflationary pressure. In both cases the behavior of the demand for money leads to unexpected results. Thus in the nonmixed regime, when (12.31) holds, the increase in the demand for money, as V_π increases, modifies the effects of the increased demand for both the consumption and investment commodities. On the other hand, in the mixed regime the reduced demand for money tends to stimulate inflationary pressure which counteracts the deflationary effect of the reduced demand for consumption commodities. The comparison is clearer with respect to current consumption of commodities which tends to increase with V_π, when (12.31) holds, in the nonmixed regime and to decline in the mixed one.

12.6 The Comparative Strength of the Effect V_π in the Alternative System

A common feature of the two systems is that an increase in V_π leads to increased investment in the physical asset q. It seems that even in the mixed system one cannot avoid some wasteful real investment designed only as a hedge against inflationary uncertainty. It can be argued that the increase in q under the mixed regime is likely to be smaller than under the nonmixed one. The basic reason for this is that under the mixed regime the increase in b_L, which is to be expected as V_π increases, absorbs already some of the increased demand for real, or linked, assets. Let us examine this argument more carefully.

There are three points on which the foregoing argument is based. First, it is taken for granted that investment in b_L increases with V_π. Examining (12.35), we find that this hypothesis is not necessarily true, although there seems to be a tendency in this direction. A sufficient condition to ensure $db_L/dV_\pi > 0$ is

$$V_x > (i\bar{\pi} - \bar{x})(\bar{x} - r). \tag{12.37}$$

Thus db_L/dV_π is positive when q is sufficiently risky. If, for example, q carries a risk premium relative to $b_N (\bar{x} > i\bar{\pi})$, then (12.36) must necessarily hold (since $\bar{x} > r$).

Assuming (12.37) holds, so that $db_L/dV_\pi > 0$, we must assume in addition that the nature of q is such that the foregoing increase in b_L reduces the necessity to increase q. It remains to be shown what is the exact nature of substitutability involved in this case.

The third point is that dq/dV_π is evaluated in the two regimes at two different points—at different sets of c, m, and other variables. In order that the comparison be meaningful, we have to assume that the foregoing does not affect the comparison. A somewhat artificial method of expressing this last assumption is by actually evaluating dq/dV_π at the same point in both systems. This can be done by starting at some equilibrium point of the mixed system and then evaluating dq/dV_π under two alternative assumptions: (1) all variables (c, m, q, b_N, b_L) are free to react to the change in V_π and (2) all variables excluding b_L are free to react, while b_L itself is constrained to remain fixed at its original value. We shall call (1) the "free variation" in q and denote it by dq^f/dV_π, while (2) will be called "constrained variation" and denoted by dq^c/dV_π. The comparison of these two variations is in fact based on a generalized Le Chatelier principle.

Having stated the problem formally, it is a straightforward mathematical problem to compare the free and constrained variations. Using a fundamental property of determinants (see appendix), we arrive at the following result:

$$\text{sign} \left(\frac{dq^c}{dV_\pi} - \frac{dq^f}{dV_\pi} \right) = \text{sign} \frac{db_L^f}{dV_\pi} \frac{db_L^f}{dV_x}, \tag{12.38}$$

where db_L^f/dV_π is given by (12.34) and db_L^f/dV_x is obtained by differentiating the first-order condition in (12.21) with respect to the variance of x (holding V_π and other parameters constant). This result shows that, if $db_L^f/dV_\pi > 0$, and in addition b_L is a substitute with respect to q in the sense that $db_L^f/dV_x > 0$, then indeed $dq^c/dV_\pi > dq^f/dV_\pi$. This is a reasonable result that does in fact support the theory that under the mixed regime the expansion of q (as a result of increased V_π) will be more moderate.

It must be noted that the foregoing result by itself does not imply that the inflationary pressure will increase more (with V_π) under the nonmixed regime. As we noted earlier, we also look at the behavior of the money market. If in the nonmixed regime the demand for money increases with V_π, then this counteracts the inflationary tendencies in the commodity market. Let us tackle, however, the more difficult problem where $dm/dV_\pi < 0$ in both systems. Assuming again that we start at the same point, we may ask under what conditions will m decline more in the free (mixed) as compared with the constrained regime?

It can be shown that the reduction of the demand for m in the mixed system (as V_π increases) will be greater when b_L and m are substitute assets in the following sense. Let γ be a parameter representing liquidity preference in the current utility function so that the latter can be written as $u(c, m, \alpha)$ with $\partial u_m/\partial\gamma > 0$, $\partial u_c/\partial\gamma = 0$. As liquidity preference, γ, increases, there will be a general tendency to increase m at the expense of other assets. If, in differentiating the system (12.21) with respect to γ, we obtain $db_L/d\gamma < 0$, then the decline in m will be greater under the free (mixed) regime, provided $db_L/dV_\pi > 0$. Analogously to (12.37), we obtain (see appendix)

$$\text{sign}\left(\frac{dm^c}{dV_\pi} - \frac{dm^f}{dV_\pi}\right) = \text{sign}\left(-\frac{db_L}{dV_\pi}\frac{db_L}{d\gamma}\right). \tag{12.39}$$

Thus, if m and b_L are substitutes in the foregoing sense, the excess supply of money created in the free system (as a result of increased V_π) will always be larger than in the constrained one, thus creating an inflationary bias in the free system.

12.7 Comments on General Equilibrium Considerations

We have analyzed the individual agent's behavior under the alternative systems and their reactions to increased variability in the value of money.

We have assumed that the parameters r, i, x, π, and p_1 are given to the individual. In a general equilibrium setup all these parameters are endogenous and determined within the system. Let us assume that the price rise π is still exogenously determined but the rest of the parameters are determined within the economic system. Then a change in V_π will affect the behavior of the individual agents and therefore the equilibrium of r, i, p_1, and the probability distribution of x. One has to take into account the supply of resources in the economy as a whole and the fact that the demand for real goods $c + q$ cannot exceed their supply. If an increase in V_π induces in a regime without indexed bonds a rise in $c + q$, the impact on the money and bonds market may induce changes in the price level, p_1, in rate of interest and rates of return on physical assets that will have impact on c, q, and m. If as an equilibrium condition we have that $c + q$ summed over all individuals has to be a constant (such as the GNP), then the change in the parameters must bring about such a situation.

Suppose, as we observed in our analysis of q and c, that, as V_π increases, the demand for q increases more in a market without indexed bonds and therefore with given parameters the individual agents will like to invest more in physical assets. This may not be the result in a general equilibrium setup. We have to find out what happens in other markets as well, and in particular to consumption goods demand. With an indexed bonds market a rise in V_π will decrease consumption c and therefore release more resources for investment purposes. The overall result may be more real investment in the indexed regime rather than in the nonindexed regime.

Moreover, as mentioned, one has to look at the impact of a rise in V_π in the money market. In the nonindexed case $dm/dV_\pi > 0$ (if V_x is sufficiently large). This may reduce the inflationary pressures and counteract $d(c + q)/dV_\pi > 0$. In the indexed case the effect on $c + q$ is ambiguous, and the impact on the commodity market of a rise in V_π is not definite, but the demand for money is reduced ($dm/dV_\pi < 0$), creating extra inflationary pressures. Thus, if we analyze all the markets and the money market as well, we may obtain, as mentioned earlier, unexpected results in comparing the two regimes. Furthermore the effect of the money market may change the equilibrium values of i and other parameters.

In sum, from this analysis of individual behavior with and without indexed bonds, the impact of the different regimes in general equilibrium, when the parameters are allowed to change appropriately, is much harder and the direction of changes is not as clear.

12.8 Summary

At the beginning of this chapter it was shown that government intermediation in the indexed bonds market has its cost either through the need
for taxation (or subsidy) contingent on the change in the purchasing value
of money or through the need to change the money supply to cover losses
(or gains) of intermediation. When the cost is taken into account, then the
claim that we can improve the position of everybody is not warranted.

We have seen that a policy of introducing governmental linked bonds,
at the expense of nonlinked ones, tends to reduce current consumption
of commodities, but it is not clear whether it tends to reduce demand for
real investment. It is also not clear whether this policy tends to reduce
aggregate demand for commodities and thus current inflationary
pressures. The latter effect will be achieved when the variance of the
value of money is sufficiently large.

As for the reaction of the mixed and nonmixed regimes to an increase
in the variance of the value of money (V_π), we have the following conclusions. If there is a considerable variability in the returns on physical
investment (which is a reasonable assumption), then an increase in V_π
will increase demand for current consumption in the nonmixed regime
and reduce it in the mixed one. Demand for investment in physical assets
will increase under both regimes, but the increase is likely to be greater
under the nonmixed regime (this is likely to be the case when physical
assets and linked bonds are substitutes in the sense defined earlier). In
general equilibrium, however, these statements have to be qualified, as
explained in the preceding section. It is not clear whether the current
inflationary pressure resulting from an increase in V_π will be smaller in
the mixed regime. This is related to the fact that there does not seem to
be a tendency for a flight from money (and into commodities) under the
nonmixed regime.

The main advantages of mixed regimes seem to lie in the tendency of
this regime to keep the demand for current consumption and investment
in physical capital at relatively lower levels under the conditions specified
earlier. If this is considered as an advantage, then it is achieved at the cost
of a relatively inefficient allocation of risk in the economy.

Appendix

We use the system described by (12.17) and (12.18) and the expected utility function $Q = u(c, m) + \alpha \bar{w} - \beta(\bar{w}^2 + V_w)$. We assume throughout that $\text{cov}(x, \pi) = 0$ and $u_{cm} = 0$. In the first experiment described in section 12.4 we freeze arbitrarily the variables b_N and b_L. This leaves us with three independent variables—c, m, and q—any one of which can be determined by the other two in view of the budget constraint in (12.17). Using this fact to eliminate c, we maximize Q with respect to m and q, obtaining the following first-order conditions:

$$u_m - u_c + (\alpha - 2\beta\bar{w})\bar{\pi} - 2\beta(m + ib_N)V_\pi = 0,$$

$$-u_c + (\alpha - 2\beta\bar{w})\bar{x} - 2\beta q V_x = 0.$$

We then differentiate this system with respect to the parameter b_L subject to $db_N/db_L = -1$. Note that, using (12.17), we have $d\bar{w}/db_L = r - i\bar{\pi}$ and $dV_w/db_L = -2\beta i V_\pi(m + ib_N)$. Some simple calculations lead to the results in (12.22) through (12.24). The value of the determinant of the system, D, is positive as a second-order maximum condition.

To obtain the first-order conditions in (12.20), we first differentiate Q with respect to c, m, and q (considering b_N as a function of these variables by (12.17) and equate the derivatives by zero, ignoring b_L altogether. After performing some manipulation with these equations, which leave the sign of the determinant of the system unchanged, we obtain the equation system (12.20). Differentiating (12.20) with respect to V_π, we obtain, in matrix form,

$$Az = g,$$

where z and g are the vectors. Thus

$$z = \begin{bmatrix} \dfrac{dc}{dV_\pi} \\[6pt] \dfrac{dm}{dV_\pi} \\[6pt] \dfrac{dq}{dV_\pi} \end{bmatrix}, \quad g = \begin{bmatrix} -2i(m + ib_N) \\[6pt] 0 \\[6pt] 0 \end{bmatrix},$$

and $A = [a_{ij}]$ is the matrix whose elements are

$a_{11} = u_{cc} - 2\beta i^2(\bar{\pi}^2 + V_\pi), \quad a_{12} = -\beta 2i(i-1)(\bar{\pi}^2 + V_\pi),$

$a_{13} = 2\beta i[\bar{\pi}(\bar{x} - i\bar{\pi}) - iV_\pi],$

$a_{21} = -(i-1)u_{cc}, \quad a_{22} = iu_{mm}, \quad a_{23} = 0,$

$a_{31} = 2\beta i\bar{x}\bar{\pi} - u_{cc}, \quad a_{32} = 2\beta(i-1)\bar{x}\bar{\pi},$

$a_{33} = -2\beta[\bar{x}(\bar{x} - i\bar{\pi}) + V_x].$

The results (12.25) through (12.29) are obtained by straightforward application of Cramér's rule. The determinant of A, denoted D', is negative by second-order conditions.

To obtain the first-order condition of (12.21), we first differentiate Q with respect to c, m, q, and b_L (considering b_N as a function of the other variables) and equate the derivatives to zero. After some manipulation with these equations (but keeping the sign of the determinant of the system unchanged), we obtain the system (12.21). Differentiating this system with respect to V_π, we obtain in matrix form

$\bar{A}\bar{z} = \bar{g},$

where

$$\bar{z} = \begin{bmatrix} \dfrac{dc}{dV_\pi} \\ \dfrac{dm}{dV_\pi} \\ \dfrac{db_L}{dV_\pi} \\ \dfrac{dq}{dV_\pi} \end{bmatrix}, \quad \bar{g} = \begin{bmatrix} 0 \\ 0 \\ 0 \\ -2i(m + ib_N) \end{bmatrix},$$

and the first three rows of the matrix $\bar{A} = [\bar{a}_{ij}]$ are given by[15]

$\bar{a}_{11} = u_{cc} - 2\beta ri\bar{\pi}, \quad \bar{a}_{12} = -2\beta r\bar{\pi}(i-1),$

$\bar{a}_{13} = 2\beta r(r - i\bar{\pi}), \quad \bar{a}_{14} = 2\beta r(\bar{x} - i\bar{\pi}),$

$\bar{a}_{21} = -2\beta(i-1)r\bar{\pi}, \quad \bar{a}_{22} = u_{mm} - 2\beta r\bar{\pi}\dfrac{(i-1)^2}{i},$

$\bar{a}_{23} = 2\beta r\dfrac{(i-1)}{i}(r - i\bar{\pi}), \quad \bar{a}_{24} = 2\beta r\dfrac{(i-1)}{i}(\bar{x} - i\bar{\pi}),$

$$\bar{a}_{31} = 2\beta(r - \bar{x})i\bar{\pi}, \quad \bar{a}_{32} = 2\beta(r - \bar{x})(i - 1)\bar{\pi},$$

$$\bar{a}_{33} = -2\beta(r - \bar{x})(r - i\bar{\pi}), \quad \bar{a}_{34} = -2\beta[(r - \bar{x})(\bar{x} - i\bar{\pi}) - V_x].$$

The determinant of $\bar{A}$, denoted D'', is positive by second-order conditions. The results in (12.31) through (12.35) are obtained by straightforward, but usually rather tedious, calculations, using Cramér's rule.

The results in sections 12.5 and 12.6 are based on the following lemma:[16] let D denote the determinant of order $n \times n$, and let D_{ij} denote the minor corresponding to the (i,j)th position. Let $D_{ij \cdot nn}$ denote the minor of the (i,j)th position in a matrix of order $(n - 1) \times (n - 1)$ which is obtained from the original $n \times n$ matrix with the nth row and nth column deleted. We then have

$$\frac{D_{ij \cdot nn}}{D_{nn}} = \frac{D_{ij}}{D} - \frac{D_{in}}{D} \frac{D_{jn}}{D_{nn}} \tag{12.39}$$

Differentiating Q with respect to c, m, q, and b_L, and using $b_N = y - c + \bar{m} - m - q - b_L$, we obtain the following system of first-order conditions:

$$u_c - f_{\bar{w}}i\bar{\pi} + i\beta A = 0,$$

$$u_m - f_{\bar{w}}(i - 1)\bar{\pi} + (i - 1)\beta A = 0,$$

$$f_{\bar{w}}(\bar{x} - i\bar{\pi}) + i\beta A - 2q\beta V_x = 0,$$

$$f_{\bar{w}}(r - i\bar{\pi}) + i\beta A = 0, \tag{12.40}$$

where $A = 2V_\pi(m + ib_N)$.

We differentiate the foregoing system with respect to V_π and assign to c, m, q, and b_L the indexes of 1, 2, 3, and 4, respectively. We also assign to V_π the notation v. Then we denote by D_{ij} the minors in the (i,j)th position of the matrix, M, obtained by differentiating the system in (12.40). We also denote by Q_{iv} the mixed partial derivative of Q with respect to i ($i = 1, \ldots, 4$) and V_π. We then obtain the following solution for q and b_L:

$$\frac{dq^f}{dV_\pi} = -Q_{1v}\frac{D_{13}}{D} + Q_{2v}\frac{D_{23}}{D} - Q_{3v}\frac{D_{33}}{D} + Q_{4v}\frac{D_{43}}{D}, \tag{12.41}$$

$$\frac{db_L^f}{DV_\pi} = Q_{1v}\frac{D_{14}}{D} - Q_{2v}\frac{D_{24}}{D} + Q_{3v}\frac{D_{34}}{D} - Q_{4v}\frac{D_{44}}{D}. \tag{12.42}$$

If, alternatively, we consider b_L as a parameter (with its value equal to the optimal value of b_L), then in the matrix M we delete the fourth row and column. The solution for dq/dV_π with b_L held fixed is given by

$$
\frac{dq^c}{dV} = -Q_{1v}\frac{D_{13\cdot 44}}{D_{44}} + Q_{2v}\frac{D_{23\cdot 44}}{D_{44}} - Q_{3v}\frac{D_{33\cdot 44}}{D_{44}}
$$

$$
= -Q_{1v}\left(\frac{D_{13}}{D} - \frac{D_{14}}{D}\frac{D_{34}}{D_{44}}\right) + Q_{2v}\left(\frac{D_{23}}{D} - \frac{D_{24}}{D}\frac{D_{34}}{D_{44}}\right)
$$

$$
- Q_{3v}\left(\frac{D_{33}}{D} - \frac{D_{34}}{D}\frac{D_{43}}{D_{44}}\right), \tag{12.43}
$$

where the last equality is obtained by using (12.39). Combining (12.42) and (12.43) and using the symmetry of the Hessian matrix ($D_{ij} = D_{ji}$), we have

$$
\frac{dq^c}{dV_\pi} = \frac{dq^f}{dV_\pi} + \frac{db_L^f}{dV}\frac{D_{34}}{D_{44}}. \tag{12.44}
$$

However, examining (12.40), we see immediately that $db_L^f/dV_x = -2\beta q$ (D_{34}/D). Hence

$$
\frac{D_{34}}{D_{44}} = -\frac{D}{D_{44}}\frac{1}{2\beta q}\frac{db_L^f}{dV_x} = k\frac{db_L^f}{dV_x}, \quad k > 0.
$$

since D and D_{44} are of opposite sign. Inserting the last result in (12.44) we obtain

$$
\frac{dq^c}{dV_\pi} - \frac{dq^f}{dV_\pi} = k\frac{db_L^f}{dV_\pi}\frac{db_L^f}{dV_\pi}, \quad k > 0, \tag{12.45}
$$

as stated in the text. The result in (12.38) is obtained in exactly the same manner.

Notes

This chapter is based on ideas, research, and previous papers by N. Liviatan and myself.

1. See, for example, G. L. Bach and R. A. Musgrave, "A Stable Purchasing Power Bond," *American Economic Review*, 1974, pp. 823–825; R. Goode, "A Constant Purchasing Power Saving Bond," *National Tax Journal*, 1951, pp. 332–340; A. Morag, "For an Inflation Proof Economy," *American Economic Review*, 1962, pp. 177–185; M. Friedman, "Using Escalators to Help Fight Inflation," *Fortune*, July 1974.

2. The model follows closely N. Liviatan and D. Levhari, "Risk and the Theory of Indexed Bonds," Research Report No. 67, Department of Economics, The Hebrew University of Jerusalem, March 1975.

3. Ibid.

4. This is so since an increase in the rate of inflation that leads to a reduction in the real value of nominal assets reduces at the same time the real value of debt.

5. This is not an equilibrium situation, and it can be shown that in equilibrium $i\bar{\pi} > r$. The purpose of the experiment is only to consider the possibility of improvement for everybody.

6. Since $V_w = (m + ib_N)^2 V_\pi$, then reducing $|b_N|$ for borrower (with $m + ib_N < 0$) and lender in exchange for an equal amount of b_L, so as to preserve the means, must reduce both variances.

7. A more complete discussion of this case can be found in the author's paper: "On the Deflationary Effect of Government's Indexed Bonds," *Journal of Monetary Economics*, vol. 5, pp. 535–550.

8. K. J. Arrow and R. C. Lind, "Uncertainty and the Evaluation of Public Investment," *American Economic Review*, 1970, pp. 364–378.

9. So that expected utility is given by $u(c, m) + \alpha\bar{w} - \beta(\bar{w}^2 + V_w)$.

10. This has been shown earlier. Suppose that $i\bar{\pi} - r \leq 0$. Then $m + ib_N \leq 0$ for every consumer, assuming identical $\bar{\pi}$. Summing over all individuals, this implies $\sum m + i \sum b_N \leq 0$. But $\sum b_N = 0$ in a market equilibrium, which implies $\sum m \leq 0$. This contradicts, however, the assumption of positive money holdings.

11. A possible intuitive explanation may run as follows. By supplying more indexing, that is, by increasing b_L relative to b_N, we provide him with more safety as far as changes in π are concerned. He may afford to enjoy therefore more liquidity despite the risk associated with it.

12. It should also be noted that, as we increase V_π, the value of the right-hand side will tend to decrease since the market is likely to react to an increase in b_L by increasing r and reducing i.

13. If $\text{cov}(x, \pi) > 0$, then the same kind of calculation shows that dq/dV_π is again positive. The condition for $dm/dV_\pi > 0$ is modified to $V_x(1 - A_{\pi x}) > \bar{x}(i\bar{\pi} - \bar{x})$, where $A_{\pi x} = [\text{cov}(x, \pi)]/V_x$ (the regression coefficient of π on x). As for the expression of db_N/dV_π we replace in (12.28) the expression $[\bar{x}(\bar{x} - \bar{\pi}) + V_x]$ by $[\bar{x}(\bar{x} - \bar{\pi}) + V_x(1 - A_{\pi x})]$; hence, if $A_{\pi x} < 1$, the sign of db_N/dV_π remains negative.

14. Note that a high riskiness of q will also tend to create a positive risk premium for q, that is, tend to make $\bar{x} - i\bar{\pi} > 0$, which is sufficient to insure that (12.30) holds.

15. The fourth row does not enter the calculations.

16. See P. H. Hanus, *Theory of Determinants*, Boston, 1888, pp. 56–60.

IV Panel Discussion

Opening Remarks

Robert J. Barro

The discussion in this book deals with indexation in several contexts. I will summarize the main points within three interrelated subject areas: indexing and business fluctuations, indexing and asset markets, and indexing as part of a positive theory of governmental behavior.

Wage Indexation and Business Fluctuations

Methods for general indexing of nominal wages matter for business cycles for the same reason that systematic monetary policy matters. Keynesian models with indexing were described by Gray and Simonsen and were perhaps motivated by the model of Blanchard. A central element is the partial predetermination of wages (and/or prices) in nominal terms. This element of nominal stickiness may derive from market processes, as in labor contracts that prespecify nominal wage rates. The stickiness may also reflect governmental fiat, as in the mandatory indexation of wages that currently prevails in Brazil, which seems to approximate a form of minimum wage. The models presented by Gray and Simonsen assume that employment is based on the spot real wage rate in accordance with the usual schedule for the marginal product of labor. In this setting nominal disturbances affect the real wage rate—because of the partial fixity of nominal wages—and thereby influence employment. The automatic linking of nominal wages to the price level affects the manner in which nominal (and other) disturbances are communicated to the real wage. Therefore indexing generally matters for the characteristics of business cycles, and full indexation of wages to the general price level insulates the real variables from purely monetary shocks.

Even in labor contracts that preset the nominal wage, it is inefficient to allow employment to vary because of perceived monetary disturbances. Sometimes the marginal product of labor exceeds the value of the workers' time, and sometimes the reverse applies. As Hall has suggested, we might see efficient long-term labor agreements where workers agree to work harder when there is more work to do (when the marginal product is high) and less hard when there is less work. In such circumstances it is unnecessary for the spot real wage to coincide with the workers' marginal product at all times; neither general indexation of wages nor systematic monetary policy matter for the characteristics of business fluctuations. Phelps's chapter discusses the "modernist" theory of labor contracts (of which we are informed that he is the father) in which not all contingencies can be specified. But he seems to agree that the general levels of money and prices are variables on which people can easily condition their payments and, more important, their work decisions. Therefore this line of contract theory does not help to explain a response of employment and output to fully understood nominal disturbances. Such responses are inefficient and are readily recognized as such by workers and firms. Further, misunderstood nominal disturbances have real effects that are well explained by models—such as those of Lucas—that do not require elaborate contracting frameworks. Hence the contracting approach seems unnecessary in the context of misperceived monetary movements.

Some consideration was given in the conference discussion to equilibrium-style models, where the real effects of monetary disturbances derive from confusion between nominal and real variables. The general indexation of wages for price changes would matter here only if there were some effects on people's knowledge about the economy. In simple equilibrium models neither indexation nor systematic monetary policy alter the information that people can derive from observed prices. For this reason the form of wage indexation (and the specification of monetary policy) is irrelevant for the business cycle. Some more elaborate models in this area, however, as constructed recently by Weiss and King, show that indexing and monetary policy affect the information content of prices in some cases. It is unclear whether this effect is quantitatively significant.

A recent study by Kormendi and Meguire estimates the effects of money shocks on output for a cross section of about fifty countries. Their findings show that the variance of measured output initially increases but eventually decreases, with increases in the variance of money. This eventual decline in the effects of money on observed business fluctuations obtains in both the Keynesian and equilibrium theories. A rising variance of money motivates shorter contract lengths, which diminishes the extent of wage-price stickiness in the Keynesian framework. In equilibrium models with incomplete information the larger variance of money means that smaller fractions of nominal shocks are misperceived as real ones. Empirically, there seems to be a positive, though imperfect association between the variance of money and the propensity to index. (As an exception, some European countries with low variances of money and prices have adopted forms of wage indexation.) As prototypical examples, Brazil and Israel have very high monetary variances and also employ extensive indexation. The Kormendi-Meguire results suggest that the variance of money is high enough for these countries to place them in a range where monetary disturbances have little consequence for observed business fluctuations.

Frank Hahn questioned the underlying motivation for governmental intervention into wage indexation or other forms of indexing for private contracts. We lack a clear expression of the underlying externalities— private market failures—that the government's policy is designed to correct. There was some discussion of class conflict—strife between workers and capitalists—as the basic rationale. However, we lack either theoretical or empirical evidence that relates this conflict to indexing or to inflation generally. The chapters by Simonsen and Macedo established some undesirable allocative effects that have resulted from mandatory wage indexation in Brazil. These effects are analogous to those produced by a system of minimum wages that can be avoided by resort to frequent labor turnover. From the standpoint of business cycles the argument in favor of compulsory wage indexation might involve the external effects that arise from monetary induced fluctuations in output. As suggested by Hahn, the government is already in the business of controlling money and the general price level but has apparently done a poor job. Wage indexation then emerges as a cure for bad monetary policy. One wonders whether the institution that cannot handle monetary matters should be entrusted with the task of implementing mandatory indexation. Perhaps a better alternative is to remove government from a position of discretionary control of money. Monetary management might be better disciplined by a rule—for Brazil a natural goal would be maintenance of a fixed exchange rate with the U.S. dollar. The use of a rule to govern monetary behavior could be usefully combined with deregulation of the private financial sector.

Indexation and Asset Markets

The conference produced a remarkable number of invariance results concerning public debt of indexed and nonindexed forms. The chapters by Fischer, Levhari, and Liviatan discuss cases where the government's issue of indexed bonds does not matter. These results obtain when the private sector is already in a position to issue similar securities. The Stiglitz chapter discusses the invariance results for cases where tax cuts are financed by government deficits. Stiglitz's basic point is that the Ricardian theorem—which says that people's capitalization of future taxes means that debt-financed tax cuts do not matter—can also be viewed as the Modigliani-Miller theorem on the public debt.

Steve Ross's discussion stresses the failure of our analyses to pinpoint interesting real-world features that limit the applicability of the irrelevance results for government-issued index bonds. For example, we would want to know whether the real effects of indexed public debt are greater in countries that are at a lower level of economic development. One feature that limits private issues of indexed debt concerns taxes in systems that do not use monetary corrections to calculate the taxable parts of interest income. The index adjustment to the bond principal may be treated as interest income for the holder and may or may not be allowable as a deductible interest payment for the issuer. A second feature that may limit private indexing arrangements concerns the government's enforcement of private contracts. Governments may be inclined—perhaps as a mechanism to support their monopoly power in the monetary area—to provide the best enforcement for contracts that are denominated in the government's designated unit of account. For example, the U.S. government failed to enforce "gold clauses" that were written into contracts before the increase of the dollar price of gold in 1933. In this context private agents may prefer contracts—for credit operations, wages, or other things —that are measured in well-enforceable units of currency rather than in less enforceable units of commodities.

Fischer's chapter shows that the equivalent of publicly issued indexed bonds arises as a counterpart of intergenerational insurance schemes that may be run by the government. The model is one where no one seems to care about their own children but where the government cares about the next generation as a whole. It is unclear how the government's behavior reflects the preferences of people who are currently alive. A basic question is whether the welfare of the next generation is a public good or primarily a private family matter. If a public good, we anticipate governmental intervention; if a private family matter, we expect to rely mainly on private intergenerational transfers, which may be assisted by various types of privately generated insurance plans. In any event it seems desirable to study public debt, social security, and other forms of governmental programs for intergenerational transfers in a model that allows also for private intergenerational transfers.

Indexing and Positive Theories of Governmental Behavior

Levhari mentions that indexation of government bonds may interact with the government's choice of monetary growth. Nevertheless, he advises against pursuing this inquiry because (1) it's political and (2) the conclusions are indeterminate. Presumably, we would not be deterred by the first consideration if it turned out that economic analysis provided significant predictive value. The second result is unfortunate—if true—but has not been sufficient reason to cease studying a host of economic problems.

The theory of governmental behavior is central for the study of inflation in two respects. First, we want to know how governments would react in various circumstances in order to predict inflation rates and, more specifically, to understand the inflationary consequences of shifts in institutions, such as indexation. Simonsen's description of monetary accommodation in Brazil is a specific example of a theory of governmental policy that allows us to forecast the effects on inflation of different forms of indexing. Secondly, our theories often involve people's expectations of variables like inflation, monetary growth, taxes, and so on. Rational expectations derive from sensible forecasts of public policy, which in turn require a model of governmental behavior. We do not want our expectations of future governmental policies to imply actions from which the policy-maker will have an interest to deviate. People will not maintain such systematically incorrect expectations for very long. But, to understand this process, we need again to model the behavior of government.

Fischer points out that indexed government debt has aspects of a rule or commitment for monetary policy. With nonindexed debt outstanding, the monetary authority has an incentive to create surprise inflation, which drives down the real value of the debt. From an ex post standpoint the depreciation of the real value of bonds amounts to a capital levy, which is an efficient form of taxation. Therefore surprise inflation enables the government to raise revenue at lower deadweight loss than otherwise. However, bondholders understand that the government has this power to create surprise inflation. Therefore the ex ante expected rate of inflation and the corresponding nominal interest rate on bonds must reflect this potential. It is not possible systematically to follow a policy of generating surprise increases in inflation. A rational expectations equilibrium must involve a competitive expected real rate of return on bonds. Further the rate of inflation must be sufficiently high—and thereby sufficiently costly as viewed by the government—so that the monetary authority is motivated not to generate systematic surprises in inflation, ex post. In this sort of equilibrium the government does not obtain revenue, on average, through surprise inflation. However, the potential for these surprises influences the average inflation rate that arises in equilibrium.

The indexation of government bonds amounts to ruling out a priori the possibility of using surprise inflation to depreciate the real value of debt. (I assume that defaulting on the bonds is a different form of breach of contract.) As suggested before, the removal of this option does not result in less average revenue for the government because the surprise capital losses cannot generate any revenue on average. (The government may lose the power to depress the real value of its debts through surprise monetary growth and inflation, contingent on a stochastic event such as a war.) The average rates of inflation and monetary growth that produce an equilibrium—where the government is not motivated ex post to create systematic surprises in inflation—tends to be lower when the ex post benefits from surprise inflation are eliminated. Therefore this theory of governmental behavior suggests that indexation of government bonds tends to lower average rates of monetary growth and inflation. (We may, however, reach an indeterminacy if the existence of indexed bonds also lowers the costs attached to inflation. This element tends to raise the equilibrium average rates of monetary growth and inflation.)

Empirically, it seems that average rates of inflation and the extent of indexation of government securities are positively correlated. Presumably, this observation reflects the incentive to index, rather than the effects of indexing on the rates of monetary growth and inflation. Porto Goncalves considered in his discussion which governments would be most likely to issue indexed bonds. Principally, governments with the least collateral—in the sense of those that have demonstrated the least restraint in producing surprise inflation ex post—will be the ones required to index their debt. These countries will also be the ones that exhibit the highest average rates of inflation.

It is of interest to pursue positive theories of the government's determination of monetary growth. This approach should lead to further testable propositions that concern the wide variety of choices that different countries have made for average rates of inflation and monetary growth. The propensity to index is also an endogenous variable form this viewpoint. Aside from learning the economic effects of exogenous changes in indexing, we would like to know which factors have actually caused governments and private agents to adopt various forms of indexing.

Comments on Indexation and Stability from an Observer of the Argentinean Economy

Domingo F. Cavallo

Several chapters in this book try to explain the existence of indexation and to understand the relationship between indexation and stability of output and prices.

From the Argentine experience, I can say that it is necessary to distinguish between mandatory indexation, on the one hand, and spontaneous indexation, on the other. I call spontaneous indexation the indexed arrangements agreed upon by economic operators in the context of voluntary contracting in free markets.

The existence of mandatory indexation, which is very common in many countries, seems to me to be mainly related to income distribution considerations. Our past president, General Domingo Perón, who used to explain Peronist ideologies and policies with very clear everyday life comparisons, once said, "Until now, prices have gone up on the elevator, and wages have had to use the stairs. From now on, I decree that prices should go up via the stairs or wages should use the elevator, too; but it isn't fair to discriminate." [1]

Prohibition of financial indexation as ceilings on interest rates was also justified in the concern to transfer income from the rentiers and savers to the enterpreneurs and investors.

The relationship between indexation and price stability can be illuminated by the distinction between mandatory and spontaneous indexation. My impression is that partial mandatory indexation (partial in the sense of not being widespread) exacerbates inflation because it benefits social groups strong enough to impose through government a scheme such as this to favor their incomes while keep under control the income of other social groups. Those powerful groups will profit from inflationary policies and will work actively for their adoption by the government.

In contrast, mandatory indexation that tends to generalize to almost every long-term contract may well work in favor of price stabilization. In terms of Perón's argument, "Now that workers can use it, the elevator will be more heavily loaded and it will move up more slowly."

You may dislike this political explanation of indexation and its relationship to stability, but mandatory indexation cannot be explained as a market phenomenon.

I can also see that there exists indexation that shows up as a result of private economic agents' decisions operating in free markets. For this kind of indexation, I can also see the relevance of the explanations offered by the discussions in this book. The Argentinean economy's experience can be useful in evaluating the realism of alternative explanations. Let me relate to you the Argentine experience with indexation in the financial markets:

There was a time when interest rates were controlled and indexation was banned. Of course there was no indexation.

In a subsequent period, interest rates were controlled, and some indexation by price indexes was permitted. By that time there was a great development of every permitted kind of financial indexation because it was a way to overcome interest rate ceilings.

There was a time when interest rates were completely free and indexation by price indexes was permitted. Indexation almost disappeared, and the length of financial contracts which were done in terms of nominal rates shortened dramatically. In this period there was a wide development of floating rates deposit and loan contracts.

There is finally a period when the Central Bank began to publish a financial index on a daily base.[2] This index increased daily by a rate equivalent to the 30-day deposit interest rate quoted in the market. This scheme of indexation was immediately adopted by most operators in the financial markets; it replaced the floating rates system and allowed a lengthening of both deposits and loans contracts.

From this experience I conclude that transaction costs associated with recontracting rather than with the attempt at ex post adjustments between expectation and facts seems to be the main reason for the adoption of indexation. For example, in Argentina, the bulk of indexation does not provide the mechanism for ex post compensation of differences between expected and actual inflation. This view is reinforced by the fact that, together with indexation, long-term contracts usually include clauses of recontracting should drastic changes occur in the general economic situation that could not have been reasonably predicted. There is also a legal procedure to force recontracting, called *teoría de la imprevision*. My impression is that, in the absence of transaction costs, an inflationary situation would be faced by economic agents by much more frequent recontracting; indexation is a form of economizing in the face of this need. This interpretation of indexation as a voluntary way to reduce the need for permanent recontracting makes the possible influence of indexation on stability less relevant.

I can also find very clear empirical evidence of risk aversion by both firms and savers playing an important role in the adoption of indexation. To make this point, let me relate another Argentinian experience.

Private firms and families have been demanding specific indexation in the loan markets. This does not necessarily reflect their expectation of a deterioration of the relative price with respect to which they can be indexed. They would be willing to pay a real specific interest rate which, added to the expected inflation in terms of the specific price, exceeds the sum of the real market interest rate plus the overall rate of expected inflation. Why would they pay this higher interest? The reason is they are demanding insurance against changes in relative prices, and they are willing to pay for it. The financial system would be able to sell this insurance with comparative advantage because it could dilute the risk by an adequate mix of assets indexed by specific price indexes within the portfolio, not necessarily backed by identical indexing of bank deposits. The market for these specific indexed loans is developing spontaneously in Argentina, but unfortunately there are several restrictions imposed by the Central Bank that prevent a rapid development of such an institutional arrangement which would be very efficient in an economy with very variable and unpredictable relative prices. It is interesting to note that these restrictions exist as a result of Martinez de Hoz and Adolfo Diz' opposition to what they considered to be the development of too many "monies".

Notes

1. In Spanish: *"Hasta ahora los precios siempre subieron en ascensor y los salarios tuvieron que usar la escalera. A partir de ahora, yo dispongo que los precios usen sólo la escalera o los salarios suban tambien al ascensor, pero no es justo hacer diferencias."*

2. The publication of this index was proposed by the author and Aldo Dadone in "Indice implícito en la tasa testigo," *Estudios* 2, no. 12 (1979).

Panel Comments

F. H. Hahn

I have learned a good deal in the last two days although I am not quite sure that I know precisely what it is that I have learned. I am in agreement with a point which has just been made by Barro which explains some of my perplexity: "What," he asked, "is the feature of the economy we are considering which would lead us to consider a government indexation policy to be desirable?" We are used in ordinary theory to propose government intervention to correct "market failure," externalities, missing markets, or monopolistic distortions. What particular market failure do we have in mind when we are considering indexation? For instance, if indexed bonds are desirable, why can they not be privately provided? Or if real wages are usefully to be insured why do labor contracts not provide them? I suspect that Barro holds the view that it is more likely that the absence of various indexed contracts points to their undesirability than to market failure. I myself with less confidence in the Walrasian invisible hand incline in the other direction. But my point is this: it does not seem to me that we have succeeded in precisely modeling the market economy and its attendant imperfections which would permit us to give a clinching answer to the questions of the consequences and welfare effects of indexation.

This is particularly clear when we consider our discussions of the welfare effects. We are far too inclined to carry over results on Pareto efficiency which depend on the abstract Arrow-Debreu formulation to the world of missing markets, etc., which we need to study when we consider indexation. Stanley Fischer made the best attempt there, but no doubt he would agree that there is still a long way to go. In any case it seems very probable that welfare propositions in this area will have to be of the "constrained" kind, that is, they will be of the sort which we encounter in the study of stock market economies. They are quite hard to formulate, and I do not think that has yet been accomplished.

But there has been another difficulty. It has not been clear to me whether indexation is to be mainly studied in the context of rational expectations equilibria or in the setting of rather more old-fashioned dynamics. For instance, Simonsen's interesting model can be given a natural dynamic setting without postulating fully rational expectations. My guess is that it would yield some interesting insights: to be more concrete, Simonsen is clearly right that in the context of rational expectations equilibrium we do not want to index wages to keep them invariant to real shocks. However, if stability is what we are considering, then some government intervention in the real wage may be desirable.

Or one could concentrate on the question of controllability. Full indexation would deprive the controller of an instrument, a circumstance which is *prima facie* undesirable. The question would then be whether it would be possible or useful to have an indexation policy—Simonsen's which, however, would not be a constant but a function of the "state of the world." As I understand it, that is what some existing indexation arrangements in fact do. Clearly, such a device provides less insurance than would otherwise be the case, and I suspect that on careful analysis may actually turn out to be "destabilizing" in certain circumstances.

At a less formal level, however, it is clear that full indexation without regard to "real" events will almost certainly be disastrous. I was in India when the monsoon had failed for two years running. Real income had to fall. Indexation in this circumstance would be pretty silly.

Accordingly, we have had proposals to index against "nominal" shocks and somehow exclude "real" shocks. It is not clear that this is very practicable although there are schemes which, for instance, exclude terms-of-trade variations from the index. But that is not what here interests me. Rather it is the seeming paradox of a government engaging in an elaborate indexation exercise against shocks of which it itself, according to the theory, is the main cause. Would it not be more sensible to control the nominal magnitudes properly in the first place? To this question I have been given the answer that, in practice, the government finds it impossible to control the nominal magnitudes. So much for monetarist prescriptions! But in any case, if that is so, then we shall have to model the endogenous monetary disturbances. This is not done anywhere in the literature, and therefore it is not clear to me why so many confident propositions are being advanced.

Suppose, just for the sake of argument, that the underlying process of inflation is to be traced to a nice potpourri of class struggle and political motives. That is, the working classes push for higher money wages as part of the "struggle" and every so often succeed, and the government "validates" this by appropriate monetary expansion to avoid unemployment and attendant electoral defeat. I dare say this model could be precisely formulated. In such a situation indexation would allow the weaker section of the working class to benefit from the aggression of the stronger. Moreover indexation might define a base real wage from which the struggle takes off, and it might well exacerbate it. Finally in such a situation it might be extremely hard to get real wage reductions appropriate to "real" shocks. In any case I doubt that there would be traditional Pareto-efficiency analysis available to pronounce on the "optimum" policy for such a world.

In conclusion, I should like to make two points:

1. If the world looked as Lucas and many followers describe it, there surely would be no need for indexation of any kind. For rational agents understand homogeneity, equilibrium is unique, and the economy is always in unique equilibrium. All we need is a firm and universally heard announcement of the money supply figures for each date. So if any of us have a case to make for indexation, then we had better not be Lucasious. Quite properly, for instance, Hellwig has concentrated on the process of price adjustment, but it is only part of the story. Until we have formulated precise models deducible from the greed and rationality of agents which are not Lucasian, we had better be circumspect in what we have to say on indexation.

2. This also brings me to my last point. Earlier I expressed doubts about the use of ad hoc log-linear macro models. I noted that they were not very robust. This rather clear and modest remark gave rise to some excitement and disagreement. I was told in particular that, unlike Arrow-Debreu theorists, macroeconomist wanted to have something to say about the "real" world. No one suggested that that something should also have some chance of not being greatly at variance with this "real" world. Witch doctors and necromancers have always claimed their art as relevant to the "real" world (in Britain we have a government under a witch's spell); I would rather do without these lovers of short cuts and stick to serious theory even it that means that we have to say to the politicians: "it all depends...."

Contributors

Robert Barro
The University of Chicago

Olivier Blanchard
Massachusetts Institute of Technology

Domingo Cavallo
Fundaçion Mediterranea, Cordoba

Michael Emerson
European Communities, Bruxelles

Stanley Fischer
Massachusetts Institute of Technology

Jo Anna Gray
Board of Governors of the Federal Reserve, Washington D.C.

Frank Hahn
University of Cambridge

David Levhari
The Hebrew University

Nissan Liviatan
The Hebrew University

Roberto Macedo
The University of São Paulo

Edmund Phelps
Columbia University

Thomas Sargent
The University of Minnesota, Minneapolis

Mario Henrique Simonsen
Fundaçao Getulio Vargas, Rio de Janeiro

Joseph Stiglitz
Princeton University

Index